D1068246

LOANS

AND

LEGITIMACY

LOANS
AND
LEGITIMACY

THE EVOLUTION OF
SOVIET-AMERICAN RELATIONS
1919-1933

◄ ►

KATHERINE A.S. SIEGEL

THE UNIVERSITY PRESS OF KENTUCKY

Editorial and Sales Offices: The University Press of Kentucky
663 South Limestone Street, Lexington, Kentucky 40508-4008

Library of Congress Cataloging-in-Publication Data

Siegel, Katherine A. S. (Katherine Amelia Siobhan), 1961-
    Loans and legitimacy : the evolution of Soviet-American relations.
1919-1933 / Katherine A.S. Siegel.
        p.   cm.
    Includes bibliographical references and index.
    ISBN 0-8131-1962-6 (alk. paper)
    1. United States—Foreign relations—Soviet Union.   2. Soviet
Union—Foreign relations—United States.   I. Title.
E.183.8.S65S56   1996
327,73047'09'041—dc20   95-26338

FOR MITCH

CONTENTS

ACKNOWLEDGMENTS ix

INTRODUCTION 1

1. MARTENS AND THE FIRST SOVIET MISSION 6

2. THE DEMISE OF THE SOVIET BUREAU 23

3. DIPLOMATIC, MILITARY, AND HUMANITARIAN INITIATIVES, 1919-1923 39

4. ECONOMIC FOREIGN POLICY UNDER HARDING 62

5. THE SOVIET COMMERCIAL MISSIONS UNDER HARDING, COOLIDGE, AND HOOVER 76

6. TRADE AND FOREIGN POLICY, 1923-1929 89

7. AMERICAN BUSINESSMEN, THE NEP, AND THE FIRST FIVE-YEAR PLAN 110

8. SOVIET-AMERICAN RELATIONS, 1929-1933 133

9. CONCLUSION 139

ABBREVIATIONS 141

NOTES 143

BIBLIOGRAPHY 187

INDEX 197

ILLUSTRATIONS FOLLOW PAGE 86

ACKNOWLEDGMENTS

Many people helped to make this book possible. My doctoral adviser, Alexander DeConde, gently diverted me from the well-traveled path of the Cold War and encouraged me to venture into the 1920s instead, for which I am very grateful. He also read all of the drafts of the dissertation from which this book emerged, and provided me with invaluable advice, assistance, and support. Professors W. Elliot Brownlee and Joachim Remak were also wonderfully helpful members of my dissertation committee. I would very much like to thank those who commented on the book in in its various forms thereafter: David McFadden, Christine White, Tibor Frank, Jonathan Coopersmith, Linda Killen, and Michael Sherry. Michael J. Hogan, editor of *Diplomatic History*, kindly gave permission for me to use portions of an article I had published in that journal. Colleagues Nina Bakisian, Fiona Harris Stoertz, Sina Dubovoj, Thom Armstrong, Eduard Mark, and Rorin Platt also offered their encouragement and support, as did the participants of the 1989–1991 Institute on Global Conflict and Cooperation Fellows Conference.

As this work evolved from dissertation to manuscript, I enjoyed the frequent inspiration, good humor, and active mentoring of my history department colleagues at St. Joseph's University. And as the manuscript turned into a monograph, I benefited from the gracious suggestions, careful oversight, and efficient operations of the editorial, production, and marketing staff at the University Press of Kentucky.

Researching the many collections used in this book would have been far more daunting a task without the generous assistance offered by librarians and archivists in the United States and Russia, including Dane Hartgrove and John Taylor at the National Archives; Dwight Miller and Shirley Sondergard at the Hoover Presidential Library; Verne Newton, Raymond Teichman, and Robert Parks at the Roosevelt Library; Joanne Hohler at the Wisconsin State Historical Society; Chris Baer, Michael Nash, and Marjorie McNinch at the Hagley Library; Elaine Barr at the Swarthmore College Peace Collection; Jennifer Rollo at the Eisenhower Library of Johns Hopkins University; Barbara Natanson at the Library of Congress, Prints and Photographs Division; Bill Gorman at the New York State Archives; and Chris Dixon and Pat Weaver at Drexel Library, St. Joseph's University. Also of great assistance were the staffs at the Federal Bureau of Investigation Reading Room; the National Archives; the Library of Congress; the

Seeley Mudd Manuscript Library at Princeton University; the Hoover Institution on War, Revolution, and Peace; the Russian State Archival Administration; the Russian Foreign Ministry Archive; the Lenin Library; and the Central Party Archive.

This book would not have been possible without the financial support of the Kennan Institute of Advanced Russian Studies; the Hoover Library Association; the Franklin and Eleanor Roosevelt Institute; the Hagley Museum and Library; the Institute on Global Conflict and Cooperation; the Society for Historians of American Foreign Relations; the History Department, Faculty Development program, and the Institute on Trade, Diplomacy and Development at St. Joseph's University; and the history department, the Interdisciplinary Humanities Center, and the graduate division at the University of California, Santa Barbara.

I would also like to take this opportunity to thank my family, including my late father, Capt. C. William Sibley, who regularly encouraged me to "suck in the valuable instruction" but died too early to see what I would do with it; my mother, Margaret M. Sibley, who banished the television to the intemperate clime of the attic and pushed books on us instead; and my siblings, who were always willing to dialogue about early Soviet-American relations.

Above all, my deepest and fondest appreciation is to my husband, Mitch Siegel, who sustained me with loving encouragement, editorial advice, technical assistance, and humor throughout the seven years we shared our lives with this book.

INTRODUCTION

In 1919 anticommunist sentiment in America was at a crest. That year saw the founding of the American Communist party and also the deportation of boatloads of suspected Bolsheviks from the United States. Attorney General A. Mitchell Palmer and his ambitious assistant, J. Edgar Hoover, laid their plans then for the large-scale raids against alleged Soviet sympathizers that were launched early in 1920. Palmer did not escape unscathed. On June 2, 1919, his house at 2132 R Street in Washington was blown up by an anarchist. Across the street, windows also shattered at the home of Assistant Secretary of the Navy Franklin D. Roosevelt.[1] At the same time, over ten thousand American troops were occupying parts of Russia, against Soviet volition, as part of an inter-Allied military intervention.

Yet this tumultuous environment did not prevent the Soviet People's Commissariat of Foreign Affairs (Narkomindel) from dispatching an unofficial "ambassador" to the United States in the spring of 1919. Despite an existing ban on Soviet trade during the Red Scare, Ludwig C.A.K. Martens, an engineer by training, was instructed to open a New York bureau in order to acquire American goods. In the aftermath of the Bolshevik revolution, Russian leaders were convinced that their country's future depended upon economic and political links with the United States. Lenin realized that there were marked differences between the outlooks of reluctant government officials and those of profit-seeking businessmen, and he sought to take advantage of them. He believed that by persuading American businessmen, the representatives of doomed imperialism, to contribute to the development of Soviet Russia, he would "promote the buildup of an international- imperialist contradiction."[2] Nearly half a century later, Soviet historian V.A. Shishkin offered a very similar analysis: "A striking example of imperialist contradiction between the U.S.A. and the other great powers on the question of economic relations with Russia was the paradoxical fact of secret, separate contacts of American agents with Soviet representatives."[3]

This book investigates the early Soviet campaign for American trade and recognition, as well as the American response, official and unofficial. It suggests that the prerecognition era, like the post–Cold War era, embraced a Russian-American relationship that was evolving rather than rigidly polarized. Despite the absence of diplomatic relations with Russia and the unflagging opposition of American officials to Bolshevism, Soviet economic initiatives and the American response to them gradually contributed to legitimizing the Russian regime in Washington.

American firms were very interested in Martens's trade efforts, though commerce with the Bolsheviks was not legalized until wartime economic restrictions were removed in July 1920. This interest encouraged Martens to perceive that his prospects were bright, despite harassment from Washington and Albany and a weak commitment from his own government. In early 1921, however, the United States forced the Bureau director to leave New York amid accusations that he was a revolutionary propagandist. In its short life, the Soviet Bureau was able to establish contact with nearly one thousand American firms and to conduct trade despite a stiff Allied embargo.[4] Martens's work laid the foundation for the more successful Soviet agencies that opened in New York during the 1920s. The story of the Martens Bureau, the first Soviet economic mission to the United States, will be discussed in Chapters 1 and 2.

As Martens returned to Russia, the dire economic conditions resulting from revolution, civil war, and Allied intervention finally prompted Russian diplomats to recognize that "temporary accommodations with the imperialist powers" were necessary. The era of Soviet "peaceful coexistence," rather than export of revolution, had begun, even as the Bolsheviks launched the quasi-capitalist New Economic Policy at home, replacing militant war communism.[5] The Western powers, particularly Britain and Germany, were also ready to deal with Russia. As Richard K. Debo points out, the British wished to promote stability in Europe, and the vanquished Germans had nowhere else to go. As early as May 1920, the Soviets had begun work on their first priority with the West, a British trade agreement, and successfully concluded it nine months later. Commissar of Foreign Affairs Georgi Chicherin, a man who deeply distrusted Britain's ambitions, nevertheless emphasized the desirability of the treaty for lessening the threat of war, for trade and credits, and for Soviet "respectability."[6] As Lenin noted, the treaty would allow Moscow "to start as soon as possible to buy machines required for our large plans of restoring the national economy. The sooner we have done this, the sooner we shall have the foundations to free ourselves from economic dependence on the capitalist countries."[7] In May 1921 the next vital goal was effected, a trade and diplomatic agreement with Germany.[8] By 1924 the Soviet government had also established trade and diplomatic links with France, Poland, Sweden, Austria, Turkey, and the Baltic states.

For the United States, the inauguration of the Soviet New Economic Policy and peaceful coexistence, along with the waning of the domestic Red Scare, offered a second chance for Russian-American trade and investment after Martens's deportation. Lenin and Leonid Krasin, commissar of foreign trade, believed that connections with American executives would bring a "big political gain" to the Kremlin.[9] Economic influence would culminate in official relations, they hoped, and facilitate financial assistance, including credits to make purchases. Yet the U. S. government steered clear of offering diplomatic recognition or financial assistance. At the same time, it became heavily involved in humanitarian efforts in

Russia that saved millions of lives and may have saved the Bolshevik regime. This early American role will be examined in Chapter 3.

Though Soviet Russia signed no treaties of political or economic cooperation with Washington, as it did with London, Berlin, and Paris, this diplomatic impasse seemed scarcely an obstacle to Soviet agents and their American brokers. These representatives set up offices in New York and other cities to buy cotton, agricultural implements, engines, and other goods, and found a welcome reception from business in the 1920s. In turn, despite their dislike for the Soviet system, most American businessmen could not help but notice the potential of Soviet Russia's 140 million people, who occupied one-sixth of the world's surface, and the incredible natural resources that lay beneath them.[10] Between 1923 and 1930 American sales to the Soviets grew twenty-fold, as total trade with the Bolshevik state surpassed the half-billion dollar mark. American firms supplied Russians with over a quarter of their imports, including oil drilling, mining, metalworking, electrical, construction, and agricultural equipment. By 1931 Moscow, in turn, purchased more than one-fourth of American industrial equipment exports. In certain fields, like power-driven metalworking equipment and agricultural implements, Moscow consumed fully two-thirds of manufacturers' foreign output that year.[11] Vital to this growing trade were large credits, from firms such as General Electric and American Locomotive Sales Corporation, as well as smaller businesses, and from banks including Chase National, Guaranty Trust, and Equitable Trust.[12]

Historians of early Soviet diplomacy have given little attention to Russia's economic interests in the United States, emphasizing instead the Kremlin's successful establishment of official ties with the European powers during the first half of the 1920s.[13] Yet over the course of the decade, Russian purchases of American goods served Soviet goals by promoting a significant change in U.S. economic policy. Most notably, Soviet trade encouraged Washington officials, no longer as reluctant as they had been in 1919, to authorize private long-term credits. This cooperation of business and government to assist American economic relations with Soviet Russia is representative of New Era corporatism, that system of public-private collaboration to ensure "order, progress, and stability" that is often associated with Herbert Hoover.[14]

Hoover played a leading role in the development of early Soviet-American relations, as director of the American Relief Administration's work in Russia, as commerce secretary during the Harding and Coolidge administrations, and during his presidency. Scholars of American foreign policy, however, have often portrayed Hoover as too ideological to capitalize on Soviet Russia's economic potential. William Appleman Williams, for example, blamed the commerce secretary's "extreme hostility toward the Soviet Union" for effectively limiting Soviet-American commerce. Peter G. Filene notes that Hoover's animosity to communism and his belief in the imminent demise of Soviet Russia led him to pressure the Harding administration to "maintain its aloofness toward trade with Russia" even as business sought to take advantage of opportunities there.[15] Yet Hoover's economic policy toward Russia evolved during the 1920s, as did that of the three administrations he served, a development that will be discussed in Chapters 4 and 6.

In general, the American government's flexibility on the Russian question before 1933 has gone unnoticed by historians. Instead, they have emphasized Washington's rigidity by citing documents such as the Colby note of 1920, a statement that has been widely depicted as the ideological blueprint for American policies until recognition.[16] Colby's uncompromising stand was a reaction to Bolshevik initiatives such as the dissemination of revolutionary propaganda, the repudiation of $250 million of Kerensky's World War debts and previous private loans to Tsar Nicholas II, and large-scale expropriation of American property in Russia, which could not be ignored or forgotten in a debt-conscious and legalistic America.[17] Yet Colby's note did not serve as a fixed compass for government action and interaction with Bolshevik agents in the 1920s and early 1930s. Although Republican officials remained committed to Wilsonian edicts on the illegitimacy of Moscow's government, they gradually facilitated efforts by the business community to pursue relations with Russia, as trade became the great palliator of Soviet-American relations during this period. As a result, the Soviet agencies that opened in the United States during the Harding, Coolidge, and Hoover administrations received far better treatment than had Ludwig Martens, and cabinet level departments increasingly referred businessmen to these agencies. These purchasing bureaus, which are explored in Chapter 5, included Alamerico, the All-Russian Textile Syndicate, and the Amtorg Trading Corporation.

There can be little question that Washington's initial policies, including restrictions on long-term credit and prohibition of direct loans to Bolshevik Russia, did at first retard trade. But the Soviet Union also presented major impediments to a flourishing commercial association. Foreign investment, the part of the Soviet-American economic relationship that the Soviet Union controlled, fared far worse overall than trade, the area that the United States regulated. In one of his speeches defending the New Economic Policy and its program for foreign investment, Lenin claimed that he would "not grudge the foreign capitalist even a 2,000 percent profit," as long as this met the Bolshevik goals of improving the living standards of peasants and workers and thus gave the regime *peredyshka*, or breathing space.[18] But no one made that kind of profit, as the policy's dictates for rapid technological development ultimately allowed for little return for investors. During the First Five-Year Plan, concessions were replaced with technical assistance contracts, which enabled firms to sell their technology on a more lucrative short-term contract basis. The unpredictable terrain for American business in Russia during the 1920s is addressed in Chapter 7.[19]

During the Cold War, scholars researching early Soviet-American relations often found that the bipolar frame of reference typical of their era was also applicable to the period before 1933. Their work emphasizes ideologically based American anticommunism as the prominent motif in the early relationship.[20] Cold War–era historians have focused upon Washington's policies rather than Moscow's not only because of the lack of available Soviet sources, but also owing to a consensus that the United States was the most active partner in shaping the relationship. Unfortunately, this American emphasis places the Soviet government of Lenin and Stalin in a reactive posture. Soviet diplomatic efforts, however, were bold and often effective during this era, as this study will show.[21]

The end of the Cold War has allowed for a new appraisal of early Soviet foreign policy initiatives with the opening of Russian archives. However, it has not ended the historiographical tendency to portray the United States as the immovable partner. In his recent study of Soviet foreign policy, Jon Jacobson suggests that along with maintaining nonrecognition, "Washington refused to discuss credits" with Moscow even as nations such as Germany offered them. Although Washington did not extend government financing to Moscow, its officials did entertain the subject of credits and responded positively to American firms' requests to offer long-term financing beginning in 1927.[22]

The great expansion of Soviet-American trade ended in 1932, when sharp cutbacks in Soviet orders, caused by the Five-Year Plan's autarkic practices as well as by American charges of Soviet "dumping", drastically shrank exports to Russia. When FDR opened diplomatic relations the following year, his considerations included both geopolitical issues and a desire to ameliorate the Depression through trade.[23] The Soviet-American economic relationship of the 1920s, by legitimizing the regime in the Kremlin, had paved the way for this opening.

Martens

and the

First Soviet Mission

In 1919, as the Soviet government slowly emerged from the combined threats and destruction of world war, revolution, and civil war, its new leadership looked to the United States. "We are decidedly for an economic understanding with America," President of the Council of Peoples' Commissars Vladimir Ilyich Lenin told a *Chicago Daily News* correspondent in October 1919. "With all countries," he was quick to add, "but *especially* with America."[1] As Tatiana N. Kargina explains, the Kremlin's keen ambition to obtain trade and diplomatic ties with "the most powerful country of the capitalist world" was a product of the complete economic breakdown in Russia. Lenin planned to entice American businessmen with "such favorable arrangements that [they] will be compelled to come to do business with us."[2] Similarly, Commissar of Foreign Affairs Chicherin declared the same year, "Our attitude toward official and non-official American representatives [is] different from our attitude toward representatives of other countries."[3]

Thus, as Washington and the European powers were offering support to the anti-Bolshevik government of Admiral Alexander V. Kolchak in Omsk, Siberia, Moscow opened its first American commercial outpost, the Soviet Bureau.[4] This office was set up to accomplish two of the Kremlin's highest goals in regard to the United States: increased trade and diplomatic recognition. Though Martens was willing to concede that recognition and its "accompanying formalities" could be postponed without serious damage to trade, he had always believed in the need for "a definite minimum of political relations" for carrying out successful commerce.[5] Despite an economic blockade, prevailing anticommunist and nativist hysteria, and harassment from the federal government's legislative and executive branches, along with a New York State probe, the Soviet Bureau succeeded in shipping more than a quarter of a million dollars' worth of products to Russia.[6] This small office signed an additional $30 million in unfulfilled contracts, for meat, textiles, and machinery.[7] The man who was chosen to orchestrate the Soviets' extraordinary American effort, "the largest and most dangerous propaganda undertaking thus far started by Lenine's party in any country outside of Russia," according to the War Department, was Ludwig Martens.[8]

Martens was a blond-mustachioed, stockily built man with a "florid complexion."[9] Born in 1874 in Yekaterinoslav, South Russia, to parents who had emigrated from Germany in 1850, Martens took a degree in mechanical engineering from the Technical University at St. Petersburg. In 1893, he joined the antitsarist movement, and within three years his revolutionary activities led him to a Russian jail after he and Lenin had organized a strike of thirty thousand textile workers in the capital city.[10] Martens remained in prison until 1899 and left then only to be pressed into the waiting arms of the Imperial German military forces because of his German citizenship. He served in the Reich's Engineer Corps for two years. During the 1905 revolution, Martens clandestinely returned to Russia. "When things grew too hot for him" he fled, first to Switzerland, where he worked for the Russian Social Democratic revolutionary movement, and then to London for the next decade.[11] The police kept Martens under surveillance while his engineering talents were put to good use in Britain, where he developed the "Mertens [sic] Machine Gun." Unfortunately, he sold his patent to an unscrupulous agent and was excluded from his rightful royalties. Martens's life in England was penurious, and after World War I began, his German ancestry got him in trouble once again. His freedom jeopardized as an "alien enemy," Martens departed for New York in 1915. There, his situation improved considerably. Martens first worked as an agent for Demidov San Donato, the largest steel maker in Russia, buying machinery and locomotives.[12] He then became vice president of Weinberg and Posner, a "wealthy Demidov engineering firm."[13]

In New York he also met Leon Trotsky, Finnish radical Santeri Nuorteva, and others active on the Bolshevik scene. In 1918 his connections led him to the executive committee of the New York Left Wing Socialist party's American Bolshevik Bureau of Information.[14] The Bolshevik Bureau was formed that February under the auspices of Louis C. Fraina and included activists in the émigré socialist community.[15] Martens was a frequent speaker before local left-wing groups and a member of the editorial board of the Bolshevik magazine *Novy Mir*. He also linked up with the Russian Federation, a group of antitsarist émigrés in the Left Wing Socialist organization who later formed the American Communist party.[16]

When Martens started his work at the Bureau in 1919, he put his revolutionary activity aside. Though his continued attendance and speeches at radical meetings attest that he never lost interest in these pursuits, he removed himself from leadership in the factionalized American communist movement, enraging the more dogmatic socialists who wished to control him.[17] His main task became the cultivation of American business contacts. He hoped to sell a variety of Russian products including caviar and furs to American customers and in return wanted to buy large quantities of tea, boots and shoes, underwear, and machinery and tools.[18] His claim that he had $200 million with which to purchase American goods drew the greatest interest in the American press.[19]

Armed with credentials signed by Chicherin in January, Martens became the Soviet "ambassador" on March 19, 1919. As the first official Soviet representative in America, Martens hoped to establish operations at the Russian embassy in Washington. He believed that his credentials gave him the right to "all moveable and real estate of the former embassy and consulates" of Russia and requested that the provisional government's commercial attaché in Brooklyn, C.J. Medzikhovsky, hand all Russian official property over to him.[20] Martens also wrote to a number of owners of private American warehouses, factories, and other facilities that were holding millions of dollars in Russian assets from the First World War. He made claims for close to $75 million for undelivered railroad supplies, cash in the National City Bank, damage claims from the Black Tom explosion in New Jersey, funds in the Russian embassy, and undelivered shoes, clothing, ammunition, and other items.[21]

Secretary of State Robert Lansing flatly rejected Martens's diplomatic credentials.[22] The Soviet Bureau chief's appeals were ignored owing to the United States' continued recognition of Boris Bakhmetev, ambassador of the defunct provisional government, and Martens was forced to share offices in Nuorteva's Bureau of Information on Soviet Russia at 299 Broadway. He nevertheless attempted to recover the Russian assets through Morris Hillquit, head of the Bureau's legal department and former socialist mayoral candidate of New York. Hillquit was aided by Charles Recht, an attorney prominent in Soviet causes. Yet there was really little that the Bureau could do to impress Washington that it had a legal claim upon the Russian money. American officials continued both to see a "Democratic Russia" as viable and to offer some limited support through Bakhmetev for Kolchak.[23] Indeed, Under Secretary of State Frank Polk "resented" the Bureau's attempt to remove Bakhmetev "as an insolent interference with American affairs."[24]

Despite these protestations on Bakhmetev's behalf, several historians have pointed out that the Russian ambassador was increasingly ignored by leading members of the Wilson administration after the Bolshevik Revolution, even as the symbolism of his office and its usefulness as a conduit for funding anti-Bolshevik causes were clearly recognized. Linda Killen suggests that by the end of 1919, the rout of Kolchak's armies and the American people's reluctance "to shoulder the whole burden" in Russia made Bakhmetev's cause hopeless. David W. McFadden contends that Bakhmetev's influence declined even earlier, during 1918, as influential men like Col. Edward M. House, Wilson's close confidant, recognized "the necessity of finding a way to work with the Bolshevik government."[25]

At the same time, Sen. William E. Borah also pushed hard for Bakhmetev's exit from the United States. Further, he introduced resolutions calling for the return of American soldiers from the Allied intervention effort in Russia. Borah was able to undermine Bakhmetev by showing the Senate how the ambassador had transferred millions of dollars to the unsuccessful White armies using Treasury credits originally meant for Russia's World War efforts. Borah's vigilance helped finally to eject Bakhmetev from his post in 1922, five years after the Bolshevik Revolution. Yet his financial attaché, Serge Ughet, maintained the fiction of provisional government representation in the United States until 1933.[26]

➤ THE SOVIET BUREAU'S OPERATIONS

Within two weeks of opening shop, the Bureau reported that large steel mill owners and machinery makers were calling, and claimed that "the largest and most influential bank in New York" was ready to finance shipments.[27] The main problem to increased sales was the ongoing inter-Allied economic embargo against Russia.[28] Not to be deterred, in April Martens moved his staff to larger quarters in the World's Tower Building at 110 West Fortieth Street, where the Bureau occupied the entire third floor.[29] Santeri Nuorteva bragged that "six hundred and twenty of 'the largest capitalists in America'" had been in contact with the office. Nuorteva, like Martens also "stockily built, florid [and] prosperous in appearance," took over the Bureau's diplomatic department. He had come to the United States in 1911 after being imprisoned for antitsarist activity.[30] Nuorteva had headed the Bureau of Information for Soviet Russia and in 1918 had also served as director of the Finnish Information Bureau, an agency of the revolutionary and short-lived "Finnish Workers' Government."[31] According to Felix Cole of the State Department, the "Hebrew" Nuorteva was the "brains" of the Soviet Bureau.[32] Nuorteva's academic training was in languages, and he had recently edited a Finnish-English dictionary.

The Bureau's general office department was headed by Gregory Weinstein, editor of *Novy Mir* and activist among New York's Left Wing Socialists, and included a large clerical staff.[33] The heart of the Bureau was the commercial department, where Abraham A. Heller was in charge. Heller had immigrated to the United States from Russia in 1891 at the age of sixteen. A long-time member of the Socialist party of America, he also ran the International Oxygen Company. Heller's publicity director was Evans Clark, husband of *The Nation* editor Freda Kirchwey. In addition to the diplomatic, general office, and commercial departments was the financial department, personified in Julius Hammer, who played an important role in financing the Bureau. Hammer also was manager of the Chemico-Pharmaceutical section of the commercial department, which served as a useful sales venue for many of his own company's medical products. Industrial data were collected in the statistical department, directed by Dr. Isaac Hourwich. Hourwich had been dismissed from the University of Chicago's economics department, according to the New York City police department, "on account of his radical views and his stubborn attitude to all persons who opposed him."[34] Martens also had attorneys on retainer, including Charles Recht, Walter Nelles, and Morris Hillquit. Although Nuorteva insisted that his Bureau had no tsarist or provisional government employees, one of the Bureau's key people was the Kerensky government's former Railway Mission head, Professor George Lomonosov, who ran the railroad department.[35]

Lomonosov had an unusual background for a Bureau employee. The New York Police Department noted that under the tsar, he had been a "reactionary and a strict disciplinarian demanding execution of all persons who would commit any acts against the government."[36] Three months after the first Russian revolution, Lomonosov became head of the Russian Railway Mission to the United States and continued in this position even after the provisional government was overturned in November. In June 1918, Nuorteva reported, "He came out for the Soviets . . . [at] a time when it was dangerous to say a word in their favor."[37] Lomonosov was identified in Soviet Bureau files as a "Menshevik intellectual," and he was thought to be "strongly opposed to the tactics of the Bolsheviki." But Nuorteva was pleased with Lomonosov's criticism of the Allied intervention, criticism that culminated in a speech Lomonosov gave at a "Justice for Russia" meeting at Madison Square Garden. Ambassador Bakhmetev, angered at his employee's disloyalty in making this speech, fired the railroad expert.[38]

In May 1919 Lomonosov also had to leave his office at the Soviet Bureau, when Maxim Litvinov ordered him back to Europe. The deputy commissar of foreign affairs was dubious that Lomonosov's work at the bureau would bear fruit "in view of the absence of all possibility of receiving railroad equipment from America." This equipment was extremely important to Soviet Russia; as Litvinov declared, "All our economic disorder is connected in a significant degree with the collapse in the area of transport." But he felt that Russian efforts would be better directed to European countries such as Germany.[39]

Litvinov's decision to send Lomonosov back to Europe in May was part of a larger policy at Narkomindel that downgraded Martens's influence. Litvinov told the Bureau chief that business would be "limited . . . taking into account the almost full impoverishment of the Russian ruble for foreign exchange and the extreme difficulty of importing gold" into the United States.[40] Thus, as late as sixteen months after Martens's credentials had been issued, he still had not been told precisely what to purchase, and this policy undermined his efforts to prove his legitimacy in the United States. The Bureau's acting commercial director, Johann G. Ohsol, complained to Moscow in May 1920, "We have been groping in the dark and trying to work out a trade policy from the fragmentary information received from you." Ohsol asked for a "complete acquisition list from you designating in the order of importance the commodities and quantities you need."[41] The Bureau's staff also needed Narkomindel to inform them of the "exact quantities and nature of raw materials you would export." American customers were lining up to buy furs, platinum, and other items.[42]

Martens was frustrated by his government's refusal to share his vision, and he regularly complained about the lack of response to his inquiries. In September 1919 he wrote, "We remain struck by your indifference to all of our proposals for better American machines, which we may receive for a payment of a small sum for storage and insurance. Our proposition for buying printing machines remains unanswered also. And all the suggestions relating to farming machinery are passed over in silence." After reading in *Ekonomicheskaya Zhizn* of difficulties in Russia in obtaining items that he could order in America, Martens wrote exasperatedly: "All the organs that we receive from Soviet Russia complain of the shortage of transportation stock and equipment. Yet, our proposals of shipments for trucks and for shipments adaptable for railroads . . . are still in need of attention."[43]

Moscow's preoccupation with the Russian civil war was the explanation given by Litvinov, who told Martens that "the successful repair of the economic apparatus, and the full implementation of the outline of social-economic tasks is strongly hampered by the . . . expanding spheres of war activities."[44] Yet in 1920, when the civil war was successfully concluded, Commissar Chicherin's focus was on relations with Britain, as Leonid Krasin, a member of the Soviet trade delegation in London, began negotiations that culminated in the Anglo-Soviet trade treaty of February 1921.[45] Chicherin believed that Washington's diplomatic importance was limited by its "provincialism."[46]

It was because Martens and his associates *did* see opportunities in America that their view of the Bureau's role remained far more ambitious than that of the Narkomindel. As Commercial Director Heller declared, "The Russian people are no fools. They want to do their shopping in America because they know that America has the largest stock of goods to choose from . . . and can supply them in the quantities needed for the enormous Russian market."[47] Despite the unsteady support that the Narkomindel offered Martens's commercial ambitions, his value as a high-profile trade representative was well recognized by the commissariat. Thus, Narkomindel fully backed him in political matters, especially during his conflicts with other activists.

Some of the socialist leaders in New York had become concerned that the Bureau chief was not sufficiently devoted to the revolutionary cause and hoped either to channel his energies more effectively or to replace him. Nicholas Hourwich of the Russian Federation told Martens that diplomacy and trade should be subordinate to the "advance guard of the movement—*the Left or Bolshevik wing of the American Socialist Party*."[48] Martens made a scathing complaint to his superiors. "Just days ago," he told the Narkomindel, "we learned that the Central Committee of the Russian Federation . . . sent around a separate statement with a list of our 'sins' against their falsely understood principles of Bolshevism. This is undoubtedly a counter-revolutionary act." The disagreement led to impassioned internecine discussions about the fate of the purchasing agency, with Martens receiving important help from Gregory Weinstein and Julius Hammer, both of whom were Left Wing Socialists and Bureau employees.[49]

The socialists' dispute over Martens reached the Comintern in July 1919, when the Russian Federation sent a delegate to Moscow to settle its tactical differences with the Bureau.[50] But the Narkomindel, knowing that Martens was more valuable as an unrecognized diplomat than he would be as an overt revolutionary, refused to give the federation what it wanted. Litvinov told Martens, "In your actions you can be guided by the exclusive directive of the Soviet Government."[51]

Litvinov's defense of the Soviet Bureau chief reaffirmed the government's decision to separate "diplomacy" from revolution. It also fit Lenin's policy of "peaceful coexistence," a term first articulated in association with the German-Soviet Treaty of Brest-Litovsk in March 1918. As Jon Jacobson suggests, the term then referred to a *peredyshka*, or "breathing spell," from war. By early 1920, with victory in the civil war assured, peaceful coexistence had evolved into a long-term strategy. Then, as E.H. Carr has noted, world revolution "began to take second place to the idea of Moscow as the centre of a government which, while remaining the champion and the repository of the revolutionary aspirations of mankind, was compelled in the meanwhile to take its place among the great Powers of the capitalist world."[52] Lenin saw it as necessary to end Soviet diplomatic and economic isolation with the West and to attract foreign investment and technology. Like Krasin, who supported this policy "as one of several alternative paths to socialism," Lenin favored the acquisition of Western equipment in order to "overtake" the capitalists.[53]

Litvinov's strong political support of Martens in 1919 showed that the success of Soviet economic development outweighed the importance of world revolution in the Soviet outlook even before the Russian civil war ended and the Allied economic embargo expired. This was well understood by U.S. intelligence agent Jacob Spolansky, a prolific analyst who was always interested in the activities of socialists in America:

> Lenin is a great tactician . . . every act of his is absolutely consistent if one has in mind constantly his fixed idea of world revolution. . . . If he can get American manufactured goods, and American capital and enterprise, he can hold on in Russia. He will therefore sacrifice his principles for the moment, and in line with this tactic might very possibly have instructed Martens to work against active Bolshevik propaganda in the United States.[54]

Spolansky's attempt to expose Martens and his office as the tools of a revolutionary government was part of a larger effort by the covert agencies of the U.S. government, the Military Intelligence Division (MID) of the War Department, and the Bureau of Investigation of the Justice Department, that continued up to the time of Martens's deportation in January 1921.[55] Intelligence agents received support from their diplomatic colleagues in the State Department, who refused to deal with Martens directly in order to avoid lending legitimacy to his mission.[56]

Despite the suspicion Ludwig Martens generated within the U.S. government, businessmen were eager to deal with him during 1919 and 1920, and he conducted high-level negotiations with some of the largest industrial firms of the United States and Canada.[57] Not all businessmen were interested, of course. After receiving a mailing from the Bureau, Charles S. Clark of Koehler Motors Company wrote the War Department, "Personally, I feel much the same sensation in having the enclosed matter before me, that I would if it were a copperhead snake."[58]

But such sentiments were not widely expressed. War Department intelligence agents worried instead that Martens and Nuorteva were "attempting and in some instances succeeding, in making American manufacturers believe that Soviet Russia wants to do business totally with America." Indeed, when a Soviet order for $6 million worth of agricultural equipment could not be placed in the United States in 1920, Soviet representative Johann Ohsol was apologetic: "It has been our sincere desire to introduce in Russia mainly American agriculture and other machinery, inasmuch as the great demands of Russia for such machinery could have been filled best by American industries."[59]

Many prominent businessmen favored the expansion of Soviet-American trade, as long as it was clear that diplomatic relations were not involved. The four-thousand-member National Association of Manufacturers declared in 1919 that "many thousands of manufacturers in this country would be in a position to do business with Russia."[60] Thus, when Nuorteva and Heller attended the Sixth National Foreign Trade Convention in Chicago in April 1919, attended by over one thousand manufacturers, exporters, and bankers, they found grounds for encouragement. Heller was particularly heartened that "the dominant tone of the convention were complaints about a lack of export markets and the difficulty of getting payment from Europe," areas where he saw Soviet trade as filling an important gap. But he was annoyed by the prominence of the anti-Bolshevik American-Russian Chamber of Commerce and the Russian cooperatives at the convention. These "counter-revolutionists" were running an exhibition booth where they "circulated pamphlets warning against establishing trade relations with Soviet Russia."[61] Foreign branches of the Russian consumers' and agricultural cooperatives, including the largest, Tsentrosoyuz, had resisted incorporation into the nationalized cooperatives in Soviet Russia.[62] The foreign branches yielded to Moscow's control, however, in January 1920, after the Allies lifted the blockade against Soviet Russia.[63]

The cooperatives and the American-Russian Chamber of Commerce were both reviled by the Soviet Bureau because of their opposition to the Bolshevik government. William Redfield, the president of the Chamber of Commerce and a former secretary of commerce, complained that the Soviet Bureau's magazine *Soviet Russia* should be kept out of the mails. The "petty-bourgeoisie cooperatives" were less open in their dislike for the Soviet regime but distrusted by that government nonetheless, as Litvinov had warned Martens, "our relations [with the co-operatives] are ambiguous and even secretly hostile."[64] Despite the presence of these unfriendly forces in Chicago, the Bureau's liaison at the trade convention tried to arrange for Heller and Nuorteva to address the gathering. He was unsuccessful. This was hardly surprising, since the convention's president, according to Heller, "warned American manufacturers against establishing trade relations with us, saying that American business men did not want 'looted money.'"[65]

In the face of such negative attention, the Soviet representatives lay low. "We established our own headquarters in the Hotel La Salle," Nuorteva told Martens, while he and Heller waited for exporters to respond to an ad in the *Chicago Tribune*. The tactic succeeded. "We were swamped with visitors for two days," Nuorteva gloated, "mostly representatives of firms all of whom were impressed with the possibility of trade with Russia." Firms including Marshall Field, Grand Rapids Underwear, National Shoe, and several meat packers stopped in, along with representatives of International Harvester and Advance Rumely, who, in addition to trade, were looking for information about their Russian factories. "We told them that if they could get cable communications for us to Moscow we can get them the information they desire," said Nuorteva. He thought it might be a good idea to establish a trading bureau in Chicago, and Gregory Weinstein decided to launch a Central Soviet Bureau at 2401 Division Street.[66] Heller measured their success this way: "Our work . . . is bearing fruit, in so far as it has brought forth attacks by the opposing forces."[67]

Heller also met Ford representative Ernest Kanseler at the New York Ritz-Carlton that April. Kanseler was interested in trading with the Soviets, going so far as to recommend an organization to handle distribution and spare parts. He invited Heller to Dearborn to inspect the plant and witness its impressive daily output of 275 tractors. But Kanseler did not wish to press the State Department on the blockade "or take any other diplomatic step," believing that export licenses could be obtained. After the Chicago convention, Henry Ford's general secretary, K.C. Liebold, hosted Nuorteva and Heller in Dearborn. There, E.L. Sorensen, manager of the Ford tractor works, told Nuorteva that the firm's Russian business was already being handled by an agent in Russia, who allegedly owned forty-five banks along with steamship lines. Nuorteva informed Sorensen that neither this agent "nor anyone else" owned any banks in Russia, and the only agency to deal with was the Soviet Bureau.[68]

The Soviets' midwestern visit did not escape the notice of Chicago's Military Intelligence Office. But little action was taken, because "after having made arrangements to completely cover [Martens] and his activities" in Chicago and New York, the Bureau of Investigation decided "to discontinue further investigation." Instead, it would limit its activities to attending political meetings. The War Department's Military Intelligence Division (MID) followed suit, and John B. Trevor's disappointment was doubtless shared by many in the intelligence community: "In view of the character of the group surrounding Martens," he sighed, "this is a most unfortunate policy at the present time."[69]

Trevor, a Harvard graduate who took over MID in 1919, fully recognized that "any investigation of Bolshevism, even in an informal way, was not to be countenanced by the Department." But he had become interested in Martens's finances and was convinced that Guaranty Trust Company's president, Henry Sabin, "one of the most unscrupulous bankers in the city," was "personally interested in Martens and his work." The Guaranty Trust Company's (GTC) interest in Russia could be traced, Trevor contended, to its holdings of $6.5 million in Russian Imperial Government and provisional government funds, rendered worthless by the Revolution. "The GTC are unable to see any satisfactory solution of their ruble problem unless the Russian Bolshevik government is recognized," Trevor reckoned.[70] He alleged that President Sabin had sent "personal funds" to Martens and paid the bureau's yearly rent of $2,500 for the next three years.[71]

On April 29, 1919, a number of bankers attended a luncheon hosted by the Council on Foreign Relations at the Hotel Astor. Martens was an invited speaker and the financing of his bureau a featured topic in this well publicized event. Despite the coverage, Trevor was convinced that "all were sworn to secrecy as to what transpired." Trevor's suspicions were raised by the attendance at the luncheon of three GTC men, including Sabin. Other bankers were also present, but "the GTC crowd constituted the backbone of this entertainment, because if there was one hundred and fifty million dollars in sight, they wanted to be present when the distribution began."[72] A Bureau of Investigation report suggested that banks were working on Martens's behalf in order to "create the belief that Soviet Russia will continue, so American manufacturers interested in foreign trade would bring pressure on the administration to recognize Soviet Russia."[73] Nuorteva insisted to reporters that the bankers' luncheon was an "informal" information meeting. He declared that the Bureau was receiving money from Russia, not the GTC. Yet when he was asked by the *New York Herald* how the funds came into the country, Nuorteva snapped, "That's our business. I don't ask you how you get your money."[74]

Trevor decided to investigate the host group, the Council of Foreign Relations. He obtained a booklet about the organization's leaders, where he detected a Guaranty Trust link in Alexander J. Hemphill, chairman of the council's finance committee, and circled board of governors' members Henry Morgenthau, Oscar S. Strauss, and Abram I. Elkus as Jews. Trevor's interest in Jews was not unusual in the intelligence community, some of whom believed in an "International Jewish Bolshevik conspiracy."[75]

The Bureau of Investigation was also interested in German Jews, making much of the fact that Trotsky's real name was not "Bronstein" but "'Braunstein.'" An agent alerted J. Edgar Hoover that "this is thoroughly German (Brownstone)." The agent produced a number of other German Jewish names in Soviet officialdom from Apfelbaum ("Zinoviev") to Gruzenberg ("Borodin"). Broadening the conspiracy to those simply of German descent, the agent recalled Martens's return to Russia in 1905, finding it "strikingly coincidental that . . . both Russian revolutions were supervised in Germany."[76]

Martens's German background was an issue for the government for other reasons. Both the War and Justice Departments, acting at the behest of the State Department, attempted to find out—six months after the war had ended—if Martens was a German "alien enemy," despite the fact that he had spent only two-and-a-half years of his life in Germany, and that unwillingly. At the end of April the War Department dispatched an agent to the Soviet Bureau to conduct an investigation into his citizenship. The Justice Department also sent an agent.[77] Martens foiled both inquiries by claiming diplomatic privilege and insisted that he be interviewed only after a letter from the attorney general or secretary of state were presented to him. Because of the "peculiarity inherent in the Russian diplomatic situation," J. Edgar Hoover recommended that the attorney general await further instructions from the State Department. W.E. Allen, acting chief of the Federal Bureau of Investigation, was frustrated by the decision against the investigation of Martens, whose "real purpose," he believed, was "to spread Russian propaganda." He sighed, "Apparently we are at the end of our rope unless it should be deemed advisable to invoke the use of a grand jury subpoena." Allen could be pleased that the New York Senate's Lusk Committee would soon "undertake a thorough investigation of Martens' organization."[78]

Despite the highly charged political atmosphere, the Soviet Bureau continued to cultivate industrialists. In May, James P. Mulvihill, a Pittsburgh shoe manufacturer, invited Heller to Washington to meet with Rep. Stephen J. Porter and the State Department counselor, Frank Polk. Polk had previously alluded to the "suspicion" under which the Bureau operated, describing Martens as "a mystery" and Nuorteva as "a very dangerous and clever propagandist." Polk told Mulvihill and Heller that "no precedent exists" for trade without recognition. Heller and Mulvihill found a more friendly government representative in Justice Louis Brandeis. Brandeis was a strong opponent of the Allied intervention in Russia and recommended that the Bureau garner "maximum publicity . . . in getting the liberal opinion of America on [y]our side."[79]

Heller began planning a Russian trade convention for the end of June in Atlantic City, which would lead to "the organization of an American Association for the promotion of trade with Russia, officered by manufacturers of national prominence." To spur interest, he sent a circular to a large number of American chambers of commerce.[80] While Heller planned his conference, his assistant, Evans Clark, also made the rounds in Washington. Clark sought to "make as many personal connections as possible and to give certain senators information relative to the desire of manufacturers to export to Russia." Armed with letters of introduction from American manufacturers, he visited Sens. Joseph France, Hiram Johnson, William Borah, and Key Pittman.[81] He relied on Paul Wallace Hanna, a journalist for the socialist *New York Call*, to find out "just what powerful men inside the Government and out are willing to give Soviet trade at least a fighting chance." In addition to the senators, a number of congressmen were sympathetic to Martens, including Joseph Walsh of Massachusetts, William E. Mason of Illinois, and Stephen J. Porter of Pennsylvania. Companies did come forth to help the Bureau's efforts in Washington. Spark plug manufacturer Apex Company wrote that its congressman, Oscar R. Luhring of the First District of Indiana, would work in Washington to help the firm gain an export license.[82]

Although the Soviet Bureau was beginning to make important inroads among both liberals and trade advocates in Washington, the Red Scare made it difficult for Martens to be tolerated. Unlike the federal government, the states were not forced to limit their tasks to "observation" of local Bolshevism. On June 12, 1919, New York State troopers stormed into Martens's offices, armed with a search warrant from the city magistrate. The state senate's Joint Legislative Committee for the Investigation of Seditious Activities, otherwise known as the Clayton R. Lusk Committee, was identified as the raid's instigator, although Senator Lusk denied ordering it and attributed responsibility to the state attorney general's office.

For two hours, everyone, including visitors, was detained. Nuorteva fumed:

> The raid was an outrage. Twenty detectives rushed into our office and at their hands we received the roughest kind of treatment, short of physical violence. They refused to let us communicate with our lawyers, they cut our telephone wires, they barred all the doors, and refused to let any of the attachés and workers leave the offices; then they seized all our papers, including correspondence in regard to commercial orders to a number of American firms, and jumbled them up in such a fashion that it will take us at least three weeks to straighten them out if we ever get them back.[83]

Although Martens was not arrested, the raid was vivid proof of the Bureau's precarious position. The Bureau's counsel, I. Horowitz, along with Martens, Nuorteva, Weinstein, and Heller, were subpoenaed to appear before the Lusk committee, which was to determine whether the Bureau "conducts agitation for the overthrow of the U.S. government."[84] Four days after the raid, Nuorteva triumphantly appeared before a huge throng of loyal supporters at Madison Square Garden. He emphasized that "we are advised by our counsels that the raid was in every way unwarranted and illegal," because of the hasty manner in which the search warrant was issued.[85]

While the raid was being conducted, Alexander M. Berkenheim, president of the Tsentrosoyuz cooperative, was allowed to ship food, clothing, and other goods to both Bolshevik and non-Bolshevik Russia.[86] Tsentrosoyuz's still autonomous American office had $3 million on deposit in the National City Bank and $1 million of credit available.[87] Abraham Heller visited Berkenheim in early May and suggested that their two agencies work together to supply Russia, "instead of at cross purposes." Since Berkenheim sought to protect his "standing with the present powers" in the United States, he was reluctant and suggested only the possibility of an "unofficial" arrangement.[88] Nuorteva was probably correct that American authorities were using the cooperative to divide the Russian people from the Soviet regime. Yet he saw the Berkenheim shipments as having a larger significance. "We welcome the news that the blockade against Soviet Russia has been relaxed, and that the Russian Cooperative societies are loading ships in New York with goods for Petrograd." To Nuorteva, it served as an opening.[89]

Six weeks after the raid, Martens told Moscow that all was quiet. Despite his recurring troubles, he again announced in the press his intentions to place large orders in the United States. But Secretary Lansing rejoined, "No arrangements have been made to permit any trade whatsoever between the United States and Bolshevik Russia."[90] Yet one month earlier, acting in Lansing's place, Polk had told the American embassy in Paris that with Germany no longer at war, he opposed a British and French plan to continue the formal wartime blockade against Bolshevik ports. Polk declared: "A blockade before a state of war exists is out of the question. It would not be recognized by this government. . . . [T]he Allies exaggerate danger of trade with the Bolsheviks in Russia."[91] Despite his cogent assessment, the United States maintained blockade-like restrictions against Bolshevik Russia for another year.

It remained vitally important for Martens and his associates to end the trade embargo. Heller made contacts with a well-connected former New Jersey senator, Thomas Martin, whose family manufactured binder twine used in farming and who was ready "to trade with Russia on the basis of a definite order of considerable magnitude." In return, Martin promised to "undertake to use his best offices to bring about the lifting of the blockade." Although the Bureau recommended this purchase to the Central Committee, and gained the backing of Lenin and Litvinov, advocates of a greater reliance on German trade, including Chicherin and Krasin, decided against it. German competition meant that Americans who wished to expedite Soviet contacts would have to work even harder toward ending the blockade.[92]

In August, Martens and Heller traveled to Ford Motor Company headquarters in Dearborn. Since Henry Ford was out of town, they were received by tractor factory director Sorensen, who followed up by writing a letter to the State Department, "in which he officially asked permission for export of tractors to Soviet Russia." After seeing the Fordson tractor demonstrated, Martens declared that "the Ford tractor will serve as the ideal machine for communist economy in Russia." He was ready to buy ten thousand of them and hoped that Ford would also "construct a factory in Russia for the production of tractors and cars." In 1922, following Martens's return to Russia, the Soviet Union ordered several hundred Fordson tractors through Armand Hammer.[93]

Another of Martens's responsibilities in New York was to recruit "specialists in all fields of technology and science" who wanted to go to Russia to help in its rebuilding. As Martens declared, "The possibility of Socialism in Russia is determined by . . . utiliz[ing] the whole technical and organizing experience of capitalism for its own purposes." Martens planned a conference for interested emigrants for July 4–6. After the June raid, the conference was moved to September 30, when it drew large numbers of committed participants.[94] By the fall of 1920 a thousand members had registered in New York with the Society for Technical Aid for Soviet Russia, and by 1923 the society had facilitated the voluntary repatriation of over five hundred emigrants, who brought their American-acquired skills and equipment back to Russia.[95]

➢ MARTENS'S FINANCING AND GOVERNMENT INVESTIGATIONS

Because the United States treated Bolshevik gold as "stolen" money and forbade imports of Russian ruble currency, Martens could not count on large infusions of cash. He had to rely largely upon the efforts of couriers, who smuggled in valuables and bank drafts to him. It was a very risky business. Only about a third of the couriers sent to him in 1919 arrived with their deliveries. They brought valuables and funds from Moscow's "disbursing agent," Frederick Strom, a socialist member of the Swedish Parliament, who belonged to the "central committee" of Scandinavian Bolsheviks in Stockholm. Author Carl Sandburg even served as a one-time courier for Martens in December 1918, bringing $10,000 in two bank drafts. He was detained by New York port authorities, who confiscated his money. Sandburg had obtained the funds in Norway, where he worked as a reporter for the Newspaper Enterprise Association.[96]

Nuorteva urged that Moscow be more generous. "Considering the extremely costly character of the activities of the Soviet bureau," he wrote to the Narkomindel, "I appeal to you with the request to call the attention of the Vesenkha [the Supreme Soviet of the National Economy] to this activity."[97] Because of the many obstacles faced by his couriers, Martens was forced to depend on local benefactors for his financial survival. Among his strongest backers was Julius Hammer, director of the Bureau's medical and financial departments. A successful businessman and owner of Allied Drug and Chemical Company, Julius Hammer provided the chief financial means for the Soviet Bureau to open and stay in operation, while garnering sales approaching $150,000.[98] When Hammer was later imprisoned, his company's business and its work with the Bureau continued with his son, Armand.

While the Lusk committee prepared for its hearings during the late summer and fall of 1919, the Justice Department's Bureau of Investigation hired a Finnish émigré, Ferdinand Peterson, to spy on Martens.[99] The federal agency suspected that Peterson was a double agent and hoped to use him to get the Soviet Bureau, and particularly Martens, involved in a divisive socialist imbroglio. Thus, upon learning from Peterson that Louis G. Fraina, the secretary of the Communist party of America, was suspected by some in the party of being a government informant, G-men played along. They left out reports and canceled checks "signed" by Fraina for Peterson to see. As hoped, Peterson fed Soviet Bureau leaders this information. Nuorteva, initially "incredulous," was apparently jealous and suspicious enough of Fraina's influence in the party to find Peterson's story credible, as did Martens. Nuorteva, who was aware of Peterson's government connections, befriended his fellow Finn and promised to pay him $1,000 if he would recover the canceled checks allegedly signed by Fraina. When Peterson tried to steal the documents, he was arrested and fired by the Bureau of Investigation.[100]

It was not until American Communists held a trial six months later that Fraina was freed from suspicion, with his top associates supporting his vigorous denial of the charges.[101] Here the Justice Department's strategy bore fruit. Martens's attendance at the "trial" contradicted the Bureau chief's claims of non-involvement in party activities, officials asserted. J. Edgar Hoover opined, "Nuorteva and Martens were instrumental in the calling of this trial, notwithstanding their public protestation to the effect that they never have interested themselves in American [socialist] affairs."[102]

The Justice Department's intrigues against the Bureau were overshadowed in the fall of 1919 by the Lusk committee's investigation into the dissemination of Bolshevik propaganda in the United States. Martens was served with a summons on November 14 and asked to report the following day. The committee wanted him to bring his "business books, documents, and chiefly, notes . . . to the Soviet Government." Upon the advice of his lawyer, Martens presented the legislators only with his account books and refused to share with them his diplomatic correspondence. The commission soon became more interested in Martens's revolutionary background as well as Lenin's inflammatory statements.[103]

Lenin's "Letter to American Workers" of August 20, 1918, introduced as evidence in the case, stated: "We are banking on the inevitability of the world revolution. . . . The corpse of capitalism is decaying and disintegrating in our midst, polluting the air and poisoning our lives." There was "only one holy and . . . legitimate war, namely: the war against the capitalists." Lenin's missive also asked workers in America to start "general strikes to help the Russian Soviet Government" and to prevent troops from being sent to Russia. The Soviet Bureau chief, however, testified that his only goal was "to win . . . to the side of Russia the big business and manufacturing interests of this country, the packers, the United States Steel Corporation, the Standard Oil Company."[104]

Martens's pursuit of big business perplexed the *New York Times*, which questioned how this could be consistent with the aims of Lenin and the Bolshevik revolution. Martens responded that his government did not promulgate revolutionary propaganda outside Russia, and that Lenin had spoken only as a "private citizen" when he "addressed Soviet propaganda to the American workingman and soldier," urging them to topple the U.S. government. The Bureau chief professed his own innocence; "I have not fostered any radical propaganda in this country . . . nor allowed anyone in my employment to do so," he told the skeptical legislators.[105]

Although Lusk could not find the Soviet representative in violation of any law, he asserted that "every act . . . [Martens] commits which is beneficial to the Bolshevik regime . . . is unquestionably an act of hostility to the United States."[106] New York State attorney general Charles B. Newton, who headed the inquiry, believed that Martens's money was used for propaganda purposes, and newspapers including the *New York Times, New York Tribune,* and *New York World* agreed.[107]

Commercial Department Director Abraham Heller attempted to capitalize on the publicity that the Lusk trial generated. He claimed that his agency had been in touch with "2,500 American business firms" to obtain needed products, from 5,000 initially contacted.[108] Not only had they "received offers from manufacturers and producers of all kinds of commodities throughout the United States," but "our offices are visited daily by representatives of different firms, and through the mails, we receive hundreds of letters." Heller released a list that included the Chicago meat packing giants Armour, Swift, Morris, Wilson, and Cudahy, the condensed milk producer Sheffield Farms, and the American Steel Export Company (a division of United States Steel).[109]

The *New York Times* promptly contacted some of these companies in order to verify Heller's allegations. The firms dismissed his claims or pleaded ignorance, possibly for political and legal reasons. U.S. Steel Corporation president Elbert H. Gary declared that there was "no foundation" for Heller's assertions. G.F. Swift of the Swift Company's export department declared, "I am sure we have never had any dealings with them of any kind." Loton Horton, the president of Sheffield Farms, stated, "If Martens has made inquiries . . . for condensed milk, I know nothing about it." Even Edward Morris of Morris and Company, the same packinghouse that would soon take a $10 million order from Martens, disclaimed any interest: "We have never had anything to do with those people [and] we would not sell them a dollar's worth of goods for cash or credit."[110]

But Martens had no trouble demonstrating that his vendors were not telling the truth. The next day, he waved a six-month-old letter from Swift that stated, "We take pleasure in quoting you market values . . . on the principal commodities we think you will be interested in." In April, Heller had met with officials of Swift in New York, who had informed him that "they would supply us with a carload of fats, lards, and canned beef as soon as we are ready. Also offered to consult the State Department on the possibility of shipments to Russia." Hammer also could produce correspondence from E.H. Boyer of Morris Meats, dated August 7, 1919, which read, "Should you be so kind as to place a contract with us, you have our assurance that it will . . . be a pleasure to give you all the assistance possible in obtaining permits."[111]

The Lusk committee, furthermore, released evidence that Martens and his associates had met or corresponded with representatives of Armour, Swift, Case Threshing Machine, Union Card and Paper, Reliance Yarn Company, and Bridgeport Rolling Mills, among hundreds of others. Although firms were reluctant to confirm their trading role during the intensely hostile atmosphere of the Red Scare, Martens had interested a great number of them. By May 1919, 853 firms had contacted Martens's bureau by letter, according to the seized files of the Lusk committee, and 235 firms had sent their representatives to the Bureau.[112]

In his first year, Martens signed over $30 million worth of orders with American firms, including meat packers, textile fabricators, and makers of machinery. In January 1920, the Soviet Bureau announced it was placing an additional $300 million worth of orders, for items ranging from agricultural implements to pharmaceutical supplies.[113] Three hundred million dollars was undoubtedly an exaggeration, but there were some sizable orders in Martens's portfolio: a $3 million contract for machinery and tools from Martens's former employer, Weinberg and Posner, and a $4.5 million contract with Lehigh Machine Company of Pennsylvania for one thousand automatic presses.[114] The Chicago meat packing firm Morris and Company negotiated a $10 million purchase for fifty million pounds of food products, and hosiery and undergarment agent Fischman and Company wrote an order for $3 million.[115] B.L. Bobroff of the Bobroff Foreign Trading and Engineering Company of Milwaukee received contracts for boots worth $4.3 million. Bobroff claimed that he had been selected "to negotiate with the Milwaukee shoe manufacturers for two million pairs of shoes for the Russian Red Army."[116] He also received an order in January 1920 for $1.4 million worth of machinery, including sixty-five milling machines, forty-five shapers, and ten thousand pairs of nine-inch and twelve-inch shoes.[117] None of these spectacular orders were ever consummated. They all ran into the same problem: no export licenses.[118]

◄ 2 ►

THE DEMISE OF THE
SOVIET BUREAU

After testifying before the Lusk committee in December, Martens was subpoenaed by a Senate subcommittee that had been established to investigate Bolshevik propaganda.[1] But before Martens appeared before the Senate, Attorney General A. Mitchell Palmer also wished to grab some headlines. Palmer, known to the public as the "fighting Quaker," issued an arrest warrant for Martens on January 2, 1920. The attorney general envisioned a spectacular public arrest of Martens for the benefit of newsreel cameras, a scenario that had the approval of Palmer's special assistant, J. Edgar Hoover. The attorney general was then in the midst of a full-scale government offensive against suspected radicals and their fellow travelers in the United States. His staff staged two broad sweeps on January 2 and January 5, arresting an estimated five thousand people in twenty-three cities. The raids were coordinated on the federal, state, and local levels.[2]

Coming just after the December deportation from Ellis Island of 249 Russians (including Emma Goldman) on the *Buford*, the January raids were the culmination of a Red-hunting whirlwind. The average number of dues-paying Communist party members declined from twenty-four thousand in late 1919 to fewer than six thousand by April 1920, and this drastic drop had long-term effects. At a meeting of the executive committee of the Comintern in 1921, an American delegate complained that although nearly four million people were unemployed in America in that recessionary year, only nine to ten thousand had joined the party.[3]

Before Martens's Senate subpoena was issued, the Bureau of Investigation also made exhaustive attempts to arrest him. After a disappointing wait outside the Bureau on January 2, 1920, agents brought along twelve cameramen and four motion picture machine operators to Santeri Nuorteva's New Jersey chicken farm. Martens's close associate termed the raid on his farm "comical" and eagerly anticipated "our 'little finale,'" the Senate hearing.[4]

Meanwhile, the War Department's Military Intelligence Division assigned Clarence Converse to watch Martens's suite in Washington at the Lafayette Hotel. But Martens was staying with a friend, *Nation* columnist Lincoln Colcord, and it was at Colcord's that he was served a subpoena on January 10.[5] The *New York*

Times reported that Martens and Nuorteva "seemed to regard the serving of the committee's subpoenas upon them last night as one of the best things that had happened to them in months." Indeed, Nuorteva crowed, "The only thing I am afraid of is becoming over-optimistic."[6] Martens's counsel, the able and prominent former Georgia senator Thomas Hardwick, devoted all his attention to Martens's case, billing the Bureau $4,000 a month for his services. The attitude of the Senate subcommittee, chaired by George E. Moses of New Hampshire, also compared favorably to that of the Lusk committee. The former was "polite and considerate," Nuorteva reported, while the latter's investigation had been "dirty, insulting and ignorant."[7]

Martens told Glover Machine Works of Marietta, Georgia, "I am glad of the Senate investigation, because I have reason to believe that it will be a real investigation and not a blind persecution and that I shall be able there to throw full light on all my doings." He added that some businessmen were going to write to Senator Moses on Martens's behalf.[8]

The Senate hearings followed an agenda similar to the Lusk committee's. The legislators in Washington, like those in New York, asked Martens about his distribution of Lenin's provocative "Letter to the American Workers." Reprints of the letter had been found in Martens's office during the Lusk raid. Martens denied knowing who had circulated the letter, but the Bureau of Investigation determined that Martens, along with Nuorteva and Weinstein, was involved and that the publication had been printed on machines belonging to the International Workers of the World.[9]

In the last week of January, MID Agent Converse reported that Martens hosted a dinner at his hotel for fifty-six guests, including lawyer Charles Recht, Colcord, the Nuortevas, and Bureau staffers Julius Hammer, Kenneth Durant, A.A. Heller, and Etta Tuch, as well as a host of others including a reporter for the *New York Call*. Nuorteva gave a speech on the occasion: "No matter what action is taken against Mr. Martens within the next few days . . . it will not be the expression of the people of this Country." He announced that after the guests were treated to a Russian song, the "Red Hog," they would be welcome to make speeches themselves. "I request that in the talks to follow that there be no criticisms of the government or its officials," he urged. Perhaps Nuorteva said this for the benefit of Converse, who was observing inconspicuously outside the doorway.[10]

While the Senate hearings continued, an organization was launched: the American Commercial Association to Promote Trade with Russia. Its founder was Emerson P. Jennings, president of Lehigh Machine Company of Lehighton, Pennsylvania, which had a $4.5 million contract for one thousand automatic printing presses from the Soviet Bureau that could not be shipped so long as the blockade continued.[11] Joining Jennings in this new association were the Borden Condensed Milk and the U.S. Steamship Companies, as well as forty-three others. They convened on January 25 in Manhattan's Raleigh Hotel, representing an alleged total of $100 million worth of Soviet orders. Their goal was to lift the blockade. The gathering was a "conference of Americans . . . independent of the Russian Soviet

Bureau," Jennings said, although one historian has suggested that Martens was instrumental in persuading the group to lobby the administration, and its agenda and name were certainly similar to the group Heller had proposed in 1919.[12] According to the Bureau of Investigation, Jennings had lent Martens $8,500.[13] Certainly the State Department found the two entities much too close and dubbed the American Commercial Association the "chief and most willing instrument of [the Soviet Bureau's] propaganda." Jennings's motivations, they declared, were based on "greed."[14]

Just as he had to the Lusk committee, Martens testified to the Senate that he had "scrupulously refrained from any interference or participation in . . . domestic affairs." Instead "the chief purpose of my mission . . . has been and is the re-establishment of economic intercourse between Russia and the United States." Although the American Communist party wished to "seize power in the United States and establish a dictatorship of the Proletariat," Martens always insisted that he was not involved in these efforts. But in late March, the Senate subcommittee concluded that Martens was not only a propagandist but also a fraud.[15] The senators contended that "the entire fabric of trade negotiations which [he] unrolled was part of an ingenious scheme of propaganda to create sympathy . . . for the Russian Soviets."[16] Nuorteva's and Martens's hopes for the Senate were dashed. In fact, the committee's final statement was written so as to enable the Justice Department to arrest Martens and deport him as an "enemy alien."[17]

Yet Martens refused to give up. He and his associates still envisioned American trade as the answer to their difficulties and saw the postwar depression in the United States as working in their favor. "The cotton farmers are crying for this trade and are threatening to diminish the next year's cotton crops," Martens declared. "The clothing industry is demanding it in order to find an outlet for their overstocked factories. The heavy industries are beginning to feel the lack of foreign markets." Martens believed that tough times would enable him to buy a wide range of goods in America, particularly leather products, textiles, chemicals, soap, and machinery, at a time when American firms were threatened by foreign competition. He wondered if America would "observe complacently how Great Britain is about to secure the greatest trade concessions in Soviet Russia? Is this country to help Japan get full control of Siberia and ridicule those Americans who are earnestly striving to obtain some share of the Far Eastern Market [and] to compel Russia to obtain all her machinery and locomotives . . . from Germany?"[18]

Martens's Bureau also worked hard to impress American bankers such as Henry E. Cooper of Equitable Trust with the abundance of natural resources in Soviet Russia. Nuorteva believed that these resources, especially gold, "will enable us within a period of six to eight months to buy, practically on a cash basis, goods up to an amount of $600 to $700 million." When those credits had been exhausted, the Russian harvest would be in, "which will give us additional purchasing power." Moscow hoped that "some American financial consortium might interest itself in the conversion of the entire Russian debt in return for vast industrial, transportation, mining and forest concessions." Trading Russia's material riches in order to wipe out debt was something that Litvinov had broached at the Paris Peace Conference in 1919.[19]

After the Dorpat Peace Treaty was signed by Soviet Russia and Estonia on February 2, 1920, Martens was able to use the port of Reval in Estonia as a trans-shipment point during the embargo. Indeed, between May and December 1920, Estonia transferred nearly 80 percent of the volume of all Soviet imports.[20] This was a lucrative business for Estonian agents, who collected 20 to 50 percent commissions from Moscow for handling Soviet orders. A representative from Morse Twist Drill complained, "They are charging the Russians such extortionate prices that they may very soon kill the goose that lays the golden eggs."[21]

Isidor Gukovskii was the general Soviet representative in Reval. The Bureau of Investigation reported that Gukovskii worked with a man named Solomon, whose task was "transmission of money to L.C.A.K. Martens."[22] In November, agents intercepted a letter and learned that "Martens [was] entirely out of funds but expecting two remittances from Solomon; the first for $35,000, and the second for $33,240." The letter also mentioned "a previous remittance of $25,000 from Solomon to Martens, which the latter received through the National City Bank."[23] Since money from Moscow was insufficient, the Soviet Bureau relied on businessmen to finance shipments to Estonia during the blockade.[24]

The United States supplied fully one-fifth of the value of all goods imported to Russia between mid-April and mid-October 1920, much of it in violation of the embargo, which ended on July 8.[25] The Soviet cooperatives Tsentrosoyuz and Selskosoyuz, whose foreign operations had been nationalized in 1920, the People's Industrial Trading Corporation, which specialized in the purchase of Ford products, and the Bureau itself contributed to this import total. In the first half of 1920, the Soviet Bureau shipped $200,000 through the blockade in goods to Russia. Notable among these were $46,000 worth of morphine and other medicines shipped by Armand Hammer. These drug shipments were provided with Hammer's personal credit, which he recouped in later dealings with the Soviet government.[26] In May and June 1920, the Bureau also sent more than $10,000 worth of soap, $2,422 in cutters, almost $11,000 in rubber galoshes, $25,000 in gauze, and nearly $100,000 worth of shoes.[27]

Because the Federal Reserve Board refused to allow American banks to make credit arrangements with their Estonian counterparts during this period, the Soviet government paid for shipments in Reval by depositing funds in gold in institutions like the Reval Industry Bank. Gold ingots were then melted down, most often in Sweden, to remove any trace of origin.[28] In July, Moscow sent $150,000 in gold to Estonia to meet the *Wheeling Mold*, a steamship unloading chisels, boots, resin, meat, camphor, and chemicals in Reval. Although this gold allowed new orders to be placed, Martens knew that the shipments could have been greater if the Estonian and New York banks been able to work out more flexible financing. "The Federal Reserve deprived us of a high potential of trade with Russia," he complained.[29]

In 1920, Gukovskii asked William H. Coombs, foreign representative of the Pressed Steel Car Company, for assistance in purchasing "railway material, mining machinery, wire rope, [and] structural steel." Gukovskii proposed that Pressed Steel would become trustees for $500 million in Soviet gold, as well as twenty thousand tons of flax, in order to open credits in the United States for Soviet purchases. Coombs informed Guaranty Trust, which found the proposal credible but would not approve it because of the American ban on Soviet gold.[30]

Shipping through Reval was difficult, and American firms were not enthusiastic about receiving payment in Estonia, "a state not recognized *de jure*." Firms wanted payment through Western banks, Martens noted, but they were "beginning clearly to understand that trade with Russia at the present moment is possible only in this condition." Babbitt Soap Company was one company that did take a $200,000 order through Reval.[31]

The American political climate continued to create difficulty for the bureau throughout 1920. Martens believed that "the American government, mindful of the opportunity of legal destruction of the Soviet Bureau, conducts a very energetic campaign against us." Martens found the new secretary of state, Bainbridge Colby, who replaced Lansing on March 23, as unfriendly as his predecessor. In June, Colby telegraphed an appeal to the members of the American Federation of Labor not to pass a resolution favoring recognition and ending trade restrictions.[32] Colby's reference to the Soviet government as "based on the denial of honor and trust" was insulting to Martens. Because Colby and his department had proved so "unrestrained," the bureau chief told his superiors, "I think it necessary to quickly protest to the American government . . . and to demand a passport for exit from America." Martens stormed to Colby, "If this is the official expression of the Secretary of State of the United States respecting the established government of the people of Russia . . . my mission here has ended."[33]

With Wilson being ill, Martens thought that "a state verging on anarchy" had emerged in the United States. During Wilson's incapacitation, his wife, Edith, acted as his proxy. Her relationship with "Russian and other émigré aristocrats" was far too cozy for Martens. Believing that "those elements, interested in a more or less honest solution of Russian question," were no longer being heard, he became convinced of "the uselessness of continuation of my activities in the U.S."[34] Martens's hints about departing led to speculation that he had been "recalled by his government." Yet when questioned, Martens insisted his government was not removing him, nor did he intend to leave.[35]

That did not stop the Bureau of Investigation from looking eagerly for Martens's supposed successor in August 1920. They already had a man in mind, along with a photograph, although they did not know the man's name. Customs and immigration authorities at the port of Baltimore were ready to "question and search all Seamen thoroughly, and will advise this office of any suspicious persons being on board."[36] But Martens would not leave until he was forced to in January 1921.

The United States remained in a postwar recession while Martens continued his operation in New York, and labor leaders began to lobby the Wilson administration to lift the trade embargo with Soviet Russia, as unions representing thousands of workers sent telegrams to the State Department demanding official trade relations.[37] More influential in the same cause were the employers of many of these workers, who used their national clout to exert great pressure to end trade restrictions. Newspapers including the *New York Commercial* and the *Journal of Commerce* reflected businessmen's bullishness on Soviet trade. So, too, did many individual firms. The Standard Steamship Company, a subsidiary of Guaranty Trust, wanted to buy flax, hemp, and manganese from the Bureau and was willing to furnish credit. The firm declared that it was ready "to force the issue between the United States Government and Russia as to trade." And medical supplier Johnson and Johnson had fifty thousand packages of surgical ligatures left over from a government order to sell to the Soviet Bureau.[38]

Robert S. Alter, the vice president and foreign manager of American Tool Works Company, lobbied particularly hard for the Bureau. He wrote to Ohio congressman Nicholas Longworth to criticize the official American position on the Soviet government. Alter pointed out that Italy, Britain, and Canada were already taking advantage of the business. He was eager to take a $1 million Bureau order, to be placed through agents Weinberg and Posner, "just as soon as the State Department will allow us to do so." He appealed to Longworth "to try and clear up this situation for the benefit of the American manufacturers." Alter noted his involvement with the Mississippi Valley Association, a business group whose area of representation "represents 55 percent of the voting power of the United States."[39]

Alter urged a colleague in the machine tool industry to take a strong stand for Soviet trade, pointing to British competition. "The matter is of such importance that manufacturers who are affected should make a concerted effort to bring Washington to its senses." S.L. Baron, the vice president of Weinberg and Posner, commended Alter on his efforts but lamented; "In spite of all the concessions which are being continually and cheerfully offered to the American people by the Russian government . . . our Government seems to pay no more attention to all of this than to a voice yelling in the desert."[40] Many other large companies wrote to the State Department petitioning for the blockade to be lifted, including Packard Motor Car Company, Duplex Machine Company, J.I. Case Threshing Company, White Truck Company, Lederle Antitoxin Laboratories, and the B.T. Babbitt Soap Works.[41] The State Department finally lifted the blockade against Russia on July 8, 1920, although officials contemplated no change in diplomatic status with Russia.[42]

One of Martens's top priorities was the purchase of railroad equipment, essential for newly industrializing Russia. In March 1920, he had visited Baldwin Locomotive Works in Philadelphia. The firm's foreign sales manager, A.W. Hinger, informed Martens, "We can assure you delivery at the rate of 100 engines per month, beginning four months after acceptance of the contract." He also invited Martens's engineers to come and inspect the factory, and discuss "the erecting and port facilities that will be necessary in Russia." But Hinger insisted that remuneration must be payment in the United States upon delivery to a U.S. port, because "your Government has not been recognized."[43]

The Soviet Bureau head wrote back a week later, "I note with pleasure your willingness to build locomotives for the RSFSR . . . upon condition that the State Department of the U.S. raises no objection . . . and that my government establishes an irrevocable bank credit in your name . . . in American gold dollars." Martens was eager to establish an agreement, since Russia needed right away "not less than 15,000 locomotives." The Soviets particularly valued Baldwin technology; the company was a prerevolutionary supplier of decapod (ten-wheel) locomotives to the Imperial Russian Transportation Ministry. The arrangement was "limited only by our ability to meet the required payments," Martens declared. Learning that company president Samuel M. Vauclain was then in Europe, Martens hoped Vauclain would travel to Russia. "His personal visit would greatly facilitate an agreeable understanding . . . inasmuch as my government would then be able to discuss with Mr. Vauclain in detail the establishment of the credits necessary."[44]

The Baldwin Locomotive president was certainly eager for foreign orders. He had predicted in 1919 that his company's international business would soon increase by more than twenty-five million dollars. Russia, along with Japan, Cuba, and Brazil, were all eyed as customers.[45]

Martens returned to Baldwin in late March with Nuorteva, Kenneth Durant, and the Bureau's locomotive inspector, Capt. Otto S. Beyer, Jr. They were met by François de St. Phalle, vice president in charge of foreign sales, Hinger, and Hinger's assistant, Rockwell. Hinger and Rockwell took the visitors on tours of the downtown Spring Garden plant and the modern, sprawling facility in nearby Eddystone. After the trip, the Soviet Bureau wrote Baldwin of the Bureau's firm intention to buy the one hundred decapod locomotives, to be delivered to Russia via "an irrevocable credit in gold" at an Estonian bank. But Baldwin insisted that "nothing further could be done" until the United States announced new regulations allowing trade with Russia.[46]

Charles Muchnic, vice president of American Locomotive Sales Company, a Baldwin competitor, was also approached by the Bureau. Although "somewhat hostile" at first, as Etta Tuch told Martens, he warmed up considerably when told that "the Russian Government is about to place orders for two thousand locomotives." Muchnic informed Captain Beyer, however, that credits were needed before any deal could be struck, and government authorization was necessary. It could not have been surprising to Martens that these large firms did not want to create any trouble with Washington. The Bureau contacted other railroad car and equipment manufacturers, including Pressed Steel Car Company, Standard Car Company, Lima Locomotive, and American Car and Foundry. All were interested in Soviet trade, but they wanted to wait for a definitive policy from the government.[47]

On May 24 Vauclain returned from Europe, and Otto Beyer came once again to Philadelphia to see him. Unfortunately for Martens, few answers on the railroad purchases were forthcoming from his superiors, Krasin and Lomonosov.[48] Martens was beginning to doubt that anything would eventuate with his locomotive contacts. Both Baldwin and American Locomotive had appealed to the State Department to gain permission to ship to Reval, but their requests had thus far been denied. Locomotives, despite the lifting of the blockade, were still restricted as "war-related material."[49]

Despite the government's obstacles, Beyer still believed that the cooling in the Bureau's relationship with Baldwin might be due to François de St. Phalle, who "did not seem to be very warm to the desirability of doing business with Russia." Vauclain, on the other hand, was more helpful and was ready to deal "as soon as the financial situation on the one hand made it possible and the government stopped interfering on the other." Vauclain, indeed, told Beyer "that space would always be available within the Baldwin Locomotive plants for Russian needs." The president insisted, however, that "he would reserve the privilege to divide all orders received from Russia on the basis of 50-50 with the American Locomotive Company."[50]

Although the Soviet Bureau badly needed to purchase railroad locomotives and boxcars, it was also an "urgent necessity," according to the Bureau, to have factories in Russia to directly produce such goods. American imports were costly. The Russian standard Decapod engine cost $75,000, a jump of more than $20,000 in price since 1918. American factories, moreover, could not provide enough cars to keep up with Soviet demand, as they produced only six thousand engines a year while Russia needed twenty thousand just to match its prewar level. The Bureau's technical department aspired for a locomotive factory to produce five thousand engines annually and a railcar factory to produce 100,000 boxcars. These factories, moreover, should "use the methods of highest specialization of American industry and the principles of automobile factories." The technical department sought to launch an entire railway equipment industry within Russia. Martens saw the development of railcar wheels, in particular, as helping to build a domestic iron industry; he knew that the United States used almost a million tons of iron annually in its production. Martens urged, "I ask you to turn to this work the most serious attention and to discuss with me the necessity of construction of foundry factories to produce wheels in Russia, and the Soviet Bureau can send to Russia all machines, necessary for production of those wheels." There is no record that he ever received an answer.[51]

While Martens was wheeling-and-dealing with Baldwin for new rolling stock, he also had the chance to purchase 113 war surplus Baldwin and American Locomotive engines. On April 27, 1920, Max Rabinov of the Revalis Company told Martens that at a price of $52,000 each ($5.9 million total) he would disassemble, pack, and ship to Estonia locomotives purchased from the War Department. But the firm demanded a deposit. In July, Martens cabled urgently to Krasin in regard to this order: "I am conducting negotiations with banks. Cable quantity and particulars regarding orders. Also amount of gold you intend to transfer here."

A contract was possible, he said, "if initial payment effected." Martens's difficulties in gaining a response from his own government were again apparent, because he also lacked specifications for parts. He asked for an "immediate transfer" of funds to Revalis through Estonia.[52]

He took this opportunity to complain about his general lack of funds. "My budget at present is equal to three to four thousand dollars per week," he reported, and with inspections of these locomotives, the budget rose an additional $1,000 weekly. "I received for the last eight months from Comrade Litvinov for support of the Bureau all of $10,000 and was forced to go into debt."[53] He did not mention the more than $90,000 reputedly sent to him by Strom in 1919, perhaps because some of it had to be disbursed to other groups, including local Communists.[54]

In August Martens told Krasin that necessary inspection of the locomotives was impossible because the Bureau was "completely lacking in financial help from you." Since November 1919, "we have spent no less than $150,000 . . . only thanks to the help of our friends did we succeed in continuing the existence of our bureau." A frustrated Martens added, "I completely am at a loss to understand the reason for the lack of financial assistance."[55]

Martens was supposed to get money "regularly," according to Litvinov. But in September 1920 the Soviet representative complained, "despite repetition [of requests], the Bureau up to now does not receive the means for its support." He wanted $5,000 immediately through three banks, and "no less than $100,000 over the course of the next month."[56]

This was a substantial sum to demand all at once, but his plea makes clear that Martens's troubles were not all traceable to his treatment at the hands of the U.S. government. Rather, his problems derived both from Washington's harassment and from Moscow's neglect. Economic conditions were then very difficult in Russia: in 1913, it took 2 rubles to equal one dollar; by 1920, it required 250. Much of the inflation had occurred only since the abandonment of the gold ruble. A pound of meat, for example, cost 35–50 rubles in 1919; it skyrocketed to 1,000–1,400 rubles in 1920. Milk had risen by a factor of ten and butter by a factor of twenty.[57]

For the Bureau chief, it was not only money but simple answers that were hard to get from the Narkomindel. "We have directed many questions to Moscow of a very important character," Martens complained to Nuorteva, who had gone to Moscow to lead Narkomindel's Anglo-American division. Martens urged rapid action on "1) questions about passports, 2) emigrants wishing to go to Russia, and 3) questions of the organization of postal relations between America and Russia."[58]

More vexing to Martens was his inability to make purchases without Moscow's official approval. In August 1920, when Martens tried to buy $40,000 worth of printing machines, he had to wait for Krasin to authorize it.[59] Krasin often did not answer Martens's queries because of his skepticism about the agent's prospects in the United States. In 1920 Krasin was in the midst of negotiations with officials in Britain, which he saw "as the leading capitalist state."[60] In the United States, by contrast, Krasin noted "the extreme difficulty of receiving foreign [Soviet] currency and the little chance for change in this position in the near future." He was particularly worried that Martens had placed orders without regard to the likelihood of completing them and ordered his agent to report "exactly what contracts you have concluded at the present time." Krasin's chief concern was "about the bringing of counterclaims from various contractors in relation with the unfulfillment of these contracts and the lack of payment of deposits." He instructed Martens to send two copies of all his signed orders and to make sure that he submitted any new contracts to Krasin before signing them. In October 1920 Krasin flatly told Martens, "Contracts may be concluded by you only with approval from me, and this must be made a proviso in the contract."[61]

Yet Martens could only see such requests as meddlesome. Regardless of the problems that faced him in America, he wanted to be the sole purchaser of American products. He was angry to hear that Soviet trade representative Victor Kopp in Berlin "had placed very large orders there for many kinds of goods from an American firm," which would supply locomotives, trucks, and other supplies for a German-Lithuanian-Russian trading organization. Martens strongly opposed Soviet sales and purchases in Europe of American goods through "the clutches of middlemen." He contended that "all our foreign representatives should never place orders for American goods, but leave this to our Bureau, or at least, take up the subject with us first."[62]

Krasin realized he had to discipline Martens and responded hoping to illuminate the Soviet view of the Bureau's subordinate position. "Your suggestion [of being sole arbiter of placement of all American orders] . . . theoretically is completely right, but until your existence ceases to be half-legal and a week does not pass, in which we learn from newspapers of some kind of persecution against you, Nuorteva, etc., of course there cannot be any talk of such centralization." Krasin informed Martens of discussions about locomotive purchases then taking place in Berlin and London, where orders would likely be placed. Martens could not be "included" in this, said Krasin, because railway expert Lomonosov and his engineers did not have visas to return to America. Martens commiserated, "I understand all the difficulty brought . . . by the conditions of our half-legal existence here." Still, he wanted Krasin to instruct all Soviet representatives placing orders for American products that they had to "send to the Soviet Bureau all data both of the price, and of the quality of the ordered goods, and that such orders cannot be placed without our approval." Martens wanted carte blanche over the making of all Soviet purchases in America. Although his Soviet superiors knew that his office was an important beachhead for them in the United States, he would never get such authorization.[63]

Nevertheless, Martens worked tirelessly to make his position more effective. By exploring trade opportunities in Canada, he hoped to build a new market and also prod jealous American businessmen to lobby their government more aggressively. It is likely, too, that he hoped to shore up his position as an important representative in the eyes of his government. "Open trade relations with Canada on a broad scale would force the American merchants to raise such a noise that the American government would decide to end the American blockade on Soviet gold," he suggested to Krasin. In May 1920 Martens wrote to Sir George E. Foster, the Canadian minister of trade, that since many railway and agricultural machinery makers were interested in trade, "the Russian Soviet Government is prepared to have its representatives visit Canadian firms in order to establish the necessary relations." That summer, the Bureau sent Johann Ohsol to Canada, attempting to get bank credits for sales to Russia. Ohsol met Canadian affiliates of American firms such as GE, Ingersoll Rand, United Shoe, and Westinghouse. He succeeded in obtaining a credit guarantee for $75,000. The plan involved using Reval as a transshipment point, and the credit would be repaid with gold shipped back to Canada, then deposited in "Treasury vaults." The money would be protected from any attachments.[64]

Soviet trade supporter Saul Baron noted, "[Ohsol] has been received by the Canadian government with the same courtesies that Mr. Krasin is now being received in England." But the widely publicized deal could only be carried out if the British government allowed the gold to reach Reval or a Scandinavian capital, where the Bank of Nova Scotia would receive it. The gold must not sully the borders of England.[65]

Unfortunately, Russia attacked Poland shortly after this discussion and jinxed the deal. Canada, still a member of the British empire, "looked up to London for its general policy in foreign affairs," Martens lamented. To make things worse, Canada had recently deported fourteen Russians for subversion. But Ohsol would not give up easily. He was gratified by the words of Undersecretary of State Thomas Mulvey, who believed that "the treatment accorded Russia . . . had been simply a shame." But it was important to act quickly if the deal was to be consummated.[66]

But Krasin told Martens to drop the discussions. He did not want to send $75,000 for what he saw as a weak guarantee and he was even more skeptical about Canada's refusal to accept a Soviet trade representative, which to Krasin was more important than anything else. Canada was far too dependent upon the whims of Britain, the commissar declared, and he compared it disparagingly to friendlier Sweden. Since "trade with Russia for the Swedish government is a question of life or death," the Swedes had "guaranteed us the inviolability of our gold." Krasin not only doubted Canada's potential for Soviet trade, but he was also concerned about Russia's vulnerability. "Until the conclusion of a solid peace, we ought in the first line to protect the exchange of our gold resources . . . . With a change of political position unfavorable to us all these deposits could be confiscated."[67]

But Martens felt that Canadian business would pan out, particularly because Ottawa had $65 million of "unfulfilled credits for trade with foreigners." Its government wanted to use this money to trade with Moscow, "not on the basis of love between Canada and Soviet Russia, but simply cold judgment." Canada was even interested in helping the Soviets to establish factories to build locomotives in Russia. Passport and postal relations might soon be possible. Even better, a "Director of a Canadian bank in New York is very interested in organizing a bank syndicate here for taking deposits and transferring money to Russia."[68]

In November Martens was even more hopeful. Ottawa was ready to establish a credit line for the Soviet Bureau for $2 million to $3 million if orders were placed soon. The credits would be used to pay firms dealing with the Bureau. They would be backed by Soviet gold deposited at Reval, and the gold would return to Canada on the same ship that brought in the goods. Ottawa, at last, wanted to see a "Commercial Soviet Bureau" opened in the country. Martens was particularly excited about the possibility of a $5 million railroad contract with manufacturers' representatives Boyer and Sloan. "This proposal seems to me an extremely important one, both in a political and economical sense, and I therefore used all force, in order to convince Comrade Krasin of the necessity to act quickly and resolutely," Martens told Nuorteva.[69]

But before he got a response, the Canadian Department of Labor, influenced by "our enemies," as Martens described them, had published a pamphlet "directed against us." In a public letter, the Soviet Bureau chief asked the Canadian prime minister to "remove it from circulation." The result, however, was that the Canadian venture collapsed. The Soviet Bureau thus did not purchase any locomotives—from Baldwin, American Locomotive Sales, Boyer and Sloan, or anyone else—by the time that Martens left the United States.[70]

➤ MARTENS'S FINAL DAYS

There was nothing Martens could have done that would have persuaded the panoply of committees then investigating him—the Lusk committee, the Senate Foreign Relations Committee, the Justice Department's Bureau of Investigation, the War Department's Military Intelligence Division, or the Labor Department's immigration division—that he was innocent of revolutionary intentions.[71] Toward the end of the Senate hearings, University of Chicago professor Samuel Harper, a consultant to the State Department and the Bureau of Investigation, predicted the fate of the Soviet representative. Although he "was surrounded by a group of clever lawyers, when the Senate is through with Martens, the Department of Justice will arrest him and the Department of Labor follow this action with deportation."[72]

Although Martens was not arrested—the subsidence of the Red Scare and the decline of A. Mitchell Palmer's influence in 1920 saw to that—the Department of Labor did launch deportation hearings two days after the Senate investigation ended in March. Between then and October, Martens reported to Ellis Island for thirteen deportation hearings that centered on his attendance at the Fraina trial.[73] On December 17, 1920, Labor Secretary William B. Wilson issued the order for Ludwig C.A.K. Martens to leave the country. Yet he supported

Martens's claim that "There is no proof that Martens . . . at any time . . . spread or gave orders to spread any kind of literature supporting such propaganda."[74]

Martens was being expelled because of his association with Moscow.[75] His attorney, Thomas Hardwick, was disappointed. "The Secretary's legal proposition is grotesquely absurd . . . and is in effect almost an act of war." Hardwick had great hope that the Harding administration would take a more balanced approach, and he was ready to help Martens through a "protracted" fight that could go all the way to the Supreme Court. Hardwick felt that an appeal had a good chance of success but also feared that the lame-duck Wilson administration might rush the case through in as little as two months, putting Martens again at its mercy.[76] Not all members of the administration agreed with its policy, as the opinion of Assistant Secretary of State Roland S. Morris demonstrates: "It saddens me so to see how completely the President—the greatest 'liberal' of his generation—is so completely out of touch with the liberal opinion on this Russia problem." Morris blamed "the unimaginative and inarticulate" policies offered by the men around Wilson, including Basil Miles, DeWitt Clinton Poole, and Felix Cole.[77]

Even if he were deported, Martens felt confident that his expulsion would not prejudice the actions of later administrations. After consultation with a man with ties to Harding's future cabinet, Martens's feelings were confirmed. He learned that "the Russian policy of the incoming administration will be diametrically different from the policy of the present administration."[78] By placing the onus of his deportation firmly on the Wilson administration, Martens urged his government "absolutely not to consider my deportation in our international policy making."[79]

While waiting to hear advice from Moscow, Martens discussed his options with Hardwick and Charles Recht. Hardwick still believed that the decision "rests on very fragile ground" and that a new administration would offer a better environment for Martens's appeal. But the realistic Martens thought he should throw in the towel "in order that the future administration will not be installed with the soiled mistakes of the old administration, so that it can begin its Russian policy without having on its hands the legacy of the old government." He recommended against an appeal in a letter to his government written on December 20. Martens was prepared to close the Bureau, transferring its business to a trusted trading firm. He also arranged for the printing of the next issue of the Bureau's magazine, *Soviet Russia.* The magazine had been launched for "fighting his own enemies with their own weapons," and its circulation had grown to twenty-five thousand.[80]

Chicherin answered his American representative on Christmas Eve. "You have during the preceding two years honorably and patiently endeavored to carry out instructions received by you to establish friendly relations with the United States, notwithstanding malicious insults and petty persecutions." Although Chicherin believed that a rapprochement between the United States and Russia would occur eventually, at present "America makes such cooperation impossible." Martens was told to return to Russia along with his Russian staff. All orders were to be canceled, and Ohsol, Hourwich, and Durant would be put in charge of the liquidation.[81] Under Harding, who freed Socialist Eugene Debs, there was a good chance that Martens would have been vindicated had he chosen to stay. Some of Wilson's advisers, including the anti-Bolshevik John Spargo, feared that Harding would open relations with Russia.[82] Yet Martens's concern that the success of future Soviet-American initiatives not be constrained by his failure prompted him to leave.

Martens was energized by the turnout of well-wishers who came to see him in his last days in New York. "You ought to have seen the crowds of financiers and commercial representatives who thronged our reception rooms prior to our departure. You ought to have heard how they abused Wilson and his advisers," he chortled.[83] Unions such as the International Association of Machinists and the Amalgamated Clothing Workers also expressed their sympathies. The International Free Trade League, an export organization, told the Bureau chief that his treatment had been "idiotic and disgraceful."[84] On January 2 ten thousand people gathered in Madison Square Garden to "condemn the action of the Department of Labor in ordering the deportation of Mr. Martens." Two nights before Martens was scheduled to leave, the National Defense Committee held another large gathering in his honor. It attracted seventeen hundred people to the Manhattan Lyceum and Astoria Hall.[85]

Chicherin took the long view of Martens's deportation. He felt it was "the product of an incomprehensible, panicked state of mind which will appear to the impartial observer as a puzzling psychological curiosity." It could not represent the opinion of working men, he contended. "We also refuse to believe it represents the viewpoint of American business interests, whose many negotiations with us demonstrate their great desire to reestablish relations with Soviet Russia." Since American relations were so difficult, Russia would target Europe. "We will be less hurt by this incomprehensible attitude of America than America will hurt herself," Chicherin declared. "We shall not impose ourselves where we are not wanted."[86]

Martens was granted a dignified deportation proceeding in which he was allowed to leave the United States "voluntarily." To Martens, the deportation itself was insignificant. "It was merely a measure inspired by the Wilson group and is to be interpreted as a last demonstration, as a parting kick. Everything seems indeed to point to a radical change in the policy of the U.S. towards Russia, so soon as Harding, the newly elected president, begins his term of office." Such thinking was based largely upon the Republican policy to restore trade as soon as possible.[87]

There was some backlash in Russia as a result of Martens's deportation. American businessmen in Tiflis, Moscow, and Kharkov were stunned to hear that their visiting privileges were being revoked when the Soviet government decided to stop their entry "in retaliation for the deportation," according to the Washington Star.[88]

Just before departing in January 1921, Martens managed to ship a final $120,000 in drugs, books, tools, locomotives, cotton, and equipment, much of it for the Soviet Russia Medical Relief Committee. As American intelligence in

Riga reported, this amounted to over three million poods (108 million pounds) of "coal, soap, agricultural implements and other cargoes" in January and February 1921.[89] Because of his quick departure, Martens was forced to cancel several large orders, not having an opportunity to obtain export licenses for them. This greatly disappointed some contractors. Emerson P. Jennings, president of the American Commercial Association to Promote Trade with Russia, tried to get a Soviet passport to further a broad scheme to restore trade. Martens was skeptical of Jennings's plans. What Jennings really wanted in Moscow, he believed, was "to receive . . . payments for contracts we entered into with him relating to his printing presses." Martens refused to issue Jennings any kind of passport or letter of recommendation, "but I told him that as soon as trade relations begin between America and Russia, I will do all in my power in order to fulfill, even if only in part, our contract with him." Jennings told Martens he was going to Europe anyway and would then travel to Russia, despite the Bureau's insistence that he would not be allowed in.[90] Martens and his family left the United States on January 22 in deluxe quarters on the steamship *Stockholm*.[91]

After returning to the Soviet capital, Martens was rebuked by Litvinov, who disapproved of the representative's unconsummated deals with Americans. Despite his support for Martens against the domestic revolutionaries' agenda, Litvinov had worked consistently to curb the Bureau's economic role and blamed Martens for "speculators and dark personalities thumping on our doors with reference to their friendship with you. . . . Judging by your propositions, I can only believe that in areas of commerce you are as badly oriented, as in your appraisal of political positions." This was apparently a reference to Martens's continuing confidence that his Bureau would flourish in the United States. Litvinov scowled, "It will not astonish you that I . . . stopped 'reckoning with your opinion.'" The torrent of abuse from the future commissar of foreign affairs went on. "You supported friendly relations with Jennings and you . . . showered praise on [him.]" Martens had, in fact, tried to warn Moscow about the printing press manufacturer. Litvinov reported, "Jennings arrived in Moscow with reference to your promised order of goods, blackmailed us over the course of six months and at the present time he abusively spews out vile libels to American firms, warning against trade relations with the Soviet government."[92]

Jennings had indeed journeyed to Russia in December 1920 to secure his order for presses but had returned six months later deeply disillusioned. He told his association that its members had been "deceived, humbugged and flim-flammed by Martens, who has acted in a most despicable manner." Jennings had once been a tireless supporter of the Bureau, and his change of heart was testimony to the difficulties of dealing with the Soviet government in the early years. He had lost hundreds of thousands of dollars in preparation for his order, and he returned to the United States one of the bitterest critics of the Soviet government.[93]

Soviet leaders had not only been besieged by Jennings; they had also been badgered by Bobroff, the Wisconsin manufacturers' representative. Bobroff had come to Moscow on the same ship as Martens, infuriating Litvinov, who hectored his agent, "You supplied recommendations . . . for Bobroff, who came to get in Moscow a contract for $6 million, an extremely disadvantageous contract for us, and this very man now blackmails us, demanding our carrying out of discussions. Sooner or later this episode will take us for many millions of gold rubles." Litvinov alleged that Martens had time and again entered into deals with people who had turned out to be unreliable. Max Rabinov, whom Martens had recommended be paid in gold for the Revalis locomotives, was now under pursuit by police in Europe. Yet, Litvinov conceded, "the truth is, knowing of the conclusion of dealings with Rabinov and Bobroff, you began to warn us concerning them." But to Litvinov, this only showed "your lack of discernment about people and the thoughtlessness with which you gave people recommendations."[94]

"Permit me to say," Litvinov concluded, "that I never asked for any kind of trade in America; that I did not contract for dealings in coal, for example, and that from the very beginning I did not approve nor did I order in America either leather shoes, or agricultural machines." These, of course, were the very items Martens had first set out to buy in March 1919. Litvinov's statement that he had never wanted trade was a blatant fabrication and reflected more accurately his disgust with the abortive nature of the mission.[95]

Historians have been much more sympathetic to Martens. As two Soviet historians note, "Ludwig Martens' creation of the Bureau of the Soviet Mission carried out great work in arranging friendly relations with the United States and establishing trade relations with American business circles."[96] Martens himself believed that his tour in New York had brought a "significant profit in the sense of attracting the attention of the American businessmen on the question of trade with Russia."[97] But he was glad to return to Russia after an absence of over two decades. Martens's engineering background fitted him well to serve as an early head of the Soviet metallurgical administration, Glavmetall, where he later assisted the Hammer family's asbestos investments. In 1922 Martens served as the head of the Subsection of Industrial Reemigration of the Supreme Economic Soviet, in charge of workers who had returned to Russia from America, including a group that had saved $50,000 to open a coat factory in Moscow. He later edited a series of technical encyclopedias. Ludwig Martens was fortunate to live out his years in relative comfort, unlike many of his old Bolshevik colleagues, before he died of natural causes at the age of seventy-four.[98]

Diplomatic, Military, and Humanitarian Initiatives, 1919–1923

The first secretary of state to deal with the Soviet regime was Robert Lansing. In 1906 Lansing had helped to found the American Society of International Law, and he later became counselor for the Department of State. His legal background was not conducive to friendly relations with the Soviets, whom he thought had done little but flout international rules. As Norman Gaworek writes, Lansing believed that "it was impossible to deal with the Bolshevik regime."[1]

With the Allied embargo still in effect and Soviet Russia seen as a transgressor of international law, all queries that reached the State Department regarding Soviet commerce received this standard answer: "No arrangements have been made to permit any trade whatsoever between the United States and Bolshevik Russia." If the Soviets imported gold into the United States to conduct trade, the State Department suggested in 1919, the gold "could be used to sustain their propaganda of violence and unreason."[2] Above all, the Soviet repudiation of international debts, nationalization of property, and spreading of revolutionary propaganda were cited as the acts of outlawry that prevented the Wilson administration from recognizing the Soviet state.[3]

Political relations between the United States and Russia were not so farfetched a concept in the early years of the Bolshevik revolution as State Department pronouncements would make them appear. The United States had dispatched to revolutionary Russia agents who hoped to further "American interests" as well as maximize opportunities there. Prominent among them was Arthur Bullard, who came to Russia in June 1917 "entirely unofficially" but with the blessing of President Wilson and his close associate, Col. Edward M. House. Shortly after the Bolshevik revolution, Bullard began working for Edgar Sisson and the wartime Committee on Public Information (CPI), which had recently opened an office in Russia to conduct "a publicity campaign to inform the Russian people as to our country and our friendship for them and our purpose in the war."[4] As an opponent of any outright efforts against the Bolsheviks, Bullard tried to convince the people of Russia of America's "good will to themselves." Ernest Poole, an associate of Bullard, noted, "it was an almost hopeless job."[5]

Bullard's attempt to persuade Russians of American good intentions was not helped by the U.S. army's intervention in Siberia and northern Russia. The intervention in Siberia was designed to assist the transportation of several thousand Czecho-Slovak soldiers in Vladivostok to join the war against Germany and Austria-Hungary in the West. The effort in northern Russia was aimed at protecting Allied war materiel and ammunition dumps from falling into German hands after the Soviets exited the war.[6]

President Wilson stood opposed to naked interference in another country's affairs. Thus, he had intervened in Russia that summer only reluctantly, after prolonged pressure from the British and French leadership, whose soldiers were already involved, as well as from Russian Ambassador Boris Bakhmetev.[7] The president insisted that he did not want American troops used in Russia for the purpose of fighting the Bolsheviks. As Betty M. Unterberger notes, this would have been a violation of point six of the Fourteen Points. The "acid test" of Europe and America's "good will" to Russia, as point six put it, was these countries' treatment of that unsettled nation.[8]

George F. Kennan points out, however, that all of the Allies, including Wilson, had an "active distaste" for the Bolshevik regime. Linda Killen agrees, noting that officials like Assistant Secretary of State Breckenridge Long "reasoned that the United States did not have the right to interfere in Russian internal affairs but that it might . . . have a duty to combat Bolshevism." The American intervention, even if "half-hearted," certainly reflected this sentiment.[9] American troops helped the anti-Bolshevik forces hold out longer than they would have otherwise, something that Ambassador Bakhmetev clearly recognized as he tirelessly lobbied for American assistance.[10] This contribution pleased some prominent members of Wilson's cabinet as well. In November 1919, with the anti-Bolshevik Russian forces in retreat, Lansing realized that "Kolchak is in danger of being wiped out" and planned to ask Wilson for permission to loan $6 million in Treasury funds to pay the Czecho-Slovak troops in Russia, "for the purpose of waging war on [the] Bolsheviks." Upon hearing of this scheme, a perturbed Assistant Secretary of Treasury Russell Leffingwell worried that the president was "not in a condition to give careful consideration to the question of authorization" because of the stroke he had suffered and would approve this "wholly irrelevant" use of Treasury funds intended for the Allies' war effort.[11] Fortunately, the troops were not paid for this purpose. Although the futility of the entire intervention in Russia became increasingly clear, American forces stayed well into 1920. They left in part owing to the lobbying efforts of some members of Congress, who believed that "troops [were] being held there through the influence of the bondholders" of tsarist debts."[12]

Confused as its aims were, the intervention hardly stopped American efforts to reach a settlement with Russia. If Wilson had reluctantly joined the Old World's struggle in Siberia, the Paris Peace Conference was at least his creation.

Here, Moscow had reason to hope for something better from the author of Point Six. Indeed, this great global gathering served as the catalyst for the first American diplomatic mission to Soviet Russia. The secret mission was the idealistic product of young William C. Bullitt, chief of the Division of Current Intelligence Summaries with the American Commission to Negotiate Peace. On January 19, 1919, Bullitt recommended to Colonel House, the American representative on the Allied Supreme War Council, that a delegation "examine conditions in Russia with a view to recommending definite action." Bullitt had long believed that recognition of Soviet Russia would serve as a ringing validation of Wilson's "uncompromising liberalism."[13] The twenty-eight-year-old Bullitt was "brilliant, inexperienced, and greatly excited" about the potential of a diplomatic breakthrough with Russia.[14] In Paris, Bullitt warned the administration of the ineffectiveness of the American military presence in Siberia.[15]

Although Bullitt wanted to send a mission to Russia, the Allied leadership weighed different approaches. At Litvinov's invitation, William H. Buckler, an aide at the American embassy in London, had gone to Stockholm for discussions on January 14–16. Litvinov had indicated to Buckler his government's eagerness to "compromise" on foreign revolutionary ambitions, in order to end the war and begin reconstruction in Russia.[16] Encouraged by this conciliatory stance, Wilson and British Prime Minister David Lloyd George wanted to invite Soviet officials to Paris to negotiate an end to hostilities in Russia. French Premier Georges Clemenceau, however, refused to host the Bolsheviks on French soil. Wilson then suggested that the meeting take place instead on the Prinkipo Islands of Turkey, where representatives from both White and Red factions in the Russian conflict would be summoned as well as from the nations of the former Russian empire. The French agreed, and invitations were radioed for all to appear at Prinkipo by February 15. But anti-Bolshevik Russian forces reacted in horror to the thought of sitting down with their Red foes.[17] The French foreign office was sympathetic to their views and soon informed anti-Bolshevik leaders in Omsk, Archangel, and Ekaterinodar that they could turn down the invitation to Prinkipo and still maintain Western support. As the Prinkipo proposal began to fall apart in mid-February, a third initiative was offered by British Secretary for War Winston Churchill, whose view of the Communist regime in Moscow was similar to Clemenceau's. He proposed that a ten-day ultimatum be extended to Moscow, requiring the Soviets to either lay down their arms or face "large-scale intervention." Wilson and Lloyd George disapproved of this aggressive expansion of the existing Allied military effort.[18]

The conferees thus reached an impasse. Then, on February 19, Clemenceau was wounded in an assassination attempt, and all discussion on Russia was postponed. It was during this lull that House and Philip Kerr, Lloyd George's private secretary, decided to implement their secret plan: Bullitt's mission to Russia. Secretary of State Lansing was an unlikely candidate to initiate dealings with the Bolsheviks, but apparently at House's urging, he furnished Bullitt with his orders for the mission. Lansing's letter indicated that the young envoy was going to monitor "conditions, political and economic . . . for the benefit of the American commissioners plenipotentiary to negotiate peace." Bullitt would be accompanied by the radical muckraking journalist Lincoln Steffens and two other officials, neither of whom were experienced at diplomacy.[19] The secretary of state did not know that House had also authorized Bullitt "to discuss terms of settlement with the Soviet government."[20] The secretary hoped that sending Bullitt to see actual conditions in Moscow might at last "cure him of his Bolshevism."[21]

Bullitt received eight bargaining points from Kerr as conditions for "the Allied Governments to resume once more normal relations with Soviet Russia." Bullitt's conditions called for the de facto governments in Russia to remain in control of their occupied areas, a provision that worked against Soviet interests. In return, a cease-fire would be called and the Allies' blockade and assistance to anti-Bolshevik forces would end. The terms also provided for amnesty for political prisoners and the future discussion of "all other questions connected with Russia's debt to the Allies."[22] John M. Thompson writes that the American president "certainly" did not know the points that Bullitt was going to discuss with the Soviet government, and Wilson was probably also unaware that Bullitt was going to "negotiate, as well as to investigate." Because it was thought that French officials had helped derail the Prinkipo proposal, they were not apprised of Bullitt's journey either. All parties including House and Wilson envisioned the trip as an "exploratory . . . attempt to sound out the Bolsheviks" rather than a serious negotiating session. Everyone, that is, except Bullitt.[23]

The American envoy met Lenin in Moscow on March 11. Although some Soviet officials, including Trotsky, initially resisted the terms, Lenin agreed to them and gave the Allies until April 10 to extend a formal offer under these conditions. Privately, Lenin compared Bullitt's provisions to those of Brest-Litovsk in their severity, but he believed that accepting them, just as he had done at Brest, would turn out to be "entirely correct." The Soviet leader would note a year later, "when we proposed a treaty to Bullitt . . . which left tremendous amounts of territory to Deniken and Kolchak, we proposed [it] with the knowledge that if peace was signed, those governments could never hold out."[24] Indeed, as Richard Debo suggests, the treaty represented "self-determination Bolshevik-style with a vengeance" since the Kremlin leaders well recognized that the authority of the Whites was limited without foreign military aid, which the treaty prohibited.[25]

Bullitt applauded what he saw in Soviet Russia during his week in that country. He pronounced that "the red terror is over" and determined that "prostitutes have disappeared from sight, the economic reasons for their career having ceased to exist." Finally, in a phrase that Steffens would later copy and popularize, Bullitt claimed he had "been over into the future, and it works."[26] Returning from Russia "bug-eyed with wonder," Steffens and Bullitt could only be disappointed with their reception in Paris.[27] Wilson had a severe headache and was unable to meet with Bullitt. The timing of their return was inconvenient also, because the conferees were busy just then discussing the more pressing German question. Although Bullitt received encouragement from American Commission members Gen. Tasker Bliss, Henry White, and even Lansing, the man who mattered most was unavailable. The president had recently suffered a minor nervous collapse, and he had also now become preoccupied with the more important and engaging German question. Lloyd George also put a damper on the agreement. Two days after Bullitt's return, the prime minister asserted that British public opinion would not allow a peace treaty with the Bolsheviks. He vaguely mentioned sending a "prominent Conservative" to Russia to garner bipartisan support. Lloyd George had clearly spurned his own creation, but his reading of the mission's unpopularity was accurate.[28]

Over the next few days, British newspapers turned up the volume of criticism of the mission. So too did Churchill, who pleaded with Lloyd George to reject any question of recognition. "I do trust that President Wilson will not be allowed to weaken our policy," Churchill wrote, apparently unaware of the prime minister's leading role in the mission. Lloyd George reassured anti-Bolshevik Britons in an address to the House of Commons in April.[29] He was constrained by the angry French leadership as well, who attacked him for his duplicity. The proposal was unpopular and its sponsors distrusted by the Allies, who were now focused on the German settlement and with Kolchak's suddenly improving prospects, and uninterested in any initiative that might lend legitimacy to the Bolshevik regime.[30]

Meanwhile, another avenue for dealing with Russia had opened. Herbert Hoover, the highly respected administrator of the wartime Committee for Relief in Belgium, recommended sending nutritional assistance to Russia, which was suffering from famine in the midst of its civil war. The scheme required that fighting cease in Russia so that food could be distributed and was based upon a much older plan first broached by Colonel House in 1918 and then dropped after the Allied intervention that summer.[31] Fritjof Nansen, a prominent Norwegian humanitarian, had also been advocating famine relief for Russia at the peace conference. Hoover favored Nansen taking the lead in the relief effort, as he represented a neutral power.[32] Hoover assured Wilson that a relief mission like Nansen's would "not involve any recognition or relationship by the Allies of the Bolshevik murderers" and would preserve Poland, the Baltic states, and Kolchak's Siberian republic from the "threat of Bolshevist invasion." Aid would also allow the Allies to see "whether the Russian people will not themselves swing back to moderation and themselves bankrupt these ideas." This alternative appeared to seal the fate of Bullitt's plan.[33]

Hoover insisted that relief would not imply relations with the Bolsheviks, but Santeri Nuorteva of the Soviet Bureau saw it differently. "If this plan was not some new intrigue against Soviet Russia it would in practice lead to the establishment of trade relations," he noted with optimism, since local authorities would distribute goods and this "would lead to the establishment of commercial relations between the Allies and Soviet Russia." Nuorteva had heard that Acting Secretary of State Polk agreed with this assessment and had said the "jig is up for the Bakhmeteff crowd."[34] But nothing would happen unless both sides stopped fighting, and Kolchak's army was advancing west. As Bullitt noted upon his return, "immediately the entire press of Paris was roaring and screaming on the subject, announcing that Kolchak would be in Moscow within two weeks." His onslaught was successful enough to extinguish much of the remaining interest in either Bullitt's or Nansen's proposal.[35]

Bullitt did not give up easily, however, and made several last-ditch attempts to combine his diplomatic initiative with the food program. Able to make only limited adjustments to the Nansen plan, and disgusted with the Allied peace treaties as a whole, he resigned on May 17 from all his official positions. The treaties contained the seeds of future wars, Bullitt declared, which "the present league of nations will be powerless to prevent," necessitating the intervention of a treaty-bound United States.[36] By then, the Bolsheviks had rejected the Hoover-Nansen plan because of the disadvantageous requirement for an immediate cease-fire with the Whites, which in Lenin's view, "linked the 'humanitarian' with the 'political.'" Lenin insisted his government was ready to deal with the Allies—and had been since Prinkipo—but not with their counterrevolutionary "pawns."[37]

In September 1919 Bullitt vented his anger and disgust with the Wilson administration and its foreign policy on the floor of the Senate. During hearings on the ratification of the peace treaty, he revealed that Lansing also did not support the proposed accord. Bullitt's testimony disclosed confidential conversations he had held with Lansing in which the secretary had said, "I consider that the League of Nations at present is entirely useless. The great powers have simply gone ahead and arranged the world to suit themselves." Bullitt, who of course agreed with the secretary, also quoted Lansing as suggesting that "if the Senate could only understand what this treaty means, and if the American people could really understand, it would unquestionably be defeated." Lansing said he had been misinterpreted but made only feeble attempts to praise the treaty elsewhere. Wilson, who had also suffered his incapacitating stroke that month, became increasingly irritated with his secretary of state. By February 1920 the rift had widened so far that Lansing tendered his resignation.[38]

Bullitt himself become part of that "lost generation" of American expatriates in France. Disenchanted with the American ideal of "normalcy" and seduced by both the high culture and low cost of Paris life, he lived splendidly near the Parc des Princes with his bohemian wife, Louise Bryant, the widow of John Reed. In 1933, when another Democrat returned to the White House, Bullitt would become the first American ambassador to the Soviet Union.

Like Bullitt, Santeri Nuorteva was skeptical about the Paris Peace Conference. He believed that it "has all the characteristics of an old fashioned diplomacy of 'give and take' and 'balance of power.' The rest of the world shall have peace, but not Russia! . . . Soviet Russia, millions of whose sons have fallen . . . shall not only be left more isolated from the world than Imperial Germany ever was, but she shall have to continue to defend herself against renewed attacks."[39] The Bullitt mission had heightened Soviet hopes for a more conciliatory approach from the United States.[40] With the mission a failure by late May, however, Litvinov charged that "America was consolidating its policy with the rabid one of Clemenceau, and actually participated in the unified military and diplomatic initiatives against us in the economic blockade." Along with the other "reactionary circles at Versailles," the United States had suggested the "laughable and clearly not acceptable proposition of Nansen, for which we in exchange for a promised delivery of provisions must agree to stop our war activities and opposition to Kolchak and Deniken." Litvinov did not trust the Allies to permit the Soviets to stay in power. "All these proposals have the goal of . . . covering up the preparation of a new intervention now starting up, a campaign for Petrograd with direct participation of English naval forces, and for strengthening the war efforts of Deniken."[41]

Despite this, Litvinov stressed that the Soviets continued to look with more favor upon Americans than they did Europeans. Moscow had freed some American prisoners of war. Moreover, Soviet officials had not carried through the sentence of execution for Xenophon Kalamatiano, who had been convicted by a revolutionary tribunal of spying for the United States.[42] As Litvinov noted: "Even in the time of last year's intervention, our relations to American officials and unofficial representatives were different from relations with representatives of other states. We did not lose a chance to make a note of our particular wish to get in contact with America. We are prepared to give any economic concession to Americans principally before other foreigners. We have in mind concessions in Siberian Russia, exploitation of forests and iron resources, construction of railroads, electric stations, remaining canals, etc."[43] Litvinov also endorsed a plan for the United States to assume all Soviet debts, including those owed to France and Britain, so that Moscow would have just one debtor. In exchange, the United States would be able to exploit resources in "an expansive area."[44]

Although the Versailles Treaty was signed with Germany on June 28, 1919, the British and French sought to continue the formal wartime blockade against Russia. Americans were opposed, though a member of the U.S. mission in Paris conceded that "we should go as far as possible with our associates in assisting Koltchak [*sic*] and preventing aid from reaching the Bolshevists."[45] Kolchak's fortunes had been reversed in May, and he lacked popular support in Siberia, his base. Nevertheless, the Allies continued to restrict trade and in September agreed upon an embargo of Bolshevik Russia that covered goods, mail, telegraph service, passports, and financial exchange. Owing to American opposition, this postwar embargo was never *officially* a "blockade."[46]

The utter failure of the White armies that fall, however, made the existing policy obsolete. Lloyd George recognized this in November and hoped to end Soviet economic isolation by developing trade with the Russian cooperatives, a development that would certainly assist British trade prospects. Clemenceau also initially liked the idea, as he thought such trade would crush the Bolsheviks. The Supreme Council lifted the embargo on January 16. Lansing, still awaiting some kind of "evolution" in the Bolshevik leadership, retained American restrictions.[47]

Britain's opening soon created pressure across the Atlantic. By March 20 the U.S. government was prepared to lift its embargo. However, Britain wanted American officials to wait until Lloyd George and other Allied officials had completed their discussions in Copenhagen with Krasin and Litvinov, who were supposedly representing a delegation from the Tsentrosoyuz cooperative. The discussions moved to London after Lenin agreed that the delegation could drop Litvinov, who had been thrown out of Britain in 1918.[48] In late May Lloyd George and the head of the British Board of Trade, Sir Robert Horne, met in London with Krasin and his associate and interpreter, N.K. Klishko, "with a view to the immediate starting of trade relations with Russia . . . through the medium of cooperative organizations." The prime minister told members of the House of Commons that it was "essential in the interests of the world to resume trade relations with Russia." The Soviets, who already had a commercial treaty with Sweden, were especially eager to establish relations with Britain, since this would create a precedent for other large powers to follow. The negotiations eventually led to a commercial treaty in March 1921.[49]

With the British beginning trade discussions, Washington was free to repeal the trade embargo. Secretary of State Colby finally authorized the measure on July 8. Undersecretary of State Norman H. Davis carried out the task while Colby was away at the Democratic National Convention. The government allowed firms to trade on a *caveat vendor* basis but retained restrictions on the sale of war materiel as well as forbade postal and passport privileges. Business organizations in the United States took immediate notice. The American-Russian Chamber of Commerce, whose members had sustained huge financial losses in the Bolshevik revolution, was pleased at the lifting of the blockade. The group's publication opined that "it would expose the real blockade of Russia, which is internal, and also conduce to mutually satisfactory relations with Russia in the future."[50] A different perspective came from the National Association of Manufacturers (NAM), which declared that this step had "aroused a great deal of interest in manufacturing and export circles." NAM nevertheless believed that a combination of European competitors and poor transportation meant that for American firms, "trading with Russia is bound for some time . . . to be a thing of the future rather than a present reality." NAM was still skeptical of the Soviets a year later. Its foreign trade department told a firm that "it is possible that concerns doing business now with ostensible agents of the Russian Government would find themselves looked upon with disfavor by the elements which we feel must eventually supplant the present regime."[51]

➤ THE COLBY NOTE

Wilson once archly declared that Bainbridge Colby was his first secretary of state who was capable of writing a diplomatic note without the president's assistance. As Daniel Smith writes, in 1920 Colby in many ways "occupied the intimate position formerly held by House."[52] In August 1920 the secretary did in fact pen a highly significant letter, although he hardly acted alone. A query about the American position on the ongoing Russo-Polish war from the Italian ambassador, Baron Camillo Avezzana, gave the secretary an opportunity to set down his views on the Soviet regime in his famous "Colby note." This document, written for Colby almost entirely by the moderate Socialist and Wilson confidante John Spargo, was a reflection of Spargo's long-held desire that Colby issue a "forceful statement" against Russia, the "'outlaw nation.'"[53] Colby did. He wrote, "We cannot recognize, hold official relations with, or give friendly reception to the agents of a government which is determined and bound to conspire against our institutions and whose diplomats will be the agitators of a dangerous revolt."[54] Although Washington had no "desire to interfere in the internal affairs of the Russian people, or to suggest what kind of government they should have," it would not open relations with the Soviet government. Colby, like Lansing before him and Hughes afterward, wanted to place the issue of recognition in the context of international law rather than domestic politics. The secretary did not specifically mention Soviet-American trade in the note, but he did believe that the Soviets would "sign agreements with no intention of keeping them." President Wilson felt the note was an "excellent and sufficient" exposition of American policy.[55]

The Colby note has become one of the most well-studied documents of early Soviet-American relations. The secretary's attempts to distinguish the nonrecognition policy from ideological anticommunism became a State Department leitmotiv in the twenties. Historians have dismissed Colby's assertions that he was not interested in reshaping the Soviet government and have described the note as one of the most ideological statements to come out of Washington during the decade. Peter Filene suggests that pronouncements such as Colby's persuaded most Americans that nonrecognition amounted to a "moral boycott." Joan Hoff Wilson agrees that this was occurring even as officials "denied they were subordinating practical economic to abstract ideological considerations."[56]

A second major thrust of scholarly analysis is that the note served as a blueprint of Washington's policy for the remainder of the period of nonrecognition, until 1933. This was, of course, Spargo's aim. He wanted the Colby note to serve as "a *fait accompli* not to be lightly done and reversed" by the incoming, and in his view suspiciously less resolute, Harding administration.[57] Historians have affirmed that Spargo was successful and that the note introduced sixteen years of diplomatic rigidity. Daniel Smith writes that Colby "formalized a policy of nonrecognition that was to become increasingly unrealistic." William Appleman Williams described the note as "a measure of the failure of American policy toward Russia." G.N. Tsvetkov avers that the note's expressed policy was "the principal weapon of American imperialism in its 'cold war' against the first socialist power." And David W. McFadden writes that the note terminated a period of significant Soviet-American interchange and "condemn[ed] Bolshevism in Russia in such an unqualified manner that it served as a policy statement of both non-recognition and non-intercourse for three successive Republican administrations." One of the few to disagree with this view is Christine A. White, who suggests that after 1920 the United States "clearly shifted away from the risks, re-focusing instead on the trade to be had in Russia."[58]

The still predominant view of a static U.S. policy in the 1920s does not ac-count for the transformations in the economic arena that shaped Washington's re-lations with Russia during that decade. Although the Colby note was the first significant official declaration of American policy toward the Soviets and its terms remained important components of official policy until recognition, this document may be viewed more accurately as a depiction of the perfervid times in which it originated than as the blueprint for Soviet-American relations during the next decade. Colby and Wilson believed that the Soviet government was faltering and saw their statements as a means to pressure reform or, indeed, to effect an end to that government.[59] Yet as Soviet Russia proved its staying power, and as its pur-chases of American goods increased, U.S. policy changed. The twenties became an era of growing American receptivity to the economic potential of the Soviet Union.

After the embargo was lifted, Washington initially maintained some restric-tions on trade that represented serious burdens to those firms interested in com-merce, though Undersecretary Davis declared that those who said the department was still limiting Soviet-American commerce after July 1920 were "less inter-ested in trade than in politics." The department believed its policies were a judi-cious response to circumstances, not ideology-based opposition. "We . . . do not recognize the Government of Russia; but we do not outlaw her citizens, boycott her trade and destroy personal relations between our citizens and hers," said Davis. Over the course of the following decade, this passive, and despite Davis's words, often limiting policy toward Russia became a more active and facilitating one, especially in relation to trade and credits.[60]

➤ CHARLES EVANS HUGHES' INFLUENCE ON FOREIGN POLICY

Harding's campaign rhetoric had indicated that his administration would concern itself less with idealistic tenets and more with economic growth, and these pillars of anti-Wilsonianism and prosperity proved "invincible" in getting him elected.[61] Ironically, the return to "normalcy" created a more progressive era than that which preceded it. Harding, the first president to have received a majority of women's votes, and Calvin Coolidge, his vice president and successor, restored civil liberties that wartime regulations and postwar hysteria had suspended, and freed political prisoners.[62] Harding had also been elected on a platform that prom-ised to modify existing policies toward Soviet Russia, stating, "We pledge the party to an immediate resumption of trade relations with every nation with which we are at peace." Albert Fox of the *Washington Post* noted that President Harding believed in "encouraging trade relationship[s] between the United States and Russia as a preliminary to adjustment of political relations." Unlike his predeces-sor in the Oval Office, Harding saw recognition as "a purely technical matter" that did not imply endorsement of a government but was instead designed to expedite international commerce.[63]

In his support of an opening to Russia, Harding had been influenced by a number of progressive Republicans, including Raymond Robins, former Red Cross chief in Russia, and Sens. Hiram Johnson and William Borah. Robins and Johnson had offered their support to Harding in 1920 in return for a promise "to reconsider" existing policy on Russia.[64] Robins recognized this was a dubious prospect once the makeup of the Harding cabinet was revealed but still made the demand for recognition in 1922 in return for taking a seat on the Coal Commission. He received only a "vague" commitment.[65] Robins, Borah, and Johnson, along with other activists including Robins's former secretary and interpreter, Alexander Gumberg, and the members of the Women's Committee for the Recognition of Russia, nevertheless counted on Harding to change policy as a means to bring about world peace. Another advocate of change was Indiana governor James P. Goodrich, whose close ties to Hoover took him to Russia for the American Relief Administration. Goodrich believed that "Communist Russia would evolve into Capitalist Russia."[66] Despite the influence of these men in Congress and in the administration, the opposition of cabinet members Hughes and Hoover to recognition proved impossible to overcome.

Even before his inauguration, the president-elect along with Secretary of State–designate Hughes and Harding's choice for attorney general, Harry Daugherty, met in St. Augustine, Florida, with a Russian named Dalinda and some of his business partners to discuss Soviet trade. Cyrus Huling, one of Dalinda's associates, declared, "The encouragement with which we met on that occasion has induced us . . . to form a syndicate for the purpose of becoming the fiscal agent of Russia in the United States, receiving gold or other commodities and exchanging them by sale or barter for goods." Daugherty took a sympathetic view toward this syndicate and encouraged Huling three months later to remind Hughes about the proposal. The State Department gave no response to Huling, however. Mikhail Kalinin, chairman of the All-Russian Central Executive Committee of Soviets, also telegrammed the White House soon after the inauguration to offer "the formal proposal of opening trade relations." Kalinin wanted to send "a special delegation to America which will negotiate upon this matter." This too went unanswered.[67] Despite his intention to resume trade relations and return to "normalcy," Harding had made no plans to open negotiations with Moscow. He was not a policy innovator but rather a president "in tow behind his two Secretaries."[68] Harding did not take an active role in policy-making and relied on those in his cabinet who did: Secretary of State Hughes and Secretary of Commerce Herbert Hoover.

As leader of Harding's cabinet, Charles Evans Hughes was a brilliant jurist who had accumulated an impressive record as a professor, lawyer, Supreme Court judge, and politician. He had served as the lead counsel in New York City's gas company investigations in 1905 and in 1906 was elected governor of the Empire

State. Four years later, Hughes was appointed to the Supreme Court, where he remained until his bid against incumbent Wilson for the presidency in 1916, which
Hughes lost in a close vote. In 1921, when he joined the Harding administration,
his credentials made him one of the "most distinguished" State Department
chiefs. One historian contends that as secretary, Hughes was an adherent of
change—but only the "slow, evolutionary" kind. The progressive of 1905 had
become rather conservative. If either Harding or Coolidge seemed open to relations with Russia, Hughes was there to "nudge them back into line."[69]

Though the president supported Hughes, Harding increasingly identified
nonrecognition as "State Department policy" rather than administration policy.
"Harding is said to be sympathetic to the [recognition] movement," as one contemporary account reported, "but is being held back by Secretaries Hughes and
Hoover." Yet there exists no indication that Harding fought to have the policy
changed, so he may have been comfortable with nonrecognition even if he did not
feel personally committed to it.[70] Although his ear was always open to those who
sought to revise the policy, including Robins and Goodrich, Harding did not
change course but rather consistently "invok[ed] Hughes's stale formula of pre-
conditions."[71]

This formula was regularly on the secretary's lips. In Hughes's first major
speech on Soviet-American economic relations on March 25, 1921, the secretary
declared that there was no "proper basis for considering trade relations" until
"fundamental changes" were effected in Russia.[72] Less than two weeks later,
Hughes received another opportunity to discuss the subject when American Federation of Labor President Samuel Gompers asked him for information on the department's policy in light of "propaganda" being circulated about Russia's plans
for orders. Hughes confirmed the union leader's own low reckoning of Soviet
trade potential, noting that during 1920 American trade with the Soviets had
amounted to an "absolutely negligible" $4 million in a year when total U.S. trade
turnover had amounted to $13.5 billion.[73]

Even though Hughes minimized Soviet economic potential for American
firms, the full extent of Soviet Bureau purchases, as well as those of intermediaries such as the Robert Dollar Company, became apparent in early 1921. Ar-
riving in Reval then were four cargo ships brimming with American products
made up largely of shoes and soap, "a cargo that must have been sorely needed in
Soviet Russia," the Commerce Department sniffed.[74] These early American shipments were small, however, compared with those originating in Britain, which
supplied half of Russia's imports in 1921.[75]

Britain's trade had been bolstered by its agreement with Russia signed in
March of that year. The treaty's immediate aim was to eradicate Bolshevik propaganda in India and other countries and secondarily to build trade. British Board of
Trade President Horne remarked that the agreement was a method to introduce
"the beginning of better relations in Europe." In terms of ending Bolshevik propaganda, the treaty was a failure, especially in areas of British interest including
India, Afghanistan, and Persia.[76] The *New York Post* quickly asserted that the

treaty had been "practically worthless" for increasing trade as well. But statistics show that Britain took the leading role in Soviet trade in the early twenties.[77]

With the opportunities of Soviet trade being eagerly seized upon by Britain, Hughes allowed that "it is unquestionably desirable that intimate and mutually profitable relations" be opened with Moscow, although "readjustments in Russia" would first be necessary. The Bolsheviks had to demonstrate "the recognition by firm guarantees of private property, the sanctity of contract, and the rights of free labor." When Hoover asked the secretary of state in 1922 about the proposed re-entry of International Harvester and Westinghouse to Russian trade, Hughes did not want "to put any obstacle in the way." He predicted failure for any business-man who tried to deal with Moscow, yet should anyone succeed, he hastened to add, all the better that the State Department did not interfere. Hughes's State De-partment found the issue of dealing with the Soviets more complex than the Colby note would indicate. The office asked, "Should private American firms seeking to trade with the bolshevik Government have the moral support of the State Department?" These were questions that introduced shades of gray to the black-and-white statement of government opposition to Soviet Russia expressed by Colby.[78]

The State Department closely followed developments in Russia. A series of new initiatives in Russia in the twenties, most notably the New Economic Policy and the Five-Year Plan, made a static approach on Soviet-American affairs unre-alistic. DeWitt Clinton Poole, who headed the Division of Russian Affairs at State, recorded that in 1922 "the Department received an average of three and one-half dispatches and one cablegram per day relating to the Russian situation," much of it originating in Riga, Latvia. The consul in this Baltic capital, the pro-lific F.W.B. Coleman, furnished reams of reports. Representatives overseas also sent in commercial information when they thought it would "prove of some value to Americans seeking trade with Russia."[79]

The State Department was particularly interested in the progress of Soviet international trade. In May 1921 Hughes had a circular mailed to commissioners and consul generals in the Baltic states, the Scandinavian countries, and Britain and Germany, telling them it was of "urgent importance . . . to keep the Depart-ment fully informed regarding the development of trade with Russia." He wanted to know which countries had opened relations, the quantities of what they were trading, how it was being paid for, and "the names of individuals and corpora-tions, whether American or foreign, prominent in this trade." He believed that "the United States is not in an unfavorable position as compared with other na-tions in the matter of trade with Russia. The difficulties of that trade are attribut-able to conditions within Russia." As Poole informed him, "we stand in a better situation with respect to British competition in Russian trade—despite the Soviet-British trade agreement—than we did in 1913."[80] The State Department requested that all American shippers to Russia report what their vessels carried.[81]

That spring, the War Department considered sending its surplus five-foot gauge locomotives to a firm that would resell them directly to Russia. Poole saw

two good reasons to allow the sale: the need for locomotives in Russia "to allevi-
ate the suffering of the people and prepare the way for eventual rehabilitation"
and the resulting drawdown of Bolshevik gold. But Poole still felt that "American
firms might well abstain from trading with Soviet institutions" as long as American prisoners were being held in Russia. The War Department locomotives were
not sold to the Soviets, even though the State Department during the same period
allowed Baldwin Locomotive to sign a $6 million order with a Russian agent for
one hundred locomotives, after advising the firm about the prisoner situation. Assistant Secretary of State Frederick Dearing was puzzled, saying it is "a little
paradoxical" that the War Department was being "prevented from doing what any
locomotive manufacturer can do." The episode demonstrates the evolving, sometimes contradictory nature of American economic policy toward Russia.[82]

Even the most steadfast enemies of bolshevism at the State Department did
not want to be perceived as being closed-minded on the issue. Thus, it bothered
Poole "that the State Department has been frequently accused of doing active
anti-Bolshevik propaganda, with the result that anything which it now puts out on
the subject of Russia is discredited in not a few circles."[83] And Loy Henderson, a
staunch anticommunist who worked at the East European Division, recalled that
his most "time-consuming" task at that post in the early twenties was watching
"developments in Soviet Russia . . . that might justify a reconsideration of our
policy of non-recognition." Officials needed to keep abreast of any revisions in
Soviet policy and practice "in order to move in the direction of recognition without having to be pushed . . . by critics in Congress," such as gadfly William
Borah.[84] Although Borah did not make a resolution for recognition of Russia in
the Senate until 1924, his regular speeches on the subject kept the issue promi-
nently in front of the public.[85]

American officials also were careful to distinguish among Kremlin representatives. Robert P. Skinner, who headed the State Department's consulate in
Britain, described Soviet trade delegate Leonid Krasin as "relatively sane and
moderate." On the other hand, he found Karl Radek, the publicist for both the
Kremlin and the Communist International, a "very pessimistic" influence on
Soviet policy. Krasin, whose work in London with the Soviet Trade Delegation
had led to the Anglo-Soviet treaty of 1921, was seen as the ideal man to work
with, and some businessmen were interested in bringing him to America. Poole
believed it was "obviously undesirable" that Krasin come to the United States, but
in December 1921 he did authorize Consul Skinner to meet with the Soviet commissar on the condition that Skinner "not take [the] initiative." Poole instructed:
"[I]f Soviet delegate calls you may receive him informally . . . listening to what he
has to say without, of course, committing yourself in any way. Use utmost discretion." The State Department was committed to its policies on debts and propaganda, but it would "let no opportunity pass of ascertaining practical means
whereby the distress of the Russian people may be relieved."[86]

Still, the State Department did not believe that trade was going to be of any
significance for the time being. A.W. Kleifoth of the Division of Russian Affairs

claimed that only "new and unknown" firms were trading with Russia. "The older experienced traders . . . to date . . . have [not] attempted to re-enter Russia, except for the purpose of investigation," he said in 1922. They were "modeling their policy on that of the Department." He attributed this reluctance to the fact that organizations and individuals had lost a total of $245 million in investments and properties during the revolution.[87]

➤ HOOVER'S EXPERIENCE IN RUSSIA

While the State Department debated the extent of American engagement in Russian trade, Secretary of Commerce Hoover was planning a huge expansion in the dimensions of American involvement in Russia. The occasion was the terrible famine, complicated by civil war and revolution, that hit the Russian countryside with horrifying force in 1921. The worst disaster of the early Soviet regime would ironically result in an American intervention that enabled the Soviet government to survive. As director of the American Relief Administration's (ARA) effort, arch anti-Bolshevik Herbert Hoover would wipe out hunger in Russia during 1921–1922 with funds from American taxpayers and private charities.[88]

Herbert Hoover's involvement in the ARA in Russia had a pivotal influence upon him. It emphasized for him something that he had recognized at the Paris Peace Conference: Russia's problems were not simply those of bad government but were based on genuine social problems compounded by centuries of oppressive authoritarian rule. Hoover empathized with the residents of the former tsarist empire and recognized that "a foundation of real social grievance" had brought about the revolution. However, he did not in the least admire the new Bolshevik government: "They have resorted to terror, bloodshed, murder to a degree long since abandoned even amongst reactionary tyrannies." Hoover's humanitarian form of diplomacy was his answer to military intervention, which he opposed in countries that had undergone communist revolutions. He believed military ventures would only lead to a reinstallation of "the reactionary classes in their economic domination over the lower classes." As he had with the Nansen plan in 1919, Hoover hoped that humanitarian aid in 1921 would derail bolshevism but do so without a reinstatement of the ancien régime. This progressive-minded administrator played a leading role in American policy-making, not only because he was a very involved commerce secretary and president, but also because he was considered approachable by those pursuing Soviet trade in a way that Hughes was not.[89]

Hoover grew up in a devout Quaker family in West Branch, Iowa. In 1895 he graduated from Stanford University with a degree in geology and was soon hired as a mining engineer by a British concern. He played an important role in the development of mining technology, contributing frequently to engineering journals and authoring a popular mining textbook.[90] His early work took him to Australia, China, South America, and Burma, where he discovered a silver bonanza worth $2.5 million.[91]

After 1908 Hoover left the British firm and turned to Russia, where, follow-ing an unsuccessful oil venture on the Black Sea, he constructed a copper-smelting facility in the Urals for the Kyshtim Corporation. Here, he metamorphosed a money-losing gold mine into a successful copper mine for Kyshtim, making "huge profits" in the process. Subsequently, he contributed to the creation of a large for-eign venture in Russia, Leslie Urquhardt's Russo-Asiatic Consolidated, where he served on the board of directors. Hoover instituted improved living and health conditions for his miners, for humanitarian reasons as well as to increase their effi-ciency.[92]

By 1912 Hoover was recognized for his "prominence in Russian enter-prises" and was invited by Tsar Nicholas II to develop East Siberia's resources. Hoover's Irtysh Corporation found rich lodes of gold, silver, copper, lead, and zinc in this region. He would later report that the Bolshevik revolution had cost him over $15 million in connection with these Irtysh holdings alone. These Rus-sian losses would often be cited by his critics as the reason for Hoover's oppo-sition to recognition, but his criticisms went deeper than these lodes.[93]

In 1914 Hoover was a forty-year-old multimillionaire involved in eighteen mining enterprises on four continents. Yet he had become tired of the business world and gravitated toward public service. With the onset of the First World War, he would have ample opportunity. In Europe when the war broke out, Hoover was by October 1914 running the Commission for Relief in Belgium, a neutral, American-dominated effort to supply that occupied and blockaded country with food. The position required him to be a skillful diplomat as well as a good organ-izer. Given this background, it was natural that Wilson would choose Hoover to be the U. S. food administrator after America entered the war. Here he was re-sponsible for overseeing the production, distribution, pricing, conservation, and consumption of food. After the armistice, Hoover returned to his European relief work by chairing the American Relief Administration and then went to Paris. There, he offered the Nansen plan for Russia, as described earlier. Hoover had similar plans for other war-ravaged European countries, regularly using food as a weapon of diplomacy. As one historian writes, he used food aid "to defeat both Bela Kun's communist regime in Hungary and a Habsburg comeback in Austria, while propping up the regimes the Anglo-Saxon powers favoured."[94]

Hoover achieved widespread popularity because of his highly publicized humanitarian work, and the Democratic party tried to recruit him as its presi-dential nominee in 1920. Among his supporters were Louis Brandeis, the Harvard faculty, and the *New Republic*, as well as many of the newest voters, women. Even after he had officially declared himself a Republican, Hoover won the Democratic primary in Michigan, and A. Mitchell Palmer, who had been expected to win easily there, found his presidential prospects obliterated.[95] Following Hard-ing's victory that year, Hoover joined his administration, enticed by the new pres-ident's offer of posts as either secretary of the interior or secretary of commerce. Hoover's interest in foreign affairs, his wish to make business and governmental practices more efficient and rational, and perhaps most of all, Harding's promise that the Commerce Department could be "as important and influential as he desired," helped Hoover make his decision.[96]

In July 1921 Russian writer Maxim Gorky made an impassioned appeal to the world on behalf of his starving countrymen for food and medicine. At that time, American and British Quakers were already in Russia providing relief, as they had been since 1916. But with conditions growing increasingly desperate, American Anna Haines and Briton Arthur Watts persuaded Gorky to issue the broad appeal for aid.[97] The American Relief Administration was the largest organization to respond, although other groups also volunteered. As the biggest and most "official" agency involved, the ARA would control the distribution of grain, while the Soviet government would provide housing and transportation for the charity organization's personnel. The agency also asked for the return of American prisoners still in Russia.[98] To organize this massive task, 350 ARA workers traveled to the Soviet Union and began distributing food financed by three sources: the U.S. government, private donations, and the Kremlin. Moscow purchased several million dollars' worth of grain in the United States with gold certified to be of "unstolen" origin, "in the possession of the Russian Treasury since the beginning of the war in August 1914."[99]

The Relief Administration's work was supplemented by the efforts of many members of other charitable organizations, among them the Mennonites, the Friends of Soviet Russia, and the Quakers. Hoover was dubious about the value of these groups' assistance in this campaign. Although sympathetic to his Quaker coreligionists, he sometimes felt that they were too easily manipulated by the Soviets.[100] As for the Friends of Soviet Russia, an umbrella organization of two hundred affiliated groups, he declared that it was "frankly communistic." Hoover urged Walter Liggett, who headed the American Committee for Russian Famine Relief, to break his group's ties with the Friends of Soviet Russia, whose letterhead urged, "Give without imposing imperialistic and reactionary conditions as Hoover and others have." Liggett refused. The Relief Administration chairman then wrote the senators on Liggett's advisory council that the Friends of Soviet Russia was "a propaganda agency for the recognition of the Soviet government, both economically and politically."[101]

Actions such as this irritated many observers. Gilson Gardner, a journalist and member of the American Committee for Russian Famine Relief, complained of Hoover that "if anybody but himself wishes to keep Russia from starving, [Hoover] finds himself running at large snorting and kicking like a bay ass."[102] Since Hoover and his organization received $20 million from the federal government, it was not difficult for the Relief Administration to dominate the charitable effort. Considering the sharp postwar domestic recession, Congress' passage of this appropriation was noteworthy.[103]

Hoover's relief effort took place during the Soviet program known as the New Economic Policy (NEP). This initiative had been developed in response to the devastating conditions that war, revolution, and war communism—a three-year push "to arrive at genuine communism"—had inflicted upon the countryside. As Hoover well knew, conditions were truly desperate in Russia, with millions dying from starvation, disease, fuel shortages, and other deprivations.[104] War, ultraorthodox economic control (including oppressive grain requisitions), and revolutionary terror combined to decimate the population between 1918 and 1922, with peasants the chief victims.

The conditions under which Russians had lived during this period were exemplified by this decree from a rural area: "The extraordinary commission hereby makes it known to the citizens of the city and district of Metelnich that for the slightest attempt to take action against the authority of the laboring people as well as every agitation and spreading of false rumors, the persons so engaged, taken as hostages and confined in concentration camps, will be shot."[105] Such ruthless policies, if necessitated by war and revolution, could not be long sustained were the country to hold together or to develop economically during peacetime. The failure of militant war communism was made manifest in March 1921 at Kronstadt. Sailors there mutinied against the government, declaring that the Bolsheviks had betrayed the revolution. They were crushed, but their rebellion led to the inauguration of the more liberal New Economic Policy. War communism had gone too far, its "errors and stupidities" alienating the people.[106]

NEP allowed more opportunities for entrepreneurial Russian peasants and also created promising trade and investment avenues for Westerners after its inception in 1921. As Washington's representative in Riga told the State Department, the New Economic Policy meant "state commercial enterprise is curtailed on every hand." This was an exaggeration, since Gosplan, the Soviet planning agency, was already well entrenched in its management of major sectors of the economy by the time this economic reform program made its debut.[107] The Soviet government also maintained a strict control over foreign commerce through the state monopoly of foreign trade. The state's management over foreign commerce was enacted just five months after the revolution to promote socialism, develop the economy, and protect the nascent Soviet republic from foreign capitalist domination and was strongly defended by Krasin.[108] Although small businesses were for a time "privatized," large firms were consolidated into huge trusts and syndicates in order to provide centralized operation of the country's key industries under a program that Lenin called "state capitalism."[109]

The capitalistic reforms of the New Economic Policy were necessary, Lenin had said, because the revolutionary leadership was in danger of leaving Russian peasants behind in the planned transformation of the economy: "That is why we have . . . had to retreat to state capitalism, retreat to concessions, retreat to trade. Without this, proper relations with the peasants cannot be restored in the conditions of devastation, in which we now find ourselves. Without this we are threatened with the danger of the revolution's vanguard getting swiftly so far ahead that it would lose touch with the peasants. There would be no contact between the vanguard and the peasants and that would mean the collapse of the revolution."[110]

Lenin believed the retreat was necessary to avoid the mistakes made by an earlier revolutionary, Robespierre, in 1794. The French leader had "failed to take into account the class nature of his enemies."[111] Lenin would not fail. Indeed, the reforms of the NEP did play a large role in the 1920s in keeping the peasants loyal to the regime by such methods as substituting a tax in kind on peasant produce, rather than relying on outright requisition of grain. The efforts of the American Relief Administration were of more immediate importance in cementing the peasants to Bolshevik Russia, however. By 1923 the agency had saved 10.5 million lives in Russia, and other organizations had saved an additional two million. Hoover, of course, had hoped that infusions of food might weaken the appeal of the Bolsheviks, since they would no longer be able to blame the oppressive conditions in Russia on the Allied blockade. It was for this reason that Hoover had opposed the embargo, believing that keeping food and other necessities from the Russians would only encourage the spread of bolshevism as well as waste the supplies then languishing in American grain elevators.[112]

Historians have viewed Hoover's relief campaign in three ways: as a self-interested effort to support the American economy, as a selfless humanitarian effort, and as a combination of both humanitarianism and a hoped-for crushing of Communism. Supporting the first point of view is N. Gordon Levin, who calls the Relief Administration a "proto-Marshall plan to establish liberal-capitalist stability," as well as Arno Mayer, who states that Hoover carried out the charitable effort as a way to hold up commodity prices in the United States. The idealistic and humanitarian concerns typifying this era, however, make this interpretation too narrow an analysis of American policy.[113]

Hoover's anticommunist proclivities and his willingness to use food as a weapon, as shown in Hungary, provide evidence for a less economically oriented and more moralistic policy. Peter Filene, for example, suggests that Hoover hoped to use the ARA for "rescuing Russia from the Bolsheviks." Benjamin Weissman's argument is more nuanced. He writes that Hoover's first goal was to end the famine, but his "collateral American goals" included the hope that "a demonstration of goodwill would enhance American influence in Russia and somehow induce changes in the Soviet system beyond those instituted by the NEP." When this proved untenable, he hoped for a "'lasting impression'" in Russia. Joan Hoff Wilson takes a similar view, noting that Hoover believed the legacy of goodwill he left might later prove useful for Americans to take a leading role in Russian economic regeneration.[114]

Aware of Hoover's mixed motives, the Soviet government was naturally suspicious. Lenin, for instance, accused him of "rank duplicity." But Lenin himself was guilty of not a little double-dealing in the matter. Two days after Litvinov had signed the aid agreement with ARA representative Walter L. Brown in Riga, Lenin instructed Zinoviev to have the Comintern "put forward a definite slogan, without coming out against the American Government . . . saying that the workers should send in their donations only directly to the address of Soviet Russia's representatives abroad." Lenin wanted aid "without strings."[115]

As the ARA effort proceeded in 1922, fears deepened that it served as a cover for military action. Alexander A. Yazikov, head of the Washington delegation of the Far Eastern Republic, the Soviet front government in Siberia, predicted, "Hoover will use the ARA to prepare a counter-revolutionary movement in the spring." Yazikov had heard Hoover say that "it follows in Soviet Russia as in Hungary." Perhaps he had also read ARA aide T.T.C. Gregory's smug assessment of the Hungarian relief effort the year before: "a handful of Americans, employing only economic weapons, brought down the Government of Bela Kun." Raymond Robins had also been informed by a friend of Hoover's that the secretary had "bragged of his having overthrown Bolshevism in Hungary and told of his getting from [Left-wing Socialist] Max Eastman just what the Bolshevists wanted so that he could make his plans accordingly." Robins had heard that Hoover had told a group of businessmen that his "'ambition was to be known as the man who overthrew Bolshevism.'"[116]

Yet among Hoover's closest advisers in the relief effort were men much more open to the Soviet experiment, including James P. Goodrich, former Indiana governor and prominent Indianapolis banker, who made several trips to Russia for the American Relief Administration. These trips ranged from surveys of famine-afflicted areas to informal meetings with representatives of the Kremlin, men whom he believed were "honest, sincere, misguided enthusiasts." His travels received wide attention in the newspapers. The *Washington Globe* called him "ostensibly an American chargé d'affaires" to Moscow. And the *Washington Star* declared, "by far the most profound impression upon American political leaders" on the Soviet question "has resulted from James P. Goodrich." The *New York Times*, too, reported that "the tone of the references to Russia at once began to change" as a result of Goodrich's positive reports.[117]

Goodrich's second trip to Moscow in the spring of 1922 led to his meeting with Soviet authorities. Harding and Secretary of State Hughes had asked him to meet "informally" with Soviet leaders "so that they might understand the attitude of Americans toward Russia."[118] This was a significant gesture at a time when the United States refused to recognize the Soviet Union. It was also noteworthy that Hoover considered sending Alexander Gumberg, a supporter of trade and recognition who had emigrated to the United States from Russia twenty years earlier, along with Goodrich. The ARA chief went so far as to have Gumberg quit his position with the Far Eastern Trade Delegation and report to Washington. There, Gumberg reported, he "got strung along for two weeks" only to learn that "bureaucracy" had prevented his trip. Hoover did, at least, pay Gumberg for his trouble, and the Russian returned to his job. But he was disappointed that he had not joined Goodrich: "I could have been very useful in healing the breach between America and Russia."[119] James K. Libbey suggests that the State Department sat upon Gumberg's visa request for reasons both ideological and personal.[120]

During his Russian visit, Goodrich spoke to a number of leaders, including Leonid Krasin, Maxim Litvinov, and Karl Radek. Radek informed him that "America cannot be prosperous as long as England and Germany are not, and these two countries cannot thrive as long as Russia is down and out." Goodrich was sympathetic. He did not press the issue of Soviet propaganda in the United States, for which he blamed domestic activists. With Russia's "pure Aryan stock," Goodrich believed that country would soon "occupy a place among the family of nations second only to that of America itself." It is not surprising that Goodrich won support among advocates of better U.S.–Soviet relations in the United States, including Gumberg, who wrote glowingly to Raymond Robins, "[O]utside of yourself I never heard a foreigner talk with more intelligence or real human sympathy or understanding about Russia."[121]

Goodrich was not shy to press his advocacy of better U.S.–Soviet relations upon President Harding, telling him in 1923 that "many intelligent Republican businessmen" were dismayed with the administration's Soviet policy. He reminded Harding that his election platform had included a promise of "resumption of trade relations with all nations with which we are at peace." This economic advantage was needed, said Goodrich, "for Republican success in 1924." He posited that heightened Soviet-American trade would bring Moscow more speedily "toward a settled democracy" and also suggested that the problems of Russia "will be solved sooner, and the Russian people more quickly relieved, by the recognition of its government . . . and the opening up of Russia to the world." As far as the debt issue, Goodrich believed that "we ought to have the courage and the wisdom to get out of the legalistic impasse in which we are now involved by recognizing the rather disagreeable fact to some that the present government is in fact the government of Russia, and then sit down with Russia and adjust the matters in dispute."[122]

Goodrich's influence on ARA leader Hoover has been questioned. Benjamin Rhodes suggests that the governor was perceived as someone "who had lost touch of reality" and "his views were ignored."[123] Hoover did not agree with many of Goodrich's counsels, particularly on the advisability of recognition. Nevertheless, the governor was a highly trusted adviser as well as a key source of firsthand reports on Russian developments. His merits were summed up by Hoover in 1921: "It will be of substantial benefit to have a man of such experience as Governor Goodrich obtain a real knowledge of what the real difficulties of this foolish economic system are." Hoover's assistant, Christian Herter, declared that his boss was "not afraid of any Bolshevik tinge" in the governor's reports. As Rhodes himself observes, Hoover often agreed with the governor, in theory if not in practice. Yet it was "too risky politically" for him to make a "public endorsement" of Goodrich's views.[124]

The American relief efforts proved their effectiveness when a grain surplus was announced in the Soviet Union in 1923. Farmers in the United States who had been shipping grain to the starving Russians were now worried about an export crop of two to five million tons of Soviet wheat. That summer, a group of farm state congressmen traveled to Russia. They hoped to offer credits, along with agricultural equipment, in order to encourage the Soviets not to sell their surplus to Germany until commodity prices rose.[125]

With this clear evidence that the Soviet regime had weathered the crisis, there were renewed calls from ARA representatives in Russia for improving relations with Moscow. Goodrich stated that the organization's leadership "almost without exception" had "reached the conclusion . . . that we ought to open up trade relations with Russia." Col. William Haskell, the head of relief operations in Russia, also became an active proponent of improved Soviet-American relations. And Frank Golder, a relief official who would later direct the Hoover War Library at Stanford University, said in 1922 that "it would be best for Russia and the world to tie up with the Soviet authorities." Such a step would help the "right wing of the Communists," he added.[126]

Goodrich was the most influential, as well as the most vocal, among these men because of his close access to both Hoover and the president. He rarely discussed the matter with Secretary Hughes, whose "technical lawyer" perspective, he said, made discussion unproductive. But he did talk to others, including the powerful Sen. Henry Cabot Lodge on the Senate Foreign Relations Committee. Lodge opposed recognition of Russia as strongly as Borah advocated it. Goodrich noted, "I called his attention to the ratification even of the Sinclair [oil] concession and told him that Chicherin had said to me that every treaty and contract made by the Government would be carried out."[127]

Although the American Relief Administration certainly had not made NEP or Soviet society more oriented to liberal capitalism, as Hoover had once hoped, it did stabilize the Bolshevik regime and thus created the opportunity for a burgeoning Soviet-American economic relationship in the 1920s. Christine White suggests that the American response to the famine so eclipsed the meager British contribution that it pushed the Soviets increasingly toward commercial relations with the United States despite the existing Anglo-Soviet agreement. Moreover, Robert Murray contends that Hoover's ARA effort "convinced him of [Soviet] trade potential." Indeed, though lacking State Department authorization, members of the American Relief Administration had served as "trade scouts" in Russia.[128]

Hoover, however, could never bring himself to agree with Goodrich on the legitimacy of the Bolshevik regime. His litmus test for recognition was one issue: debts. Shortly after seizing power, the Soviets had renounced the $187 million that the U.S. Treasury had extended to the provisional government as well as the $86 million that American banks had lent to the tsarist regime.[129] Central to Herbert Hoover's outlook, and a reflection of his Quaker upbringing, was a passion for cooperation and voluntarism, whether among nations abroad or businesses at home. Soviet Russia, in his view, had showed it would not cooperate with the maxims of international law by its repudiation of foreign debts and nationalization of properties. Hoover's emphasis on the debt issue suggests that his objection to the Bolsheviks was less related to anti-Soviet ideology than it was to Moscow's refusal to conduct itself in what he considered civilized international behavior. Despite these beliefs, in a gesture of humanitarianism in 1921, Hoover suggested to Harding that the international war debts be canceled. The European countries collectively owed $9.6 billion to the United States. This suggestion "shocked his colleagues," writes David Burner, and by the fall of 1922, perhaps owing to public pressure, Hoover was urging that they be repaid in full, although he was willing to make concessions on interest payments. Hoover served as one of five members of the World War Foreign Debt Commission, which operated between 1922 and 1927. The commission, along with the more significant Dawes and Young Plans, set up a number of payment schedules, almost none of which were met. Since the Soviet Union was not recognized by the United States, its debt did not come up for negotiation by the Foreign Debt Commission, although the principal and interest of Russian debts totaled $260 million by 1926.[130]

ECONOMIC FOREIGN POLICY
UNDER HARDING

Herbert Hoover brought up his concern with Soviet unpaid obligations almost immediately after he entered the Commerce Department. He pronounced that "communism and long term credits are incompatible" because "no one would trust men who repudiated debts and agreements whenever it suited them."[1] Nevertheless, within a few years, Hoover's own department would be among the vanguard of Washington agencies in facilitating Soviet-American trade, both financed and unfinanced. Hoover is known for his successful practice of corporatism, first at the Commerce Department and later in the White House. During Hoover's eight years at Commerce, as Robert H. Zieger writes, this once soporific agency revived to become "the epitome of progressive government . . . combining scientific management, organized cooperation and private initiative." In this way, Hoover carried Progressivism into the 1920s.[2] Businessmen were pleased at Hoover's steps in the department, and they especially welcomed his aggressive efforts to promote foreign trade by finding markets for domestic products at the Bureau of Foreign and Domestic Commerce (BFDC).

In an effort to professionalize this division, Hoover selected Julius Klein, an eminent economics professor, to direct it. The bureau became very successful. In late 1921, seven thousand inquiries flowed in weekly. Within a year, this figure had doubled and by 1924, more than quadrupled. Foreign trade was now a priority for many businesses, and the U.S. Chamber of Commerce lobbied Congress to appropriate an additional $250,000 to support foreign trade functions and staff for the Commerce Department. The American Manufacturers' Export Association wanted a separate department of overseas commerce established. Hoover boasted about his department's contribution to the strength of American foreign trade and was pleased that exports, only ten percent of the economy's gross national product before the war, were growing significantly. He was especially gratified that British trade journals "credit our stronger position in this matter very considerably to the service built up by the Department of Commerce."[3]

This campaign did not neglect Soviet-American trade. Hoover, according to his secretary, was "very much interested in any trade relations with Russia." Raymond Robins reported that Hoover had told him "confidentially" in early 1921 that he saw Soviet-American trade as being "right and necessary without delay." In his first month in office, the commerce secretary announced in a press conference that for the health of the global economy, nothing was more vital than "the recovery of productivity in Russia." But in the same breath, Hoover predicted that American firms would have "no consequential trade" with Moscow. Russia had traditionally relied on food exports to finance its purchases abroad, and its current severe grain shortage would preclude much trade.[4]

In pursuit of what he felt was the right policy for Soviet-American relations, Hoover did not mind stepping on the toes of other cabinet-level colleagues. Early in his term, he complained that other federal departments were restricting potential growth of American sales to Moscow. He attacked the Treasury's ban on Soviet bullion, pointing out that firms wishing to trade with Russia had to compete with British companies not subject to a ban. "We could immediately start up some export to Bolshevik Russia if our people were allowed to receive Bolshevik gold," he declared. Hoover was well aware that market forces eventually attracted to the United States much of the Soviet gold initially shipped to other countries. This gold could enter the United States as long as it came under "the mint mark or coinage stamp of any friendly recognized nation." As a Treasury undersecretary conceded, such gold was accepted "as free from any suspicion or possibility of Soviet origin." The Federal Reserve confirmed that by the end of 1922, French and Swedish purchases and payments had supplied the United States with nearly $300 million in Soviet gold, making bullion supplies "largely Russian" in origin. In 1928 the Soviet news agency Tass pointed out that Reserve officials were "always . . . confident that whatever gold Soviet exported would ultimately arrive [in] American coffers." Tass asserted that this gold had served to compensate for the 1921 depression. But Treasury Secretary Andrew W. Mellon was adamant that no Soviet gold had been assayed by his staff for eight years.[5]

In addition to his opposition to the ban on gold, Hoover also disagreed with Secretary Hughes's proposal that German intermediaries resume their prewar practice of brokering America's Russian trade. Hoover protested that renewing this system contradicted his department's "policies . . . for [a] commercial and economic relationship to Russia." He declared that compared to Germans, "Americans are infinitely more popular in Russia and our Government more deeply respected." Owing to Russians' "racial sympathy" toward Americans, they would find German intermediaries a "crushing disappointment," he added.[6]

In an internal State Department memo, Assistant Secretary Frederick Dearing sharply dissented from Hoover's statements, particularly his idea of "racial sympathy." Direct commerce with the Soviets was preferable, Dearing agreed, but indirect sales through Germany should not be discouraged where they were the best available option. Moreover, Dearing criticized Hoover for completely overlooking the importance of German economic rehabilitation to the United States. Washington wanted to use Russian trade to build up Germany and thus strengthen the entire European economy.[7] If Hoover had decided on some other, "definite" scheme for Soviet-American trade, he ought to make the State

Department aware of it since "his broad policies are of such a nature that they involve the conduct of this nation's foreign affairs."[8] The State Department had good reason for concern about Hoover's involvement. Throughout the 1920s, the commerce secretary was the most influential official in matters relating to Soviet-American economic relations.

The challenge of German competition continued to concern American representatives. Samuel H. Cross, acting American commercial attaché in Belgium, intimated in 1922 that "this conception of the Germans as the chosen people to rebuild Russia for the rest of the world should be fought down with all possible means." If the United States allowed German "domination of Russian economic life," warned Cross, it would lose the ability to wield its own "desirable future economic influence." At a conference of commercial attachés in Europe that year, attendees agreed that although American firms would use German middlemen to aid in the reconstruction of Russia, "the U.S. Government should not support existing German-British plans for a greater German expansion into Russia than those two countries can jointly finance, nor encourage American capital to furnish Germany or Great Britain credits for those plans which . . . may be detrimental to the future interests of the United States and Russia." As it turned out, the Dawes Plan certainly helped finance German-Soviet trade via private American loans to Germany.[9]

In order to learn what possibilities existed for trade with Russia in 1921, the Bureau of Foreign and Domestic Commerce assigned three trade commissioners to the Baltic region and central Europe, including Felix Cole, who had headed the State Department's Division of Russian Affairs during 1920. Frederick Dearing carefully advised diplomatic and consular officers in Europe about the Commerce Department's delegation: "It is not so much the purpose of the investigation to promote immediate trade with Russia as to enable this Government later to inform American business interests when the proper time shall have arrived for large scale commercial operations and investments." The Commerce Department could get no closer to Moscow than its consulate in Riga, Latvia, an outpost six hundred miles from the Bolshevik capital that nevertheless became the center of intelligence on Russian developments.[10]

In November 1921, as part of the BFDC's reorganization effort and in recognition of the breakup of the old tsarist empire, its Russian Division became part of a new Eastern European Division, run by Dr. E. Dana Durand. A former professor at Harvard, Durand had worked for International Harvester in Russia before the revolution. He had later served as a trade commissioner in Vladivostok and Riga, as well as joined an investigative mission in Bolshevik Hungary. Durand recommended to Hoover that the "quickest way to bring about the desired reforms is by participating in commerce and investment." To enable businessmen to learn more about Russian opportunities, his division issued bulletins and circulars, based largely on Soviet publications, and drew an eager response. A survey by the Russian Division in 1921 attracted replies from "nearly 8,000 concerns that declared themselves interested in the Russian field."[11]

While all of this energetic fact-finding was under way in his department, Hoover remained wary. In December 1921 he noted, "for the first time I now see signs of change with regard to Russia." Eventually, he believed, "Americans will be in position to take a great leadership in reconstruction work."[12] President Harding agreed with his commerce secretary's assessment. "I hope the day will soon be at hand," he wrote, when "we may . . . resume commercial relations." But five months later, Hoover was still convinced that "discussion of economic relationships are a waste of time" until conditions in Russia changed.[13]

His cautious approach reflected reality. As the Soviet Trade Delegation in London acknowledged at that time, Russia "is obligated to limit foreign trade to fundamental necessaries" since the treasury was short of hard currency.[14] This situation was reflected in trade figures. In 1921, for instance, while Soviet Russia was suffering from famine, its total imports amounted to only $120 million, less than one-fifth of the prewar tally.[15]

Although Hoover adamantly opposed the philosophy and operation of the Bolshevik regime, he looked forward to the opportunity of trading with Moscow and saw economic intercourse as one of the more effective ways of bringing Russia into the "civilized" world. As he contended in one of his more famous pronouncements, "whatever goods could filter to Russia would relieve just that much individual misery and . . . it would be well for the world to lift the curtain on this experiment in economics." Hoover's views of the Soviet Union developed from an amalgam of beliefs, one of which was his strong opposition to communism, but another of which was his equally vigorous conviction about Russia's potential as a trading partner. Businessmen joined him in this outlook, intermingling their dislike for the Bolshevik regime with an avid desire for that government's "real money" and an appreciation for its commercial opportunities, particularly with the onset of NEP.[16]

The members of his department promoted Soviet trade aggressively, and the BFDC was at the forefront of these efforts. In 1922 the head of the Bureau's Automotive Division, Gordon Lee, declared, "If there is any business . . . for American motor truck manufacturers, we want to help them." Soviet-American trade began to rise dramatically in 1923, and with Moscow's need for increasing levels of credit, the BFDC's Finance and Investment Division stepped forward with a special circular about Soviet financing. Commerce Department staff also made a point of familiarizing themselves with the Soviet agencies that opened in the early twenties in New York, including Allied American Corporation (Alamerico) and Amtorg, and sending interested businessmen their way. Such efforts did not go unnoticed by the Soviet agents. S.D. Winderman of Alamerico was gratified that "the Chief of the Department in Washington thinks so well of us . . . it shows what can be accomplished."[17]

By 1924 U.S. sales to Russia were $42.1 million, out of a total U.S.–Soviet trade turnover of $50.3 million, and within four years overall trade had doubled to $100 million.[18] This compared favorably to the prewar record. Between 1910 and 1914 American exports to Russia averaged $25 million annually.[19] Hoover was pleased that the American positive trade balance with the Soviet Union had sur-passed that of countries that had opened relations with Moscow, including several of its traditional prewar trading partners. He believed that withholding recognition contributed to the growth of trade by encouraging Moscow to try to win Washing-ton's favor.[20]

Hoover's basis for rejecting recognition of Russia was anchored to the Colby note of August 1920 and the Hughes statement of March 1921. These docu-ments were not materials with which to build a thriving trade relationship. Never-theless, Hoover did so. Contemporary observers, as well as historians, have contended that Hoover's protrade posture was a contradiction of his own antirec-ognition policy.[21] This view is now undergoing some revision. Andrew J. Williams recently explained Hoover's distinct views on trade and recognition this way: "to have banned trade with Russia would have implied a degree of state intervention in the economic life that Hoover and most Americans would have found unaccept-able, while Hoover's refusal to recognize Russia was widely accepted."[22] But this interpretation does not go far enough. Rather than refraining from banning trade, Hoover actively worked to facilitate it by pushing for eased fiscal regulations to allow firms to offer long-term financing to the Soviet Union.

The growth of financial ties between the two nations despite the absence of relations is evidence of the success of policies of the Commerce Department fol-lowed later by the State Department. Large credits came from banks, including Chase National, Guaranty Trust, and Equitable Trust, and from firms like General Electric and American Locomotive Sales Corporation, as well as from smaller businesses.[23] Supporters of better Soviet-American relations were impressed by Hoover's actions. Norman Hapgood, former ambassador to Denmark and a lead-ing supporter of Soviet recognition, declared in 1923 that "Hoover has swung around on the Russian situation." His attitude compared favorably to Hughes's, who, as Gumberg complained, "learned his lesson from Colby and sticks to it." Isaiah Hurgin, a Soviet trade representative in the United States, was also heart-ened by Hoover's declaration that no ban on Soviet commerce existed. Hurgin felt that this was "a direct blessing on trade with the United States." In September 1925 Alexander Gumberg met with Hoover and came away convinced that the secretary was "very much interested in the Russian situation" and "fully aware of the economic revival" that had taken place in the Soviet Union. Gumberg attrib-uted this to Relief Administration leaders Goodrich and Haskell's continuing ad-visement of Hoover.[24]

Such was the interest of the Commerce Department in matters Russian that E.C. Ropes had announced to D.D. Borodin of the Soviet agricultural agency in New York that he was "deeply interested" in sending a department agent to Russia to help conduct the preliminary census of 1926 and, along with an Agriculture Department agent, "help the Russian government whip its annual agricultural sta-tistics into shape."[25]

So strong, indeed, was the belief that the Commerce secretary's views on the Soviet Union were being shaped by pro-Russian counsels that Gumberg was shocked when rumors surfaced that Hoover had expressed an opposing perspective. The *New York Times* leaked a story in 1925 that a Washington "high official" who was active in the promotion of foreign trade had denounced Soviet plans to purchase $300 million annually in the United States as being "propaganda pure and simple." Suspecting that the unnamed prominent official could only be Hoover, Gumberg was outraged. Sales to Moscow were then over the $70 million yearly mark, and "with proper credits and with good crops" there was no reason why the figure of $300 million was not attainable, in his view. Senator Borah, too, suspected that a two-faced Hoover was the newspaper's source: "A certain prominent gentleman who is talking one way to one class of people and talking another way to another class of people flatters himself that he is doing so without being uncovered. . . . In my opinion, he is an unmitigated hypocrite." George Barr Baker, Hoover's publicist, rushed to Hoover's defense. Confessing to feeling "touchy" about the whole matter, Baker declared that the secretary could not possibly have been the person quoted since Hoover had only recently refused to discuss the trade issue with Walter Duranty, the *Times* correspondent who wrote about Russia. "He has not talked with a newspaper man for some time," Baker asserted. He added, "It would be typical of Mr. Hoover to speak with frankness to you but it would have been totally untypical of him then to have talked in a different vein for publication in a newspaper." Gumberg was much relieved and told Goodrich, "I am very glad that Mr. Hoover is not to blame for that interview, and that we can count him among our friends."[26]

➤ THE GENOA CONFERENCE

Although the United States would be only peripherally involved in diplomatic moves to reintegrate Moscow into the world economic system, Europeans were less dissuaded from dealing with the Bolsheviks because of their greater need for past payments from and future trade with Moscow. In London, Paris, and Brussels, banks, firms, and bondholders had experienced huge losses in the Russian revolution, and they continued to feel acutely the weakened Russian market, now hobbled by war and starvation. In early October 1921, twenty-one nations (but not Russia) had sent representatives to Brussels for a conference on the Russian famine. The conferees agreed upon aid to Russia, but only if the Soviets acknowledged their debts and made commitments on the security of future credits. The Soviets were interested, particularly now that NEP had encouraged a retreat from revolutionary foreign policy. On October 28, Chicherin responded by announcing that his government was ready to acknowledge the debts owed to the Allied powers with the quid pro quo that the Soviets be awarded loans, recognition, and a peace treaty as well as reciprocity between Allied claims against Russia and damages caused by the Allied intervention. He proposed an international conference on the entire issue.[27]

This Soviet opening toward the West also gained a receptive response. German foreign minister Walter Rathenau, prominent leader of A.E.G. Corporation, had since 1918 been eager to create in Russia "an economic dominion which would enable the Reich to . . . eventually become again a world power of the first rank." Rathenau still saw Russia in semicolonial terms as both a market and a source of raw material. Well aware that it was necessary to act together with the Allies in order to raise sufficient money, he approached British and French representatives to suggest that they join in a consortium in which Germany would rebuild the railway system, refurbish industrial installations, and exploit mines in Russia. One-half of Germany's profits from the venture, Rathenau proposed, would be used to pay reparations.[28] In December, Lloyd George, Prime Minister Aristide Briand and Finance Minister Louis Loucheur of France, and Rathenau and other German business representatives held discussions on a plan for an international syndicate with British, French, and German participation to promote reconstruction in Soviet Russia.[29]

Lloyd George packaged together elements of both Chicherin's debt initiative and the Western consortium and, at a meeting of the Allied Supreme Economic Council in Cannes in January 1922, persuaded Briand to agree to a European economic conference at Genoa that April for the purpose of rebuilding European trade. The "Cannes Conditions" insisted that the Soviet government must pay Russian debts in order to receive credit assistance. Yet as Carole Fink notes, the French hope for "a straightforward Anglo-French military alliance" was spurned by Lloyd George, who dealt "heavy-handedly" with Briand. The French prime minister resigned from his government soon thereafter.[30]

Lloyd George had a very different view from the French on the postwar European order, as Jon Jacobson points out. The British prime minister saw Genoa as part of his "Grand Design" of British-led European reconstruction and disarmament. He rejected the existing mechanisms of collective security, including Versailles and the League covenant, because he saw them as destabilizing. Lloyd George believed that a general peace treaty with Russia and economic reconstruction of the Soviet state would encourage international investment and trade, as well as generate more British jobs and exports. He further hoped that this would "bring the United States—attracted by the promise of European disarmament—back to Europe both as a generous creditor . . . and as a guarantor of peace." Raymond Poincaré, who replaced Briand, was certainly interested in Soviet reconstruction. He also wanted a repayment schedule from Moscow before any credits were offered. Unlike Lloyd George, however, he had no interest in general disarmament or any other "schemes to supplant the League of Nations" and refused to allow this subject, along with the issue of reparations, on the agenda.[31]

While the French and British representatives were meeting in Cannes, Soviet officials Krestinskii, Krasin, and Radek were in Berlin in an attempt to reach a diplomatic and economic settlement with German government and business representatives. Chicherin was not interested in the imperialistic-sounding consortium and hoped instead to detach Germany from the Allies with a signed financial agreement. Soviet newspapers had applied pressure with angry articles decrying foreign exploitation, even suggesting that Russia should sign the Versailles treaty and take reparations from Germany. Yet as Robert Himmer suggests, Germany could not pay for "both substantial *and* independent aid as the Soviets wished." Rathenau, moreover, wanted to wait until the Genoa conference before acting.[32] The German-Soviet agreement thus hit a roadblock.

These various proposals would unravel at the Genoa conference. Even before the meeting, Lenin had asserted that his government had no obligation to follow the Cannes conditions.[33] At Genoa, Chicherin and Krasin expressed their keen interest in obtaining significant financial assistance immediately; Chicherin told the conferees that he needed "a big loan" of about $2 billion.[34] If this was not possible, the Soviet representatives would accept credits to purchase Western goods. Only if they gained "credits to an amount approximating their requirements" would the promised recognition of Western debts be considered and the Kremlin's own counterclaims for the Allied intervention be renounced.[35] British and French representatives assured Russia of its right to German reparations.[36] But they also insisted that there could only be extensive credits after the Kremlin made a commitment on the old obligations, and Chicherin rejected these terms, insisting on reciprocal treatment for the Soviet claims. This impasse proved to be unbridgeable.[37]

The United States had been invited to Genoa, but Hughes sent only an unofficial observer, American Ambassador to Italy Richard Washburn Child. The secretary would not allow his envoys to sit with their Russian counterparts.[38] The *Free Press* reported that the Genoa discussions and their potential for accelerated British-Soviet trade brought "enormous pressure . . . on the administration to 'liberalize' its Russian policy." Advocates of Soviet-American trade, meanwhile, "bombarded Congress and cabinet officers with appeals." Secretary Hughes successfully countered this pressure by enlisting the support of Samuel Gompers, the president of the American Federation of Labor.

Gompers was in the midst of fighting a communist takeover of his organization and vehemently opposed the opening of relations between the United States and Soviet Russia. Referring to the Anglo-Soviet trade treaty, he declared, "The British government . . . succumbed to the 'trade with Russia' propaganda, but it got no trade and admits that it got no trade." Despite the interest of many American workmen in Soviet orders, confirmed at the State Department where dozens of union resolutions calling for trade relations were received, Gompers continued, "American labor is uncompromising in its opposition . . . and it sees no reason for going to Genoa to do what America elsewhere has refused to do." Gompers had reason to distrust the Soviets and their friends in the United States. The executive committee of the Comintern had proclaimed in 1921, "The attraction of the broad proletariat masses to the movement of the revolutionary class struggle is one of the many tasks of the American Communists at the present moment . . . the party must with all its strength rapidly create a split in the AFL and establish strong centralized economic organizations of the working class."[39]

Chicherin was dismayed at the United States' absence at Genoa. "What is the matter with America? America would be a favored nation in Russia and we are desirous of establishing relations," he lamented. Ambassador Child was told that "Russia has more faith in the United States than in any other nation" because Chicherin saw the United States as better equipped to help his country.[40]

Raymond Robins was convinced that what happened at the Genoa conference could be very important. "If any sort of agreement is arrived at there between Russia and England . . . our policy on Russia will change." But if nothing happened, he fretted, "we will revert to the old policy with more enthusiasm than ever before." His concerns were so strong during the conference that they interrupted his sleep. He wanted Alexander Gumberg to persuade Borah to make a rousing speech in the Senate in support of recognition. Robins exclaimed, "This is the Hour to Strike for Free Russia!" The timing was crucial, he believed. "We are nearer results than at any time in the past, and yet if we fail now [it] very well may be used at the critical moment against Russia."[41]

But it was the Germans and Soviets who were closest to reaching results at Genoa, rather than any of the Allies. On April 16 Soviet and German diplomats signed a pact at the nearby resort of Rapallo that officially restored Russo-German diplomatic and economic relations. This was a disastrous development for the Western powers, who found their leverage over Russia now much reduced. It ultimately would lead to the breakup of the conference, as Lenin recognized.[42] For Chicherin and for his government, as one historian notes, the Rapallo agreement was "a great diplomatic and moral triumph" through which "the Soviets were able to prevent the formation of a common front against Bolshevism."[43] It matched Chicherin's strategy "not only to unearth separate interests but also to play on the rivalry of separate countries" and would be the sole discernible accomplishment of the Genoa conference. Bilateral negotiations like those with Germany, Chicherin believed, were "the best means of struggle against the international united enemy front. Above all, it is necessary to make good use of the influence of politics over economics, and we arrived at this in Germany."[44] The Russian government had demonstrated that it could overcome its failure to gain general European investment at Genoa by making individual arrangements with Western countries and firms.[45]

Nevertheless, at the end of the conference, the Soviets made one last plea for an arrangement on foreign debts and claims in the hopes of obtaining financial assistance from the Allies.[46] The British were somewhat flexible, but the French and Belgians were immovable, and the Soviet representatives did not get their loan. Progress at Genoa thus ground to a halt, and this failure led the Allies to propose a second conference at the Hague the following month. When it became clear that the British would not deal with Russia separately from France and Belgium, as Chicherin wished, the Hague conference similarly stalemated over the issue of debts and credits.[47]

Carole Fink suggests that the U.S. government was actually pleased that Lloyd George's goal of unifying Europe through "activist British commercial and political leadership" had aborted. Its failure gave Washington the freedom to make its own demands for debt repayment and to influence more directly reparations payments, tariffs, and immigration policies.[48] The United States indeed "accepted a degree of responsibility for keeping the world economy on an even keel," Paul Johnson writes. American banks extended $9.5 billion in loans to foreign governments and firms by 1924, a figure that increased to $12 billion only three years later. This money purchased government-backed paper abroad as well as investments in foreign enterprises, especially public utilities, mining, oil, and railways.[49] However, as both contemporary observers and historians have affirmed, this lending was "reckless and indiscriminate" and contributed to the stock market crash of 1929.[50]

➤ HOOVER PROPOSES AN ECONOMIC MISSION TO RUSSIA

Herbert Hoover was very interested in addressing "the primary question of determining what purpose America can serve in the broad, economic regeneration of Russia." In July 1922 Hoover suggested an exploratory economic mission to be sent to Russia, in part to determine whether his American Relief Administration's assistance was still needed. This mission would serve as the American alternative to Genoa. It would include two to three dozen businessmen and would gather information regarding "the application of American capital for restoring industry, transport, and other items."[51]

Alexander Gumberg was the originator of this idea, which he persuaded Robins to impress upon Hoover.[52] Robins had contacted Hoover in June, suggesting a commission "to consider the economic necessities of the Russian people with a view to advising the U.S. Government with respect to the necessity for additional measures of relief during the coming winter . . . [and] with a view to recommending to the Russian Authorities concrete remedies, and to the United States Government the basis . . . upon which the Government and its citizens may cooperate in the economic restoration of Russia."[53]

Robins suggested that Dwight Morrow, George Sutherland, James P. Goodrich, Thomas D. Thacher, and Allen Wardwell should serve on the commission, with Alexander Gumberg serving as attaché. Hoover did not generally agree with Robins's approach toward Soviet Russia, but the idea of combining a relief trip with an investigation struck him as a good one.[54]

Secretary of State Hughes willingly signed on to the Robins-Hoover proposal, noting that the trip would demonstrate the United States' commitment to "find out the facts and shape our policy in accordance with them." The State Department instructed its ambassador to Germany, Alanson B. Houghton, to contact Commissar Chicherin to gauge his government's interest in hosting a contingent of American businessmen on this exploratory economic mission. Houghton was not the ideal candidate for this task. He felt that the United States ought to remain "passive" rather than initiate action with Moscow, lest Soviet representatives think that Washington was capitulating, which would damage the chances of a more "conservative" group from getting into power in Russia.[55] Nevertheless, he carried out his duties.

Washington's proposal was examined by a foreign affairs commissar highly sensitive to the way foreign bourgeois elements treated his government. The organizers of the nine-nation Washington Armaments Conference sponsored by the United States that past winter had neglected to include Moscow even though the meeting's agenda contained issues of vital concern to Russia.[56] This slight had angered Chicherin. However, he still saw the United States as a junior partner to Britain, "'the cream of capitalist society.'"[57] He was, moreover, reluctant to embrace the very notion of a foreign investigation of virtually every facet of the Soviet economy. The plan was, he said, "an attempt to transform Russia into Turkey or Egypt," and no Soviet official was prepared to see the country so carved up and colonized. Nonetheless, the commissar did not immediately reject the idea, since he felt it had prospects of meeting "various aspirations" of his government. The investments and credits that the newly proposed mission might generate, for instance, would be welcome. In order to take advantage of this potential bounty, Krasin suggested that a Soviet commission be established to work with the visiting Americans. This commission would include representatives of the National Commissariats of Foreign Trade and Foreign Affairs, Gosplan (the state planning board), and the Chief Concessions Committee. By pairing these official agencies—all integral components of the economic machinery of the Soviet Union—with the visiting delegation, Moscow underscored its view of the significant prospects of the mission.[58]

Despite Ambassador Houghton's suspicions about the value of his proposal, he approached Commissars Chicherin and Krasin as an enthusiastic envoy. At a breakfast meeting with them, the ambassador declared he would recommend "with confidence" that Secretary of State Hughes should "appeal to Russia and suggest the sending . . . of [the] American committee of experts for the preparation of economic relations." Chicherin did not want the commission admitted, however, before the two governments involved had met to discuss Moscow's "concrete conditions." One of these was that the visiting delegates should stay out of Russia's internal affairs. Then came the quid pro quo. In order to be sure that the American visit was not tainted by any perception of Soviet inferiority, Chicherin pronounced that the delegation could come to his country "only under condition of the admittance in America . . . of our representatives for investigation of the American market."[59] This Soviet insistence on "national honor" was surprising to some veteran observers, like Gumberg.[60]

Chicherin's request was echoed in the Soviet press, where a reporter complained that the "one-sided dispatch of an inquiry committee clearly is a contradiction to the principles of the equal rights of both sides." Reciprocity was very important to the fledgling Soviet state, as had been evident at Genoa. Krasin pointed out to the Central Committee that American representatives had already been in Russia with the American Relief Administration, and therefore the United States should be willing to meet Moscow "halfway" with a bilateral exchange.

Krasin did acknowledge, however, that "without a preliminary . . . or even re-peated acquaintance with general Soviet landscape, American capital will not come to work in Russia."[61]

Although the Soviets desired reciprocity, at least one of their representatives liked the idea of an American mission. The head of the former Far Eastern Repub-lic mission to the United States, Yazikov, found the idea of a visiting delegation reason for optimism, believing it would "hasten a favorable decision on the Rus-sian question in the United States. I think the next meeting in the cabinet will stand for restoring relations with Soviet Russia."[62] But facing both a demand for a reciprocal commission and the expectation of a new American policy, Ambassa-dor Houghton was displeased. "So far the only result of our proposing a commis-sion has been to convince the Russians that the United States is changing its attitude." Secretary Hughes would have nothing to do with Moscow's counterof-fer. Soviet leaders had not made it "desirable" to "make any proposition to them," he sniffed.[63]

While the Secretary of State had been pursuing this commission through his German ambassador, the Secretary of Commerce was also working on the effort via unofficial channels. In August, Hoover persuaded his friend Goodrich to lobby Raymond Robins to contact the Soviet government. This was a mistaken strategy, because Robins distrusted the secretary's motives. He was, moreover, taken aback at the "Hoover-centric" proposal that Goodrich presented to him. As he described it to Alexander Gumberg, Robins was to contact the Soviet government "to ask for a commission and to ask that Hoover be chairman. . . . If this is done Russia will be recognized at least in the matter of trade relations within 60 days. . . . [Goodrich] spoke of Hoover as willing to give two years of his life to the 'help' of Russia. It was all Hoover from beginning to end." Robins could only scoff, "I would not wish Hoover on the Soviet in a million years. Russia is a rich morsel for the hungry wolves of the capitalist world!"[64]

Robins was soon pestered again by Goodrich, and again he vented to Gum-berg in disgust: "Your friend said that I should help to get the Soviet Government to accept the Hughes note. In other words, have them confess all that the propa-gandists have said and then ask for mercy, a commission, and Mr. H.H. as chief." Robins was increasingly convinced of an ulterior motive in Hoover's support for the commission. "I have regarded the purpose would be Kyshtim and the Russo-Asiatic Corporation—not freedom for the Russian people." Robins, who won-dered if Hoover's commission might try to overthrow the Soviet government once it arrived, did not think the Soviets "should ask for Herbert Hoover without other courageous free men on the Commission."[65]

In the end, the commission never went to Russia. Hughes interpreted the Soviet request for permission to send a delegation to the United States in Sep-tember as a "definite refusal" of Washington's proposal, and he considered the matter closed. This failure came as no surprise to President Harding, who had correctly predicted that the Soviet government would want reciprocal treatment. Still, the president wished the matter had been handled with more discretion. "I should have preferred to intimate [to the Soviets] in a diplomatic way," he told a member of Hughes's staff, "that the investigation . . . was to furnish the understanding essential to the proper consideration of the relations between America and Russia."[66]

Soviet Communist party officials were critical of the way that American "fumbling" had made it necessary for them to reject the mission. But ultimately, as a party report noted in late 1922, the overture had revealed Washington's desire for influence in Russian reconstruction. "Our refusing the one-sided commission and our emphasis on the principle of reciprocity . . . did not prevent the press from looking into the matter of finding some way for official rapprochement with Russia." The proposed mission had kindled a different outlook in political and business circles as well, demonstrating "an undoubted shift from the shrill negative approach toward entry into negotiations with the Soviet government."[67]

Above all, the party believed, the commission's origin was based on American financial need, "an inevitable consequence of the West European crisis, which had economically isolated the U.S. and resulted directly in a great social-economic shock in America." Political consequences of this crisis were already apparent, the report stated. "If this situation continues, it will be a large minus for the Republican Party in the next presidential election." The Republicans had already suffered "partial defeat" in recent midterm elections. The party analysis held that Russia's opportunity lay squarely in this poor economic environment. "Rapprochement with Russia, as a large market, is dictated with particular persistence. It becomes still more urgent in view of Russia's gaining entrance to the Pacific Ocean, where Japanese-American relations are the object of constant disturbing concern with the U.S."[68]

This sanguine outlook was based upon a common conception in Soviet thinking. Officials believed that economic imperatives drove the foreign policy of the capitalistic United States. This focus on economic factors neglected the idealistic and moralistic components of New Era foreign policy. Yet the party's geopolitical understanding was prescient. Japanese expansionism would be an important factor in bringing American recognition to Russia, although it would not occur for another decade.

The party's official analysis zeroed in on the forces behind the aborted commission, but it did not ignore the motivations of the individuals involved. Harding and Hughes "'completely if unofficially' gave in to thoughts of the desirability of rapprochement" by their authoring of the mission. In addition to planning a delegation, the party pointed out, the administration had already resorted to "that favorite method of the American government, dispatching 'its little man'." This was unofficial liaison Meyer Bloomfield, a friend of D.C. Poole. Bloomfield worked discreetly between the State Department and Moscow, communicating with the Bolsheviks without the need for either side to formally acknowledge him. He had made two trips to Moscow in 1922, the first for information for the State and Labor Departments, and the second on his own.[69]

The continuing if quiet role of Bloomfield was a sign that the mission idea was not entirely dead. Moreover, the Soviet government had been informed privately that if its leaders would make the next overture, Soviet reciprocity would "possibly" be respected. Deciding to act, Chicherin revived his plan for a Soviet mission to the United States in late 1922, suggesting that a "Russian Bureau for Trade Information" be established in New York as a first step toward trade relations. Bloomfield, working as Chicherin's intermediary, asked Poole if the United States would be willing to approve such an office "provided that a similar American bureau will be admitted to Russia." But Hughes again opposed such an exchange because it would appear that America was preparing the way for diplomatic recognition.[70]

Meanwhile, American-Russian Chamber of Commerce president S. R. Bertron suggested to Hughes that because of the increased interest in trade in both countries, it might be beneficial to dispatch a mission of businessmen to Moscow. The secretary told Bertron that he was not sure the situation merited "much hope" but said his department would nonetheless "lend . . . assistance in all suitable and practical ways." An internal State Department memorandum noted, however, that since the American-Russian Chamber of Commerce "has done much anti-Bolshevik propaganda," the mission would be "less effective" if it were conducted solely under the chamber's auspices.[71] The State Department's concern about this issue was curious but was in all likelihood sincere.

In December, Bloomfield met with Boris Skvirskii to discuss the idea of a Russian mission. Skvirskii had previously represented the Far Eastern Republic, absorbed into Soviet Russia in 1922, which was why he was permitted to have an office in Washington. Two months later, Maxim Litvinov sent Bloomfield to see Poole, Hughes, and Harding. Bloomfield later informed Gumberg that these officials had told him that the trade delegation "was dead because of the reciprocity requirements."[72]

The Soviet government's disappointment with this decision was demonstrated by Chicherin, who took the opportunity to lecture an American official, Julian Gillespie. The occasion where both men were present was the Lausanne Conference in Switzerland, which was held to negotiate a peace treaty between the World War Allies and Turkey. "By refusing to accept a Russian trade delegation," Chicherin told Gillespie, Washington "was treating Russia as an unequal . . . inferior nation." When Gillespie responded that Russia "should be willing to be regarded as an unequal, at least temporarily," because it desired recognition and trade more than Washington did, the commissar of foreign affairs found this "degrading and unpleasant." Despite the mission's failure, Chicherin pointed out to Litvinov that it had demonstrated the American "desir[e] for rapprochement" in the area of trade, confirming a gradual evolution in Soviet-American relations that bombastic statements such as the Colby note only masked.[73]

THE SOVIET COMMERCIAL MISSIONS UNDER HARDING, COOLIDGE, AND HOOVER

When the Soviets had requested that a trade mission be accepted in America, a Russian group was already in the United States: the Special Trade Delegation of the Far Eastern Republic (FER), headed by Alexander A. Yazikov and Boris Skvirskii. This Siberian delegation had attempted to gain diplomatic recognition at the Washington Conference of 1921–1922, but failed, as the conference recognized that "the delegation . . . is closely allied with the present Soviet Government of Russia." The FER was indeed linked with Soviet Russia; diplomatically and militarily, in order to counter the Japanese occupation of Siberia, as well as politically and economically. The Bureau of Investigation discovered that the Soviet government had extended two loans to the FER, including one for $3 million in the spring of 1922, with $10,000 set aside for "the use of the delegation in the U.S." A cablegram announcing the $10,000 credit, addressed to "Yazikoff, Washington," had somehow reached the old Russian embassy, redoubt of Boris Bakhmetev. He dutifully supplied the State Department with a copy.[1]

Few knowledgeable observers were surprised when on November 12, 1922, not long after the Japanese had committed to leaving Siberia as a result of the Washington conference, the national assembly of the Far Eastern Republic issued a proclamation at Chita dissolving itself and joining the Soviet Union. This effectively made FER representative Skvirskii Soviet Russia's "second unofficial ambassador to the United States."[2] Skvirskii pointed out to his superiors that because of the union of the FER and Moscow, the representative of the FER "actually will represent part of Soviet Russia." But Secretary Hughes showed no intention of recognizing Skvirskii except as a "private citizen." The State Department staff met with him on an informal basis, hoping to keep its consular offices in Siberia.[3] The absorption of the FER into the Soviet Union forced a reassessment of the role of the two American representatives. Albert Fox, the enthusiastic advocate of Soviet-American relations who reported for the *Washington Post*, doubted that U.S. authorities would withdraw Vice Consul Edward B. Thomas, stationed in

Chita, and S. Pinkney Tuck, in Vladivostok. But Soviet officials mandated that the American consuls in Siberia had to be registered with the Soviet government, and "the State Department, rather than be humiliated by associating with the Bolsheviks, [withdrew] their consuls," Fox wrote. They left in 1922.[4]

Like Martens before him, Skvirskii was limited by his lack of funds. He needed $3,000 to $4,000 each month, he told Litvinov, and like his predecessor, Skvirskii also lamented the "chronic seizures of deliveries of money which put me in a very difficult position." He was unlikely to get more funds, for despite his title as Soviet "commercial representative," Maxim Litvinov told Skvirskii to stay out of Soviet-American trade. Litvinov declared that the trade was not worth it, since Skvirskii's dealings would "not capture even the payment of telegrams." Instead, if businessmen wanted to trade with Moscow, they would need to contact Soviet representatives in Berlin directly. "I understand that this creates a bigger inconvenience for Americans, but it is not our fault if we cannot have a representative in America who could conduct preliminary discussions for us," he declared. Yet Litvinov overlooked the unofficial discussions being conducted on Moscow's behalf by Armand Hammer, who was already making extensive Soviet contacts and contracts with American businessmen, as will be discussed later.[5]

Skvirskii's prospects for an important post improved dramatically in 1923 when Litvinov and his colleagues decided to expand their goals for the representative. The director of the Justice Department's Bureau of Investigation, William J. Burns, learned in July that Skvirskii had "received instructions from the People's Commissariat of Foreign Affairs to proceed immediately to legalize himself in the United States." Skvirskii, Burns reported, was "under orders to work silently and undercover endeavoring to secure the recognition of the Soviet Government by the U.S. Government. He has been particularly interested in arranging for trips to Russia by U.S. Senators."[6]

Indeed, that month a group of senators had traveled to Russia, some of whom were briefed by Skvirskii's assistant, Alexander Gumberg.[7] According to Burns, the Narkomindel's new initiative for the Washington delegation was based on a perception that conditions were improving for Soviet emissaries in America. The commissariat "did not believe that the U.S. would again repeat the action taken in the deportation of Martens." Yet intelligence agents also learned that Soviet officials had cautioned Skvirskii "to proceed very slowly." In September 1923 Skvirskii and his associates at the Soviet delegation boldly opened a Russian information bureau in the nation's capital. *Washington Post* reporter Fox was pleased: "American business men and others, including those who have visited Russia recently, have asked that some such agency be established in the U.S." Fox continued somewhat naively, "There is nothing political about the Bureau, according to the Soviet representative here." Skvirskii began publishing a magazine called "The Russian Review," which was modeled after the similarly named Arcos agency publication in England.[8]

Another Soviet representative also heightened his profile in 1923, Burns discovered. Isaiah Yakovlevich Hurgin, a representative of Narkomindel who was employed in New York by the Soviet-German-American shipping venture Derutra, had been advised by the commissariat "to abandon his illegal status and to officially announce his position." Agent Burns believed that Hurgin was also targeting legislators to hail the benefits of recognition. He further alleged that Hurgin was awaiting imminent word of being named "the official ambassador for the Soviet Government." Although some of Burns's notions were speculative, his concerns about Skvirskii's and Hurgin's lobbying of congressmen show that he was aware, as were they, that the legislative branch was more open to reconsideration of diplomatic policy than was the executive branch.[9]

The intermediary work of Skvirskii and Hurgin would soon develop into three much larger Soviet ventures in New York. The first was Alamerico, which was launched by American Armand Hammer. This was followed by the All-Russian Textile Syndicate, led by Alexander Gumberg, formerly of Skvirskii's agency. Finally, there was the large and influential Amtorg trading agency, formed from the successor agencies of Martens's office and relying initially upon the talents of Isaiah Hurgin as its chairman of the board.

➤ ARMAND HAMMER AND ALAMERICO

Armand Hammer was born in New York City in 1898 to Russian-born Dr. Julius Hammer and his wife, Rose, who named him in honor of the symbol of the Socialist Labor party. When Armand was nine, his father met Lenin at the International Socialist Congress in Stuttgart. By 1919 Julius was chairman of the New York Left Wing Socialists, then one of the most militant factions on the American scene, and used the earnings from his successful pharmaceutical firm to bankroll its successor, the American Communist party. He also worked without salary at Martens's bureau to which he sold a large stash of surplus drugs for Soviet Russia, where morphine, codeine, chloroform, and other painkillers were in short supply. The Hammers shipped "hundreds of cases" of drugs to Russia through the Soviet Bureau. In just two months, May and June 1920, the amount of medicines that Hammer shipped through the bureau amounted to $46,000.[10] Although Armand Hammer described his father as merely an "unofficial trade adviser" to the bureau, the senior Dr. Hammer was one of Martens's strongest supporters, providing him with important backing when a fight erupted among the Left Socialists in New York over Martens's fate. This Russian connection would stand Armand in good stead, as he went on to become not only the most well-known American businessman to deal with Russia, but also the only one whose acquaintanceship spanned every Soviet leader from Lenin to Gorbachev (Stalin was the significant exception). Armand Hammer did not, however, carry on the radical political tradition of his father.[11]

During the summer of 1919, Armand's involvement in Soviet matters steeply increased when his father was arrested for manslaughter and the family's business, Allied Drug and Chemical Corporation, became Armand's chief responsibility. Dr. Hammer had performed an abortion that allegedly resulted in the death of his patient, the wife of a tsarist official in the United States, and he was imprisoned at Sing-Sing in September 1920.[12] Despite his new tasks, young Hammer was committed to graduating from Columbia College of Physicians and Surgeons, which he did in 1921. Meanwhile, his firm earned over one million dollars. Allied Drug held a monopoly on the supply of "tincture of ginger," a highly potent legal drug that was often abused during Prohibition to make "really powerful ginger-ale highballs."[13]

Compared with the successful commerce in "jake," as this sometimes deadly mix was called, Russian drug sales were a money loser for Allied Drug and Chemical. They were also illegal during the trade embargo. Hammer had little respect for the regulations, recalling later that "my family . . . supplied the Soviet with medicine and chemicals denied them by Clemenceau's 'barbed-wire fence' blockade."[14] But lack of financial compensation from the Kremlin, on top of an expensive legal defense for his father, led Armand Hammer to depart for Moscow in July 1921 to try to recoup some of the family's earnings from the Russian sales. He carefully left his destination off his passport because the State Department then restricted most travel to Russia.[15] He hoped to collect the $150,000 that the Soviet government owed his family's company for supplies including drugs and oil-drilling equipment, and wished to make "arrangements about further shipments and terms of payment." An important aspect of his trip was his offer of humanitarian assistance, which included delivery of an ambulance and inventory for a fully stocked field hospital worth $60,000.[16]

After an exciting journey—including a detention in Britain at the hands of Scotland Yard owing to a film he was carrying and in Germany because of Soviet red tape in granting him a visa—young Hammer arrived at the Kremlin, where Lenin granted him a one-hour interview. The impressionable twenty-three-year-old was highly flattered to be in the presence of the charismatic Bolshevik leader. Hammer recalled that he "felt embraced, enveloped" by Lenin, "as if I could trust him completely." Lenin thanked Hammer for his kind offer of medical assistance. But as the Bolshevik leader urgently explained, "What we really need is American capital and technical aid." Lenin had virtually conceded that "Communism was not working," Hammer recalled. Armand did not disagree, describing what he saw as a "revolution in tatters." Hammer likely perceived that new investment would enable his family to recoup their past financial advances to Moscow. He immediately ordered one million poods (thirty-six thousand tons) of American grain for the starving country in exchange for caviar, hides, and furs, which he sold back home for a reasonable profit. He also made plans to develop an asbestos mine in the Urals. This was the start of Hammer's ventures in Russia, ventures that would yield profits dwarfing the sum his father had lent the Bureau.[17]

Lenin was convinced of the significance of Hammer's asbestos mine, the first American concession to Russia. "It is extremely, extremely important that his whole undertaking should be a complete success," Lenin wrote in his letter of introduction for Hammer, which the American would carry with him into the hinterlands of Russia. Lenin was so impressed with Hammer's "efficiency" that he hoped the young man would be willing to bring electrification to the Urals. Hammer did not, but his concession paved the way for others to do so and fulfilled Lenin's hope that his venture would serve as "a small path leading to the American 'business' world."[18]

Early in 1922 Hammer convinced Henry Ford to work through him in implementing the sale of twenty-five thousand Fordson tractors to Soviet Russia. With the New Economic Policy's emphasis on agricultural modernization, Ford became a major client for Hammer. The young agent soon signed up three dozen other American firms interested in representation in Russia, including Union Twist Drill, American Tool Works, U.S. Machine Company, Allis-Chalmers, U.S. Rubber, Parker Pens, and Underwood Typewriter Company.[19] Hammer decided to devote himself to his Soviet ventures and sold the family's drug concern for just over $1 million. He set up a New York–based company called Allied American Corporation, or Alamerico, in order to sell manufactured goods in the Soviet Union. In July 1923 Alamerico inked a $2.4 million agreement with Moscow to sell American finished goods in Russia in exchange for Soviet raw materials. Soon, Alamerico had signed more than $1 million in business contracts with domestic firms. In return, it exported from Russia such commodities as furs, asbestos, horsehair bristles, timber, flax, caviar, and semiprecious stones.[20]

In March 1924 the New York office of the Commerce Department dispatched an intelligence agent to investigate Alamerico and learned that the firm's officials had already made overtures to top department staff in Washington. These included Durand and Lewery of the Eastern European Division, who were "thoroughly familiar with the Allied American Corporation." Not all officials were so open to Soviet opportunity. Carl J. Mayer, the American trade commissioner in Riga, Latvia, protested that Alamerico was "in reality a propaganda organ of the Soviet Government" and run by a "communist."[21]

Mayer received a stiff rebuke from his superiors in Washington for expressing these sentiments. Leonard J. Lewery reminded Mayer that "it is not the object of the Bureau to interfere with the business relations of any American concern in Russia or with any of their agents doing business with Russia" unless actual suspicions of fraud were a consideration. Lewery had received "direct complaints" about Mayer's negative comments, from Armand Hammer as well as from H.W. Watts, president of the United States Machinery Company. Watts was "doing a highly satisfactory business" with the Bolsheviks, Lewery reported, and did not appreciate Mayer's immoderate comments. Allied American's agents were already "the largest exporters to Russia of automotive and electrical equipment," and they had recently purchased over $500,000 worth of cotton "at one clip." The trade commissioner was admonished to be more careful about his sources and to use "a great deal of reserve" when weighing the opinions of "Russian exiles and refugees" on the Soviet Union. Lewery's dressing down of Mayer clearly shows the priority that the Commerce Department put upon Soviet trade, and its concern to protect American firms from departmental insinuations that their trading efforts were somehow improper. Lewery's invocation of "a highly satisfactory business" with Moscow indicated how much the government's position had changed since the Martens era.[22]

Indeed, Alamerico experienced little interference from authorities and until 1925 handled a substantial amount of Soviet-American trade, though not "all the trade," as Hammer had claimed. Its import and export turnover reached a total of $10 million through April 1924, but there were competitors, such as the Robert Dollar Company. After Lenin's death in May 1924, the Kremlin established its own purchasing agency in Manhattan—Amtorg—to replace Alamerico.[23]

➤ ALEXANDER GUMBERG AND THE TEXTILE SYNDICATE

Hammer's exports, while important early successes, were modest in size. A more impressive record was compiled by another Soviet agency, the All-Russian Textile Syndicate, launched in the United States by Alexander Gumberg in 1923. The textile syndicate's cotton purchases were the largest Soviet orders in America until the mid-1920s and were only surpassed by Amtorg. The Russian-born Gumberg, who had immigrated to the United States as a youth in 1903, was quite a remarkable character. After struggling to make a living, he eventually landed a job as business manager of a Russian newspaper published on New York's Lower East Side, a paper to which Trotsky also contributed. During the first Russian revolution, Gumberg traveled to Russia with the Root Commission as its interpreter. He was then hired by Raymond Robins as his personal secretary and interpreter while Robins was head of the American Red Cross in Russia during 1917–1918. In May 1918 Gumberg returned to the United States, and soon began working for the Far Eastern Trade Delegation.

A diligent advocate of improved Soviet-American relations, Gumberg's influence grew as he worked closely with Sen. William E. Borah and others active in the prorecognition cause.[24] Gumberg always emphasized commerce as crucial to improved relations between the United States and Soviet Russia. Despite his sympathies for Russia, he was no ideologue. William Henry Chamberlain, a close friend of Gumberg and reporter for the *Christian Science Monitor*, asked Gumberg why he did not wish to return to Russia, perhaps "to be a nepman." Gumberg explained:

> Well, I have been there before. I could not be as crazy as some of our American "idealists" and kid them in Russia (and even myself) that I could be a sincere member of the party of the revolution. If after all the years of my associations in the *Novy Mir* and after I did not get converted, and went through the revolution in 1917 unscathed, there is not much chance of my becoming a convert at this late hour. And frankly, I have seen so many of the post-1917 bolsheviks, that I have no desire to look like them. I prefer to remain a free lance, a sympathetic bystander and well-wisher.[25]

Gumberg was also greatly enjoying Washington. He had attended a Gridiron Club dinner, along with Harding, Coolidge, Harry Sinclair, and other industrialists, "the cream of the cream of the country. . . . So why hurry away from here?" he asked. Such an evening had provided him with more insights than he could have obtained in five years, he told Chamberlain. Despite his attempt to detach himself from the Bolsheviks, his role in the United States in the 1920s greatly contributed to the health of Soviet-American relations. Working to gain American recognition for the Soviets, Gumberg would also begin to furnish Russia a commodity it urgently needed: cotton.[26]

Textile production had long played an important role in the Russian economy, and by the time of the revolution it represented the country's most industrialized sector. In 1922 the government consolidated approximately 350 textile plants in Russia into the giant All-Union Textile Syndicate.[27] The syndicate was said to be "the first combination of big industrial groups in the economic field in the post-Revolutionary epoch." It controlled 117 sales branches in Russia that distributed cotton on both the wholesale and retail levels. As Soviet authorities confidently hailed the "revival of Russian-American business relations," the textile syndicate and the Soviet Chief Cotton Committee made plans to buy almost 175,000 bales of American cotton. The orders were placed through European brokers, just as they had been before the war.[28]

In 1923 the president of the textile syndicate, Victor P. Nogin, decided to open an office in New York. He hoped that this would eliminate the cost of middlemen and, believing that economics and policy were closely linked in the United States, also bring favorable official attention to the Soviet Union. James P. Goodrich helped arrange Nogin's visit to New York and then to Louisiana and Texas. Nogin was struck by "how much the relation of American business circles to Soviet Russia had changed." He also noted disapprovingly, however, that blacks were not permitted on his train car south from the nation's capital. While in the South, Nogin was impressed by the new attentiveness to Soviet Russia, as meetings with cotton dealers, bankers, and other "bourgeois" representatives showed an attitude "dictated purely . . . [by] commercial, business, and practical positions," not the least of which was his plan to purchase 200,000 bales of cotton. W.L. Clayton, head of the United States' largest cotton brokerage, was enthusiastic. "These purchases have come at a time when our own textile industry has been passing through the greatest depression perhaps in its history. . . . We have found a sorely needed outlet in Russia."[29]

The New York offices of the All-Russian Textile Syndicate (ARTS) opened in October 1923. Gumberg at different times served as the firm's secretary-treasurer, general manager, vice president, and director. The Soviet press believed that the new office would be auspicious "not only in commercial, but in political circles."[30] The cotton buying did not result in the hoped-for transformation in Washington's policies, despite the lobbying efforts of cotton magnates such as Clayton. But it did change the face of Soviet-American commercial relations by transcending political barriers. Despite the lack of relations, Herbert Hoover himself was interested in meeting with Nogin.[31]

The most significant change that the Soviet textile syndicate brought was its ability to generate bank credit for the cotton purchases. Syndicate executives were confident that their organization's $1 million capitalization and its other resources would enable it to obtain financing. Because of the cooperation of the Rockefeller-controlled Chase National Bank and its vice president, attorney Reeve Schley, they were proved right. In 1923 Chase offered short-term financing of $2 million to ARTS for cotton shipments and warehouse stock, backed by the guarantee of Gosbank, Russia's state financial institution. Sherrill Smith of Chase praised the "prompt, orderly and satisfactory" practices of the syndicate.[32]

Schley's former law firm, Simpson, Thacher, and Bartlett, arranged the incorporation of the textile syndicate in New York. The first cotton shipment, worth $2 million, went to Russia in February 1924. In its first nine months, ARTS was able to purchase $36.7 million in American cotton. The syndicate did not use American ships to carry its cargo but instead commissioned foreign vessels to transport cotton from Houston and Galveston, Texas, to Murmansk. Foreign steamers were used because Russia levied port charges five times higher on American vessels to retaliate for the lack of political relations.[33]

The syndicate's credit initially covered only shipment to Bergen, Norway, pending final payment. In 1925 conditions improved significantly. First, the syndicate's financial position stabilized and cotton shippers were allowed additional credits as insurance premiums dropped. Using the cotton as security, ARTS could ship as much as $25 million worth of the fiber at a time to Murmansk. That year, too, Chase Bank granted $15 million in credit, and as a result the syndicate bought a total of $43 million worth of American cotton in 1925.[34]

To Nogin, Chase's investments were "proof of a new tendency among American financial circles." Chase was the second largest financial institution in the United States, with almost $800 million in deposits. The bank had not been a major investor in the tsarist empire and had not experienced the heavy losses of other institutions such as National City Bank, the nation's largest. National City, with assets worth $1.25 billion, had over $33 million worth of assets in Russia at the time of the Revolution. Its leaders wanted compensation and were disturbed by Chase's Soviet financing. Accordingly, Chicherin viewed National City as "one of our leading established enemies in the American capitalist circles." Charles E. Mitchell, the president of National City, headed the Committee for Protection of Creditors, which urged the State Department not to deal with the Soviets until the issue of claims had been resolved.[35]

But National City could not prevent the Soviets from getting financial help from competitors. In 1926 Chase arranged an additional $30 million credit line for Moscow. Equitable Trust Company, ninth in size in the United States with $500 million in deposits, also entered Soviet financing operations, enticed by a 50 percent guarantee from the Soviet state bank. This financing helped the All-Russian Textile Syndicate buy almost $117 million worth of American cotton over its first three years.[36]

Other prominent individuals also took a role in enabling Soviet-American business relations. Dwight Morrow, a close friend of President Coolidge, was director for the syndicate of banks and industrial companies that J.P. Morgan controlled. Morrow's interest in the "Russian question" spurred him to meet with Nogin to discuss financing. The Morgan banks "usually did not finance commercial transactions," Gumberg noted, and so "they cannot give credit to the Textile Syndicate." Still, Morrow's commitment to "recommend" that banks work with the ARTS was heartening. Despite the success of the cotton purchases, the discreet Nogin did not want his offices to be used for lobbying for closer relations between the United States and Russia. He warned against a "repeat [of] the mistakes of 1919 and 1920." After Nogin died in 1924, his caveat was ignored and Gumberg became an active lobbyist for the cause.[37]

American officials were well aware of the importance of cotton in the Soviet-American trade mix. Frederick W.B. Coleman of the American legation in Riga warned his government in 1925 that reports of Russia curtailing its cotton and flour imports by 1929 "will tend to reduce the Soviet-American trade . . . to an insignificant figure." As American cotton shipments to Russia increased from 60,408 bales in 1922–1923 to 322,617 bales in 1924–1925, domestic cotton production in Russia had increased even faster, from 63,136 bales to 391,828. At the end of the decade, however, the Soviets were still buying "large amounts" of cotton in the United States, though in 1928 exports of cotton to Russia were surpassed by exports of manufactured goods. Nevertheless, cotton had played an extremely important role in pioneering a credit relationship between the United States and the Soviet Union.[38]

➤ THE AMTORG TRADING AGENCY AND THE AMERICAN-RUSSIAN CHAMBER OF COMMERCE

In the fall of 1924 Hammer's Alamerico agency entered its final months in business. The Amtorg (short for *Amerikanskii Torgovlaia*) Trading Agency, which had opened the previous May, would take its place.[39] With a capital base of $1 million furnished by Gostorg, the Soviet state trading agency, Amtorg would purchase durable goods including agricultural implements and railroad equipment. At first, Amtorg planned to purchase goods with the proceeds of its sales in the United States. However, since America bought scant quantities of Soviet goods, the purchases were financed instead by Soviet sales to Europe as well as by American banks. Amtorg superseded Hammer's trading agency, but it did not replace all of the Soviet commercial bureaus in the United States. The Soviet-controlled Tsentrosoyuz cooperative, for instance, was flourishing. Tsentrosoyuz received credits in the United States "at a highly favorable percentage rate" based on the value of its export cargo on docks in Russia. In January 1924 Tsentrosoyuz got a credit from National City Bank to purchase $400,000 worth of International Harvester reapers. The normally reluctant National City offered the credit because it had the security of a $2.5 million deposit from the prerevolutionary Moscow Union of Consumers' Societies.[40]

Amtorg was the most important Soviet trading agency of the era. The National Association of Manufacturers (NAM) fittingly made Russia "the principal topic of discussion at the foreign trade section" of its annual meeting the very month that Amtorg opened in 1924. Its program was entitled "The Truth About Russia, Industrially." It attracted a large audience, as well as the involvement of E. Dana Durand, the chief of the Commerce Department's Eastern European Division, who provided NAM with suggestions of individuals and organizations to participate in the panel.[41]

As the session began, Chairman Norman J. Gould declared that his group had no official opinion on the controversial issues under discussion. This silence on the merits of Soviet trade and recognition has led historians to criticize the association, as well as other business groups of the era, for giving "implicit support" to the United States' policy toward Russia. Earl Constantine, a top assistant in NAM, indeed had contacted Hoover to encourage him to have Durand "stress" Hoover's views at the panel. These views included Hoover's conviction that "it was high time the manufacturers of our country knew the truth about Industrial Russia and disillusioned themselves as regards its immediate potential as an export market."[42]

Despite its politically astute antennae, the association's panel on the "The Truth About Russia, Industrially" is evidence of NAM's recognition of a widespread interest among its members. If the views of Washington were solicited, so too were the perspectives of Moscow. Amtorg vice president Sherman was invited to give the opening address on the panel in 1924 and also in 1926, when NAM held a similar panel. In 1924 the dapper, pince-nezed Sherman acknowledged the many problems that his country had encountered and then announced that Soviet Russia "has shown really remarkable improvement." Russian-American trade was growing, but so too was a European presence in Soviet trade, he cautioned. The Soviet Arcos agency in London had placed over $200 million in orders there since 1921, "while we in New York lag hopelessly behind," Sherman lamented.[43]

In 1926, Sherman's second appearance at NAM, the Amtorg official claimed that in 1925 Russian economic production was 82 percent of what it had been in 1913—an amazingly rapid achievement, he pointed out, since in 1921 production was barely 15 percent of the prewar figure. Russia was ready for the introduction of mass-production machinery. Sherman told the audience that with its shortage of capital, his nation needed long-term credits from the United States, credits that European firms were offering. He was gratified that more firms were recognizing "that the Soviet credits are a good business, financial and moral risk."[44]

As returning panel chairman Norman Gould noted in 1926, the earlier session had shown that "a large proportion of our businessmen are alive to what is going on in Russia." Referring to the gathering of two years before, he recalled that "at no session of that convention . . . was the attendance larger than at the Russian session." Gould pointed out, however, that in 1924 the topic of "unsecured credits" to Moscow had not even come up, while in 1926 Soviet buyers were regularly obtaining two-year financing. The panel chairman was again careful to emphasize that his association "in no way questions the attitude of our Federal Government." Firms should remember that their credits "to Russian agents are credits . . . to the Socialist Soviet Government itself," said Gould, but he did not propose that these be limited.[45]

Much indeed had changed between 1924 and 1926. Most importantly, Soviet-American trade had moved into the mainstream, thanks to Amtorg's large purchases, including five thousand tractors in 1924–1925. Among the indications of change was the decision made by *Journal of Commerce* editor H. Parker Willis to spend over $7,500 for publicizing two "Special Russian Editions" in 1926. The issues were designed "for the promotion in the U.S. of the financial, commercial, economic and industrial interests of Russia," and the journal planned to send representatives to Russia and to obtain Soviet advertising.[46]

That year, too, the defunct American-Russian Chamber of Commerce was reborn. The old chamber had closed down in 1922 despite its president's efforts to revive it. In 1924 C.H. Carver, an associate of Averell Harriman, began discussing the formation of a new chamber with Alexander Gumberg and urged the Russian to try to persuade attorneys Allen Wardwell and Thomas Thacher to join them in a proposal for a "Board of Trade for Russian-American Commerce." Commissar Krasin was pleased to learn about it, noting, "I can only welcome such an association, which I trust will . . . help reestablish normal trading relations between our countries." Allen Wardwell, a prominent liberal and former member of Robins' Red Cross mission to Russia, agreed to serve as vice president of the chamber. Civil engineer Hugh L. Cooper, "the great apostle of American-Soviet friendship," became its president. The chamber went on to become an important player in Soviet-American trade. Among other actions, as Saul Bron noted, the American-Russian Chamber of Commerce gained a "favorable reception" with its lectures in fifty major cities.[47]

Cooper was tremendously excited about the possibilities of American scientific and technological involvement in Russia, describing them to the members of NAM in 1926. As the architect of a colossal hydroelectric power plant on the Dnieper River, which he predicted would support $500 million worth of manufacturing in the Ukraine, he had good reason to be bullish. His project was a veritable armamentarium of American manufacturing know-how. It would be powered by four 880-ton generators manufactured by General Electric, each of which would be driven by water turbines from the Newport News Shipbuilding and Dry Dock Company. So huge was the scale of the project that the entire collection of General Electric parts for Cooper's hydroelectric station filled 130 railroad cars.[48]

The success of Cooper, and the chamber, was mirrored in the sales racked up by Amtorg. The agency's orders alone doubled from $13.1 million in 1925–1926 to $26.3 million in 1926–1927. To the trading agency's purchases can be added those of the All-Russian Textile Syndicate, which bought $117 million worth of southern cotton for the Soviet Union between 1923 and 1926 with financing supplied by Chase and other banks. Soviet sales of raw materials to

The home of Attorney General A. Mitchell Palmer at 2132 R Street in Washington was blown up by anarchist Carlo Valdinoci on June 2, 1919. Valdinoci died in the blast, which also shattered windows across the street at the residence of Assistant Secretary of the Navy Franklin D. Roosevelt.

Soviet Bureau chief Ludwig C.A.K. Martens (right) and the director of the Bureau's diplomatic department, Santeri Nuorteva, are pictured in Washington in January 1920 during Senate hearings on the Bureau's suspected pro-revolutionary activities.

Unless otherwise noted, all photos are from the Library of Congress.

Santeri Nuorteva, his wife, and Martens pose for newsmen in Washington, 1920.

Boris Bakhmetev, the Russian Provisional Government's ambassador to the United States, remained in that post until 1922, despite the collapse of his government in the fall of 1917.

Robert Lansing replaced William Jennings Bryan as Secretary of State in 1915 and was thus the first in that post to encounter the Soviet regime. He served until 1920, when he had a falling out with President Wilson.

American businessman Armand Hammer, a pioneering and unusually successful concessionaire in Soviet Russia in the 1920s, imported grain, mined asbestos, produced pens and pencils, and exported art.

Bainbridge Colby (left) succeeded Robert Lansing as Secretary of State in 1920. His famous "Colby note" expressed the U.S. government's refusal to recognize the Soviet regime. At right is Under Secretary of State Frank Polk.

Charles Evans Hughes (left), Secretary of State under Harding and Coolidge from 1921 to 1925, greets his successor, Frank B. Kellogg, and Kellogg's wife, Clara, on February 27, 1925, in Washington. While Hughes largely continued the American policy toward Russia created by his predecessor, Kellogg oversaw significant changes, including the first officially sanctioned arrangements for private long-term credit to the as-yet-unrecognized Soviet regime.

Soviet officials at the Genoa Conference, April 20, 1922. Left to right: Commissar of Foreign Affairs George Chicherin, Comintern publicist Karl Radek, Deputy Commissar of Foreign Affairs Maxim Litvinov, Commissar of Foreign Trade Leonid Krasin, and an unidentified man.

Suffragist Lucy Gwynne Branham protests the treatment of National Woman's Party leader Alice Paul in the fall of 1917. Imprisoned for picketing, Paul had been force-fed and confined to a psychopathic ward before protests brought her release. Branham went on to lobby for recognition of Soviet Russia in the early 1920s. Courtesy of the Smithsonian Institution.

Robert F. Kelley was chief of the East European Department of the State Department in the late 1920s and a convinced critic of the Soviet Union.

Col. Raymond Robins was a prominent progressive Republican and humanitarian and a vigorous advocate of Soviet-American diplomatic relations.

Former Indiana governor James P. Goodrich, a close associate of Herbert Hoover, visited Russia for the American Relief Administration. Like Robins, he was a strong supporter of recognition of the Soviet government.

Boris E. Skvirskii (left), director of the Soviet Information Bureau in Washington, is shown with Soviet envoy Maxim Litvinov in New York, November 19, 1933, during Litvinov's visit to negotiate diplomatic relations with the United States.

Engineer Hugh Cooper, builder of the Dnieprostroi dam and active promoter of Soviet business opportunities, welcomes Litvinov at the American-Russian Chamber of Commerce dinner on November 24, 1933, in New York.

William C. Bullitt, U.S. ambassador-designate to Russia, greets President Franklin D. Roosevelt, November 17, 1933, in Washington.

Americans rose from $13.2 million to $14.1 million in the same period.[49] In 1928 Americans shipped $75 million in products to Russia; in 1930 U.S. exports to the Soviet Union were $114 million, and Amtorg's overall share of Soviet-American trade was 85 percent as compared with only 11.3 percent in 1923–1924. At the end of the twenties, the agency could claim to be "the largest single buyer of American agricultural and industrial equipment for export."[50]

To facilitate this trade, in 1927 the chamber had established an office in Moscow under the direction of Charles H. Smith. Smith had been connected with Russia since the war, first as a member of the Inter-Allied Railway Commission and then as a concessionaire. He was extremely impressed with Soviet progress and told the chamber in 1928 that "the American way is being disseminated throughout the land."[51]

➢ AMTORG: ILLICIT ACTIVITIES

Some of Amtorg's procurement activities raised suspicions among American officials, including J. Edgar Hoover, who became director of the Bureau of Investigation in 1924. Hoover learned in 1925 that Isaiah Hurgin of Amtorg had approached Robert Cuse, a Brooklyn dealer, and asked him "to make negotiations for the purchase of Liberty Motors and other air plane motors." Cuse confirmed that he was supplying Amtorg with reconditioned war surplus engines made from Liberty Motor spare parts supplied by Packard Automobile Company in Detroit. He told the New York office of the Bureau that he was selling the engines for $1,000 each and noted that "there is an enormous amount of stealing going on" of such materiel.[52]

Seeking further information about Cuse and his connection with Amtorg, the Bureau of Investigation interviewed N. Streloff, who had worked for Cuse occasionally since 1915. Streloff reported that Cuse had tried to recruit him to obtain drawings of airplane catapults from the Chance-Vought Corporation, Streloff's employer. He also described Cuse's factory in Jersey City, where four hundred of the reconstructed motors were built, some of which were shipped through Britain to Russia. The Bureau learned that Cuse's firm had also written to McCook Field to get drawings of bombsights, ships, and gun synchronizers, among other items. Amtorg's appetite for war materiel demonstrates that the Soviet Union was concerned with developing its military strength as well as its industrial might in the mid-1920s. But these sales concerned American authorities, not only because of their sensitive nature but also because Amtorg was working through intermediaries, attempting to evade detection of its purchases. In 1930 Basil W. Delgass of Amtorg testified in Congress that his agency had indirectly purchased four hundred motors from the War Department and then had them "repaired, crated, and shipped illegally to Russia in the general category of machinery" along with "secret instructions for their reservicing."[53] Yet despite Amtorg's success in obtaining war supplies, its regular dissemination of pro-Soviet information, and its development by the early thirties of an espionage operation, the agency consistently received better treatment than the earlier Soviet Bureau, a reflection of the government's recognition of its important trading role.[54] Where Martens faced a blockade and harassment, Amtorg saw Washington refer firms to its offices and permit these firms to offer short- and long-term credit.

Through three chief agencies in the United States—Alamerico, ARTS, and Amtorg—Soviet leaders had succeeded in launching a growing Soviet-American economic relationship. As a result, they had fulfilled not only Martens's hope that his legacy would prove positive, but also Lenin's wish that the "path leading to the American 'business' world . . . should be made use of *in every way*."[55]

⊀ 6 ⊁

TRADE AND FOREIGN POLICY,
1923–1929

Soviet representatives have named 1923 as the year marking the "resumption of trade relations" with America. That year Russia's grain crop was at last large enough to supply exports for hard currency. Armand Hammer's agency, Alamerico, was in full operation, and the All-Russian Textile Syndicate opened. The year was also notable for a milestone in Soviet-American legal relations. Remaining diplomatically unrecognized by the United States, Russia's national sovereignty was acknowledged in American courts in 1923, when the Soviet government was found not to be subject to U.S. civil laws. The case arose in a New York suit brought by furriers Wolfsohn and Son, who had stored $800,000 worth of merchandise in Siberia when it was still under the control of Admiral Kolchak. The furs were seized by Communist authorities in Irkutsk in 1920, and the company sought a court order to obtain reimbursement for its losses from Soviet property held in the United States. A New York State court denied Wolfson's claim, stating that "foreign powers cannot be subject to [U.S.] laws," a ruling that pleased Moscow's lawyer, Charles Recht.[1]

The court had decided that the United States' refusal to grant diplomatic recognition to Moscow was irrelevant to establishing Soviet Russia's legal existence. Recognition, the court concluded, "does not create a state" nor did its absence prevent such an entity from existing. Recht was relieved that his Soviet clients could now make deposits, and hold property, in the United States "without the risk . . . [of] confiscation."[2] Indeed, despite nonrecognition, the U.S. government had consistently affirmed the "territorial integrity" of Russia's boundaries.[3]

The Wolfsohn furriers did not throw in the towel. In 1925 they appealed the ruling to the U.S. District Court for the Southern District of New York. This time, Wolfsohn sued Amtorg's vice president and treasurer in New York as "managing agent of the defendant, R.S.F.S.R." Recht represented Amtorg and the Soviet Union and, using the previous New York State court ruling, argued that the Soviet regime was "the de facto government of Russia, constituting the foreign State of Russia and is, consequently, immune from any suit in American courts without its consent." Judge Knox of the U.S. Appeals Court agreed and confirmed the lower court decision that "without its consent, the Soviet Government may not be held to be subject to the suit of American citizens in American courts." The complaint against Amtorg was dismissed as well.[4]

At the same time Soviet representatives in the United States continued their efforts to improve relations. Agent Isaiah Hurgin suggested that his government's best strategy was to "play our economic propaganda" and alert businessmen to the Soviet Union's potential. Hurgin's intent was shared by a Soviet representative in Britain, P. Berzin, who pointed out that Westerners, "especially those of England, France, and America," had only an "extraordinarily vague" impression of the opportunities waiting for them in Russia "in spite of our printed and spoken propaganda."[5] Perhaps this was because Western countries were inundated with Soviet propaganda of a different sort, although Moscow authorities insisted that the responsibility for that campaign lay with the Third International, ostensibly a separate organization. Nevertheless, State Department administrators repeatedly insisted that Soviet Russia must stop the political propaganda as well as make unilateral concessions on the renounced Russian debts and property claims of Americans in Russia before any discussions could be held.[6] Soviet officials just as regularly stipulated that the United States should pay compensation for the damages caused by America's role in the military intervention and blockade of Russia.[7]

The New York–based *Daily Worker* believed that Hughes's opposition to recognition was having "its effect on American public opinion." Most Americans supported the administration's policy, but the public was not especially excited about the issue if the limited number of letters to President Harding on the subject are any indication. It would take the Great Depression to turn public opinion in favor of diplomatic relations.[8]

Secretary Hughes and his colleagues did face some vocal domestic opponents. One of them was Sen. William Borah, who tirelessly promoted the cause from his influential position on the Senate Foreign Relations Committee, where he became chairman in 1924. Although one historian has described Borah as a "curious combination of isolationist and advocate of international cooperation in limited areas," Borah's biographer, Robert Maddox, suggests that the senator's isolationism was consistent with his push for recognition. Borah wanted to practice "the diplomacy of abstinence" and stop meddling with the course of the Soviet government.[9] He strongly pushed the recognition issue in front of the public. On June 27, 1922, he gave a speech in Philadelphia at the first mass meeting of the Women's Committee for the Recognition of Russia and followed this with encores in Boston and Chicago.[10]

Borah was joined by many other advocates of Soviet-American relations, including textile syndicate head Alexander Gumberg, lecturer Scott Nearing, professor Jerome Davis, former governor James P. Goodrich, author Sherwood Eddy, and suffragist Lucy Branham. These individuals were active in groups such as the Foreign Policy Association, with its credo of a "liberal and constructive American foreign policy," and the Women's Committee for the Recognition of Russia, a new organization formed by the Women's International League for Peace and Freedom (WILPF) in 1921.[11] The Women's Committee was led by Lucy Branham, "the suffragette history professor" of Columbia University, who had accompanied Armand Hammer on trips in the Soviet Union in 1921.[12] Branham, with contacts on the East Coast and in Chicago, was executive secretary and chief organizer of the committee, which lobbied congressmen and the administration from a small office in Washington. It also planned meetings throughout the country, inviting prominent advocates like Raymond Robins, Borah, and other congressmen to speak. Alex Gumberg was impressed with Branham: "I have seen her on the job and know that she is an ideal person for it." Gumberg apparently found Branham an unusual woman, because he also believed that "one cannot use proper political lingo with ladies around."[13]

Branham's organization had sufficient credibility to gain two interviews with Secretary Hughes, and their second meeting, on March 21, 1923, gained wide attention. Hughes received the women with "great pleasure" but pronounced that there would be no change in U.S. policy, using the occasion to deliver a major statement on the subject. Asserting that the United States had no wish to intervene in the internal affairs of Russia, as "such interference would be futile," the secretary declared it was Moscow's policies that stood in the way of U.S.–Soviet ties. He told the committee that he appreciated its interest in peace, "a cause which is very close to my heart," but noted pessimistically that "there is no hope for the success of the gospel of brotherly kindness while the world is run on a policy of hate." He added that it was a "fallacy" to think that recognition would favorably influence trade and furthermore dismissed prospects of trade as "insignificant." The secretary was not entirely closed to Soviet-American rapprochement. "We are just as anxious in the Department . . . as you can possibly be, to have a spirit of mutual understanding." But he added, "The world we desire is a world not threatened with the destructive propaganda of the Soviet authorities." Recognition was off-limits without "good faith and the recognition of obligations." At the end of the secretary's jeremiad, one woman challenged him, "Mr. Hughes, what would happen if the United States did recognize Russia?" The WILPF *Bulletin* recorded his evasive reply: "the Secretary hesitated a moment, then said in substance: 'Ladies, I do not care to be questioned,' and withdrew."[14]

Hughes's declaration on Russia was front-page news the next day.[15] It was a disappointment not only to the Women's Committee but also to Soviet observers. The journal *Izvestiia* protested, "In 1918 Hughes' speech would not surprise anybody. In 1923 it is very much out of tune and is an anachronism." Gumberg groused, "Mr. H. is like a stone wall."[16] Hughes's posture on the issue did not discourage Women's Committee leaders from sending an open letter to both Harding and his secretary of state in early April, asking for the United States to invite Russian representatives to meet "in a friendly atmosphere . . . [to] try to find a basis for friendly relations acceptable to both countries."[17] Nothing happened, and after a series of attacks on peace groups by the government and the popular press, the Women's Committee was eventually dropped by WILPF in an attempt by the larger organization to defuse attacks from conservatives that WILPF was a pro-Communist organization.[18]

Yet Gumberg had not given up entirely on the secretary of state, who remained the pivotal player in any change in policy. Two days after Hughes's speech, Gumberg echoed the Women's Committee by urging Borah to request Hughes to have a "conference with Russian representatives . . . not a back door conference; rather, one in which his terms could be frankly discussed. I have no doubt that if approached in the proper spirit, the Russians would be very reasonable, and . . . a great stride toward peace would be made." Although Borah had already lambasted U.S. policy in the Senate, he should raise the issue again, Gumberg declared, and "demand a hearing before the Foreign Relations committee." The committee would then appoint a subcommittee to look into the matter, which Borah could chair, giving him an opportunity to "call a lot of witnesses who would be favorably inclined towards recognition." The time to act had arrived because "1923 would be a year of decision in Russian-American affairs."[19]

Of all the advocates of Soviet-American relations in the twenties, none was more assiduous in his efforts than Raymond Robins. A friend of Harding, he aimed his efforts squarely at the Oval Office. The president proved difficult to budge, however. On one occasion in 1922, Robins seemed ready to give up. "This last appeal of mine was based upon his letter to me of a most friendly and appreciative character. [But] we have probably broke for good now. He left the door open but I don't think I would find anybody home!" Despite his frustration, Robins did not flag. Instead, he worked closely with Goodrich and Gumberg in a concerted attempt to change policy in the spring of 1923.[20] The Soviet government undermined their efforts, however, by placing a Catholic priest, Father Constantine Buchavich, on trial for treason in March. Buchavich was accused of collaborating with the Poles during Russia's recent war with its former possession, and he was executed. The judicial murder (for Buchavich's trial was more show than substance) caused a huge outcry in the West. Gumberg agreed with Borah that this violent act had been occasioned by "the policy of intervention and blockade," since "hate is what feeds extremists on both sides." But he was both disgusted enough and realistic enough to see what damage the Soviet judges had done. "These fellows still seem to be sitting up nights trying to think up some scheme that will get them in dutch with the world," he lamented.[21]

By early June the furor had died down, and Gumberg again felt the time was appropriate to lobby Harding, whom he believed would be sympathetic. The president was then making plans to leave for a speaking tour of the West Coast and Alaska. Gumberg told Goodrich that "if the right move is made now it will be met in the spirit of sincere cooperation." The governor dutifully talked to Harding but reported to Gumberg that "the Chief . . . won't take this matter up until he returns in August." Goodrich did write Harding an eighteen-page memorandum on the subject, largely based on a report that Robins had written the previous month. Robins had alluded to the importance of Russia's vast size, great resources, and excellent investment and trade opportunities, as well as its improved economic position owing to the recovery of its agricultural sector. He clinched the argument by saying that Soviet trade would bring increased prosperity, "essential for Republican success in 1924." He finally recommended that the United States should send a commission to meet with Russian representatives to settle outstanding issues, especially since Germany, Great Britain, and other countries were taking advantage of Soviet opportunities.[22]

Robins himself visited with Harding in June and urged him to move quickly to end "the Wilson non-intercourse policy." Instead of putting off Robins again, Harding finally decided to send him to Moscow on a fact-finding mission. Secretary Hughes was not consulted. Robins traveled to Berlin, where he awaited instructions to proceed to Moscow to begin discussions on a new Russian policy for the president. William Appleman Williams believed that this trip brought the Harding administration remarkably close to recognizing Russia.[23] Robins was not the only envoy to be dispatched to Russia without Hughes's authorization. With Harding's encouragement, Interior Secretary Albert B. Fall also traveled there. He went on behalf of Sinclair Oil, one of the two firms from which he had collected bribes in Wyoming, and "quickly became a convert to the cause of Russian recognition." Unfortunately, Fall's oil interests also played a role in the demise of Harding, the most hopeful prospect for early recognition of Russia. The Teapot Dome oil scandal, in which the interior secretary was later implicated, may have precipitated Harding's sudden collapse that summer as he journeyed to Alaska, although it is clear that the president was already dying from cardiovascular disease.[24]

If Harding was not able to recognize Russia, it seemed difficult to imagine that his successor Coolidge would. Indeed, Gumberg, already sick that summer, lost ten pounds in five days after Harding's death on August 2, 1923. It was not until the fourth day that he could even choke down an egg and a slice of toast.[25]

➤ COOLIDGE AND SOVIET-AMERICAN TRADE

Harding's vice president, Calvin Coolidge, had impressed some recognition adherents as a "non-entity" and others as an unalloyed reactionary. He appeared a very unlikely candidate for introducing an improvement in Soviet-American relations. In 1919 the former Bay State governor had been pushed into national prominence when he halted a Boston police strike. He had been applauded then by the National Association of Manufacturers for his "successful vindication of the supremacy of the forces of true Americanism."[26]

But Coolidge was also planning to have a conference with those "Senators, Congressmen, and other prominent individuals who investigated conditions in Russia," Gumberg reported. There were indications that the new president was more interested in foreign affairs than his predecessor had been. Coolidge had urged a "close study of the Russian question . . . without prejudice" soon after taking the oath of office. Such plans encouraged Soviet representative Isaiah Hurgin to suggest that "a certain stunted spring" had commenced with the president's entry into the White House.[27] Hurgin was too pessimistic; Coolidge's season in the Oval Office actually included remarkable growth in trade relations.

The first year of Coolidge's administration saw the opening of two major Soviet purchasing bureaus, ARTS and Amtorg. And in his first speech to Congress on December 6, 1923, Coolidge announced that he was "willing to make very large concessions for the purpose of rescuing the people of Russia." He added that "while the favor of America is not for sale," if Soviet Russia took the requisite steps in the areas of debts, claims, and propaganda, the United States should "be the first to go to [its] economic and moral rescue." Coolidge, moreover, was not opposed to "doing business with the Russian people."[28] Chicherin responded to the speech in a cable he authored jointly with Alexander Gumberg and American recognition advocate Raymond Robins. The wire advised the president that as long as "Soviet dignity and interests" were taken into account, the Kremlin was eager to address "all questions, touched on in your message." On the issue of claims, Moscow was "entirely ready to enter into discussion . . . on the basis that the settlement will be based on the principle of mutual reciprocity." If these stipulations were addressed, said Chicherin, his government was willing to do everything possible to bring about a "restoration of friendship" with the United States. The Soviet leadership clearly expected an approaching shift in American policy, as its desire for equal treatment and respect continued.[29]

Within two days Charles Evans Hughes, whom Coolidge had retained as secretary of state, quashed all hopes by declaring, "There would seem to be at this time no reason for negotiations." The Soviets were expected to make financial and political settlements before any discussions could be held.[30] Senator Borah was disgusted at this continued official recalcitrance and tried once again to push his recognition initiative through the Senate. But in January his resolution was "overwhelmingly" torpedoed when Robert Kelley of the State Department introduced evidence of Soviet propaganda inciting revolution. Hughes formally commended Kelley for his impressive collection.[31] Not only did Borah face the stiff opposition to recognition of senators like Henry Cabot Lodge, but the Teapot Dome scandals were then also coming to the fore, pushing Russia to the back burner in Congress.[32] Borah could only complain in frustration, "the opposition to the recognition of Russia is so pronounced that I have been unable to make any decided progress."[33]

The Coolidge speech had beneficial results for Moscow nevertheless. The address, and Hughes's brusque retort to Chicherin afterward, bolstered trade by increasing publicity for the Soviet representatives in the United States, suggests James K. Libbey. Executives from "no fewer than four banks" made arrangements for lunch with textile men Gumberg and Nogin within a week after the secretary of state sent his rejection to Chicherin. Herbert Hoover also met with Nogin and Gumberg. Soviet historian Tatiana Kargina agrees that the speech had a positive outcome, describing it as the pivotal juncture between the limited Soviet-American trade relationship before 1923 and the expansion of commerce that followed. Beforehand, few Americans believed in "equal rights and mutual advantages" between the two countries, and fewer contracts were worked out. After Coolidge's address, which "officially permitted [Americans] to enter into 'trade relations with

Russia,'" such rights were recognized as essential to support trade. This recognition of rights helped legitimize Moscow's American missions.[34]

To Narkomindel, Coolidge's speech indicated a new priority on trade for the United States. Economically attuned Soviet officials cited "large trends in the world market" that had made exports an "American national problem." They predicted that Washington would have to become more involved in supporting commerce abroad; thus, the "reformation of American capitalism" was at hand. Soviet representatives hoped for much from the progressive wing of the Republican party, which showed signs of strengthening in Congress after the 1922 elections. Boris Skvirskii believed that the formation of a new Progressive party was possible. Stalin was more cautious. "Must we work with each disadvantage, which reckons itself left or progressive? No. In particular, in America, which has so many false progressives, speculating with progressive policy—it is necessary for us to distinguish between progressives and progressives."[35]

Narkomindel representatives disagreed with Stalin. Their faith in the Progressives, and particularly the Farmer-Labor party supporters of Sen. Robert M. La Follette of Wisconsin, led them to believe that a Progressive victory in the 1924 presidential election could change matters significantly, bringing a "transformation of all aspects of American political life" and a reassessment of the whole Soviet issue. The growing Progressive movement encouraged Rosta, the Soviet news agency, to predict that labor leader Gompers, the "instrument of anti-Soviet agitation," was in the process of losing his moorings against a growing wave of prorecognition sentiment. Because of this imminent and "inevitable defeat," Gompers's lobbying had assumed "an almost hysterical character." Gompers had angrily blamed Moscow that year when the Farmer-Labor party was "captured by the Communists" at its convention in Chicago.[36] Alexander Gumberg urged La Follette to ensure that the Farmer-Laborites demand Soviet recognition in their election campaign. Rosta grumbled, however, that La Follette "abstains from publicly speaking out on his opinion of Russia, not wishing to set himself against Gompers." The La Follette Progressives, like the two major parties, gave scant campaign attention to the recognition question.[37]

Raymond Robins did not believe that La Follette had a chance of being elected in 1924. But he disparagingly referred to the Coolidge-Dawes ticket as "The Golddust Twins, Address Wall St." To Robins, Harding was "the only conservative that could have been elected in 1924." He was, of course, mistaken. Coolidge won the election in a landslide, polling nearly sixteen million votes to just over eight million votes for Democrat John W. Davis. La Follette received almost five million ballots but only 13 out of 531 electoral votes.[38]

➤ THE ROLE OF THE PRESS IN THE SOVIET-AMERICAN RELATIONSHIP

Soviet leaders' hopes for incipient recognition and trade relations were fanned periodically by members of the American press. In mid-1923, *Washington Post* reporter Albert W. Fox reported, "There is genuine hope in many quarters that the President's desire to see America's foreign relationships established on a benefi-cial . . . basis may be fulfilled, even with respect to Russia." He added, "The idea that such a relationship would encourage extreme forms of bolshevism . . . is no longer seriously entertained."[39] William Randolph Hearst's papers were also sup-portive. Hearst's *New York American* editorialized that in the area of relations with Russia "America . . . lags behind," as did the "daily account of the American press." Chicherin told Ambassador Child that he and his colleagues appreciated the *American*'s efforts and believed that the "Hearst press was fair," but worried that Hearst did not have enough influence in a Republican administration.[40] Hearst's efforts and attacks were resented by the administration, particularly when the *American* suggested it was "authoritatively known" that Hughes has "been unable to ascertain definitely [Coolidge's] views in relation to Foreign Affairs." This was "absolutely false," Hughes protested to Coolidge, accusing the publisher of "scurrilous abuse."[41]

Early in 1924 Rosta observed with pleasure that a major "daily organ of conservative business circles" had joined the fight for diplomatic relations. *Finan-cial America* editorialized that Washington's professions of openness toward commerce with the Soviet Union were "entirely superfluous and senseless" since "without relations . . . the work of American capital in Russia is impossible." Fi-nancial journals, in fact, had long been prominent among the newspapers support-ing Soviet-American relations. As early as 1919 H. Parker Willis, editor of the *Journal of Commerce* and the *New York Commercial*, declared that his paper was running a "publicity campaign . . . in the hope of precipitating the resumption of commercial relations." Willis became one of the most active business supporters of Soviet-American trade in the next decade.[42]

The American media often rushed to print their hunches about shifts in offi-cial policy. Because Soviet journalists relied heavily on American accounts, these positive reports were soon printed in Soviet newspapers as harbingers of change. Rosta's Kenneth Durant worried that this was harmful to Russia's prospects. Not only did it "misrepresent official [U.S.] opinion in Moscow regarding the question of recognition," but in the United States it was "exploited with the purpose of em-barrassing Senator Borah and others." An example of this effect occurred follow-ing Hughes's resignation from the State Department in February 1925. American journalists initially "showed a greater tendency to expect a speedy change of the American policy than did the Moscow press," Durant noted. But soon the Soviet press was predicting that the "longed for recognition by America" was at hand. The recently completed Soviet-Japanese treaty, *Izvestiia* suggested, would also spur Washington to seek relations.[43] Similar reports started pouring into the American consulate in Riga, where Moscow's minister was reporting that con-tacts between the two governments had actually begun. Stories appeared about meetings between American and Soviet officials that had allegedly taken place in three separate cities.[44]

Some American journalists, meanwhile, were going so far as to report that Senator Borah had influenced Hughes to resign and that his replacement, Frank B. Kellogg, was "more open" on the issue of Soviet-American relations. Such opinions were unfounded because Kellogg was as opposed to recognition as Hughes had been: he was Hughes's hand-picked replacement. A few days before Hughes left office, as if to cement the link between him and his successor, the State Department issued a memorandum reiterating that trade treaties or political agreements with Russia were unlikely to garner the United States any more business than it was already getting. Further, the memorandum declared, nations recognizing Russia were not spared propaganda of an "extreme, vicious" nature; Berlin's chief of political police, for example, reported that the Rapallo treaty had not stopped revolutionary propaganda in Germany.[45]

The notion that links with the Soviets might be hazardous to American domestic tranquility was shared by some outside the State Department. These included Elihu Root, the former secretary of state, Nobel Peace Prize laureate, and president of the Carnegie Endowment for International Peace, who had journeyed to Russia with his "Root Mission" under the provisional government. He felt that recognition of Russia would bring an "inevitable decrease of faith in our own institutions." Most opponents of recognition professed more confidence in the strength of American organizations than did Root. Perhaps they realized too that nonrecognition was hardly a barrier to communist advocacy in the United States.[46]

As secretary of state, Kellogg quickly put all speculation of abrupt change to rest. He telegraphed Coleman in Riga that there had been no policy change and sent all consular and legation offices in Europe the same message. Soviet trade was strictly at firms' own risk, just as before. Those who asked for advice or information on the subject were "invariably [told] that . . . they must be their own judges." Nevertheless, Borah did find Kellogg's department to be more conciliatory than Hughes's.[47]

➤ THE REGIME OF FRANK B. KELLOGG

Secretary Kellogg, like Hughes, had worked as a trustbuster for the government, targeting Standard Oil and General Paper Company. A native of Minnesota, Kellogg had long been active in the Republican party, and in 1916 he was elected to the Senate, where he served one term and, allying with Borah, helped to defeat the League of Nations. Afterward he obtained the prestigious post of ambassador to the Court of St. James, where he stayed until his appointment as secretary. Kellogg did not "cut an impressive figure," according to one contemporary. Unlike his dignified and erect predecessor, he was short, "gnarled," and nervously disposed, a condition that he controlled with generous amounts of golf. His biographer, L. Ethan Ellis, wrote that he is "most fairly viewed as a busy mediocrity." Yet Loy Henderson, who worked under Kellogg, remembers this administrator as inspiring others with the vision that the United States, "in spite of its policy of noninvolvement, was contributing its share to the maintenance of world peace." Indeed, the secretary would win the lustrous Nobel Peace Prize for the well-intentioned, if ineffectual, Kellogg-Briand Pact of 1928.[48]

In 1926 the department's old laissez-faire approach to Russian trade was articulated by Robert Kelley, a hard-boiled opponent of bolshevism who ran the State Department's Eastern European Affairs Division, in a speech to officers at the Foreign Service School. America could "enjoy the benefits of commerce" with the Soviets so long as recognition was not involved, he told the audience. Secretary Kellogg, however, soon made significant adjustments in the policies that determined economic relations with Soviet Russia. Growing Soviet-American trade spurred him to shift from Hughes's policy. In 1927, for the first time, the State Department authorized long-term credit for an American sale to Moscow. The American Locomotive Sales Company, which had received a large contract from the Soviet government, was permitted to offer five-year terms of payment, the kind of credit that is essential for a sizable heavy equipment order. Kelley, who was advising the department on the matter, had declared that the proposed financing violated the carefully preserved distinction between the established and acceptable practice of offering short-term credit to Moscow and the unprecedented and, in his view, unmerited practice of granting long-term credit. But he was overruled by three men equally anticommunist in their outlook: President Coolidge, Commerce Secretary Hoover, and Treasury Secretary Andrew W. Mellon. They decided that the State Department "would not look with disapproval upon banking arrangements incidental to the financing of contracts concluded . . . with the Soviet authorities" as long as securities sales were not involved. This was a significant breakthrough. Herbert Hoover, who had said in 1921 that "trade with Russia on credit was out of the question" and even more specifically that "communism and long term credits are incompatible," had now endorsed a different approach.[49]

So too had the State Department leadership. In 1924 Evan E. Young of the East European Division had dismissed the potential of Soviet-American commerce, scoffing at the idea that anyone would offer large credits and questioning why any country would send a trade representative to Moscow.[50] But in February 1928, Secretary Kellogg issued a four-page statement on his department's Russian policy, which revealed that long-term credits had become routine. The secretary vaunted the higher level of trade enjoyed by the United States as compared with Britain and Germany, both of which had already recognized and signed trade treaties with Moscow. Kellogg declared that his department "endeavored to reduce to a minimum difficulties affecting commercial relations" between the United States and the Soviet Union.[51] Yet Kellogg's trumpeting of trade did not stop Robert Kelley from continuing to "promote a hard line toward the Soviets." Kelley's training of Soviet experts for the department, including George F. Kennan and Charles E. Bohlen, was designed to inculcate "the values against which to judge Soviet behavior," and this emphasis was maintained well after recognition.[52]

Although long-term credits and even an occasional loan had now become available to Russia, some commercial restrictions stayed in place.[53] America's ban against Bolshevik bullion was galling to Moscow since the policy was based on the assertion that gold originating in Russia had been stolen from its prerevolutionary owners. Also at issue was the inequitable way the ban was enforced. Although Russian gold was not permitted entry, Western European nations routinely serviced their accounts in the United States using remolded Soviet bullion. The Moscow State Bank decided to test this prohibition in February 1928 and transported $5 million in gold bars directly to New York, consigning the shipment to the Chase National Bank and the Equitable Trust Company. Despite long acceptance of "laundered" Soviet gold, this more straightforward use of the metal became an international issue. Within two weeks, the French ambassador told the State Department that his government would sue whomever took this gold, because he claimed it was owed to France. Chase National Bank and Equitable Trust refused to certify the Soviets' title to the gold shipment bearing the Bolshevik seal because they feared a French lawsuit.[54] The Treasury Department ultimately rejected the gold bars on the attorney general's advice that "acceptance might imply United States recognition of Soviet ownership." Although Soviet officials had proof that the gold had been manufactured in the mid-twenties and not, as French representatives alleged, ten years earlier, they were wary of a court battle. The gold was recalled to Moscow.[55]

The Tass correspondent covering the event was furious. He declared bitterly that this was "the only Soviet gold which the American government refused during recent years. The bourgeoisie imagined itself carefully protected from taint of Bolshevik gold by the vigilance of Treasury officials," he bristled, yet "hundreds of millions" worth of gold had "entered unprotested" since the early twenties.[56] This was completely accurate, as the Federal Reserve itself had noted.[57]

Yet in other areas there were important successes. In 1928 the International Civil Aeronautics Conference, which carried U.S. sponsorship, requested permission from the State Department Division of Protocol to invite representatives from Amtorg to an upcoming meeting. The conference's executive officer explained, "The Amtorg Trading Corporation is placing special orders for aircraft equipment in this country, and undoubtedly there are Russian technical men whom the Conference might like to meet and hear." East European chief Kelley was willing to allow the networking to proceed, while preserving existing policy of official nonintercourse with Soviet representatives. Knowing full well that Amtorg men were all affiliated with the Soviet government, he responded disingenuously, "This Department does not desire to interpose any objection to the presence at the Conference, in a private capacity, of Russian aeronautical experts or technical men."[58] The State Department thus permitted American businessmen to speak to their Soviet colleagues at an officially sponsored event.

The aeronautical conference was evidence of the growing access that Soviet representatives were gaining to the United States. In 1925 Amtorg had complained that as many as forty-two Soviet purchasing agents wanted to come to the

United States but were prevented by visa regulations.[59] Three years later the American military attaché in Paris reported that "about 100 men" had passed through France from Russia on their way to the United States. "While some of these men are doubtless going to America for the purpose of buying goods, establishing credits and other financial arrangements, advantage is being taken of this legitimate business for the purpose of introducing into our country a large number of Bolshevik political workers," alleged T. Bentley Mott. Soon after, J. Edgar Hoover noted that three men were coming to lobby for recognition of Russia, but "they will enter the U.S. ostensibly for the purpose of negotiating for the purchase of automobiles and other machinery."[60]

Stalin claimed that these fears of political intrigue were exaggerated. In 1929 he stated that "No representative of the USSR has the right to meddle in the internal affairs of countries in which he is directed, not directly, not indirectly." This had been expressed in the "most firm and strict orders to all our personal staff in Soviet agencies in the U.S." He mentioned the Amtorg staff specifically: "Bron and his colleagues are not the least bit connected with propaganda in any way." Unlike Amtorg, however, the executive committee of the Comintern faced no such constraints. It had an ambitious agenda for the American Communists. "The Workers Party must actively struggle with the imperialist policy of the American capitalist class," the executive committee resolved in 1929. The party "must energetically help national-revolutionary movements in countries which are now colonies," including the Philippines, Cuba, and Puerto Rico, since "the American capitalist class . . . using the Dawes plan as its principal big stick" was trying to subjugate North and South America as well as Asia. The Comintern's leadership blamed this imperialism on "the gigantic industrial expansion of the U.S."[61] This expansion was being fueled, ironically, by Soviet orders, which continued to increase thanks to greater access to credits.

➤ CREDITS BECOME THE CURRENCY OF TRADE

Initially, American firms had tightly restricted their financing in accordance with Washington's posture toward the Soviets.[62] But in 1924 Soviet reports noted an "undoubted improvement in conditions of credit," although it was short-term. Credits to Russia averaged just over five months then, and many firms required 50 to 75 percent of the order amount up front. By fiscal year 1925–1926 the average length of American-based financing had almost doubled, and the amount of credit available had also significantly increased, as Soviet accounts confirm.[63]

International Harvester was among the first major American firms to offer financing to the Soviet Union. Shortly after the revolution, one of the managers of the firm's struggling Russian plant, Sidney McAllister, had told a company official in Chicago that "in a business sense, our people and our government, whether they like [it] . . . or not, if they want to do business, must get into the game immediately." Harvester began selling American-made products to the Soviet cooperative Selskosoyuz as early as 1920. By 1924 Harvester was offering financing to several of the New York-based Soviet cooperatives for binders, trucks, reapers, and mowers. The arrangement required 50 percent down and monthly payments so that the purchase would be completely paid for one year after delivery.[64]

In October 1924 Amtorg sought a $1.5 million to $2 million credit from Harvester with no money down. Amtorg officials Isaiah Hurgin and Paul Ziev informed Harvester's O.H. Browning that "in none of their transactions are they asked to pay 20 percent cash with their orders." Ziev declared that Harvester was impelling Russian business to go to German factories, where terms were "very liberal," as were Canadian requirements. Ziev showed Browning a letter from the Massey Harris Company indicating that the firm granted Amtorg two years' credit with no money down and the first payment of 20 percent due six months after the goods were received in Russia. Harvester's less liberal terms made Amtorg vituperative. "Mr. Ziev advised us that if we had the very best truck in the world, and at the very lowest prices of any, he would not, under the present circumstances, buy ours," Browning related.[65]

Yet Harvester machines were, as always, highly desired in Russia, and the company's terms were actually better than those of its chief rival, Ford Motor Company. The Dearborn firm offered no credit until late 1925 yet still managed to get the lion's share of the Soviet tractor market through that year owing to the efforts of Armand Hammer's export agency and the passion for all Ford products and methods, which were thought to be the wave of the future.[66] Realizing the advantages Harvester offered, Amtorg placed a $1.5 million order with Harvester in late 1924 with terms of half payment, half credit. The Harvester officials were pleased to report that payment "was made promptly at maturity."[67]

International Harvester was "the first of any importance to extend credit to the Russian Government," according to Fayette Allport, representative of the Bureau of Foreign and Domestic Commerce in Brussels. Harvester's action prompted Ford to offer 25 percent credit beginning in late 1925. George Sandomirsky, Harvester's Russian agent, wrote, "The Commissar of Foreign Trade had been dealing with the Ford Co. and trying to get Ford tractors on a credit basis, with the hope that, if they offered Ford an order for 10,000 tractors, they might expect to receive them with a fifty percent [credit] from 6–9 months."[68]

Thus, the Soviet Union "used the [Harvester] arrangement in many countries as a lever to obtain similar or more advantageous arrangements," Allport observed. Harvester was contacted by many foreign firms, as well as the French Ministry of Commerce, requesting details. Harvester, gun-shy from its losses through nationalization, did not permit the outstanding amount at any given moment to exceed $4 million and always received a bank guarantee for its credits from the Soviet banks in London. Yet, Allport intimated, "the bank guarantee is of course little more than a fiction" because these financial institutions were Soviet-linked. Although firms in other countries, including Canadian, Swedish, German, and Czechoslovakian manufacturers, were besting the Harvester terms—the Swedes offering up to two years' credit with no cash down—the Soviets still liked to brag about their Harvester credits "because it is undoubtedly the most responsible concern from which the Soviet Government has been able to obtain credit," noted All-port. Yet Soviet purchasers always desired better conditions and Harvester official E.A. Brittenham related that he was "constantly under pressure" to ease credit.[69]

This pressure came internally as well. Sandomirsky believed that Harvester could still get a share of the Soviet tractor business, estimated at $7.5 million or about eighteen thousand tractors for 1925–1926, if only the "percent of cash payments were reduced." German firms were taking away much of the business. Deutsche Works and Krupp shared a $10 million order that year, and Sandomirsky feared that "the fulfillment of these orders will result in German machines being forced on to the Russian farmer, who still is trying to get a McCormick or Deering Machine."[70]

Because of these competitive pressures, Harvester for the first time in 1925 extended its payment terms beyond one year, granting an eighteen-month, $2.5 million credit to Amtorg. This accelerated a significant move by the Soviets away from Fordson tractors to other makes. Ford continued to be very tightfisted with financing and also experienced problems in its production of spare parts after 1926.[71]

Harvester's financing contributed to a larger trend, and by 1925–1926 the length of financing offered to Russia by the average firm had significantly increased.[72] Even as company-supplied credits were becoming common, however, unsecured financing was not. When W. Averell Harriman and Company wanted to extend a $35 million credit to German industrial firms to promote German exports to Russia in May 1926, the firm ran into roadblocks at the State Department. Harriman's effort was part of a 300-million-mark credit to Russia to permit purchases of German light equipment and heavy machinery, and his credit was of course pushed by the German government and the Reichsbank.[73] Leland Harrison explained that the State Department objected to the proposal because it would entail "the employment of American credit for the purpose of making an advance to the Soviet regime." The government declared that its disapproval of a loan to Moscow was key in the decision, rather than opposition to German-Soviet trade.[74]

However, there are indications that fear of aiding a competitor was a principal reason for the rejection of Harriman's financing. American officials were beginning to see Germany as an important rival for Soviet business. Every year between 1923 and 1930, with only two exceptions, Germany edged out the United States in exports to Russia.[75] Since Washington already facilitated private American loans to Germany under the Dawes Plan, and these loans partly financed Soviet-German trade, the State Department's decision to prohibit Harriman's involvement was also contradictory.[76] In 1926 journalist H. Parker Willis warned members of the NAM that the Germans were using American bank loans to finance their exports to Russia. He asked critically, "Will [the Russians] get their funds from American bankers, or will they get their goods from American manufacturers?"[77]

Washington's position against Harriman's loan, however, dimmed German hopes for effecting "economic pioneer work in Eastern Europe." According to a German newspaper, greater access to the Eastern markets was necessary since "Germany's hopes for a benevolent attitude of the Western Powers toward importing German goods have not been fulfilled." In 1928 Chase National Bank backed an even more ambitious, and similarly unsecured, effort to finance railway bonds for the Soviet State Bank at 9 percent. It too was denied by the State Department. These difficulties did not prevent Germany from offering sizable long-term financing to Russia. In 1929 Berlin hoped to offer an additional large credit to support Russo-German trade, as the German ambassador to Russia, Dr. Herbert von Dirksen, informed American ambassador to Germany Jacob Gould Schurman. In a further demonstration of the irrevocable connection between American financing of Germany and German financing of Soviet trade, Berlin was told to wait until "the Young plan and associated questions have been definitely settled" before extending the credit.[78]

The government's opposition to unsecured Soviet financing—that is, financing that was not tied to orders for American goods—should not obscure the importance of Washington's decision to loosen its policy on long-term credits. Authorizing such credits was clearly the most important innovation in U.S. economic policy toward Russia in the late twenties. In 1928, following American Locomotive Sales' five-year financing arrangement with Moscow, International General Electric offered an even larger five-year credit—$25 million toward the Soviet purchase of massive electrical apparatus. It made a "profound impression" among businessmen, according to gleeful Soviet sources. General Electric required only a 25 percent down payment, far better than the deposits often demanded by other firms, with the balance to be paid five years from the scheduled shipping dates. Clark R. Minor, president of International General Electric, announced that the contract, because of its "higher rate of interest charged," would settle all nationalization claims against the Soviets, which then amounted to $1.75 million.[79] Certainly this was a violation of the spirit, if not the letter, of State Department policy that all claims be repaid before new financial assistance was offered. As a Tass correspondent crowed, "General Electric considers new business importanter [sic] than pre-Revolutionary claims."[80]

The contract had taken more than a year to hammer out and was negotiated under the watchful eye of the State Department. Assistant Secretary of State William R. Castle Jr. noted, "As this was merely a financial credit not involving Russian securities in the American market, it was not a thing that we would disapprove formally." This appears to be an example of diplomatic double-talk. It is difficult to imagine the department accepting such a liberal financing proposal just two or three years before, when such arrangements were discouraged. The State Department had its own reasons for approving the deal, and one of them was the notion that "hopes awakened by the GE contract" would undermine the German-Russian trading relationship.[81]

In 1928 Saul Bron of Amtorg reported, "About fifty first-class firms, each of which is a leader in its particular sphere, have offered considerably improved conditions for short-term credits." As long-term credits were also becoming more frequent, "all of this gives reason for a certain optimism in estimating the immediate prospect of development of the business relations between the USSR and the United States."[82] Bron's hopes were fulfilled. In 1929 he reported that his agency had received one-year credit terms from over two hundred companies and longer terms from many others.[83]

Isaac Sherman's Industrial Credit Corporation, founded in 1927, greatly aided this effort. Since Amtorg had been unsuccessful in selling its acceptances to banks, Sherman would "assume the risk of postponed payments," using a $3 million fund, by purchasing Amtorg acceptances and then trying to sell them to others. William R. Corson and Robert T. Crowley write that Sherman's credit company was completely subsidized by the Soviet trading agency and did not entail Sherman's "own money," as he had claimed. It was "simply intended to provide access to that part of the U.S. business community that did not want to deal directly with Amtorg."[84]

The trend toward greater accessibility in credit enabled the import-export trade to increase from 1923 to 1930 by more than 2300 percent, from $6 million to nearly $140 million. The great bulk of this was American exports, and most of the increase took place after the Five-Year Plan had replaced the New Economic Policy in 1928.[85] The plan's economic blueprint was largely oriented to heavy industry. By the end of the decade, Soviet orders represented a significant share of several sectors of the American economy, including oil drilling and refining equipment, agricultural implements, construction and mining machinery, and electrical and metalworking apparatus.[86]

Between 1925 and 1929 the largest item the United States sold Russia was fifty million rubles' worth of farming machines, including twenty thousand tractors, mainly Fordsons, but also lesser quantities of International, Harris, Keyes, and Advance Rumely models. Together these shipments amounted to 25 percent of all American tractor exports. Metal and electrical equipment—including grinding machines, high-speed precision lathes, and mining, boring, and quarrying implements from firms such as Cincinnati Milling, American Tool, Pratt and Whitney, and Brown and Sharpe—was worth twenty-five million rubles in total sales. The oil industry purchased fifteen million rubles' worth of American equipment and technology, and the automobile industry ordered three and one-half million rubles' worth of Fords, Buicks, Packards, Dodges, and Harley Davidsons.[87]

American products were preferred in Russia because of their advanced technological design, although U.S. firms had to compete with German ones, which had the advantages of proximity as well as a trade treaty that included extensive government-backed long-term credits for Moscow. Overall, American and other Western technology acquired during the First Five-Year Plan had a tremendous impact upon the industrialization of the Soviet Union, contributing in a major way to the plan's success.[88] So dependent was the Soviet Union on foreign technical assistance that International Harvester claimed in 1930 that the Soviets were trying to get 150 American engineers and other technical workers at Harvester and GE to leave their jobs and work in Russian plants by offering raises of 50 to 100 percent.[89] Despite such suspected double-dealing, technical assistance contracts and the expansion in exports during the early plan were beneficial for both American suppliers and their Soviet customers.

Herbert Hoover could take some credit for his Commerce Department's contributions to the Soviet-American trade relationship that peaked in 1929–1931. Nevertheless, Soviet sources were convinced that Hoover's refusal to distance himself as president from Hughes's old demands on debts, claims, and propaganda was evidence that Hoover remained "hostile" to the Soviet government. Officially, American diplomatic relations with Russia had changed little since the end of the First World War. When Rep. C.B. McClintock asked Secretary of State Henry L. Stimson what kind of safeguards existed for several of his Connecticut constituents who were going to work in Russia in the fall of 1929, Stimson answered tersely, "Persons who proceed to Russia in present circumstances must do so at their own risk." The secretary reassured McClintock, however, that he had received no reports of harm to "the not inconsiderable number of American citizens" already in Russia. Similarly, Worthington Pump and Machinery wished to send a Russian-born, naturalized American citizen to install an order of machinery in Russia. But Robert Kelley informed the company that since the State Department lacked a naturalization treaty with Russia, it "can give no assurance that such a person would not be treated as a Russian citizen should he place himself within the jurisdiction of Russia."[90]

Despite such difficulties, those who wished to trade with Russia were doing well. In late 1928 the American-Russian Chamber of Commerce surveyed its membership for information regarding their experiences in doing business with the Soviet Union. More than half of the members responded, and in a positive fashion, as the organization noted: "The majority of the replies stated that credits had been extended and that all obligations were carried out meticulously." The Bausch and Lomb Company was typical, reporting that "payment has invariably been prompt" in their dealings with Amtorg. The export manager of Black and Decker Manufacturing similarly stated, "We feel very optimistic about the possibilities of securing business in that territory. . . . We have had 100% help and cooperation from the Amtorg organization, and are going to continue to keep a representative permanently in the USSR."[91]

H.J. Freyn of the Freyn Engineering Company, which served as technical adviser to the iron and steel industry of Russia, offered a glowing report. The firm was planning to broaden its consulting agreement and noted that "the aim of the Soviet Government is Americanization on as broad a scale as possible." But, Freyn cautioned, "If American bankers, engineers, industrials and merchants are unwilling to furnish the aid for which Soviet Russia stretches out its hand, other nations will have to do it, and will do it." Other firms offered similarly positive sentiments. Samuel Newberger, whose firm supplied the All-Russian Textile Syndicate, found his customer "most punctilious and correct in its manner of handling both actual cotton transactions and contracts of all forms." Charles E. Stuart, of Stuart, James, and Cooke, Inc., technical advisers of the coal industry of Russia, was very upbeat. His firm had "the largest individual group of foreign engineers in Russia." Although Stuart had heard rumors of starvation and other difficulties, he could find little evidence of them. Moreover, he affirmed that the Soviets paid their bills. This consistently positive response on Soviet payments and potential was drawn from a group devoted to Soviet trade. But those who sold to the Soviet Union rarely found reason to complain about payments on current accounts. It was the old debts that were unmet.[92]

In July and August 1929 the chamber with much fanfare sent a delegation of one hundred—including businessmen, their wives, socialites, and tourists—for a month to the USSR to explore economic possibilities.[93] Alexander Gumberg, who organized the trip along with Chase National Bank's Reeve Schley, remarked, "Our delegation was the first large group of foreign travelers to make such an extensive trip in Russia under comfortable conditions." In the first leg of the trip, travelers stopped in Leningrad, Moscow, and Nizhni Novgorod (Gorky), where Ford was making plans to erect an automobile factory. The group then floated down the Volga to Stalingrad and went on to the Caucasus resorts and oil regions in Georgia. Finally reaching the areas of heavy industry, they saw the Donetz coal mines, the Dniepropetrovsk steel mills, the Kichkas-Dnieprostroi dam, which was the showpiece of Hugh Cooper, and the cities of Kiev and Kharkov before returning to Moscow.[94]

The 95 guests, each of whom paid $1,000, traveled almost six thousand miles by luxurious train, steamer, and automobile. The junket received wide coverage in American papers, and Alex Gumberg heralded the trade potential of the trip.[95] It also drew the attention of the Russian public, especially when some of the women on the train donned their silk pajamas to cope with the heat. *Time* magazine poked fun at the "sack suits" male delegates had to wear to avoid "vanities that might strike a bourgeois note in the communist paradise."[96]

Serious business was conducted during the trip too, and these initial contacts led to some of the major construction and consulting contracts of the First Five-Year Plan. Most spectacularly, the Austin Company of Cleveland agreed to build the Ford automobile plant near Nizhni Novgorod. Ford had already signed a four-year technical assistance contract for the construction of an $18 million factory, for which Ford would contribute approximately 40 percent, as well as supply technical experts and train Soviet workers and engineers. Using parts that Ford would sell (worth up to $30 million over the life of the deal), the plant would be capable of assembling thirty thousand cars and twenty thousand trucks annually by 1933. The Soviet Union had in 1929 only twenty thousand cars on its roads, half of which were in working condition. The first Ford was built in Nizhni Novgorod in 1932.[97]

Westinghouse representatives also agreed to provide equipment for a power plant in the Stalingrad tractor factory, and twenty other firms began negotiations during the trip, including the Animal Trap Company, Bristol Patent Leather, Remington Rand, International Business Machines, Underwood Elliott Fisher, and Gillette Safety Razor. MacDonald Engineering Company of Chicago used the opportunity to contract to build grain elevators and refrigerator plants.[98]

The Soviets treated the Americans well. Better, indeed, than they treated the British, despite the fact that Great Britain imported more from Russia than the United States did. The Swedish newspaper *Stokholms Tidningen* editorialized that this Soviet attitude was intended to make the British "frightened by the success of the Americans into being more accommodating." Britain had broken diplomatic relations with Russia in 1927 after alleging seditious and propagandistic activities at Arcos, the Soviet purchasing agency in London. Moscow's favorable treatment toward the Americans had also been bestowed "to gain the benignity of the United States and to obtain their goods."[99]

In 1929 Stalin was concerned that a burgeoning Soviet-American commercial relationship would be undone by treacherous European rivals. "Germans constantly cry that the position of the Soviet Government is precarious and that it is not justified to open serious credits with Soviet economic organizations, but at the same time, they try to monopolize trade relations with the USSR, and offer credit." Stalin accused British businessmen also of conducting "an anti-Soviet campaign" even as they "made an attempt to organize credit for the USSR." Stalin asked, "How to explain these two-faced German and English businesspeople? They want to monopolize to themselves the trade relations with Russia, abusing and driving away the United States from us." Stalin regretted that "the United States is entirely distant from this struggle" but remained convinced that the United States and the Soviet Union still had a "great basis for broad business relations."[100]

The contracts signed under the auspices of the American-Russian Chamber of Commerce in 1929 served to confirm the Soviet dictator's hopes for American business. Yet D.C. Poole, observing the returning delegates from his post as counselor at the embassy in Berlin, was skeptical. Although he conceded the importance of the Austin factory-building deal, he pointed out that International Business Machines "did no business. IBM found that some of the ideas of the company had been pirated and some of their patents copied." Moreover, John L. Senior of Cowham Engineering, who had harbored ideas about building a cement plant in the Soviet Union, had been convinced by the trip to "give up any idea of entering the Russian field," Poole noted. As for Westinghouse, its representatives "are understood to have come out of Russia with the somewhat obvious conclusion that while sales to Russia should be increased, credit facilities should not."[101]

The tour itself had certainly been Potemkinesque. "Practically all the members" agreed that they had been through a staged performance and "only at nights, in bed, were they left alone," a German newspaper reported. The unrelenting "cleanliness of the entourage, the lack of beggars, the efficient supply of factories and mines and the satisfaction of peasants . . . became obvious" as carefully scripted. The chamber's officials could hardly have missed this themselves, and they did not publicly disagree with these assessments.[102]

Yet Alexander Gumberg had been visiting Russia for the Chase National

Bank regularly, and the chamber's journey struck him "more favorably than any previous visit, chiefly because of the increased industrial activity in the country since the inauguration of the five-year industrial program." The organization did not intend to prepare a formal report about the trip, as had a delegation of British industrialists earlier that year. The British delegation had been traveling under official auspices to explore the restoration of relations between Britain and the Soviet Union. A similar report from the American Chamber of Commerce might be seen as provocative, because its mission had not carried official sanction. Schley noted, "Our Chamber . . . has endeavored not to be drawn into controversy on political subjects."[103] The chamber's primary orientation certainly was trade, not politics. Nevertheless, the organization became active when its leaders saw it as necessary to promote commerce. In 1931, chamber members helped to roll back stiff restrictions on Soviet raw material exports to the United States. On the more purely "political" issue of recognition, however, the group took little part until the summer of 1933, when its agent in Russia served as a go-between for American officials and the Soviet government.[104]

After returning from its Russian mission in November 1929, the chamber reassessed the effectiveness of its agent in Moscow, Charles H. Smith, and the location of his office. Neither was deemed satisfactory. Smith himself was considered too old and passive for a post where the chamber needed dynamic leadership. He also lacked a "clean slate". A former member of the International Peasant Soviet, Smith had mining and lumber interests in the Soviet Far East and according to the State Department was "more or less an agent of the Soviet Government," an opinion confirmed by Raymond Robins.[105] Smith was perceived as too radical to be properly businesslike. Also, he was not helping develop the business of the group's members, and the chamber had a financial deficit and could ill afford an ineffectual administrator. To make matters worse, his quarters in Moscow were in an inconvenient location. Declining finances meant that the chamber had not been able to pay Smith since January 1929. Although the chamber's ranks had grown to 156 members, its highest number ever, this was still not enough to cover the expenses of the summer Russian delegation, the publication of a yearbook, and Smith's operation. To make up the difference, the chamber would lean on its major members. The chamber received no funding from Russia, the only organization of its kind not supported by the country with which it was affiliated.[106]

The chamber decided to move its offices to the Soviet Union's Chamber of Commerce for the West, or Torgpalata, which would provide rent-free space and a better location. The organization also agreed to pay Smith $7,500 in back salary and look for a new agent. The desirable hire would be someone who was "not over 40, active and energetic, who has had business experience and who will be able to establish contacts in Russia and keep in touch with all business developments there." At Gumberg's suggestion, and to protect Smith's feelings, he would be told only that the office was closing. Smith was warmly congratulated on his "pioneer work in developing American-Russian relations."[107] Tatiana Sofiano, a secretary at the USSR Chamber of Commerce who had served the delegation the previous summer, temporarily took Smith's place. The Soviet government did not mind sparing Sofiano, "an astute and omnipresent Soviet figure among Americans working in Moscow." In her many capacities, she remained loyal to the Soviet security apparatus. The chamber eventually hired Spencer Williams, a young newspaper reporter who had joined the trip to Russia, for Smith's post in 1930.[108]

Some were unhappy with this change in personnel. The head of the Torgpalata, L.M. Khinchuk, wired the chamber expressing his displeasure about Smith's resignation. The departure of this "sincere friend of the Soviet Union" was considered a "serious loss to the establishment of relations." Khinchuk was joined in his sentiments by six American newspaper correspondents, including William Henry Chamberlain of the *Christian Science Monitor,* Walter Duranty of the *New York Times*, and Eugene Lyons of the United Press. They had come to rely upon Smith as their liaison with the Kremlin. Spencer Williams proved to be an asset to the chamber, however, serving in Moscow until 1940, when the Nazi-Soviet alliance made Soviet-American trade vexatious. Many of the American goods exported during that brief period were resold to the Nazis and in December 1939 President Roosevelt ordered a "moral embargo" against shipments of aircraft and weaponry to Russia.[109]

During the 1920s, the groundwork had been laid and the financial scaffolding erected for a burgeoning trade relationship between the United States and Russia. Although Washington remained intransigent on the subject of diplomatic relations, officials such as Hoover and Kellogg had facilitated trade with the Soviets by permitting the extension of once forbidden long-term credits. Economic pressure had influenced foreign policy and helped legitimize the Soviet regime in the United States.

AMERICAN BUSINESSMEN,
THE NEP, AND THE
FIRST FIVE-YEAR PLAN

The great expansion in Soviet-American trade relations discussed in the previous chapter was accompanied by an equally significant growth of American investment in Russia, related to the launching of the New Economic Policy. By the end of 1920 the ideological zeal of war communism had reached its apogee. As Alec Nove suggests, by then Lenin himself had "gone right off the rails" in pursuit of peasant surpluses and supposedly wealthy "kulaks" in order to feed the soldiers and the urban workers.[1] But growing unrest among the peasants, as well as a revolt by sailors at the Kronstadt base in March 1921, helped the Soviet leader and some of his colleagues see that war communism had reached its limits.

The New Economic Policy (NEP), launched in 1921, allowed peasants to pay a tax in kind on their goods rather than face outright requisitioning; it also permitted small businesses to operate and invited foreign investors into Russia to build up the country's industry. By December 1921 Lenin could declare that Russia's domestic crisis was finally being addressed: "We have placed on a correct footing the problem we have been handling this year and which up to now we have handled so badly—that of forming a sound economic alliance of the workers and peasants." But a lasting economic solution also required international engagement: "Without definite relations between us and the capitalist countries we cannot have stable economic relations."[2] This turn toward capitalism at home and abroad was of course a step backward for the revolution but was necessary nevertheless, as Lenin explained to the Seventh Moscow *Gubernia* Conference in 1921: "We shall go on retreating until we have completed our [economic] education; until we have made our preparations for a definite offensive."[3]

NEP's scheme to attract foreign investment found a strong supporter in Commissar of Foreign Trade Leonid Krasin. He knew that Soviet Russia needed capitalists to finance and operate industrial facilities and recognized that Russia's dearth of experienced production managers was endangering the country's economic health and its future. During the Revolution and war communism, many of the country's educated and experienced supervisors and technicians had become "demoralized" or had simply "disappeared," he noted. The ever-practical Krasin recommended foreign concessions as a means to provide "hard currency, technology, and administrative direction with the obligation of definite development of production" in the USSR. Like the Treaty of Brest-Litovsk, which was also signed with a foe, deals with the capitalists would allow the Bolsheviks to "start putting things in order at home and deepening the socialist revolution," as Lenin put it.[4]

Although concessions drew a great deal of interest in the early twenties, attracting nearly three thousand applicants, only 6 percent of them actually began operations between 1921 and 1923. Lenin was perplexed. "Our concessions policy seems to me to be excellent. But despite that, we do not have any profitable concessions." The situation had significantly improved by the mid-twenties. The initial flurry of "speculators" dissipated, as V.A. Shishkin notes, and 482 applications yielded 110 operating concessions in 1925–1926. Although these foreign investments comprised only one-half of one percent of production in 1926–1927, their peak year, they made a very significant contribution to the technological development of the Soviet Union.[5]

Once NEP had been instituted, Lenin had to continue to defend its provisions for international investment in Russia. As he acknowledged, offering concessions "look[ed] like a bloc with foreign capitalism," but he vowed that "the property of the landlords and capitalists would not be restored." To those who might disagree, he lectured, "To think that we can get out of this [desperate economic] state without crutches is to understand nothing!" But he also intended to limit the power of concessionaires, reassuring critics: "There is nothing to fear in concessions so long as we retain possession of all the state enterprises and weigh up exactly and strictly the concessions we grant, and the terms and scale on which we grant them. Growing capitalism will be under control and supervision, while political power will remain in the hands of . . . the workers' state."[6] These political limitations, along with a deeply rooted disdain for foreign investors and a growing advocacy of state-run enterprises to effect rapid industrialization, would prevent the Soviets from developing a lasting relationship with the capitalists.

In the beginning, foreign investment was vital, regardless of the inconsistencies it created. In a speech he gave in early 1921, Lenin declared, "So long as revolution is not complete, bourgeois capital will be useful to us as we can accelerate the development of our economic life." At the same time, the Chief Concessions Committee of the Supreme Soviet of the National Economy (Vesenkha) recognized that in order to bring an increase in exports of raw materials and native industry, improvement in domestic transport and in manufacturing capability was required. Indeed, it was a vicious circle, for it was impossible to "restor[e] transport and industry without improving exports, and improving exports can't be imagined without preparing to receive from abroad the necessary locomotives, rails, machines, and other equipment of industry." Yet the Vesenkha also recognized the drawback to allowing foreigners to export Russia's "natural riches" and exploit its workers. "The principal disadvantage of concessions . . .

is the recognition for concessionaires of the right to partial property in equipment of the undertakings and products . . . granted them by the right to export abroad products of the concessions." But the committee recognized that without the concessionaires, there might be no machinery from abroad "to equip factories and plants, materials necessary to us for technical, organizational, and administrative strengths." Foreign capital was thus the prerequisite for financing imports, infrastructure, and, finally, the manufacture of exports.[7]

Although the NEP has been portrayed as the "encouragement, by the state, of a private business sector," concessionaires soon found that this "private sector" was a highly public matter. After Lenin's death, opposition to concessions, both ideological and opportunistic, increased. The "fundamental dilemma of NEP"— the potential enriching of groups such as peasants, Nepmen, and foreign investors, "whose basic outlook was inimical to the regime"—became more and more unacceptable.[8] By 1926 "increasing emphasis on the need to industrialize the Soviet Union on its own resources restricted the scope for concessions," as Carr and Davies write.[9]

This change in policy was unfortunate not only for Western businessmen, but also for Leon Trotsky, who became head of the Chief Concessions Committee in 1925. Trotsky, a former foe of concessions who had once argued for reliance on internal resources instead, had by 1925 come to embrace foreign investment. In his new post, he was concerned about the slow pace of industrialization and the low output of Soviet workers. As Richard Day points out, Trotsky recognized that capitalist investment would ensure "'the transfer to our country of foreign plant, foreign productive formulae, and the financing of our economy.'" Trotsky believed, notes Jon Jacobson, that "importing the most sophisticated and expensive technology . . . would catapult the USSR into the industrial future and allow it to create the objective basis for true economic independence from capitalism."[10] Stalin and Bukharin, however, had now taken up Trotsky's former position against concessions and in favor of autarky, and it was dangerously provocative for the former Red Army chief to advocate the opposite course so strongly. Trotsky knew Stalin's views were highly influential in the party and accused his rival, who had placed Trotsky in his new post, as aiming "purposely to compromise [me] in the eyes of young communists." He added acidly, "It's already being said that I'm on Averell Harriman's payroll."[11] In character, Trotsky tried to use the post as a springboard for his "attack on [Stalin's] reactionary theory of 'socialism in a single country.'" He declared, "We are becoming a part, a highly individual but nevertheless component part of the world market." But in his new incarnation as foreign investment enthusiast and world integrationist, Day suggests, Trotsky "committed political suicide."[12]

The New Economic Policy's promise of improved Soviet trade and investment opportunities initially caught the imagination of American businessmen, unaware of the difficulties and party battles that were to come. In terms of actual financial benefit, however, the plan brought disappointing results. As Evan E. Young of the Department of State's Division of Eastern European Affairs noted,

"The experience of foreign business men has been that the practical working out of concessions has fallen far short of expectations with the result that many firms have withdrawn from their Russian enterprises."[13]

➤ INTERNATIONAL HARVESTER AND THE NEW ECONOMIC POLICY

Young was writing in 1924, the same year that the International Harvester Company finally pulled out of Soviet Russia, and the history of that firm's Lubertzy works near Moscow well illustrates the conflict between American businessmen and Soviet economic planners during the NEP era. One of the few large private enterprises to survive war communism and its wide-scale nationalizations, Lubertzy faced a new threat during the New Economic Policy when the Soviet government pressured Harvester to turn Lubertzy into a concession and thereby make a major investment in its plant.

Since its opening in 1910, the Harvester factory had manufactured thousands of inexpensive, rudimentary reaping machines known as *logobreiki* (literally, "brow-sweaters"), as well as more sophisticated Deering reapers and engines. As the predominant prewar producer of agricultural machinery in Russia, Harvester manufactured 97 percent of that country's reapers and binders for what became by 1914 the firm's largest foreign market. As the largest prerevolutionary investor in Russia, Harvester managed to turn a slight profit at Lubertzy up until the First World War.[14]

In November 1917 Lubertzy still had a work force of more than two thousand, ranging from engineers, draftsmen, and factory workers to secretaries, bakers, doctors, nurses, and teachers, among whom, as the firm readily acknowledged, "we no doubt have many [socialists]."[15] After November the plant continued to gain government contracts despite the upheaval in Russia, first from the farmers' cooperative, Selskosoyuz, and after 1919 from the new government agricultural machinery agency, Selmash.[16] Even so, the company's leaders had to cope with lagging sales, labor disruptions, and food and transportation shortages. In the earliest days of the revolution, the bloody street fighting in Moscow interrupted daily operations and resulted in at least one unsuccessful takeover attempt.[17]

In the ensuing months, government decrees undermined Harvester's ability to operate the factory. The situation for Harvester was even worse in the provinces, where the firm maintained a network of branch houses that delivered implements to local farmers. Lacey G. Gray, who worked for the company in Omsk where he also served as a U.S. vice consul, protested that "the combined worry of keeping this, that, and the other of our personal effects from being requisitioned and the shortage of food had made [Harvester agent F.J.] Brown, Mr. Jordan, the British vice-consul, and myself decide it was not a place for white men [*sic*]."[18]

Harvester's main plant got some help from Raymond Robins, head of the American Red Cross in Russia. Robins developed close connections with Soviet leaders, including Lenin and Trotsky, during the first six months of the revolution. "Colonel Raymond Robins . . . has a very good and clear understanding of this situation and its necessities as relating to the American government and American commercial interests," manager Sidney McAllister noted. This greatly benefited Harvester. Robins's "entrée with the Bolsheviks" helped the firm fend off several takeover threats and assisted it to secure contracts for Lubertzy. During one takeover attempt, McAllister reported, "[Robins's] speaking of the matter at headquarters resulted in [government representative] Kosmin coming to us with instructions, as he stated, to straighten out all difficulties of our Company." Robins's efforts helped keep Harvester from being immediately nationalized, and it continued to receive orders from the Soviet government.[19]

The Soviets spared Lubertzy from nationalization during their initial drive to control the economy's "commanding heights" in 1918–1919, not only owing to Robins's efforts but also because of Harvester's position as the major producer of machinery for agriculture, the most vital economic sector in the Soviet Union. Because large industry was, in Lenin's words, "incredibly devastated," the government required some factories that were operational.[20] George Sandomirsky, Russian manager of the plant, informed Harvester officials in Europe that Lubertzy had "established good, cordial relations with the . . . Vesenka and with the Commissariat of Food and Supplies [the distributor of Harvester machines]." Harvester had avoided the seizure of any company assets by emphasizing that "our Company means real work," and it made an important contribution to the Soviet economy.[21]

Harvester's situation in the USSR remained uncertain nonetheless into the early years of the New Economic Policy. The country was in a "transitional phase," Lenin acknowledged, and "we are forced to seek highly complex forms of relationships." Harvester officials realized that their status in Russia was as "precarious" as it was "exceptional." Harvester's delicate position is confirmed by the Soviet government's refusal in 1920 to let the firm import $50,000 worth of medical goods and clothing for Lubertzy. As a company official reported, authorities "could not allow our factory at Lubertzy (which is unnationalized) to take better care of its workmen than the nationalized concerns could take." T.H. Anderson offered a realistic appraisal: "Our position in Russia calls for a different and more conciliatory policy than firms whose property has been confiscated. Our Company should invest a reasonable amount to assist Lubertzy and show our good intentions . . . and thereby in a measure further secure our assets in Russia." It was for this reason that the firm decided neither to financially support nor to participate in a proposed exploratory mission to Russia sponsored by the U.S. Chamber of Commerce. "I believe we have too large [an] interest in Russia to let up in furthering any plan of this nature and we have, perhaps, more at stake than many other companies," said Harold McCormick.[22]

In 1922 the company's outlook on investment in the USSR changed when the Soviet authorities began aggressively pushing Harvester to update and expand the Lubertzy factory. According to the principles of the recently created New Economic Policy, plants had to operate under conditions of "advanced production as against backward production." It was no longer acceptable for Harvester to continue operating the factory in its prerevolutionary state. Initially, authorities simply requested that Harvester invest additional capital in Lubertzy.[23] By 1924, however, Soviet goals were more grandiose: Harvester must transform Lubertzy into a state-of-the-art concession, completely electrified, its production line capable of modernizing Soviet agricultural methods and producing forty-two thousand items of machinery annually within five years.[24]

Harvester opposed establishing such a significant stake in Russia for several reasons. The plant had not been profitable since 1914, and there was little reason to think it would become so after a large infusion of private capital. There was always the hazard of nationalization, and the rules for running concessions meant that Harvester would have very limited control over Lubertzy. Finally, the government demands hit Lubertzy when a 2000 percent inflation rate was making it difficult for the factory even to pay for supplies and labor. As a result, a mower manufactured at the plant in 1922 cost $108 versus $62 for one shipped from the United States. In September 1922 the State Department received word that the plant had been closed "because the Soviet Government, which takes all its output, has been unable to dispose of the products at their high cost price."[25]

The plant had not shut down, but it faced continuing difficulties. Later that year, a state investigative commission determined that half of the Harvester plant now belonged to the Bolshevik government. It was alleged that Soviet supplies of new materials were high enough so that when depreciation of existing stock was factored in, Harvester's ownership of Lubertzy dropped to a fraction. Manager Hans Emch wrote that he felt "quite sure that a certain plan exists to investigate and attack . . . the running of the factory, with the idea of finding matter for criticism in past business."[26]

In December the metalworkers union, with Selmash's blessing, advocated the takeover of the Harvester plant.[27] In the union's view Lubertzy was too vital to be shut down, and its owners threatened just that by their "refusal to put floating capital into the production." The metalworkers' goal matched that of the New Economic Policy: to obtain new infrastructure and technology from foreign investment.[28] And as the State Department confirmed, "The Harvester Company has put no outside capital in its Russian business since the Revolution but has heretofore kept it going on a turnover of its Russian assets. . . . The object of the Harvester Co. was simply to keep the plant going and intact." Confident that Russian engineers were capable of operating the plant, the metalworkers declared that it was "necessary to nationalize the factory and transfer it to the institution supervising the construction of agricultural machinery in the Republic," the Selmash trust.[29]

Still, Emch was guardedly optimistic. He advised company officials that "the general opinion in higher circles" was "that there cannot be any question of nationalizing an American enterprise at the present time." Harvester's general manager, Alexander Legge, remained apprehensive, however, and contacted Secretary of Commerce Hoover to tell him of the problems at Lubertzy. Hoover informed Charles Evans Hughes, who expressed concern but could do little owing to the absence of relations between the two countries.[30]

On the first day of 1923 the Soviet government enacted a new law requiring that "owners of large industrial establishments may run such only on a concessionary basis." Lubertzy would no longer be allowed to operate without the express authorization of the Chief Concessions Committee. The plant's managers were well aware that this authorization would not come without an investment of capital.[31] Harvester's difficulties were rooted in the government's decision not to renew the factory's yearly contract in October 1922, a contract that had been renewed routinely for four years. Selmash, already late in its payments, refused to send any more rubles. Emch and Sandomirsky desperately wrote to the chairman of the presidium of Vesenkha in early 1923, pleading for renewal of the production contract and asking for prompt payment of 180,000 prewar rubles owed for past deliveries. If payment was not forthcoming, McAllister was prepared to shut down the factory.[32] By this point, the number of employees had shrunk to just 689. Although this was equal to 33 percent of the prewar staff, Lubertzy's output was just 14 percent of prewar production.[33] Even so, there were 3,540 mowers sitting in Lubertzy's warehouses. Wishfully, the firm wanted the Soviets to extend peasants credit for machinery purchases and also to establish "a proper government sales organization."[34]

Selmash chairman Davidov was unsympathetic. "If the Russian government is compelled to furnish capital to finance the Lubertzy factory," he demanded, why transfer this money from Russia's "lean purse" to the Americans' "bulging pocket"? After all, "the government could retain the entire advantage of the investment by nationalizing the factory." But he emphasized that the factory need not be nationalized if Harvester would only invest in it. McAllister, who was now running Harvester's European manufacturing operations, was adamantly opposed to such a step. "We will absolutely not put any good money into Russia, nor will we negotiate anything along the lines of a concession." Instead, the company would "do the best we can to keep things alive and when we cannot do this we will inform the officials that we find it impossible to operate . . . and propose to close down temporarily." McAllister clung to a long-standing Harvester belief that "the Russian government cannot afford to do anything along the lines of nationalization of the Lubertzy works in the face of their . . . necessity of creating a favorable impression on the American government, capital, and business." But he was mistaken.[35]

In March 1923 Harvester received permission from the State Department to meet with Soviet representatives to try to keep the plant operating.[36] This effort was unsuccessful, and within two months the company suspended operations, cutting off water and steam lines to the plant. After Lubertzy shut down, Harvester officials tried once more to avoid nationalization. Hans Emch met in

London with a Soviet representative, Sudakov, who insisted, as had Lenin, that his government was "very anxious to make business connections with America." Harvester continued to insist, however, that it would not invest further in the plant, which contradicted the goals of the New Economic Policy and made Lubertzy's demise as an American enterprise inevitable.[37]

Late in the afternoon of September 24, 1924, a commission from Glavmetall, the state metal industries agency, entered the factory armed with a document from Vesenkha ordering Emch to surrender the plant. With little choice, Harvester simply requested "formal documents and proper receipts." The company was instructed by its lawyer never to acknowledge that the nationalization had been legal.[38]

Harvester personnel wondered if they had done all that they could to prevent nationalization. Vice President Herbert F. Perkins reported that Harvester treasurer Austin Ranney "expressed some anxiety that we may not have been clearly understood by the Soviet authorities in Russia to be very willing indeed to consider an opening of the Russian factory." Perkins disagreed, writing McAllister: "I would like to ask you if you have any doubt whatever . . . that both our representatives in Russia and you yourself . . . have consistently and continually indicated our willingness and desire to negotiate."[39]

Although Vesenkha had assumed control of the plant, Soviet officials still wanted the Harvester managers to stay. They asked the company to sign a thirty-year concession agreement at the end of which Lubertzy would be transferred to the Soviet government. The agreement specified that Bolshevik authorities would determine output, quality, and prices, and Harvester "shall deliver in kind for the benefit of the State ten percent of [its] manufactured productions first." The arrangement also prohibited Harvester from leasing or selling Lubertzy. This sounded to McAllister and Legge as if the facility already belonged to the Soviets, and they were not interested in an agreement on such terms.[40]

In Washington, the Coolidge administration told Harvester to forget about filing a claim with the U.S. government for the factory until the United States reestablished relations with the Soviet Union.[41] Undoubtedly, diplomatic relations would have made it easier for Harvester, and other firms, to look after their Russian interests. The firm did enter a claim on its 1924 tax return, charging off $2,291,000 in "depreciated book value" for Lubertzy.[42] In fact, the company lost over $43 million from its Russian operations.[43]

The Lubertzy works went on without Harvester, although it did not produce in the quantities that it once had. In the United States, the International Harvester Company in Russia, a subsidiary of International Harvester, continued its paper existence. One of Harvester's spokesmen noted in 1932, "We have kept this company going now for 15 years since the Revolution. It is some expense and trouble to hold the annual stockholders' meetings and directors meetings and believe it would be safe to omit these." By the 1940s Harvester in Russia was holding meetings only every three years. As late as 1959 the company was still making active efforts to recoup its Russian losses with the U.S. government.[44]

➤ AMERICAN CONCESSIONAIRES IN THE SOVIET UNION

Harvester did not turn its plant into a concession because its leaders believed that they would lose control of the plant. Other American firms, however, did yield to the siren song of concessions. These businesses had never invested in Russia before, and the promise of quick economic gain in a highly populated, rapidly industrializing country proved particularly enticing. Unfortunately, the logic of investment in the Soviet Union undid most of them also. The Bolshevik government could not long allow capitalists, and foreign capitalists at that, to remove products and "excess capital" from Russian shores.

American engineer Washington Vanderlip launched the first attempt at a concession in the fall of 1920. When Vanderlip arrived in Russia, the Soviets had him confused with the wealthy Frank Vanderlip, former president of National City Bank, and believed also that he came with the backing of the incoming president, Warren G. Harding. The journal *Novy Put* divulged that Vanderlip represented "twelve of the largest concerns and banking corporations on the Pacific coast." These included Harry Chandler of the Los Angeles *Times* and Edward L. Doheny, the oil magnate. Although Washington Vanderlip was linked with some of these wealthy West Coast businessmen, he was himself a man of modest means, a well-traveled geologist, engineer, and prospector, excitable but not the "billionaire" the Soviets believed him to be. Moreover, there is no evidence that he had any connection with Harding.[45] He had long had an interest in Kamchatka's riches, however, and the concession that the Narkomindel authorized him was gargantuan, a sixty-year lease of 400,000 square miles in Siberia, including the resource-rich Kamchatka Peninsula. It included "extraction of oil, rock coal and fish." Vanderlip was to deliver a certain percentage of his products to Russian ports, where the Soviet government would have the right to purchase what he could not sell. In order to carry out these requirements, Vanderlip would build railroads, highways, harbors, and twenty fish factories. There was one problem, however, with the Kamchatka location: the Japanese still controlled it. This did not deter the ambitious Vanderlip. He wanted to buy all of Kamchatka, and he recklessly promised American recognition of Russia for it. Moscow, however, had no interest in selling. Instead, Lenin relished the potential American-Japanese rivalry in the Far East. "We will utilize the growing hostility between America and Japan and offer Kamchatka on lease instead of losing it without proper compensation, especially in view of the fact that Japan already has taken from us vast territory in the Far East," the Bolshevik leader declared. "Already we are sowing discord among our enemies," said Lenin slyly. "The concessions do not represent peace, but war of a profitable economic nature."[46]

In addition to his vast Siberian concession, Vanderlip had agreed to obtain $1 million worth of credit for Russian purchases in the United States through a banking syndicate, and to find markets in the United States for Russian exports. But Vanderlip's concession was "conditional . . . only after establishment between U. S. and RSFSR [of] normal relations and by the establishment of such no later than 2 July 1921." Ludwig Martens, who had returned to Moscow, noted the Vanderlip "treaty" with great enthusiasm, declaring that with the imminent arrival of Harding to Washington "everything seems indeed to point to a radical change in the policy of the United States toward Russia." Despite Martens's hopes, "normal relations" did not transpire in the allotted time, and the Vanderlip concession in Japanese-controlled Kamchatka turned out to be little more than a pipe dream, as the engineer returned to California.[47]

In early 1922 Sinclair Exploration Company also tried to open a Siberian oil concession. Harry Sinclair signed a deal with the Far Eastern Republic, later subsumed by the Russian Soviet Federated Soviet Republic, for reserves in the area of Russia then occupied by the Japanese but claimed by Russia. Unlike Vanderlip, Sinclair did have close ties to the Harding administration, but he got no help from the State Department in his attempts to press the Japanese to permit him to operate on the island of Sakhalin. Hughes was more interested in maintaining cordial relations with Japan than in recognizing the legitimacy of Soviet Sakhalin, where Sinclair's concession lay. This was so even as Japan continued to occupy Russian Sakhalin in violation of the Washington Conference requirements to evacuate it. Sinclair was unable to press its claim to the oil, and Japanese interests eventually got the very lucrative concession.[48]

By now the first American concession in Russia had *really* opened. Armand Hammer came to Russia in the summer of 1921 to collect the debts the Bolsheviks owed his family as well as to bring charitable assistance.[49] Owing to his family connections, Hammer received help directly from Lenin, who steered him through the nettlesome Soviet bureaucracy so that Hammer would be able to swiftly establish an asbestos mine at Alapayevsk, in the Ural Mountains. The Chief Concessions Committee approved Hammer's concession in October 1921. His venture was required to produce 80,000 pounds of asbestos in the first year of operation, 100,000 in the second, 120,000 in the third, 140,000 in the fourth, and 160,000 in the fifth. The Soviet government would get 10 percent of the output. The U.S. government was largely uninformed about the project, and as late as October 28, 1921, the Commerce Department did not know who Hammer was.[50]

Lenin needed Hammer for more than simply capital investment. As the Soviet leader told Ludwig Martens, who had become head of the state metallurgical agency, the American doctor's financial involvement in Russia was "politically" significant.[51] Lenin accordingly went out of his way to assist him, telling Zinoviev, "I beg you to help the comrade Armand Hammer; it is extremely important for us that his first concession would be a full success."[52] As the first American concession operator, Hammer would serve as "the bellwether to induce other American capitalists to invest." Lenin believed that "we must make a special effort to *nurse* the concessionaires; we must *woo* [them] energetically."[53] But he also seemed convinced of his minions' ability to make a botch of the venture. "I am sure that *not a damn thing will be done* unless there is *exacting* pressure and supervision," Lenin hectored Ivan Ivanovich Radchenko of the People's Commissariat of Foreign Trade on Hammer's behalf.[54]

Indeed, even with Lenin's friendly influence, establishing the asbestos mine in Russia was not an easy task for Hammer. The Soviet authorities impounded a vital shipment of German equipment on one occasion, and Hammer had to push hard to import this material duty-free as had been promised under the agreement. When he first arrived, he also had to deal with the terribly backward conditions in the mine. Its five thousand workers were digging holes for dynamiting the ore with long iron rods and then lugging away the chunks of asbestos for further processing. To speed up this operation, Hammer supplied the laborers with hydraulic drills and built a new railroad to move the ore. This done, he laid off half of the mine's work force. Hammer did offer his remaining employees relatively good benefits; in addition to a salary of approximately $7 per month, they received free utilities and subsidized clothing and food.[55]

When the facility was complete, however, Hammer's mine ran into economic problems. High production of asbestos abroad, particularly in Canada, combined with low demand for the ore in Russia meant that his venture stayed disappointingly in the red. By 1926 Hammer had relinquished control of the concession and had turned his attention to other prospects in Russia, where, unlike most concessionaires, he ended up doing very well.[56]

While Hammer dug for asbestos in the Urals, another American entrepreneur drilled for oil in the Caucasus. Mason Day and his associates at the Barnsdall Corporation began efforts to set up an oil concession in Soviet Georgia in 1921. The firm, newly christened International Barnsdall, dispatched three men to the Caucasus: Day, trade representative Frederick G. Menard, and assistant secretary Eugene F. Connors. In Tiflis, the Soviets presented them with two options: either start a "mixed corporation" or form a concession. A mixed company arrangement involved equal ownership with the Soviet government, and the company rejected it. Barnsdall wanted "monopoly rights in the region and to export all kinds of raw materials from the Caucasus." The firm thus decided upon a concession that included raw materials ranging from tobacco to coal, but the primary interest of the firm was oil exploitation.[57]

The Barnsdall group would have to wait for word from Moscow on their concession, because the Soviet leaders responsible for such deals, including Krasin, were at the Genoa Conference, where Standard Oil and Royal Dutch were also competing for oil rights in the region. Standard Oil's recent acquisition of Nobel's nationalized holdings in the Caucasus was hotly disputed by the British at Genoa. Soviet representative F.Y. Rabinovich, president of the Union of Georgia, Azerbaijan, and Armenia for Foreign Trade, suspected that the Barnsdall delegation was doing more than prospecting for profitable opportunities. Rabinovich inferred, "It has the task from Hoover to investigate the economic status of the Transcaucasus republic, independently of the interest of the separate firms."[58]

By January 1923 Barnsdall vice president Philip H. Chadbourne wrote cheerily to Gumberg, "Have closed contracts for all the machinery, etcetera, and everything looks fine." The agreement reached in Tiflis was favorable to the company. Barnsdall would have the "exclusive right to handle, sell, and market all or any of these goods: oil, tobacco, wool, skins, silk, timber, lumber, coal, licorice root, cocoons, manganese." Barnsdall got the right to all of these products tax-free, and it would also have "preference over any other shippers over all railway lines, steamship lines and pipelines at reasonable rates." Subsequent agreements added to the amount of land involved and broadened the scope of the operation. The Russians and Georgians would get a 30 percent commission when the goods left the country.[59]

The Barnsdall people were impressed with the oil industry and the government in Russia. They were also conscious of their role as investment pioneers. Chadbourne professed, "I am moved not only by personal considerations, but I know that a large portion of the American public is following with close attention this opening of industrial relations with the soviet republic." Chadbourne believed that American recognition was imminent. He along with Day thanked the Central Executive Committee (Ispolkom) for their help, stating, "We are now but awaiting the arrival of our tools and equipment to commence work."[60]

In early March 1923 the Barnsdall representatives, including Chadbourne and Brown, the vice president of Barnsdall New York, arrived with their oil-drilling equipment specialist from the Lucey Manufacturing Corporation. They met with the president of the Azerbaijan Soviet, Comrade Mousabekoff, who offered his felicitations: "It is difficult for us to rebuild everything ourselves, and therefore the proletariat of the Soviet Federation in general, and that of Azerbaijan in particular, heartily desires the cooperation of representatives of cultured nations, in the front rank of which America stands." Brown returned the pleasantries, and Chadbourne chimed in that the work was but the "first swallow" in a "new era in the economic relations between the U.S. and Soviet Russia." As the agreement was signed between the Soviet oil agency Azneft and the Barnsdall Corporation, Mousabekoff nearly choked up: "The Americans are the first to reply to the . . . need from Soviet Russia."[61]

Soviet functionaries were greatly impressed with Barnsdall's commitment. As a Comrade Serebrowski noted in the *Baku Workman*, "the Americans are going at the matter very seriously. They are acquainting themselves thoroughly with those parts of the oilfields where they wish to bore." He was encouraged by the significant involvement of the Lucey engineering firm, whose president was due to arrive presently. "It is clear that if Mr. Lucey himself is coming here with Mr. Day, the Americans attach very great importance to their future operations in Baku." Serebrowski crowed, "We can therefore look forward to seeing American machinery and piping follow closely upon the coming of their engineers, and this . . . will greatly augment the production in those fields."[62] The Soviet interest in using foreign investment to enhance their technological arsenal was once more evident.

In May Chadbourne wrote to Gumberg again, noting that conditions had become difficult for his venture in Russia but adding gamely that "nothing worthwhile comes without a struggle." He reported how busy he was, "getting buildings, office, quarters etcetera ready for arrival of machinery in July." Gumberg, in the midst of the campaign to persuade Harding to send a diplomatic commission to Russia, responded with encouragement. "Things are getting better and better as far as American attitude to Russia are concerned. While we are not yet arrived, I really think that there may be something doing this year."[63]

Barnsdall's leaders were bullish on the project, and for the Soviets, Barnsdall's venture was a tremendous "propaganda effort" that succeeded in "keeping the major oil companies off balance," particularly Standard Oil, notes Floyd Fithian. It even drew in Harry Sinclair, who attempted to follow Barnsdall's success in the Caucasus while avoiding a repeat of his failure in the Far East. Sinclair planned a $150 million investment in Central Asia, but then the Teapot Dome scandal bubbled around him, preventing him from raising the necessary funds. And Barnsdall, despite its promising beginnings, left Russia in 1924 having lost money. Its record was another in the annals of overambitious and unfulfilled Western concessions in Soviet Russia.[64]

Nevertheless, the State Department had to occasionally cool the ardor of some of its more enthusiastic representatives for American investment in Russia. Even before the formal signing of the Barnsdall concession, for example, the high commissioner in Constantinople, Mark L. Bristol, wrote to Washington that Henry Mason Day had been made "virtually the fiscal agent and Minister of foreign trade" for the Autonomous Soviet Republics of Azerbaijan, Georgia, and Armenia. "[This] means that the United States controls and dominates the commercial activities . . . of one of the richest territories in the Near East," crowed Bristol, ignoring the fact that the United States had nothing whatsoever to do with a private arrangement between an American individual and these Soviet states. He was soon chastened by Acting Secretary of State Dearing: "Unusual care should be taken that the action of American officials should not be construed as extending the official sanction of the Government to the negotiations between Mr. Day and the Caucasus republics."[65]

But D.C. Poole was more interested in Day's plans, likely because he recognized the strategic import of Barnsdall's product, oil. In a report to Secretary Hughes, Poole related that he had told Day, "We will do anything possible to assist any legitimate American enterprise in securing these materials" in the Caucasus, which had only recently come under Soviet control. The government could help, Poole thought, by establishing "official representation at Tiflis" and sending U.S. Shipping Board vessels to ports in the region. The Commerce Department had already unofficially dispatched a representative to the Georgian capital. Poole added discreetly that the Shipping Board should consult the State Department for authorization and that the department would respond as favorably as possible, weighing "commercial considerations" against "paramount political considerations." Approval was seen as likely, because the State Department had recently authorized the Shipping Board to ship to Soviet ports.[66]

The profit potential of transoceanic traffic to Russia was also discovered at this time by Averell Harriman, who had long been interested in Soviet Russia.[67] When he graduated from Yale College in 1911, Harriman had at first planned to follow his father, Union Pacific magnate Edward Henry Harriman, into a career with the railroad. But after a short stint on the firm's board of directors (he was probably the only member of that august body to also work as a "gandy dancer"), Harriman turned instead to ocean shipping and operated the successful American Ship and Commerce Corporation during the First World War. By 1920 he headed an investment firm, W.A. Harriman and Company, and served on the boards of several leading American corporations, including Guaranty Trust Company. This combination of transportation, financial, and administrative experience, along with an ebullient curiosity, made Harriman eager to buy a share of Derutra, the German-Soviet shipping line, in August 1921. Derutra was the first mixed company, or joint venture, in Soviet Russia.[68]

Harriman had previously dabbled in Soviet trade, having assisted Hamburg banker Max Warburg in financing Soviet orders in Germany. Warburg consistently assured him of the safety of doing business with Russia. Harriman recalled that his desire to better "understand the Revolution" also spurred him to greater financial involvement in the Soviet Union.[69] In the spring of 1922 Harriman's associate, Clifford Carver, negotiated final arrangements for the new shipping firm with Soviet representative Leonid Krasin and Derutra's German partner, the Hamburg-Amerika Line. At the first of these meetings, Krasin insisted that as a condition for the establishment of the new shipping line, the United States must officially recognize his government. Like many Soviet leaders, he believed that business and government in the United States were closely linked. Carver, however, was able to convince Krasin of the merits of making some kind of "beginning" without waiting for a change in the political situation.[70]

The new freight service gradually gained notice. The *New York Times* reported in 1924 that the company in large part "account[ed] . . . for the already impressive movement of trade between unrecognized Russia and this country." Isaiah Hurgin, the Soviet representative at Derutra's New York office, declared that Derutra demonstrated the potential of Soviet-American trade. Derutra shipped cotton, timber, scrap iron, asbestos, flax, furs, and charity freight, including that of the Russian Red Cross. It got $3.50 per box for shipping Hebrew National Kosher Sausage relief packages.[71]

In 1926 Harriman disclosed that his New York branch of Derutra was doing better than any of the line's offices in Europe. Still, he had not been able to recoup his investment. Harriman's American Ship and Commerce Corporation and its German partner divested their holdings in Derutra that year and returned full ownership to the Soviet government.[72]

By this time Harriman was already deeply involved in a more ambitious Russian venture, a concession to exploit manganese ore at Chiaturi in Soviet Georgia, which he hoped would dwarf Derutra in its success. Russia had supplied more than half of the world's manganese production before the war, and three-fourths of that output had come from Chiaturi. The war greatly boosted demand for the ore because it was needed for the production of steel as well as for batteries, paint, dyes, and glassmaking.[73] Harriman's interest in the mine was encouraged by an optimistic view of its potential return. As one of his telegrams proclaimed in 1925, "PRICE MANGANESE ASSURES LARGE PROFIT." Harriman sensed an "exceptional opportunity to control enormous basic industry with very limited capital and risk." He believed that his earnings from Chiaturi, the largest such concession the Soviets had made with an American, would reach $120 million.[74]

Harriman did not bother to contact the State Department about Chiaturi.[75] He signed the concession contract in June 1924 and by the summer of 1925 had paid $3,450,000 for excavation rights. To guarantee his commitment to spend $3 million on railroad construction and mine mechanization at Chiaturi, he was also required to deposit $1 million in Gosbank, the Soviet state bank.[76] The entire arrangement was confirmed on July 27, 1925, and a new firm, the New York–based Georgia Manganese Company, was created to operate at Chiaturi.[77]

To Harriman, who would be the chairman of this new company, the concession was more than just another investment. Not only was his company's money at risk, Harriman declared, but so were "our reputations as conservative businessmen." A successful Soviet venture would serve as an example for other American firms, "including several of the most important interests who have already talked to me," whose representatives were monitoring the situation. One of Harriman's advisers predicted that, should the operation be successful, "it would have a bearing on even the attitude of the Foreign Department of the United States."[78]

Chiaturi appeared to be a promising venture, as demonstrated by the international following it attracted in the investment community.[79] Even before Harriman officially purchased the Chiaturi concession, Georgia Manganese had received orders for over 110,000 tons of manganese from large American concerns including Bethlehem Steel. The ore fields contained an estimated eighty million tons of manganese, as well as two to three million tons of peroxide, a more valuable compound.[80] An additional boost came when Capt. T.T.C. Gregory, a former member of the American Relief Administration who was described as the "closest friend of Mr. Hoover," reported that the commerce secretary had given his blessing to the operation.[81] Even Henry Ford was interested in the manganese project, being "the world's largest consumer of this metal."[82]

Yet within the first six months of the concession's life it was apparent that problems were developing. A competing mine at Nikopol in the Ukraine, run by a German concern, Rawack and Grunfeld, was starting to produce manganese ore in quantities sufficient to erode Harriman's price. The German firm had also been given responsibility for the distribution of the entire Soviet state monopoly of manganese abroad, putting Harriman in a vulnerable position. Although a memorandum of understanding between the two mines stipulated that Harriman would ship 60 percent of all manganese exports from the USSR and Nikopol only 40 percent, the "combination of German-Soviet competition" soon overwhelmed the American businessman. While Chiaturi's production mushroomed from 52,177 tons in 1922–1923 to 775,700 tons four years later, Nikopol's output increased from 74,177 tons in 1922 to 615,000 tons in 1927. It was little wonder that world prices plummeted.[83]

In an attempt to resolve the problem, Harriman met with Chief of Concessions Trotsky in December 1926. Trotsky, the now fervent concession supporter, had been removed from the Politburo just one month earlier, in part for his unorthodox views. Given his precarious status, Trotsky was in no position to take action on behalf of Harriman; nor did he particularly want to.[84] It did not help that Harriman's mine was situated in Soviet Georgia. As Robert H.M. Robinson, Georgia Manganese's president, pointed out, many local citizens were eager to take control of the mine themselves, and "through Stalin the Georgians have just now immense power."[85]

The predictions of large profits from manganese turned out to be "in some degree inaccurate," as one of Harriman's close associates noted with great understatement. In addition, there was increasing hostility toward concessionaires from officials, and Moscow remained stubbornly inflexible on royalties and output requirements in the face of fluctuations in the world price. The Chiaturi workers were also well paid and well supplied by Soviet standards and because of frequent government inspections of the mine, enjoyed over 125 days off per year.[86]

In early 1927 Robinson recommended to Harriman that he negotiate out of the deal as soon as possible, even though the firm had not yet fulfilled its obligations by building a railway from the mine to the Black Sea. Before giving up, however, Harriman tried to renegotiate. He asked the Soviet authorities for cutbacks in production, a "sliding scale" of royalties based on market prices and shipping costs, and a steep reduction of the ambitious rail construction called for in the original plan.[87] Soviet officials agreed to consider these proposals but were disturbed at Harriman's suggestion that his firm not pay for the railway work. The rail line was to be a concrete result of NEP's program of using "foreign capital for working out our riches." As they reminded Harriman, "according . . . to the 'bourgeoisie' morals," their right to hold him to the agreement was "incontestable."[88]

Eventually, the concessions committee did decide to cut back Nikopol's production significantly in favor of Chiaturi's. It also released Harriman from some of his contractual obligations. In return, Georgia Manganese was required to increase its total output by 25 percent, from sixteen million to twenty million tons of ore over the twenty-year life of the contract. Robinson protested that these production figures were not feasible. In addition to these requirements, Moscow was making it difficult for Harriman's foreign staff to exchange their hard currency for rubles at favorable rates. In September 1928 it finally became apparent to Harriman that he could not make the mine a going concern, and he terminated the deal.[89]

Despite his troubles, Harriman claimed that Georgia Manganese had left him "with a small profit." Because the mine's actual operations lost money, this profit was based on the unprecedented loan that the Georgia Manganese Company had granted to the Soviets. At the termination of the concession, Soviet representatives agreed to give back Harriman's $3,450,000 investment only if he would assist them by purchasing Soviet bonds for $4,450,000. Harriman promised to buy the specified amount of Soviet state notes, which yielded 7 percent interest and had a fifteen-year maturity. Shrugging off the profound difficulties he had experienced, Harriman claimed that this loan had secured him a "reasonable profit" on his earlier investment. This bond purchase, as the Soviet purchasing agency Amtorg was proud to note, was "the first American loan received by the Soviet Government."[90]

Control of the Chiaturi excavation went to Rawack and Grunfeld. After this experience, Harriman stayed out of Soviet affairs and did not turn his attention to Russia again until the Second World War. Once he left, his former employees saw their wages cut 20 percent, and the clothing and shoes that Harriman had imported for them seized and sold by local authorities for quite a good profit.[91]

Concessionaire Armand Hammer's asbestos mine had also become untenable during this period. Hammer's losses at the facility followed another defeat, when the Soviet government established Amtorg to eclipse his import-export office, Alamerico, in New York. But Hammer refused to give up and instead turned his attention to new opportunities in Russia. On October 8, 1926, he opened a concession in an old soap plant in Moscow, where he produced pencils and pens, to which he soon added three more facilities manufacturing items including celluloid and asbestos roofing tile. To expedite his pencil output he turned to Germany, where he recruited technicians and engineers employed by the highly regarded manufacturer Eberhard Faber. Hammer's pencils were more expensive than those issued by the Soviet government, but they were of a higher quality and far more in demand. Hammer's workers produced the writing implements on a piecework basis, and the factory was able to export some of them.[92]

The American entrepreneur's four plants employed up to one thousand people in peak periods and, unlike his other Russian concession, reaped generous profits, ranging from $550,000 to $600,000 annually on gross sales from $2.5 million to $4.5 million. Historian Antony Sutton reports that Hammer's plants represented one of only two foreign-owned concessions among the 340 established to make such substantial earnings in the Soviet Union during this era.[93]

By 1929 Stalin was tightening the screws still further on foreign concession operators. His extreme distrust of international influence in Russia had already been manifested in the Shakhta affair of 1928.[94] Within a year Hammer found himself heavily taxed and unable to secure credit in the United States to support his businesses in Russia. On February 18, 1930, he relinquished his concessions in exchange for "several million dollars paid in rubles cash, [and] Soviet bonds." In addition, he was permitted to take his valuable art masterpieces, precious jewelry—including the exquisite Fabergé Easter eggs—and ornate icons. This "Romanov Treasure" had been collected by Hammer and his brother Victor during their Russian residence. A 15 percent export tax was levied on this personal art collection, but at the same time many additional artworks went duty-free to the United States with Hammer. These he would auction off in America for the Soviets, earning a 10 percent commission on each sale. Hammer would not return to the Soviet Union for more than thirty years.[95]

The NEP program of foreign concessions was constrained by high state demands for investment and output, limits on repatriation of profits, and requirements for pay and benefits that far exceeded the standards Moscow set for its own plants. Operators like Harvester that could not or would not comply with the technological imperatives of the NEP soon found themselves out of business. This suggests that even had Cyrus McCormick assented to Soviet demands to modernize Lubertzy, International Harvester would likely have been compelled to leave Russia by the end of the 1920s as did Hammer, a favored concessionaire. Harvester thus made a prudent business decision when it decided instead to cut its losses in 1923. Moscow so strictly defined conditions for American firms in the Soviet Union that its policies usually led to failure.

➤ THE FIVE-YEAR PLAN AND TECHNICAL ASSISTANCE CONTRACTS

The experiences of Harriman and Hammer signal the end of the NEP and its policy of bringing in foreign concessions to reconstruct the Soviet Union. From its inception, the policy had been self-contradictory for the Soviet regime. Even Lenin had admitted that the concessions were "a foreign thing in our system."[96] The domestic side of NEP was unraveling by this time too, as grain collections collapsed in 1927–1928. Grain exports had been envisioned as the best means by which to pay for Soviet industrialization under NEP, but it had become increasingly clear that they would not be sufficient for this purpose under existing production and marketing conditions. Moscow thus launched brutal collection methods—"extraordinary measures"—under Stalin's leadership in 1928. Nikolai Bukharin and Alexsei Rykov, supporters of "limited collectivization" of agriculture, rejected these strong-armed tactics. They called for grain imports instead, as well as more effective inducements for farm output so that "NEP could be rescued and sustained." This importing option was contradictory for NEP advocates, however, since it would restrict Moscow's ability to buy the Western technology needed to industrialize, one of the main goals of NEP.[97]

Bukharin's protests were drowned out, as Alan Ball notes, by NEP opponents who convinced many that the program "was incapable of sustaining a sufficiently rapid tempo of industrialization, in large measure because of the difficulty of acquiring grain."[98] The two factions battled it out in the Politburo, and after denouncing Bukharin the party confirmed its acceptance of the Five-Year Plan in April 1929. Peasants, small business owners (the Nepmen), and foreign concession holders became targets of a ferocious and implacable "socialist offensive" designed to root out "enemies" at home. At the same time, Stalin identified an even more menacing threat from "international capital" that led to an emphasis on defense-related production within the accelerated industrialization of the plan.[99]

The plan's development of large-scale industries would be far greater in scope and far faster in implementation than the New Economic Policy's initiatives. Foreign expertise would still be needed, but it would be used for the development of *Soviet-run* plants and installations to promote self-sufficiency in production. Technical assistance, which involved the procurement of Western information, processes, or training—or at most, construction of a plant or other facility—swould replace the long-term, foreign-owned concessions of NEP.[100]

The new emphasis on technical assistance to develop the Soviet economy was more beneficial to American companies than the concession system had been. In 1925 Americans had just eight out of ninety active concessions in Russia. Four years later, the number of new technical assistance contracts held by American firms had reached forty, surpassing the number held by any other country, and there were over thirteen hundred engineers and technicians, mainly Americans and Germans, working in Russia as consultants.[101]

The Soviets knew that the Americans, "who had taught the world speed and efficiency and for whom obstacles do not exist," were the world's technological leaders, and even better, "they do not guard manufacturing secrets so jealously."[102] As an *Izvestia* columnist pointed out, "While many manufacturers in Western Europe and Japan were in every way endeavoring to 'secrete' from us even the most innocent processes of manufacturing, their American colleagues freely admit within the walls of their factories and mills the representatives of Soviet industry." Moreover, the article continued, "the United States has the *highest technical development* in the world. In the production of machines in which the Soviet Union happens to be particularly interested at present (agricultural, electric, equipment for heavy industries, etcetera), America stands today outside all competition. In this connection it is exceedingly important that American industry, which has expanded by virtue of an enormous domestic market and immense concentration of capital, is employing methods of *standardization and mass production* on a vast scale."[103]

America was "the model for Soviet industrial development," one scholar writes, because the Soviet Union "chose to enter the ladder of industrial development on the top rung." Opportunities were plentiful for those who wished to sell their expertise. A.A. Heller, head of the Newark-based International Oxygen Company and Martens's former commercial director, publicized this when he launched the Russian American Compressed Gas Company (Ragas) in Russia. He raved, "The demand for our products, oxygen and acetylene gases for welding, equipment, and material, as well as welded products . . . is growing so rapidly that it will soon exceed our capacity." Ragas, a $1 million venture, constructed oxygen plants in three major Soviet cities and provided welding assistance to the oil pipelines "from Tuapse to Grozny and from Baku to Batum."[104] Competition also induced U. S. corporations to contribute important technical processes to the Soviets. The executives of industrial firms knew that if they refused a Soviet order, several rivals—foreign and domestic—would compete for the job.

Chemical giant E.I. Du Pont de Nemours and Company had previously rejected Bolshevik overtures. When Amtorg had tried to attract Du Pont with a celluloid, paper, and artificial silk concession in 1927, company president Lammot Du Pont refused. "Under present conditions . . . [we] hardly feel that we would be interested," he replied.[105] The Soviet representatives were persistent. They wanted the chemical firm to assist them by constructing new plants in Russia and by training Soviet engineers and technicians at Du Pont's facilities in the United States. In early 1929 the company finally yielded, agreeing to sell its ammonia oxidation process, used to produce fertilizer, to the Soviet chemical agency Chemstroi.[106]

Several factors influenced Du Pont to move ahead with this new customer. The work would be financially rewarding and, because the deal was no longer a concession calling for a massive investment inside Russia, the company was not exposed to great risk. Also, many other large corporations were entering Soviet Russia at the end of the twenties. Rival chemical makers, such as Imperial Chemical of Great Britain, were picking up Soviet accounts. Du Pont entered the Soviet Union partly as a way to defend its market share. In addition, other American businessmen already in Russia were encouraging Du Pont to join them. They felt that a larger American presence would give them more clout in the USSR.

One of the men trying to convince Du Pont to make a significant commitment to the Soviet market was Col. Hugh L. Cooper, the chief construction engineer for the $75 million Dnieprostroi hydroelectric power station in the Ukraine. Cooper campaigned indefatigably for American trade and investment in the Soviet Union. Hailing Lammot Du Pont as one of the "big men of the world," Cooper urged him to help solve the world's "greatest unsolved problem," that of Russia. In March 1929 he forwarded to Du Pont a cheering report about the Soviet Union. The chemical executive responded by sending back a newsletter that gave a more negative view. Cooper dismissed it as "written by some ignoramus who probably gets fifty dollars a week" and stated that his views on the Russian situation had been corroborated by "very substantial men of more important organizations."[107]

Du Pont's director of development, Dr. Fin Sparre, was interested in Soviet "efforts . . . to spread Communism in other countries" and exchanged letters with Cooper and H.H. Dewey, the vice president of International General Electric, which had recently signed a $25 million, five-year contract with the Soviets. Dewey told Sparre that he believed that Stalin's commissars were "much less radical than they sound. . . . But as yet [they] do not feel strong enough to admit openly that communism, as advocated by Lenin, is impossible." Dewey was also optimistic about the Five-Year Plan, which he thought would get the Russian people so "interested and involved" that they would "modify their radical ideas and . . . accept a more rational program."[108]

Cooper agreed with Dewey that the Soviet leaders were not the zealous revolutionaries many people thought. Cooper was persuaded by party leader Rykov's argument that one could no more criticize Russia for hosting the Third International than criticize Holland for hosting its predecessor, the Second International. Cooper was convinced that Russia would eventually turn to capitalism and in the meantime it was "perfectly safe" to do business there. The engineer again pressed Du Pont to expand his Soviet operations. He urged the chemical executive to send his biggest "pessimist" to the Soviet Union for ninety days, so that Cooper might have an opportunity to convince even the most disbelieving skeptic. Cooper's exhortations finally had an effect. At the end of July Lammot Du Pont set up a meeting with Saul Bron of Amtorg at the company offices in Wilmington, Delaware, to discuss expanding Du Pont's ties to the Soviet Union.[109]

At this conference Du Pont and the Soviet representatives worked out a draft of an agreement entitled "For Construction of Chemical Plants and Apparatus in the U.S.S.R." Under its terms, Chemstroi engineers and workers would receive training in the United States. Du Pont also agreed to sell the Soviets the process for making lithopone, a zinc-based white pigment used for the manufacture of paper, paints, and inks. But the firm declined to sign any blanket arrangement with Moscow. "We do not regret at all the steps we have taken so far, and will be very glad in the future to discuss with you the sale of plans or processes . . . but each of these negotiations must contemplate an agreement independent of any other," said Lammot Du Pont. The executive committee of Du Pont's board of directors reaffirmed company policy on this issue. The firm would not invest any money in Russia nor would it sign any broad agreements. Any deal would have to be based on a "substantial" payment in American dollars with the balance payable on a short-term basis. Thus there would be no comprehensive "establishment of industry in Russia under Du Pont guidance."[110]

In the case of lithopone manufacture, Soviet engineers would be allowed to come—three at a time—and observe Du Pont's American plants in operation. In return, the Soviet Union agreed to pay the chemical company $85,000 for designing the lithopone plant, $70,000 of which would be paid in advance.[111] The Grasselli Chemical Company of Cleveland, a Du Pont subsidiary, would design the plant. Fin Sparre foresaw complications in Russia and wanted T.S. Grasselli to boost his fee to $100,000. Grasselli wanted even more: $350,000. Stiff competition, however, meant that it was unrealistic to demand such large payments. Also, many of these chemical processes were fully developed, meaning that any additional money Du Pont could get for the established technology would be largely profit. Thus, although ammonia oxidation technology had cost Du Pont $27 million to research and develop, it agreed to receive only $150,000 plus engineering expenses from the Soviet government.[112]

Even with these low prices, the company could not take Moscow's business for granted. Du Pont specialist William M. Richter held extended negotiations with the Soviets over Du Pont's lacquer technology only to learn that a competitor, Hercules Powder, "had been in close touch" with the Soviets regarding the production of nitrocellulose, which was needed for manufacturing lacquer. With Hercules's help, the Soviets planned to triple their output of nitrocellulose "from 2,000 kilos to 6,000 kilos" and thus make Du Pont's participation unnecessary.[113]

One way to ensure that Soviet orders would not be lost to competitors was through cooperation with other firms. Du Pont and Imperial Chemical Industries had an arrangement by which they shared information about the chemical processes each firm had sold to the Soviets. This helped them to apportion their business. Du Pont would make certain that Imperial was not selling some product or technology to Moscow before it went ahead with its negotiations, and vice versa.[114]

Du Pont's negotiations with Soviet Russia did not mean that its managers' ideological allegiance had changed. On the contrary, the firm's leadership frequently expressed an antipathy for the communist system, even after the contract with Moscow had commenced. "As time goes on, I am coming more and more to the conclusion that business relations with Soviet Russia by American corporations are undesirable, but have not yet come to the point where we should refuse to sell them goods," said Lammot Du Pont.[115]

Yet just as Cooper had hoped, Du Pont's presence in Russia mattered more than the firm's misgivings. The chemical giant's visible role inspired firms in other industries. James D. Mooney, General Motors vice president in charge of overseas operations, pointed to Du Pont's Russian involvement in order to persuade company president Alfred P. Sloan to increase GM's business with the Soviet Union. Mooney also cited "other American companies with a reputation for conservatism and foresight . . . [that] have already gone into this tremendously interesting and potential market." The warnings about Soviet trade that Sloan may have heard were "bunk."[116]

Mooney was wary of losing an important emerging market for his automobiles. As Stalin had pointed out, Russia had "peasants and workers delivered now from their former landlords and capitalists . . . and their demand is huge, both for personal and for industrial use." In 1930 Mooney traveled through Russia for twelve days of business discussions in the hopes of setting up some kind of technical assistance agreement. In his report to Sloan, he noted that he had deliberately "confined [his] official observations . . . to the economic considerations" of General Motors and did not care "whether that Government is autocratic or democratic or bolshevik." More important to Mooney was whether the Soviets would pay for the cars and trucks they bought. He was convinced, regardless, that the government was "stable."[117]

Mooney recommended that General Motors build and operate a final assembly plant for imported Buicks, Chevrolets, and Bedford trucks in the Soviet Union. Unlike Ford's Nizhni Novgorod facility, this factory would refrain from full-scale manufacturing, despite the desire of the Soviet government, since Mooney felt it would only bring "a rather useless amount of goodwill." The Buick passenger car had a preeminent reputation in Russia, and commissars "battled" hard to build the cars there, but Mooney was adamant. The Bedford trucks could possibly be made in the USSR but not the much-coveted Buicks.[118]

Mooney, a thoroughgoing capitalist, put in a good word for the centralized planning of the Communist party that "accounts for the rapid progress the country has made." The party "provides the coordination and driving power, and keeps the unions in line; the leaders have vision; their ability as a nation to *pay* is self-evident."[119] Lammot Du Pont never held such a view about the Soviet order, no matter how many processes his company sold to the Kremlin. "These people seem to have no realization whatever of the virtue of trustfulness, integrity, and property rights," he groused. His firm continued to oppose extending long-term credits to Moscow at a time when many other companies were offering them. In 1936—three years after the United States had opened diplomatic relations with Moscow—he continued to maintain that "the Russian government was looked somewhat askance at, if not distrusted by, American business people generally."[120] Fortunately for both the Soviets and Du Pont stockholders, the president's ambivalence about this trade relationship did not prevent his firm's continued involvement in what was a beneficial association. Once the company had launched trade with Moscow, its profit margins took precedence over the president's predilections. Vice President F.W. Pickard predicted in the early thirties that "Russia will be a fairly important market for the United States." He naturally included his own E.I. Du Pont de Nemours and Company among those that would get "our share."[121]

The experience of Du Pont affirms the success of technical assistance for American suppliers and Soviet customers. By selling processes in the short-term, rather than making long-term investments, firms found Soviet business both profitable and manageable, and Moscow got the technology it so badly needed, often at discount prices. In contrast, the fate of concessionaires like Averell Harriman, the largest American investor under the NEP, reveals a pattern of lack of control and losses in Soviet dealings. As Khrushchev-era historian M.E. Sonkin explained, "foreign capital introduced conditions which for the most part were unacceptable in the workers' and peasants' state."[122]

SOVIET-AMERICAN RELATIONS,
1929–1933

During the First Five-Year Plan, Soviet-American trade reached a peak, although the high sales were short-lived. From 1927 to 1930, spurred by the industrialization imperatives of the plan, U.S. exports to Russia increased from $65 million to $114 million. In 1931 sales dropped to $104 million, but the Soviet government's orders still made it America's seventh-largest customer.[1] Soviet purchases of American manufactured goods in 1931 were 22 percent higher than those in 1929, a significant increase when compared to the more than 50 percent drop in overall American exports during this very depressed period. While $104 million amounted to only .14 percent of American GNP in 1931, it still represented 4.3 percent of American exports that year.[2] Russia had become the largest foreign customer for American industrial machinery.[3]

These sales had repercussions outside the United States and Russia. Frederic M. Sackett, American ambassador to Berlin, reported in 1931 that the undersecretary of the German Ministry of Finance had told him that "in view of the long term credits granted by American industry to Soviet Russia, Germany would be forced to increase its terms for the present calender year." The German twelve-month credits were no match for the American terms of eighteen months or more. Yet for Americans, sales grew so fast between 1929 and 1931 that Alexander Gumberg felt compelled to write, "The magnitude of the Five-Year Plan probably scares more people than it attracts. The thing is too stupendous and complex. Russian business is concentrated in too few firms." Companies that had been repeatedly favored with Soviet business sometimes reached the "saturation point" in extending credits. Gumberg related a story that he had heard from the president of a large firm that had granted $700,000 in financing to Russia over two years and was then asked for more. The frustrated executive declared, "I have to wait until at least a part of this money is paid off before I can take this matter up again."[4]

Soviet orders were highly concentrated in certain industries. In 1931, for example, Amtorg and its Soviet affiliates purchased the following hefty amounts of American industrial exports: 58.7 percent of all locomotive equipment, 59 percent of metalworking equipment, 65.6 percent of lathes, 73.8 percent of foundry equipment, and 97.4 percent of turbines. Sixty percent of all Soviet orders in the United States in 1930 and 1931 were placed in just five states in the American Midwest.[5] Much of the equipment would enable the Soviets to produce their own machinery, consistent with the autarkic goals of the plan.

In the midst of this successful trading relationship, and after a period of dormant interest in the issue, congressional allegations of revolutionary activity were again leveled at Soviet officials in the United States, this time by New York Republican Hamilton Fish Jr. Fish's charges were based on documents obtained by New York City police commissioner Grover Whalen in 1930, linking Amtorg officials with the Comintern. Whalen had a list of "thirty Amtorg attachés" believed to be "undercover agents of the Communist International." Boris E. Skvirskii, the head of the Soviet Information Bureau in Washington and the "unofficial Soviet envoy" to the United States, stood accused of running Amtorg's "Ogpu [Soviet Secret Police] section." At the hearing in Congress, Amtorg chairman Bogdanov was treated "very roughly" by the congressmen, Alexander Gumberg reported. "[They] yelled at him [and] demanded that he answer 'Yes or No.'" Bogdanov got a vociferous defense from the American Communists, who were also at the hearing and "acted in their usual imbecilic manner," Gumberg scowled. He lamented, "all this noise has seriously interfered with development of Russian credits in our country."[6]

What looked like it might have been a replay of the Martens Senate hearings, however, turned out differently and was evidence of the significant change in the United States' outlook toward Russia over the previous decade. In the late spring of 1930, when Whalen began his crackdown on Amtorg for "subversive revolutionary propaganda," the American-Russian Chamber of Commerce launched its own investigation of Whalen's documents. Suspecting these records to be forgeries, the chamber appointed a committee of its top officials, including Chairman of the Board S.R. Bertron, Vice President Allen Wardwell, and Directors Hugh Cooper and H.H. Dewey, to meet with Commerce Secretary Thomas P. Lamont on May 27. The committee requested the Commerce Department to investigate the documents' "genuineness" and were pleased when the secretary told them that his views about Soviet trade had not changed "by reason of the publication of the so-called 'Whalen' documents." The chamber was vindicated when the papers were shown to have been so badly faked that, as Gumberg joked, opponents of the Soviet Union had supposedly claimed that "Amtorg deliberately manufactured the 'documents' in order to get Whalen in trouble!"[7] The Fish committee agreed that the Whalen evidence was bogus. It also found that "there is not sufficient competent legal evidence in the record to prove the connection of the Amtorg Trading Corporation . . . with subversive activities."[8]

Although Fish and Whalen had created a wave of negative publicity for Amtorg and Soviet-American trade, other government attacks were more damaging. In 1930 Congress enacted the ultraprotectionist Smoot-Hawley Tariff Act with provisions that targeted the Soviet Union; specifically, section 307, which placed an "embargo for goods made by convict or forced labor." Soviet officials believed with some justification that this was designed more to cushion American businessmen than to protect Russian workers. Soviet pulpwood products, asbestos, manganese, and sausage casings were all cited for having been "dumped" on the market, even though American exports to Russia were more than three times the amount of Russian exports to America, with a favorable balance of trade of $500 million between 1923 and 1930. Depressed commodity prices had spurred the Soviets to ship even more raw materials to pay for foreign equipment. But Soviet lumber still amounted to less than 1 percent of American production, while Russian matches in the United States satisfied one-tenth of American consumption and Russian pulpwood composed less than 5 percent of total pulpwood imports. These new tariff provisions drove the American-Russian Chamber of Commerce to complain bitterly in the capital.[9]

On July 28, 1930, when two shiploads of Russian pulpwood were held in New York because of allegations that they had been produced by convict labor, the chamber interceded. Its leaders protested to President Hoover, Treasury Secretary Mellon, and Commerce Secretary Lamont. After a hearing on August 1 with the Treasury Department and a leading pulpwood importer, the ban was lifted immediately.[10] Hoover had overruled Assistant Secretary of the Treasury Seymour Lowman, a strong supporter of the import restrictions, and this pleased both Raymond Robins and Alexander Gumberg immensely.[11] The issue did not subside as the Depression worsened. In 1931 the Senate entertained another protective tariff, the Kendall bill, H.R. 16517. Again the chamber became involved, sending a delegation to make its views known to Ogden L. Mills, undersecretary of the Treasury.[12]

The combined subversive propaganda and "dumping" charges were a setback for Amtorg and, as Amtorg's Bogdanov wrote to Gumberg, they "hamper[ed] the normal development of commercial relations between the United States and the Soviet Union."[13] It was the Depression-inspired tariff, more than the propaganda allegations, that contributed to the contraction of the Soviet-American trading relationship at the end of the Hoover administration. As historian Robert Paul Browder has pointed out, the Soviet government had a "highly sensitive national honor," and this prickliness made Moscow representatives react angrily to American charges that they had "dumped" goods.[14]

In 1932 total Soviet purchases in the United States plunged to a paltry $12.6 million, one-tenth of the previous year's tally.[15] American economic nationalism was not entirely to blame, however, since the Soviet Union had its own reasons for cutting back. The country was heavily in debt. By 1931, following the initial flurry of large purchases under the Five-Year Plan, Russia owed $500 million in credits, largely to Germany and Britain. These foreign purchases, along with a sluggish demand for Soviet raw materials and slow delivery of grain from peasants who had been forcibly collectivized the year before, had contributed to a $150 million trade deficit, making continued large-scale purchases in Western countries difficult.[16] This move away from foreign trade also fit the "rhetoric of autarky" of the Five-Year Plan with its insistence on Soviet self-reliance.[17] Thus, between 1930 and 1932, Soviet orders abroad dropped by one-third. Yet certain countries maintained a strong share of the existing orders, facilitated by trade agreements. German sales to Russia in 1932 and 1933 amounted to 45 percent of the goods imported by the Soviet Union over those two years, while the United States' comparable figure was only 5 percent.[18]

Political retaliation did play a part in the steep drop in American purchases after 1931. Deputy Commissar of Foreign Affairs Nikolai N. Krestinskii told Politburo colleagues, "The loss of Soviet markets . . . will be an incentive to American business and political circles to review their traditional position of nonrecognition of the USSR."[19] President Hoover, however, refused to be moved by such pressure, even as his secretary of state, Henry L. Stimson, saw the advantages of recognition for strategic and peace considerations after Japan's annexation of Manchuria in 1931. Stimson's predecessor, Frank Kellogg, also began to support recognition, citing economic and security factors. Yet Hoover was steadfast.[20] He did make one final and remarkable concession, however. In 1932 his newly created Reconstruction Finance Corporation, designed to help reenergize the depressed American economy, extended a $4 million publicly financed credit to Amtorg to finance cotton purchases, which was implemented early in the Roosevelt administration.

Recognition remained controversial, and in 1932 Franklin D. Roosevelt did not emphasize it in his campaign. Soon after his election, however, he consulted with Secretary of State Cordell Hull and Yale professor Jerome Davis in "a careful study" of the issue that generally "assumed recognition would be realized," although some officials in Hull's department cautioned about potential disagreement with Russia. Meanwhile, popular support grew in favor of the opening, as Peter Filene notes, with newspaper editorials most commonly advocating the move to promote "Soviet-American trade and international peace." New York Times correspondent Walter Duranty noted that "there is a good deal of interest and a general feeling that recognition might help . . . where immediate business interests of groups or individuals are involved. For instance, the General Electric and General Motors people are quite keen on finding a way, if it can be done with proper dignity—I might almost say on finding a way anyway."[21] Many businessmen did believe that diplomatic relations would improve the faltering Soviet-American trade picture, and Roosevelt was "sensitive" to this consideration. Yet as Joan Hoff Wilson points out, there is little evidence that business pressure directly contributed to FDR's decision to recognize Russia.[22] Government officials believed that trade would be modest, about $40 million annually. Fantastic figures were bruited about in the press, however. R.J. Baker, secretary of the American Steamship Owners Association, saw Russia taking "up to $5,000,000,000 worth of American goods within the next four years." The more sober New York Times noted that "even if the $1,000,000,000 [annual] estimate of prospective Russian purchases in this country is high . . . the amount would assuredly be large enough to act as a spur to both factory and farm."[23]

The president's most compelling reason for recognition matched Stimson's peace argument. American recognition of the Soviet Union would counter a Japanese invasion of Siberia, which had become more likely since Japan brought its "Co-Prosperity Sphere" to the Asian mainland. As Senator William E. Borah declared, "To restore amity between 120,000,000 people on one hand and 160,000,000 on the other is a thing of supreme moment. . . . It would be great to have now at least one realistic move toward a friendlier and more tolerant world." Edward M. Bennett affirms that FDR hoped to use recognition as the linchpin in his peace policy, symbolically "lining up" Americans and Russians against the militaristic states of Japan and Germany. He suggests, too, that Roosevelt "publicly encouraged" the Soviet view that diplomatic relations had been opened to foster "American-Soviet cooperation against Japanese aggression."[24] Interestingly, Soviet chief propagandist Karl Radek had predicted in 1922 that events in the Far East would cause America to recognize the Soviets; when the Soviet Union was strong enough to be useful against Japan, the United States would "be eager enough to make friends with Russia," he had augured. Following more than a decade of building up trade in order to obtain recognition, Soviet leaders found instead that a slump in American orders, combined with Japanese imperialism and German militarism, at last brought them formal notice.[25] Yet the Japanese government, the purported target of these initiatives, professed a lack of interest. An official at the American Embassy in Tokyo reported that recognition had "arroused little comment" in the capital. The Japanese minister of war was quoted as saying that "he did not see how Japan was affected, that he considered that the motive was economic, and he supposed that the two nations would have to resume diplomatic relations at some time in any case."[26]

Washington extended recognition under conditions stipulating Soviet non-interference in American domestic affairs, religious freedom and legal rights for Americans in Russia, and acknowledgment of Russian war debts. Aware of how intractable some of these points might be, Secretary Hull wished to carefully and discreetly settle them before the United States offered recognition. Roosevelt felt differently. He wanted "a brilliant political success," not "difficult impasses" and "interminable" discussions. Thus, in Roosevelt's easygoing manner, recognition was negotiated with Soviet commissar Maxim Litvinov in November 1933, leading to a "gentleman's agreement" on the outstanding issues. The debt—over $600 million of Imperial and Provisional government obligations owed to the U.S. Treasury and American creditors—was drastically reduced, and both parties agreed that the actual figure would be between $75 million (the Soviet reckoning) and $150 million (the American). Roosevelt did not press for a firm payment schedule, and the work of extracting the funds was left for the State Department and the first ambassador to Soviet Russia, William Bullitt.[25]

After the president had agreed to terms of recognition with the foreign affairs commissar, it was only appropriate that the American-Russian Chamber of Commerce was given "the honor of feting Maxim Litvinov." The businessmen welcomed the Russian at New York's tony Waldorf-Astoria Hotel, where he gave the last speech of his successful trip. After the attendees had enjoyed a sumptuous banquet, which included braised Long Island duckling and cranberry pie, they directed their "rapt attention" to Litvinov. He gave a bold narration of the USSR's potential for enormous profits, which had singular allure in the midst of the Great Depression.[28]

The cozy atmosphere at the Waldorf-Astoria was a distant memory just a few months later, however, as Bullitt, now ensconced in Moscow, faced a daunting task in ironing out the details of the Soviet-American agreement. Litvinov's government had no intention of paying the old obligations without a loan. The Soviet leaders could logically argue that if they met the American obligations without financial assistance, they also would have to pay French and British debts—which were much larger.[29] The Roosevelt administration was unlikely to grant such a loan, and unable to once the U.S. Senate enacted the Johnson Debt Default Act in 1934, which prohibited loans to governments that had not paid their war debts. Congress applied the Johnson provisions to the American Export-Import Bank, which had recently opened and was "designed to promote Soviet-American commerce."[30] The debt issue thus remained unresolved.[31] In 1935, a meeting of the Comintern Congress in Russia occasioned further American protests, with Bullitt denouncing the meeting and its discussions as a violation of the 1933 agreement on "non-interference in the internal affairs of the United States."[32] Bullitt's high expectations for a new Soviet-American relationship ultimately led him to become severely embittered. No longer an effective representative, in August 1936 he left Moscow to become ambassador to France.[33]

Although the debt issue prevented economic assistance to Moscow until World War II, diplomatic relations meant that a trade agreement was finally possible. In July 1935 the Soviets commited to spend $30 million per year on American goods in return for most-favored-nation status. The agreement was renewed annually, with subsequent upward adjustments, until the war.[34] Soviet-American trade recovered from the trough of 1932–1934, yet the treaties could never recreate the high sales of the decade preceding 1933. For the eight years before recognition, 1924–32, American exports to Russia had averaged close to $70 million each year, but between 1933 and 1939, annual sales to Moscow were only about half that figure.[35] Recognition was not to be the economic panacea that many had hoped for.

⋖ 9 ⋗

CONCLUSION

As this study has emphasized, the commercial opportunities that Moscow offered after the revolution drew an interested response from American companies and government officials. As a result, the Soviet Union had an important influence on U.S. foreign economic policy between 1919 and 1933 despite its lack of diplomatic status in the United States. The expansion of trade, particularly during the NEP era, facilitated the extension of financing to Moscow and also served to legitimize the Soviet regime in the United States.

From the time Ludwig Martens opened his office until Franklin D. Roosevelt opened diplomatic relations, the United States and the Soviet Union underwent a subtle but significant shift in their relationship. This evolution of Soviet-American relations before recognition has often been overlooked by historians, who have portrayed ideologically charged documents like the Colby note as blueprints for American policy during this era. But even as American troops marched in Russia, President Wilson spurned William Bullitt, and Secretary Colby drafted his thundering missive, Ludwig Martens built a busy office in New York City. His contacts with entrepreneurs such as Armand Hammer, Henry Ford, and Abraham Heller and firms such as American Locomotive, Baldwin Locomotive, and International Harvester were not lost when he was deported in 1921. By the mid-twenties, with the New Economic Policy in full swing, new Soviet agencies in New York were purchasing millions of dollars' worth of American machinery, equipment, and raw materials. Martens's contacts were revived and vastly augmented. At the same time, the U.S. government had taken a leading role in extending humanitarian aid to Russia.

Firms responded quickly to Soviet opportunities, and by 1925 International Harvester and other manufacturers were offering credits of up to one year to Russian agencies. This trade was accompanied by American investment in Russia under NEP's concession program. International Harvester's General Manager Alexander Legge aptly described the difficulty with these investments: "As soon as the business commences to show any returns the Soviet authorities will put them out of the running, either by taxing the business to death or imposing restrictions of various kinds."[1] For American firms, the unsatisfactory concessions of NEP were followed by the far more rewarding opportunities of the First Five-Year

Plan, where American firms sold technical processes, provided consulting services, built factories, and trained Soviet engineers.[2]

During the 1920s, Soviet purchases drew a favorable response in Washington, where the rigidly anti-Soviet laws and practices of the Wilson administration were gradually changed during the Harding, Coolidge, and Hoover administrations. Commerce Secretary Hoover, whose department was already actively seeking out Soviet trade opportunities for businessmen, recognized that trade would greatly increase with the aid of long-term financing. He worked with other members of the Coolidge administration to loosen restrictions, and long-term credits were approved in 1927. Large Soviet purchases had more effectively influenced American policy than had the lobbying of Borah, Robins, Gumberg, and Branham. Permitting the use of long-term credit was the most important innovation in U.S. economic policy toward Russia in this period and confirmed official support of trade. Even Robert Kelley, perhaps the most committed hard-liner at the State Department, recognized the importance of being pragmatic on the issue. In 1930, as Soviet agents flowed into the country with purchase orders, he rejected a proposal to exclude Communist party members from joining Amtorg delegations. Kelley realized that "such an instruction would have a very ill far-reaching effect on the United States commercial relations with Russia."[3] The Soviet search for trade and financing in America was a success, not only in its acquisition of needed goods but also in increasing the prominence and legitimacy of the Soviet Union in the United States.

ABBREVIATIONS

ABP	Arthur Bullard Papers
AGP	Alexander Gumberg Papers
AHP	W. Averell Harriman Papers
ARCCP	American-Russian Chamber of Commerce Papers
AVPRF	*Arkhiv Vneshnei Politiki Rossiskoi Federatsii*
CP	Commerce Papers, Hoover Presidential Library
CW	Lenin, *Collected Works*
DPP	E.I. Du Pont de Nemours and Company Papers
DVP	*Dokumenty Vneshnei Politiki SSSR.* Vols. 1–6.
FBI Martens	U.S. Department of Justice, FBI Records, Ludwig Martens Papers.
FRUS	U.S. Department of State. *Papers Relating to the Foreign Relations of the United States, 1920-1928.*
GARF	*Gosudarstvennyi Arkhiv Rossiiskoi Federatsii*
JGP	James P. Goodrich Papers
HHPL	Herbert Hoover Presidential Library
IHP	International Harvester Papers
L0032	Lusk Committee (Russian Soviet Bureau Seized Files)
MID	Military Intelligence Division, War Department
PCP	Pre-Commerce Papers, Hoover Presidential Library
PSF	President's Secretary's File, Roosevelt Presidential Library
RGAE	*Rossiskii Gosudarstvennyi Arkhiv Ekonomiki*
RTsKhIDNI	*Rossiiskii Tsentr' Khraneniia i Izucheniia Dokumentov Noveishei Istorii*
RRP	Raymond Robins Papers
WCRRP	Women's Committee for the Recognition of Russia Papers
WILPF	Women's International League for Peace and Freedom
WSHS	Wisconsin State Historical Society

NOTES

INTRODUCTION

1. Murray, *Red Scare*, 78–79; Coben, *Palmer*, 205–6.
2. Lenin as quoted in Kargina, *"Politika Americanskogo Kapitala v Otnoshenii Sovietskoi Rossii,"* 171, 172.
3. Shishkin, *Sovetskoe Gosudarstvo i Stranyi Zapada*, 194–95.
4. For the full list of firms that dealt with Martens, see transcript of Lusk file, RG 165, 10110–1194/185, and list in L0032, box 1.
5. Uldricks, *Diplomacy and Ideology*, 69; Ball, *Russia's Last Capitalists*, 10.
6. Debo, *Survival and Consolidation*, 414; O'Connor, *Diplomacy and Revolution*, 115.
7. Lenin as quoted in Yanson, *Foreign Trade in the U.S.S.R.*, 69.
8. Carr, *Bolshevik Revolution, 1917–1923* 3:339–40.
9. Kargina, *"Politika Americanskogo Kapitala v Otnoshenii Sovietskoi Rossii,"* 172.
10. Hugh L. Cooper, "Possibilities in Russia," National Association of Manufacturers, *Proceedings of the Thirty-first Annual Convention of the National Association of Manufacturers*, October 5, 1926, 206.
11. Budish and Shipman, *Soviet Foreign Trade*, 10–11, 20–21, 33, 153; American-Russian Chamber of Commerce, *Handbook of the Soviet Union*, 353, 363, 365; "Prospects of Soviet-American Trade," S.G. Bron, *Ekonomicheskaya Zhizn*, June 10, 1928, attached to Cole to secretary, June 25, 1928, RG 59, 661.1111/20. For additional discussion of this trade, see Bron to Harriman, October 31, 1927, AHP, box 14, and Amtorg Trading Corporation, *Soviet-American Trade Outlook*, 25.
12. See Rosta (Russian Telegraph Agency), April 2, 1924, *GARF, fond* 391, *op.* 2, *del.* 69, *l.* 234; *Rosta* report, July 18, 1925, *GARF, fond* 391, *op.* 2, *del.* 21, *l.* 91. On the American Locomotive Sales and General Electric financing see M.J. McDermott, State Department memo of press conference, November 30, 1927, RG 39, box 188, file 134; press release, October 16, 1928, Hammond file L3597, G.E. historical file; Tass, 1928, *GARF, fond* 4459, *op.* 2, *del.* 329, *l.* 387.
13. See, for example, Uldricks, *Diplomacy and Ideology*; Debo, *Survival and Consolidation*; O'Connor, *Diplomacy and Revolution*.
14. See Hogan, "Corporatism: A Positive Appraisal," 363.
15. W.A. Williams, *American-Russian Relations,* 179; Filene, *Americans and the Soviet Experiment*, 110.
16. See, for example, Hoff Wilson, *Ideology and Economics*, 29; Smith, *Bainbridge Colby*, 68; W.A. Williams, *American-Russian Relations*, 173; Tsvetkov, *Shestnadtsat' Let Nepriznaniia*, 240.

17. For an example of this outlook see Hughes to Quarton (American consul at Reval), December 18, 1923, RG 59, 711.61/71. On the tsarist loans see Edward F. Gray to Sen. Charles E. Townsend, August 9, 1919, Leffingwell Papers. On the Soviet debt to the Treasury see *Annual Report of the Secretary of the Treasury on the State of the Finances for the Fiscal Year Ended 30 June 1920* (Washington, 1921), 329, and on seizures of property see W. Kliefoth to Hughes, August 1, 1922, RG 151, 448-U.S.

18. Lenin, *CW* 32:315.

19. In one of the first post–Soviet Russian analyses of the concession policy, Elena Semenovna Kosikh suggests that there was a bitter division between the supporters of the New Economic Policy and those who wanted to "curtail" it, since "the drawing in of foreign capital and foreign specialists was perceived as one of the channels of influence for ideological opposition to the working class." Kosikh, "Concession Policy of the Bolsheviks," 1, 6.

20. See, for example, W.A. Williams, *American-Russian Relations*, 177–79; Hoff Wilson, *Ideology and Economics*, 18; Libbey, *Gumberg and Soviet-American Relations*, 140; and Propas, "Creating A Hard Line toward Russia," 209.

21. Recent books have given full attention to the Soviet side of the relationship. Two excellent ones are C.A. White, *British and American Commercial Relations*, and McFadden, *Alternative Paths*.

22. Jacobson, *When the Soviet Union Entered World Politics*, 245.

23. Bishop, *Roosevelt-Litvinov Agreements*, 7–8; Seppain, *Contrasting U.S. and German Attitudes to Soviet Trade*, 27.

CHAPTER 1.
MARTENS AND THE FIRST SOVIET MISSION

1. Lenin, *CW* 30:51.

2. Tatiana N. Kargina, "Soviet-American Trade," 3; Associated Press clipping, November 21, 1922, JGP, box 17.

3. Chicherin as quoted by Nuorteva, "Memorandum on the Establishment of Trade Relations with Russia," June 17, 1919, *AVPRF fond* 507, *op.* 5, *del.* 17, *papka* 2.

4. In May 1919 the Supreme Allied Council—France, Britain, Italy, Japan, and the United States—told Kolchak that provided he met certain democratic requirements, "they are . . . disposed to assist [his] government . . . with munitions, supplies and food to establish themselves as the government of all Russia." Three months later the State Department said that it had no objection to loans to Kolchak by National City Bank or Kidder Peabody of $5 million and £10 million respectively. See G. Clemenceau, Lloyd George et al. to Admiral Kolchak, May 26, 1919, in Cumming and Pettit, eds., *Russian-American Relations*, 338; Lansing to National City Bank, August 18, 1919, Lansing to Kidder, Peabody, and Company, August 18, 1919, RG 39, file 79. Kolchak was soon routed.

5. "Statement of Martens, Representative of RSFSR in the United States," *RGAE, fond* 413, *op.* 3, *del.* 515, *l.* 5.

6. Products included soap, shoes, and mining equipment. See bills of lading confirming these shipments in the *AVPRF fond* 507, *op.* 5b, *del.* 5, *papka* 35. These show that State Department representative Felix Cole was misinformed when he declared that Martens "proffers . . . proved to be wholly tentative." See memorandum, RG 59, 661.1115/68 as quoted in Hoff Wilson, *Ideology and Economics*, 53. On the harassment Martens faced, see Talbert, *Negative Intelligence*, 180.

7. U.S. Senate, *Russian Propaganda*, January 30, 1920, 71; Sonkin, *Okno vo Vneshnii Mir*, 128, cites a figure of $15 million.

8. Masteller, memo for L. Lanier Winslow, State Department, April 16, 1919, RG 165, 10110-1194/38.

9.   J.E. Hoover, "Memorandum for Office," January 4, 1919, FBI Martens, vol. 1, file 353815.
10.   Wrisley Brown, memorandum for Colonel Masteller, April 12, 1919, RG 165, 10110-1194/25.
11.   *New York Tribune*, April 1, 1919, RG 165, 10110-1194/27.
12.   See Charles E.J. Newman, ADS-2, and Cornelius J. Browne, report, Police Department, City of New York, bomb squad, April 21, 1919, attached to letter, John B. Trevor to Office of MID, April 29, 1919, RG 165, 10110/1194; C. Pilenas, memorandum for Captain Issacs, April 12, 1919, RG 165, 10110-1194; K.C. Masteller, memo for L. Lanier Winslow, State Department, April 16, 1919, 10110-1194/38; Wrisley Brown, memorandum for Colonel Masteller, April 12, 1919, RG 165, 10110-1194.
13.   See *New York Tribune*, April 29, 1919; *New York Times*, March 28, 1919, RG 165, 10110-1194/10.
14.   See Evgen'ev and Shapik, *Revolyutsioner, Diplomat, Uchenyi*, 9; Draper, *Roots*, 107, 162.
15.   Their organizations included "the Russian Socialistic Federation, the New York Group of Social Revolutionists, the Russian Branch of the Socialist party, the New York Section of the Russian Bolsheviks, *Novy Mir*, the local Russian daily, and the Socialist propaganda league." See *New York Call*, February 3, 1918, RG 165, 10110-1194/13; Louis Jasper Vaissee, postmaster, to Col. R.H. Van Deman, War College, February 4, 1918, RG 165, 10058/24-16.
16.   R.C. Williams, *Russian Art and American Money*, 199; U.S. Senate, *Russian Propaganda*, January 19, 1920, 7–16.
17.   Between March and May 1919 Martens was honored at meetings sponsored by the New York County Committee of the Socialist party, the executive committee of the Socialist party of the United States, and the Communist Labor party. See Wrisley Brown, memorandum to Colonel Masteller, April 12, 1919, RG 165, 10110-1194/25, Secret Martens Mission Propaganda for the Overthrow of Governments—Facts and Circumstances Relating to His Activities in the United States, FBI Martens, vol. 4.
18.   See Commercial Department brochure, RSFSR Bureau of the Representative in the U.S.A., Hoover War Collection; Martens and Nuorteva to State Department, March 19, 1919, in Cumming and Pettit, eds., *Russian-American Relations*, 329; *New York Times*, April 8, 1919, RG 165, 10110-1194/28; Heller to Martens, August 7, 1919, *RGAE, fond* 413, *op.* 3, *del.* 515, *l.* 18.
19.   The *Chicago Herald-Examiner* was dubious about this claim and reported that "all the gold that can be at the disposal of the Russian Bolsheviki is $27,900,000," though the potential of an additional $125 million, "the amount that may have been seized in Moscow belonging to the banks of Roumania," was acknowledged. *Chicago Herald-Examiner*, April 3, 1919, April 5, 1919, RG 165, 10110-1194. The Bureau had always claimed that the $200 million was in banks abroad, not in the United States. See press release, "RSFSR Bureau of the Representative in the USA, Commercial Department," L0032, box 1.
20.   U.S. Senate, *Russian Propaganda*, January 19, 1920, 16; case report, L.S. Perkins, April 16, 1919, on Martens, RG 165, 10110-1194.
21.   See, for example, Martens to president of Pennsylvania Railroad, April 14, 1919; Martens, Hammer, and Lomonosov to Bankers Trust, "Soviet Aims to get Russian Funds Here," April 8, 1919, *New York World*; Lomonosoff, proclamation, May 21, 1919, L0032, box 1.
22.   *New York Times*, March 24, 1919.
23.   Killen, "Search for a Democratic Russia," 251.
24.   Recht to Hillquit, April 1, 1919, Polk as quoted by Nuorteva in letter to Hillquit, April 20, 1919, L0032, box 1.
25.   Killen, "Search for a Democratic Russia," 252–53; McFadden, *Alternative Paths*, 49–50. On Bakhmetev's role in supporting the White armies, see Maddox, "Woodrow

Wilson, the Russian Embassy, and Siberian Intervention," 440–44; Killen, "Search for a Democratic Russia," 251.

26.   See Borah to Recht, June 9, 1922, Recht to Borah, June 8, 1922, C.H. Smith to Borah, June 12, 1922, Borah Papers, box 121; Maddox, *Borah and American Foreign Policy*, 194–96. The Russian ambassador had responsibility for signing for all of the monies that the U.S. Treasury loaned to his government. Of the total $187,729,750 extended to Bakhmetev, all but $62 million went directly to the Provisional Government finance minister in Petrograd, according to Treasury Secretary Andrew W. Mellon. The balance was spent in the United States on war materiel. See Mellon to Charles Evans Hughes, June 2, 1922, *Annual Report of the Secretary of the Treasury on the State of the Finances for the Fiscal Year Ended June 30, 1922*, 284, and Frank L. Polk, cited in U.S. Congress, *Russian Bonds*, 16.

27.   FBI report, March 31, 1919, FBI Martens, vol. 1, 353815.

28.   In August 1918, the Allied powers—Britain, France, Italy, and the United States—had enacted a naval blockade against Soviet Russia to accompany their military intervention in that country. Ostensibly to prevent goods from falling into German hands during the war, it was continued long after the armistice that November. Even as the Allies began to realize the ineffectiveness of their military intervention in Russia during the Paris Peace Conference, they maintained various forms of "economic warfare" against Soviet Russia in support of General Kolchak. See O'Connor, *Engineer of Revolution*, 169; Gaworek, "From Blockade to Trade," 39–69 passim.

29.   The *New York Tribune* described Martens's new quarters as "sumptuous." *New York Tribune*, April 22, 1919, RG 165, 10110-1194/46.

30.   Chicago Herald Examiner, April 3, 1919, April 5, 1919, RG 165, 10110-1194/21; "Synopsis of the Case of Ludwig C.A.K. Martens," December 31, 1919, RG 165, box 1440, 10110-1194/263; *New York Times*, June 13, 1919, RG 165, 10110-1194/112.

31.   Santeri Nuorteva form letter, Bureau of Information on Soviet Russia, L0032, box 1.

32.   Felix Cole to Colby, April 29, 1920, Colby Papers, box 2.

33.   See Louis E. Stander to Heller, April 10, 1919, L0032, box 1.

34.   Morris Hillquit report, n.d., 1919, order no. 1, representative in the U.S.A. of the People's Commissariat of Foreign Affairs, New York, April 11, 1919, L0032, box 1; Charles E.J. Newman, ADS-2, and Cornelius J. Browne, report, Police Department, City of New York, bomb squad, April 21, 1919, attached to letter, John B. Trevor to Office of MID, April 29, 1919, RG 165, 10110/1194; "Personnel of the Bureau of the Representative of the Russian Socialist Federal Soviet Republic, April 22, 1919," L0032, box 1; Draper, *Roots*, 162–63; Sutton, *Wall Street and the Bolshevik Revolution*, 202.

35.   *New York Tribune*, April 22, 1919, RG 165, 10110-1194/46.

36.   See Charles E.J. Newman, ADS-2, and Cornelius J. Browne, report, Police Department, City of New York, bomb squad, April 21, 1919, attached to letter, John B. Trevor to Office of MID, April 29, 1919, RG 165, 10110/1194.

37.   Cable of Minister of Ways of Communication Nekrassoff to Count Schulenburg, May 15, 1917; *New York Tribune*, April 22, 1919, RG 165, 10110-1194/46. On Lomonosov, see Russian Soviet Recognition League to Lincoln Steffens, July 2, 1918, RG 165, 10110-1194.

38.   Lomonosov speech, June 11, 1918, Bakhmetev to Lomonosov, June 12, 1918, Lomonosov to Bakhmetev, June 12, 1918, L0032, box 1.

39.   Litvinov to Martens, May 27, 1919, *AVPRF fond* 507, *op.* 5, *del.* 2, *papka* 2.

40.   Litvinov to Martens, May 27, 1919, *AVPRF fond* 507, *op.* 5, *del.* 2, *papka* 2.

41.   See Chicherin, credentials for Martens, January 2, 1919, L0032, box 1; Ohsol to the Narkomindel, May 14, 1920, *AVPRF fond* 507, *op.* 5b, *del.* 1, *papka* 3a. Martens lacked priorities and specifics on the goods he should buy: $150 million in railway equip-

ment, $30 million of agricultural implements, $10 million of other machinery and tools, $5 million for hardwood and metals, $30 million for boots and shoes, $20 million for textiles and dry goods, $25 million for cotton, $25 million for foodstuffs, and $5 million for paper and rubber. See statement of the Soviet Bureau, June 1919, *AVPRF fond* 507, *op.* 5, *del.* 5, *papka* 2; commercial department brochure, RSFSR Bureau of the Representative in the U.S.A., Hoover War Collection; Heller to Martens, August 7, 1919, TsGANKh, *fond* 413, *op.* 3, *del.* 515, *l.* 18.

42.   Martens to Chicherin, September 26, 1919, *AVPRF fond* 507, *op.* 5, *del.* 11, *papka* 2; Ohsol to the Narkomindel, May 14, 1920, *AVPRF fond* 507, *op.* 5b, *del.* 1, *papka* 3a.

43.   Martens to the Narkomindel, September 16, 1919, *AVPRF fond* 507, *op.* 5b, *del.* 5, *papka* 35.

44.   Litvinov to Martens, May 27, 1919, *AVPRF fond* 507, *op.* 5, *del.* 2, *papka* 2.

45.   There are a number of excellent treatments of the Anglo-Soviet treaty. See, for examples, C.A. White, *British and American Commercial Relations*, Ch. 5, passim; S. White, *Britain and the Bolshevik Revolution*, Ch. 1, passim; O'Connor, *Engineer of Revolution*, Ch. 11, passim; and Ullman, vol. 3, *The Anglo-Soviet Accord,* Ch. 10, passim.

46.   O'Connor, *Diplomacy and Revolution*, 115.

47.   "Notes by Mr. A.A. Heller," May 27, 1919, L0032, box 1.

48.   Hourwich, "Problems of the Soviet Representative," in *Revolutionary Age*, April 19, 1919, 6 (emphasis in original), as quoted by Draper, *Roots*, 163.

49.   Martens to the Narkomindel, July 2, 1919, *AVPRF fond* 507, *op.* 5, *del.* 3, *papka* 2; Gitlow, *I Confess*, 28. On Weinstein's role, see FBI report, May 28, 1919, FBI Martens, vol. 1; on Left Wing support, see Maximilian Cohen, "Resolution Adopted by City Committee Left Wing Section, Socialist Party Local New York," RG 165, 10110-1194/230, April 14, 1919.

50.   See report of Comrade Hourwich, representative of the Communist party of America, at the plenary session of the Executive Committee of the Communist International (IKKI), August 20, 1920, *RTsKhIDNI, fond* 495, *op.* 1, *del.* 9.

51.   Litvinov to Sletov, August 1919, *AVPRF fond* 507, *op.* 5, *del.* 3, *papka* 2; Litvinov to Martens, May 27, 1919, *AVPRF fond* 507, *op.* 5, *del.* 2, *papka* 2. Also see Draper, *Roots,* 163.

52.   Jacobson, *When the Soviet Union Entered World Politics*, 17–18; Carr, *Bolshevik Revolution* 3:289–90.

53.   O'Connor, *Engineer of Revolution*, 172; Lenin, *CW* 32:480, as quoted in Jacobson, *When the Soviet Union Entered World Politics,* 19.

54.   Spolansky (unidentified) to Hoover, November 18, 1919, FBI Martens, vol. 2. Spolansky's role is discussed in Brown and MacDonald, *Field of Red*, 162. Spolansky's book about his work in the FBI is *The Communist Trail in America.*

55.   For the full dimensions of the War Department's role in rooting out domestic radicalism before World War II, see the excellent study by Talbert, *Negative Intelligence.*

56.   Wrisley Brown, major, Air Force, MA (DMI) to intelligence officer, April 18, 1919, RG 165, 10110-1194/43. An important player in the State Department's effort against Martens was the anti-Bolshevik Russian studies professor Samuel N. Harper of the University of Chicago; see McFadden, *Alternative Paths*, 37–39, 300–302.

57.   *New York Times*, March 28, 1919, RG 165, 10110-1194/10.

58.   Charles S. Clark to MID, July 7, 1919, RG 165, 10110-1194/126.

59.   Re Ludwig Martens et al. (May 1919), RG 165, 10110-1194/81; Ohsol to Jennings, April 23, 1920, *AVPRF fond* 507, *op.* 5b, *del.* 14, *papka* 3b.

60.   William B. Burney, manager, Foreign Trade Department, to secretary of state, July 12, 1919, RG 59, 661.1115/5.

61.   Heller memo, April 29, 1919, L0032, box 1; Martens to Nuorteva, April 29, 1919, *AVPRF fond* 507, *op.* 5, *del.* 5, *papka* 2.

62.   Kayden and Antsiferov, *Cooperative Movement in Russia*, 224.
63.   Gaworek, "Allied Economic Warfare against Soviet Russia," 67. Also see discussion in Uldricks, *Diplomacy and Ideology*, 57; Norman H. Davis, "Conversations with Diplomats," June 24, 1920, Davis Papers, box 9.
64.   Redfield, "Russia's Position in World Production," minutes of the eighth Annual Meeting, April 27, 1920, group IV (foreign commerce), 401–15, accession 160, U.S. Chamber of Commerce records; Litvinov to Martens, May 27, 1919, *AVPRF fond* 507, *op.* 5, *del.* 2, *papka* 2.
65.   Memorandum by Mr. Heller upon his return from Sixth National Foreign Trade Convention, April 29, 1919, L0032, box 1; T.W. Van Schoiack to MID, July 7, 1919, RG 165, 10110-1194/127.
66.   Nuorteva to Martens, April 29, 1919, *AVPRF fond* 507, *op.* 5, *del.* 5, *papka* 2.
67.   Charles E.J. Newman, ADS-2, and Cornelius J. Browne, report, Police Department, City of New York, bomb squad, April 21, 1919, attached to letter, John B. Trevor to Office of MID, April 29, 1919, RG 165, 10110-1194; Heller memo, April 29, 1919, L0032, box 1.
68.   Memo of conference between A.A. Heller and Ernest Kanseler, April 12, 1919, Memo of interview between A.A. Heller and I. Halpern, April 14, 1919, F. Campbell to Martens, telegram, April 25, 1919; Nuorteva to Martens, April 29, 1919, L0032, box 1.
69.   John B. Trevor to director of MID, April 8, 1919, RG 165, 10110-1194/17; FBI report, April 4, 1919, William M. Offley to W.E. Allen, acting chief, Bureau of Investigation, April 20, 1919, FBI Martens, vol. 1, 353815; John B. Trevor to director of MID, April 8, 1919, RG 165, 10110-1194/17.
70.   John B. Trevor to director of MID, April 11, 1919, RG 165, 10110-1194/29; Re Ludwig Martens et al. RG 165, 10110-1194/81; John B. Trevor to Division of Military Intelligence, April 29, 1919, RG 165, 10110-1194; synopsis of the case of L.C.A.K. Martens, December 31, 1919, RG 165, 10110-1194/263; John B. Trevor to Office of MID, May 14, 1919, RG 165, 10110-1194/64; also see Brown and McDonald, *Field of Red*, 133. On Trevor, see Talbert, *Negative Intelligence*, 26, 140.
71.   See handwritten note, RG 165, 10110-1194; report, W. Finch, April 30, 1919, RG 165, 10110-1194/101; statement from Guaranty Trust, L0032, box 1. Trevor received confirmation from Alexander J. Hemphill of GTC that Sabin had privately funded the bureau. Trevor to director of MID, April 24, 1919, RG 165, 10110-1194/41. Martens had $6,800 on account at Guaranty Trust and $9,506.96 at Public National Bank; see statement, Guaranty Trust Company, April 1919; statement, Public National Bank, May 1919, L0032, box 1.
72.   *New York Sun*, April 11, 1919; *New York Times*, April 8, 1919; Re Ludwig C.A.K. Martens et al., RG 59, 10110-1194/81; Synopsis of the case of L.C.A.K. Martens, December 31, 1919, RG 165, box 1440, 10110-1194/263; Trevor to director of MID, April 11, 1919, RG 165, 10110-1194/29; *New York World*, April 8, 1919, RG 165, 10110-1194/18; Trevor memo, April 11, 1919, RG 165, 10110-1194/32.
73.   "Martens Mission Propaganda for the Overthrow of Governments—Facts and Circumstances Relating to His Activities in the United States," FBI Martens, vol. 4 (hereafter cited as "Martens Mission Propaganda").
74.   *New York Times*, April 8, 1919, *New York Herald*, April 1, 1919, RG 165, 10110-1194/28, /27.
75.   *New York Sun*, April 11, 1919, RG 165, 10110-1194/32. John B. Trevor to director of MID, April 12, 1919, RG 165, 10110-1194/33; "Martens Mission Propaganda," FBI Martens, vol. 4.
76.   Memorandum for Mr. Hoover, Martens examination by Lusk committee, October 23, 1920, FBI Martens, vol. 2.
77.   MID Report, RG 165, 10110-1194/100, April 30, 1919; Basil Miles to Frank Polk, June 24, 1919, RG 59, 701.6111/648; Report of the Commercial Department for week

of April 23–30, 1919, L0032, box 1. On Martens's spell in the German Imperial Army, see William Wallace Flynn report, June 19, 1919, FBI Martens, vol 1.
78.   J.E. Hoover to attorney general, May 15, 1919, L0032, box 1; Allen, Memorandum to Mr. O'Brien in Re Ludwig Martens, May 15, 1919, FBI Martens, vol. 1, 353815.
79.   Report on trip to Washington, May 19, 1919, Nuorteva to Hillquit, April 20, 1919, L0032, box 1.
80.   Memo, Heller to Martens, May 22, 1919, Heller round-robin, June 4, 1919, L0032, box 1.The June raid on the Bureau prevented the conference, but in January 1920 the American Commercial Association to Promote Trade with Russia was launched in New York.
81.   The companies whose letters he carried included International High Speed Steel, American Screw, Ford Motor, Duplex Truck, Interstate Pulp and Paper, and Dennison Manufacturing. See Evans Clark,"List of Letters Taken to Washington," June 3, 1919, Konta, Kirchwey, France, and Michael to J.I. France, May 22, 1919, Lincoln Colcord to Hiram Johnson, May 29, 1919, Dudley Field Malone to Borah, to Pittman, and to Frank Polk, May 30, 1919, L0032, box 1.
82.   Clark to Hanna, May 16, 1919, L0032, box 1; Savitt, "To Fill a Void," 61; A.A. Heller to Nuorteva, June 11, 1919, L0032, box 1.
83.   *New York Times*, June 13, 1919, RG 165, 10110-1194/112. See also U.S. Senate, *Russian Propaganda*, January 26, 1920, 34. On the raid see also Reikhberg and Shapik, *Delo Martensa*, 7; statement by the Soviet Bureau, June 13, 1919, *AVPRF fond* 507, *op. 5, del. 5, papka* 2.
84.   Statement by the Russian Soviet government, no date, *AVPRF fond* 507, *op. 5, del. 5, papka* 2; Martens to the Narkomindel, July 2, 1919, *AVPRF fond* 507, *op. 5, del. 3, papka* 2.
85.   Speech of Nuorteva at Madison Square Garden, June 16, 1919, L0032, box 1.
86.   Report on Berkenheim, October 1919, *AVPRF fond* 507, *op. 5, del. 11, papka* 2; Wrisley Brown for John M. Dunn, March 29, 1919, to L. Lanier Winslow, Office of the Counselor, Department of State, RG 165, 10110-1194/38.
87.   See Fithian, "Soviet-American Economic Relations," 118–19; W.L. Moffat, Jr. to John B. Trevor, March 22, 1919, RG 165, 10110-1194.
88.   Heller, "Interview with Mr. A.M. Berkenheim of the All-Russian Central Union of Consumers' Societies," May 9, 1919, L0032, box 1.
89.   Nuorteva to Martens, August 7, 1919, *RGAE, fond* 413, *del.* 515, ll. 22–24, as cited in McFadden, *Alternative Paths*, 284. See discussion in idem, 283–84, and statement of the Soviet Bureau, August 6, 1919, *AVPRF fond* 507, *op. 5, del. 5, papka* 2.
90.   Martens to *tovarishchi* [comrades], August 7, 1919, *RGAE, fond* 413, *op. 3, del.* 515, *l.* 17; *New York Times*, August 13, 1919, 2.
91.   Ammission [White] to secretary of state, July 15, 1919, Polk to Ammission, July 18, 1919, RG 59, 661.119/433.
92.   Heller to Martens, August 7, 1919, *RGAE, fond* 413, *op. 3, del.* 515, *l.* 18, 19; McFadden, *Alternative Paths*, 283.
93.   Martens to Chicherin, August 13, 1919, *RGAE, fond* 413, *op. 3, del.* 515, *l.* 16, 20; C.A. White, *British and American Commercial Relations*, 209–10.
94.   Martens to Russian citizens in America of the Russian Soviet Republic, May 10, 1919, *AVPRF fond* 507, *op. 5, del.* 21, *papka* 3; McFadden, *Alternative Paths*, 281.
95.   Martens to MID, September 9, 1920, *fond* 507, *op.* 5b, *del.* 5, *papka* 35; See also Sovnarkom (Smol'ianinov) to V.I. Molotov, May 12, 1923, *RTsKhIDNI, fond* 84, *op.* 84, *del.* 568.
96.   Hoff Wilson, *Ideology and Economics*, 41–42; Libbey, *Gumberg and Soviet-American Relations*, 56; U.S. Senate, *Russian Propaganda*, January 30, 1920, 80; Savitt, "To Fill A Void," 25; Marlborough Churchill to George W. Ashworth, March 13, 1920, RG 165, 10110-1194/289; *Chicago Socialist*, December 27, 1919, RG 165, 10110-1194/220.

97.   Soviet Bureau Technical Department to *Vesenkha*, n.d., *AVPRF fond* 507, *op.* 5b, *del.* 1, *papka* 3a.

98.   Gitlow, *I Confess*, 28; Wolfe, *Life in Two Centuries*, 166; Weinberg, *Armand Hammer*, 23. One entry in the Lusk file shows that Hammer paid $1,039.58 for payroll in May 1919.

99.   "Important Disclosures on the Soviet Bureau in New York," *Russky Golos*, June 7, 1920, FBI Martens, vol. 5.

100.   J.E. Hoover to Colonel Hicks, May 24, 1920, RG 165, 10058-24/111; Draper, *Roots*, 229. On the FBI's work with Peterson, also see Spolansky, *Communist Trail in America*, 142–45.

101.   On the party's defense of Fraina, see *New York Call*, June 10, 1920, *AVPRF fond* 507, *op.* 5b, *del.* 4, *papka* 3a. Also see Fraina's own defense, in letter to the executive committee of the Communist International, August 7, 1920, read at the second session of the executive committee, August 8, 1920, *RTsKhIDNI, fond* 495, *op.* 1, *del.* 4.

102.   J.E. Hoover to Colonel Hicks, May 24, 1920, RG 165, 10058-24/111.For Martens's reaction, see Martens to Nuorteva, November 4, 1920, *AVPRF fond* 507, *op.* 5b, *del.* 1, *papka* 3a.

103.   Martens, memorandum, November 20, 1919, *AVPRF fond* 507, *op.* 5, *del.* 3, *papka* 2.

104.   "Letter to American Workers," August 20, 1918, in Lenin, *CW* 28:75, 72, 70; memorandum submitted by———to Special Agent———in Newark, N.J., February 24, 1920, FBI Martens, vol. 2; Secret, "Martens Mission Propaganda," FBI Martens, vol. 4; *New York Times*, November 17, 1919, 1, as quoted in Sutton, *Wall Street and the Bolshevik Revolution*, 119.

105.   *New York Times*, November 17, 1919, 2; November 18, 1919, 1; November 17, 1919, 1.

106.   The Lusk committee noted that Martens's office had written checks to the Russian Socialist Federation, the Russian Federation Socialist party, and the Communist party in amounts ranging from $2.00 to $668.75. *New York Times*, November 27, 1919, 73; FBI report, May 6–8, 1920, FBI Martens, vol. 5.

107.   See *New York Times*, November 27, 1919, 3, November 19, 1919, 12; November 18, 1919, 1; FBI report, November 24, 1919, FBI Martens, vol. 1. On the Lusk committee's activities, see discussion in Talbert, *Negative Intelligence*, 175–81.

108.   *New York Times*, November 18, 1919, 1; Report of the Commercial Department for week of April 23–30, 1919, L0032, box 1.

109.   Heller, 1919, n.d., L0032, box 1; *New York Times*, November 17, 1919, 1.

110.   *New York Times*, November 17, 1919, 2.

111.   Report of interview, April 14, 1919, L0032, box 1; *New York Times*, November 19, 1919, 9.

112.   See "Number of firms offering to do business with the Russian Socialist Federated Soviet Republic," May 21, 1919, memorandum to Miss Tuch, May 29, 1919, L0032, box 1.

113.   Transcript of Lusk file, RG 165, 10110-1194/185; U.S. Senate, *Russian Propaganda*, January 30, 1920, 71.

114.   These last five contracts had been signed between July 1919 and May 1920; see Etta Tuch to Martens, June 8, 1920, June 9, 1920. Also see Morris and Company contract signed January 22, 1920, by Harry E. Bayer and Martens; and Bobroff contract signed January 26, 1920 by Bobroff and Martens, *AVPRF fond* 507, *op.* 5b, *del.* 14, *papka* 3b.

115.   Sutton, *Wall Street and the Bolshevik Revolution*, 158; U.S. Senate, *Russian Propaganda*, January 30, 1920, 71.

116.   See U.S. Senate, *Russian Propaganda*, January 30, 1920, 71; report of J. Spolansky, Chicago, April 4, 1919, RG 165, 10110-1194/15.

117.   Etta Tuch to Martens, June 8, 1920, June 9, 1920; see also Bobroff contract signed January 26, 1920, by Bobroff and Martens, and Isaac A. Hourwich, memorandum, June 9, 1920, *AVPRF fond* 507, *op.* 5b, *del.* 14, *papka* 3b. Firms included the Kempsmith Manufacturing Company of Racine, Wisconsin; Milwaukee Shaper Company, Mayer Boot and Shoe, and the Steel Sole Shoe Company.

118.   "Memorandum for Mr. Heller," April 23, 1919, *AVPRF fond* 507, *op.* 5, *del.* 11, *papka* 2.

CHAPTER 2.
THE DEMISE OF THE SOVIET BUREAU

1.   See State of New York, "In the Matter of the application of L.C.A.K. Martens for the return of a thousand dollar Liberty Bond . . .," August 23, 1920, FBI Martens, vol. 6.

2.   See Wolfe, *Life in Two Centuries*, 167; Draper, *Roots*, 204; Warth, "The Palmer Raids"; Coben, *Palmer*, Ch. 12 passim.

3.   Draper, *Roots*, 206. The existence of two competing Communist parties—the American Communist party and the United Communist party (the former Communist Labor party)—was blamed for this "ridiculous" situation, but the Department of Justice's attacks certainly did not help. See meeting of Ispolkom (executive committee) of Comintern, March 17, 1921, *RTsKhIDNI, fond* 495, *op.* 1, *del.* 26; on the parties, see Howe and Coser, *The American Communist Party*, 71.

4.   Nuorteva to Grenville S. McFarland, January 12, 1920, *AVPRF fond* 507, *op.* 5b, *del.* 4, *papka* 3a.

5.   Converse to Major Strauss, January 13, 1920, RG 165, 10110-1194/216; *New York Times*, January 11, 1920, FBI Martens, vol. 2.

6.   *New York Times*, January 11, 1920, FBI Martens, vol. 2; Nuorteva to McFarland, January 12, 1920, *AVPRF fond* 507, *op.* 5b, *del.* 4, *papka* 3a.

7.   Hardwick to Martens, June 8, 1920, *AVPRF fond* 507, *op.* 5b, *del.* 14, *papka* 3b; Nuorteva to McFarland, January 12, 1920, *AVPRF fond* 507, *op.* 5b, *del.* 4, *papka* 3a.

8.   These included Rahn Larmon and Lehigh Machine Companies, the Antheus Trading Company, and the National Storage Company. See Martens to Glover, December 28, 1919, RG 165, 10110-1194/270.

9.   Memorandum submitted by————to Special Agent————in Newark, N.J., February 24, 1920, FBI Martens, vol. 2; Secret, "Martens Mission Propaganda," FBI Martens, vol. 4.

10.   Secret report signed by C.L.C. (C.L. Converse), January 28, 1920, RG 165, 10110-1194/290.

11.   Emerson Jennings to Woodrow Wilson, November 5, 1919, RG 59, 661.119/471.

12.   *New York Times*, January 26, 1920, 1; Wolfe, *Life in Two Centuries*, 166.

13.   Letter, October 18, 1920, no names given, FBI Martens, vol. 6; See fascimile copy in records of FBI, January 20, 1920, FBI Martens, vol. 2. The source of the loan was blacked out but likely it was Emerson Jennings (a bank statement from January 22, 1920, for $6,014.69, is from Citizens National Bank of Lehighton, Pennsylvania).

14.   Felix Cole, memorandum, May 11, 1920, RG 59, 661.1115/68, as cited in Hoff Wilson, *Ideology and Economics*, 54. The MID also was keeping an eye on Jennings; see S. Perkins, report, February 5, 1920, RG 165, 10110-1194/300

15.   U.S. Senate, *Russian Propaganda*, January 26, 1920, 7–16, 54; captured document as quoted in Paterson *Guardian*, March 31, 1920, FBI Martens, vol. 2. For contemporary commentary, see Lincoln Colcord, "Absolutely No Russian Policy," *The Nation* 110 (April 3, 1920): 428.

16. Cited in Hoff Wilson, *Ideology and Economics*, 53.

17. Martens to chairman of Senate subcommittee, May 6, 1920, *AVPRF fond* 507, *op.* 5b, *del.* 4, *papka* 3a; McFadden, *Alternative Paths*, 318.

18. Memorandum on the "Legal Aspects of the Importation of Russian Gold Rubles into the United States. . . ," *AVPRF fond* 507, *op.* 5b, *del.* 16, *papka* 3b; Martens to Krasin, September 7, 1920, *AVPRF fond* 507, *op.* 5b, *del.* 5, *papka* 35.

19. Nuorteva to Henry E. Cooper, April 21, 1920, *AVPRF fond* 507, *op.* 5b, *del.* 14, *papka* 3b; also see Litvinov letter, May 24, 1920, *AVPRF fond* 507, *op.* 5, *del.* 11, *papka* 2.

20. C.A. White, *British and American Commercial Relations*, 149; John C. Wiley to secretary of state, December 22, 1939, Wiley Papers, box 3.

21. Memo attached to letter, H.E. Cushman, Treasurer, Morse Twist Drill and Machinery Company to Hoover, May 16, 1921, RG 151, 448-U.S.

22. See Martens to Isidor Gukovskii, June 2, 1920, *AVPRF fond* 507, *op.* 5b, *del.* 14, *papka* 3b; Bureau of Investigation report, January 17, 1921, 61-640-0, FBI Martens, vol. 4, 353815.

23. Memorandum of telephone message received from Mr. Yardley, December 24, 1920, FBI Martens, vol. 6; On the $33,240, see also London to Martens, November 15, 1920, *AVPRF fond* 507, *op.* 5b, *del.* 16, *papka* 3b.

24. New York manufacturers' agent Aron Berkman, for example, lent the Bureau $20,000 while shipping over $43,000 worth of soap, gauze, and drugs to Estonia. See Martens to Gukovskii, June 7, 1920, Martens to Berkman, June 16, 1920, *AVPRF fond* 507, *op.* 5b, *del.* 14, *papka* 3b.

25. See Wilton to Foreign Office, March 24, 1921, enclosure, "Goods Available for Export from Russia and Goods Ordered by Russian Representatives Abroad, Purchase and Sales Commission, Foreign Countries, Moscow"; "Translation of Confidential Report Compiled by Soviet Authorities for Their Own Use," Foreign Office correspondence file, British Public Record Office, file 371/6877, both as cited in C.A. White, *British and American Commercial Relations*, 156.

26. See *Tallina Tolliwalitsus* bills of lading, April 29, 1920, May 19, 1920, May 17, 1920, *AVPRF fond* 507, *op.* 5b, *del.* 5, *papka* 35; manifest, SS *Lake Frumet* and *Wheeling Mold*, June 30, 1920, *AVPRF fond* 507, *op.* 5b, *del.* 14, *papka* 3b. On the People's Industrial Trading Corporation, see C.A. White, *British and American Commercial Relations*, 155.

27. Agents included Heller (galoshes), A. Berkman (soap and gauze), and Elias Berlow (shoes). See manifest, SS *Lake Frumet* and *Wheeling Mold*, June 30, 1920, *AVPRF fond* 507, *op.* 5b, *del.* 14, *papka* 3b; E. Tuch to Martens, May 21, 1920, *AVPRF fond* 507, *op.* 5b, *del.* 1, *papka* 3a; Martens to Nuorteva, November 4, 1920, *AVPRF fond* 507, *op.* 5b, *del.* 1, *papka* 3a.

28. On gold, see C.A. White, *British and American Commercial Relations*, 160–62, and also *Krasnaya Gazeta*, March 2, 1921, paraphrase, cable message from the American consul at Viborg, March 16, 1921, RG 59, 661.1115/263.

29. Chairman of Vneshtorg to Isodor Gukovskii, August 20, 1920, *AVPRF fond* 507, *op.* 5b, *del.* 5, *papka* 35; Martens to Nuorteva, November 4, 1920, Martens to the Narkomindel, June 21, 1920, *AVPRF fond* 507, *op.* 5b, *del.* 1, *papka* 3a.

30. William F. Coombs memorandum re Russia, attached to president to Charles E. Hughes, May 24, 1921, RG 59, 661.1115/333. The State Department found this $500 million figure unrealistically high. See Poole, note, on A. W. Kliefoth letter, June 13, 1921, RG 59, 661.1115/330.

31. C. Essy Ehsing to J.A. Hutmacher (Brussels), April 4, 1920, IHP, BA1-01, box 2, 1364; Martens to the Narkomindel, June 21, 1920, *AVPRF fond* 507, *op.* 5b, *del.* 1, *papka* 3a. Consul Albrecht in Stockholm "reported that an American named John Chretien, manager of B.I. Babbitt Company, is negotiating with the Soviet Mission in Stockholm for

the sale of Babbitt soap in exchange for platinum." Monnett B. Davis, an American consul in training, had visited Martens's bureau posing as an interested manufacturer and also learned of this arrangement. See Boris Baievsky to director, BFDC, July 1, 1921, RG 151, 448-U.S; Davis memo, January 21, 1921, RG 59, no file number.

32. Martens to the Narkomindel, June 21, 1920, *AVPRF fond* 507, *op.* 5b, *del.* 1, *papka* 3a; *New York Times*, June 6, 1920, as cited in D.M. Smith, *Aftermath of War*, 58.

33. Martens to the Narkomindel, July 16, 1920, June 21, 1920, *AVPRF fond* 507, *op.* 5b, *del.* 1, *papka* 3a; Martens to Colby, June 19, 1920, *AVPRF fond* 507, *op.* 5b, *del.* 5, *papka* 3a.

34. Martens to the Narkomindel, June 21, 1920, *AVPRF fond* 507, *op.* 5b, *del.* 1, *papka* 3a.

35. "Martens refutes false reports," June 20, 1920, Martens as quoted in "Memorandum for Mr. Hoover," July 7, 1920, FBI Martens, vol. 5.

36. FBI report, Baltimore, August 27, 1920, FBI Martens, vol. 5.

37. For a sampling of labor appeals for an end to restrictions on Soviet trade, see RG 59, 661.1115/P81. An extensive list of unions "demanding trade with Russia" is also found in U.S. Senate, *Relations with Russia*, 57–61.

38. J.G.C. at Bureau to Heller, April 8, 1920, Heller, "Report to Martens, Washington," April 3, 1920, FBI Martens, vol. 2.

39. Alter to Longworth, June 26, 1920, *AVPRF fond* 507, *op.* 5b, *del.* 14, *papka* 3b.

40. Alter to Mr. N.P. Lloyd, Newton Machine Tool Works, June 10, 1920, S.R. Baron to Alter, June 29, 1920, *AVPRF fond* 507, *op.* 5b, *del.* 14, *papka* 3b.

41. A large record of letters from businesses seeking to end the blockade and to open trade relations may be found in RG 59, 701.6111, 661.119 and 661.1115.

42. On the department's policy, see Colby to Minister Camillo Avezzana, *FRUS, 1920* 3:468. For discussion of Colby and his note, see Ch. 3.

43. A.W. Hinger to Martens, March 19, 1920, *AVPRF fond* 507, *op.* 5b, *del.* 14, *papka* 3b.

44. Martens to Baldwin, March 25, 1920, *AVPRF fond* 507, *op.* 5b, *del.* 14, *papka* 3b.

45. Synopsis of minutes, Baldwin Locomotive Works, July 17, 1919, Austin Papers, box 6; "Siberian Report," M. Bunting to Sample, June 16, 1922, 9, 12, Austin Papers, box 7.

46. Baldwin to Bureau, April 2, 1920, Inspector Beyer, memorandum to Vanderlip, through Martens, December 31, 1920, *AVPRF fond* 507, *op.* 5b, *del.* 16, *papka* 3b.

47. Tuch, report to Mr. Martens, March 27, 1920, memorandum for Mr. Martens, April 10, 1920, FBI Martens, vol. 2.

48. Martens to Lomonosov, July 22, 1920, *AVPRF fond* 507, *op.* 5b, *del.* 5, *papka* 35.

49. This classification included "locomotives, railway materials, rolling stock, motor cars and their component parts, etc." Firms hoping to sell these items to the Bolsheviks after the blockade had lifted had to apply for export licenses from the State Department's War Trade Board Section, where "each application . . . will be considered on its own merits." See Alvey A. Adee to Alexander Hinchuck Company, January 29, 1921, RG 59, 661.1115/253.

50. Inspector Beyer, memorandum to Vanderlip, through Martens, December 31, 1920, *AVPRF fond* 507, *op.* 5b, *del.* 16, *papka* 3b. Baldwin and American Locomotive Company had been dividing their business at least since 1914. See Abramson, *Spanning the Century*, 108.

51. Technical Department to *Vesenkha*, no date, *AVPRF fond* 507, *op.* 5b, *del.* 1, *papka* 3a; Martens to MID for transfer to *Vesenkha*, September 9, 1920, *AVPRF fond* 507, *op.* 5b, *del.* 5, *papka* 35.

52. Agreement between Max Rabinov and Martens, April 27, 1920, *AVPRF fond* 507, *op.* 5b, *del.* 16, *papka* 3b; Martens to Krasin, George Lomonsov, July 23, 1920,

AVPRF fond 507, *op.* 5b, *del.* 5, *papka* 35. The Soviet government initially had difficulty coming up with the necessary deposit, Krasin complained, because the continuing absence of an Anglo-Soviet treaty created currency restrictions that made it "technically impossible" to sell Soviet gold in Reval. See O'Connor, *Engineer of Revolution,* 236.

53. Martens to Krasin, George Lomonsov, July 23, 1920, *AVPRF fond* 507, *op.* 5b, *del.* 5, *papka* 35.

54. The Communists were feeling pinched themselves. In late 1919 MID learned that "conditions [were] very bad in Communist Labor Party. [Party leader] Gitlow asked why Martens had not sent the usual remittance. [Funds] from Stockholm had not arrived." See MID Chicago report, RG 165, 10110-1194/294. On the party's reliance upon funds from Russia, see Klehr, Haynes, and Firsov, *Secret World,* 21–26.

55. Martens to Krasin, August 11, 1920, *AVPRF fond* 507, *op.* 5b, *del.* 5, *papka* 35. See also U.S. Senate, *Russian Propaganda,* January 30, 1920, 80.

56. Litvinov to Tov. Sletov, August, 1919 (n.d.), *AVPRF fond* 507, *op.* 5, *del.* 2, *papka* 2; Martens to Krasin, September 7, 1920, *AVPRF fond* 507, *op.* 5b, *del.* 5, *papka* 35.

57. I. Gurevich, "The Rate of the Russian Ruble," 1920 (n.d.), *AVPRF fond* 507, *op.* 5b, *del.* 19, *papka* 3b.

58. Martens to Nuorteva, November 4, 1920, Martens to the Narkomindel, November 23, 1920, *AVPRF fond* 507, *op.* 5b, *del.* 1, *papka* 3a.

59. Martens to Krasin, August 6, 1920, *AVPRF fond* 507, *op.* 5b, *del.* 5, *papka* 35.

60. O'Connor, *Engineer of Revolution,* 171.

61. Krasin to Martens, August 31, 1920, Martens to Krasin, August 30, 1920, Krasin to Martens, October 8, 1920, *AVPRF fond* 507, *op.* 5b, *del.* 5, *papka* 35. Martens dutifully sent Krasin quotes from the Belting and Leather Products Association, Detroit Twist Drill, and Rosendal Reddaway Belting and Hose.

62. Martens to Krasin, August 6, 1920, *AVPRF fond* 507, *op.* 5b, *del.* 5, *papka* 35; on Kopp, see C.A. White, *British and American Commercial Relations,* 149.

63. Krasin to Martens, August 20, 1920, Martens to Krasin, August 30, 1920, *AVPRF fond* 507, *op.* 5b, *del.* 5, *papka* 35.

64. Martens to Krasin, September 7, 1920, *AVPRF fond* 507, *op.* 5b, *del.* 5, *papka* 35; Martens to Sir George E. Foster, May 4, 1920, *AVPRF fond* 507, *op.* 5b, *del.* 14, *papka* 3b; Martens to Krasin, August 11, 1920, *AVPRF fond* 507, *op.* 5b, *del.* 5, *papka* 35.

65. S.R. Baron to Robert Alter, June 29, 1920, Robert Alter to Nicholas Longworth, enclosing clipping from Associated Press in *Cincinnati Commercial Tribune,* June 26, 1920, with headline, "Martens Signs Contract for Canadian Supplies," J. Ogle Carss to Sir George Perley, May 26, 1920, Perley to Carss, May 27, 1920, *AVPRF fond* 507, *op.* 5b, *del.* 14, *papka* 3b.

66. Martens to Krasin, August 11, 1920, *AVPRF fond* 507, *op.* 5b, *del.* 5, *papka* 35.

67. Krasin to Martens, August 28, 1920, *AVPRF fond* 507, *op.* 5b, *del.* 5, *papka* 35.

68. Martens to Krasin, September 7, 1920, *AVPRF fond* 507, *op.* 5b, *del.* 5, *papka* 35.

69. Martens to Nuorteva, November 4, 1920, *AVPRF fond* 507, *op.* 5b, *del.* 1, *papka* 3a.

70. Martens to Nuorteva, November 4, 1920, *AVPRF fond* 507, *op.* 5b, *del.* 1, *papka* 3a; Inspector Beyer, memorandum to Vanderlip, through Martens, December 31, 1920, *AVPRF fond* 507, *op.* 5b, *del.* 16, *papka* 3b.

71. See, for example, the outlook expressed in Bureau of Investigation reports, Chicago, May 5, 1919, Los Angeles, July 8, 1919, FBI Martens, vol. 1.

72. Memo, conversation between McCormick and Sam Harper, March 19, 1920, McCormick Papers, box 116.

73. See *New York Call,* June 10, 1920; Martens to Nuorteva, November 4, 1920, *AVPRF fond* 507, *op.* 5b, *del.* 1, *papka* 3a. On the decline of Palmer and the Red Scare, see Coben, *Palmer,* 230–45.

74. See Martens to Nuorteva, November 4, 1920, *AVPRF fond* 507, *op.* 5b, *del.* 1, *papka* 3a, and discussion in *AVPRF fond* 507, *op.* 5b, *del.* 4, *papka* 3a.

75. "Declaration of Representative of the RSFSR in the USA Martens on the Occasion of the Decision of the Ministry of Labor on Sending Him from the United States of America," December 17, 1920, file 225, *DVP* 3:389.

76. Hardwick to Martens, December 18, 1920, Martens to the Narkomindel, December 20, 1920, *AVPRF fond* 507, *op.* 5b, *del.* 4, *papka* 3a. Also see Hardwick to Borah, November 11, 1921, Borah Papers, box 101.

77. Roland S. Morris to Bullard, August 4, 1920, ABP, box 1.Miles, for example, declared that Martens "should be interned." See Miles to Polk, June 24, 1919, RG 59, 701.6111/648.

78. Martens to the Narkomindel, December 20, 1920, *AVPRF fond* 507, *op.* 5b, *del.* 4, *papka* 3a.

79. Martens to the Narkomindel, December 20, 1920, *AVPRF fond* 507, *op.* 5b, *del.* 4, *papka* 3a.

80. Hardwick to Martens, December 21, 1920, Martens to the Narkomindel, December 20, 1920, *AVPRF fond* 507, *op.* 5b, *del.* 4, *papka* 3a; *Krasnaya Gazeta*, March 2, 1921, paraphrase, cable message from the American consul at Viborg, March 16, 1921, RG 59, 661.1115/263.

81. Chicherin to Martens, December 24, 1920, *AVPRF fond* 507, *op.* 5b, *del.* 4, *papka* 3a.

82. Radosh, "Spargo and Wilson's Russian Policy," 555.

83. "Interview with Martens—Russia—Service Report, Political Factor," RG 165, 10110-1194/375.

84. Kenneth B. Ellman to Martens, December 31, 1920, *AVPRF fond* 507, *op.* 5b, *del.* 14, *papka* 3b. The league had elected Martens and Nuorteva Russian representatives to its honorary advisory committee in 1919; see Ellman to Nuorteva, November 12, 1919, *AVPRF fond* 507, *op.* 5, *del.* 35, *papka* 3.

85. U.S. Senate, *Relations with Russia*, 61; also see protests, United Mine Workers to Woodrow Wilson, Mitchell Palmer, L.E. Wheeler, January 22, 1921, Cigarmakers' Union to Colby, January 22, 1921, RG 59, 661.115P81. On National Defense Committee gathering, see Matthew C. Smith, colonel, General Staff, chief, Negative Branch, to L.J. Baley, chief, Bureau of Investigation, January 27, 1921, RG 165, 10110-1194/350.

86. Interview, Adlon Hotel, Berlin, December 25, 1920, RG 165, 10110-1194/372.

87. Martens to London, December 17, 1920, *AVPRF fond* 507, *op.* 5b, *del.* 4, *papka* 3a.

88. "Interview with Martens—Russia—Service Report, Political Factor," RG 165, 10110-1194/375; RG 59, 701.6111/538; "U.S. Trading with Soviet Blocked," *Washington Star*, February 24, 1921.

89. Manifests dated November 15, 1920, November 26, 1920, December 28, 1920, December 31, 1920. *AVPRF fond* 507, *op.* 5b, *del.* 16, *papka* 3b; Commercial Relations of Soviet Russia Economic Factor, monograph report, May 3, 1921, Riga, RG 165, 2515-D-39.

90. Martens to Nuorteva, November 4, 1920, *AVPRF fond* 507, *op.* 5b, *del.* 1, *papka* 3a.

91. Report, January 10, 1921, on Martens departure on SS *Stockholm*, RG 165, 10110-1194/338.

92. Litvinov to Martens, October 22, 1921, *RTsKhIDNI, fond* 5, *op.* 1, *del.* 2080.

93. See Poole to Hughes, October 4, 1921, RG 59, 661.11/7; Jennings, letter to the members of the American Commercial Association to Promote Trade with Russia and other interested American manufacturers, August 31, 1921, RG 59, 661.001/30. On his way home, a Commerce Department representative reported that Jennings stopped in Germany to "recite to us his experiences in attempting to do business with the Soviet Government." See Howard W. Adams to Julius Klein, September 21, 1921, RG 151, 448-U.S.

94. Litvinov to Martens, October 22, 1921, *RTsKhIDNI, fond* 5, *op.* 1, *del.* 2080.
95. Litvinov to Martens, October 22, 1921, *RTsKhIDNI, fond* 5, *op.* 1, *del.* 2080. Lenin found the disagreement between the two men "regrettable and harmful." See Lenin to Chicherin, October 22, 1921, *CW* 45: 355.
96. Evgen'ev and Shapik, *Revolyutsioner, Diplomat, Uchenyi,* 14. Also see McFadden, *Alternative Paths,* Chs. 11–12 passim.
97. Martens to the Narkomindel, June 21, 1920, *AVPRF fond* 507, *op.* 5b, *del.* 1, *papka* 3a.
98. "Interview with Martens—Russia—Service Report, Political Factor," RG 165, 10110-1194/375; "The Return Rush to Russia," interview with Mr. Recht, translation from *Novy Put,* March 17, 1922, included in letter, commissioner in Riga to secretary of state, March 22, 1922, RG 59, 701.6111/582; Lenin to Martens, June 27, 1921, August 2, 1921, *CW* 45:196–97, 236–37.

Chapter 3.
Diplomatic, Military, and Humanitarian Initiatives, 1919–1923

1. Gaworek, "From Blockade to Trade," 60.
2. *New York Times,* August 13, 1919, 2; "Intercourse with Territory under Bolshevik Control," Acting Secretary of State William Phillips to Senator Wadsworth, November 1, 1919, Russian series, no. 2, RG 59, F.W. 661.119/471. On this policy, which prohibited the granting of export licenses but was, according to Phillips, "no blockade," see also Frank L. Polk to Mark O. Prentiss, April 22, 1919, RG 59, 701.6111/301, and State Department notices of April 28, 1919, and May 6, 1919.
3. Since 1913, diplomatic recognition had acquired a new meaning in Washington, connoting an *endorsement* of a new government rather than an acknowledgment of that state's existence. Woodrow Wilson had set a precedent by his crusading emphasis on the need for "legitimate governments" in Latin America.
4. McFadden, *Alternative Paths,* 45; Ernest Poole, "Arthur Bullard in Russia during the War," ABP, box 1.
5. Poole, "Arthur Bullard in Russia during the War," ABP, box 1. McFadden argues that Bullard and Robins, among other Americans in Russia after the revolution, joined Soviet representatives including Trotsky and Chicherin in conducting a significant, if ultimately unsuccessful, "probing search for a means of coexistence," which continued until 1920 through other channels after the Americans left Russia. See McFadden, *Alternative Paths,* 338, and full discussion in Chs. 3–5, passim.
6. On the movement of goods to Berlin, see discussion in Bullard, "Dealing with the Bolsheviki, June 1918," ABP, box 6.
7. Killen, "Search for a Democratic Russia," 241–43.
8. Unterberger, "Woodrow Wilson and the Bolsheviks," 83.
9. Kennan, *Russia and the West,* 117; Killen, "Search for a Democratic Russia," 242. A study that puts the responsibility for the intervention squarely upon the Allies, "to overthrow the Bolshevik regime," is Mayer, *Politics and Diplomacy of Peacemaking,* 294 and Ch. 10, passim. One that places the blame on the Bolsheviks for "failure to avoid war with the Allies" by insufficient attempts to appease their fears of Soviet-German collaboration is Debo, *Revolution and Survival,* 299 and Ch. 11, passim.
10. Killen, "Search for a Democratic Russia," 241, 242, 250–51.
11. Leffingwell to Carter Glass, November 1, 1919, Leffingwell Papers, reel 30.
12. See testimony of Rep. Isaac Siegel in U.S. Congress, *Russian Bonds,* part 1, 12.
13. Thompson, *Versailles Peace,* 151; Brownell and Billings, *So Close to Greatness,* 80; Bullitt to House, February 3, 1918, as cited in ibid., 67.

14. Kennan, *Russia and the West*, 130. Also see *FRUS, 1918, Russia* 1:395, as cited in Kennan, *Soviet-American Relations, 1917–1920*, 510.
15. See Bullitt to House, January 30, 1919, cited in Bullitt, *Bullitt Mission to Russia*, 15–17.
16. Mayer, *Politics and Diplomacy of Peacemaking*, 424–25. Also see discussion in McFadden, *Alternative Paths*, 180–89.
17. Mayer, *Politics and Diplomacy of Peacemaking*, 434.
18. Kennan, *Russia and the West*, 127; Brownell and Billings, *So Close to Greatness*, 78, 79; Ullman, *Anglo-Soviet Relations* 2:121–28.
19. Thompson, *Versailles Peace*, 152, 150; Lansing to Bullitt, February 18, 1919, as cited in Bullitt, *Bullitt Mission*, 4.
20. Thompson, *Versailles Peace*, 156.
21. See Robert Lansing, *Desk Diary*, January 18, 1919, February 16, 1919, as cited in Thompson, *Versailles Peace*, 150.
22. P.H. Kerr to Bullitt, February 21, 1919, as cited in Bullitt, *Bullitt Mission*, 36–37; on Lloyd George's involvement in the mission, see Thompson, *Versailles Peace*, 154–55.
23. Thompson, *Versailles Peace*, 155, 158. See also Debo, *Survival and Consolidation*, 45. The French intelligence community nonetheless closely monitored Bullitt's trip. See Kennan, *Russia and the West*, 131.
24. Thompson, *Versailles Peace*, 167; Lenin, *CW* 24:59–60, 25:603, as cited in Thompson, *Versailles Peace,* 164–65. Also see Ullman, *Anglo-Soviet Relations* 2:149.
25. Debo, *Survival and Consolidation*, 48.
26. Bullitt, *Bullitt Mission*, 59–60; Brownell and Billings, *So Close to Greatness*, 90.
27. This was William Allen White's description. See Brownell and Billings, *So Close to Greatness*, 89.
28. Kennan, *Russia and the West*, 131–33. Lloyd George based this assessment on Henry Wyckham Steed's highly critical editorial in the *Daily Mail*. Steed's piece reflected great alarm at the thought that through Bullitt, the Allies were considering "whether . . . to accredit an evil thing known as Bolshevism." As Lloyd George responded, "As long as the British press is doing this thing how can you expect me to be sensible about Russia?" Steed as quoted in Brownell and Billings, *So Close to Greatness*, 91; Lloyd George as quoted in Debo, *Survival and Consolidation*, 50.
29. Ullman, *Anglo-Soviet Relations* 2:153–57.
30. Kennan, *Russia and the West*, 134; Debo, *Survival and Consolidation*, 48.
31. See discussion in McFadden, *Alternative Paths*, Ch. 10 passim.
32. Ullman, *Anglo-Soviet Relations* 2:157–58.
33. Nansen directed the peace conference's newly established Commission of Relief. See Hoover to Woodrow Wilson, April 7, 1919, March 28, 1919, PCP, box 20.
34. Nuorteva to Hillquit, April 20, 1919, L0032, box 1.
35. Bullitt, *Bullitt Mission*, 90. Also see discussion in Ullman, *Anglo-Soviet Relations* 2:160–61. Although staying clear of Bolshevik Russia in 1919, Hoover's relief administration did open missions in locations ranging from Warsaw to Trieste to Tiflis.
36. McFadden, *Alternative Paths*, 249–51; Bullitt to Wilson, May 17, 1919, in Bullitt, *Bullitt Mission*, 96.
37. Lenin to Chicherin and Litvinov, May 6, 1919, *CW* 44:224–25; Mayer, *Politics and Diplomacy of Peacemaking*, 486–87; Ullman, *Anglo-Soviet Relations* 2:160.
38. Lansing as cited in Ambrosius, *Wilson and the American Diplomatic Tradition*, 188; Bullitt, *Bullitt Mission*, 103; Brownell and Billings, *So Close to Greatness*, 98; see Pratt, "Robert Lansing," 609–10.
39. Statement by the Russian Soviet Bureau, May 8, 1919, *AVPRF fond* 507, *op.* 5, *del.* 5, *papka* 2.
40. Lenin to Chicherin and Litvinov, May 6, 1919, *CW* 44:225; Lenin to Ninth All-Russia Congress of Soviets, December 25, 1921, *CW* 33:150.

41. Litvinov to Martens, May 27, 1919, *AVPRF fond* 507, *op.* 5, *del.* 2, *papka* 2.
42. Litvinov to Martens, May 27, 1919, *AVPRF fond* 507, *op.* 5, *del.* 2, *papka* 2. On Kalamatiano, who was imprisoned from 1918 to 1921, see Foglesong, "Xenophon Kalamatiano," 154–95.
43. Litvinov to Martens, May 27, 1919, *AVPRF fond* 507, *op.* 5, *del.* 2, *papka* 2.
44. Litvinov to Martens, May 27, 1919, *AVPRF fond* 507, *op.* 5, *del.* 2, *papka* 2.
45. American mission, Paris, to secretary of state, July 15, 1919, Polk to Ammission, July 18, 1919, RG 59, 661.119/433.
46. Killen, "Search for a Democratic Russia," 250; Gaworek, "From Blockade to Trade," 53–54.
47. Gaworek, "From Blockade to Trade," 58, 61–66.The cooperatives by then were under the control of the Bolsheviks, however. See Gaworek, 67 n. 101.
48. See Hoff Wilson, *Ideology and Economics*, 35; Polk to Wallace, March 7, 1920 *FRUS, 1920* 3: 703–4, as cited in Smith, *Colby*, 57; Foreign Office memorandum, March 20, 1920, enclosed with letter from Wigler, March 23, 1920, RG 59, 661.1115/50; O'Connor, *Diplomacy and Revolution*, 118.
49. "House of Commons Premier's Statement," June 3, 1920, *Manchester Guardian*, June 1, 1920, in *RGAE, fond* 413, *op.* 2, *del.* 1517, *l.* 106, 105; "House of Commons Premier's Statement," June 7, 1920, *RGAE, fond* 413, *op.* 2, *del.* 1517, *l.* 109; S. White, *Britain and the Bolshevik Revolution*, 5. For full discussion of the preliminary discussions held between May and November, see Debo, *Survival and Consolidation*, Ch. 15 passim.
50. State Department, press release, July 7, 1920, *FRUS, 1920* 3:717; *Russian Economic Bulletin* 2 (July 1920): 1.
51. Archibald J. Wolfe, "Lifting the Trade Embargo on Russia," *American Industries* 21 (August 1920); NAM Foreign Trade Department to Standard Underground Cable Company, June 21, 1921, RG 59, 661.1115/331.
52. Wilson, as quoted in interview with William W. Hawkins, vice chairman of the Board, Scripps-Howard Company, on September 27, 1920; see Hawkins to Colby, August 11, 1933, Colby Papers, box 2; Smith, *Colby*, 20.
53. Radosh, "Spargo and Wilson's Russian Policy," 556; Spargo as quoted in ibid.
54. Colby to Camillo Avezzana, August 10, 1920, *FRUS, 1920* 3:468.
55. Colby to Avezzana, August 10, 1920, Colby Papers, box 3A; Radosh, "Spargo and Wilson's Russian Policy," 553; Wilson's handwritten note to Colby, on Colby's letter to Wilson, August 9, 1920, Colby Papers, box 3A; also see discussion of note in John Spargo, "Bainbridge Colby," 201–8.
56. "Russia Approaching Recognition," *Literary Digest* 73 (April 15, 1922): 10–11, as quoted by Filene, *Americans and the Soviet Experiment*, 90; Hoff Wilson, *Ideology and Economics*, 29.
57. Spargo to Colby, July 31, 1920, as quoted in Radosh, "Spargo and Wilson's Russian Policy," 555.
58. D.M. Smith, *Bainbridge Colby*, 68; W.A. Williams, *American-Russian Relations*, 173; Tsvetkov, *Shestnadtsat' Let Nepriznaniia*, 240; McFadden, *Alternative Paths*, 295; C.A. White, *British and American Commercial Relations*, 140.
59. D.M. Smith, *Bainbridge Colby*, 68.
60. Davis, quoted in U.S. Congress, *Conditions in Russia*, 215; Davis to Alton B. Parker, January 8, 1921, RG 59, 861.01/400.
61. Murray, *Politics of Normalcy*, 15.
62. Eugene Debs, freed on December 24, 1921, was the outstanding example.
63. See Savitt, "To Fill A Void," 234; Womens' International League for Peace and Freedom, Bulletin no. 6 (June 1923): 6; Records of the WILPF, U.S. Section, reel 130.93, series E, serial publications; *Washington Post*, July 1923 (no date given), *Washington Post*, June 20, 1923, JGP, clippings file.

64. Libbey, *Gumberg and Soviet-American Relations*, 73. Also see Maddox, *Borah and American Foreign Policy*, 184; Salzman, *Reform and Revolution*, 310–11.
65. Libbey, *Gumberg and Soviet-American Relations*, 102–3.
66. Maddox, *Borah and American Foreign Policy*, 189; Lucy Branham, "From the Women's Committee for the Recognition of Russia Affiliated with the WILPF," Records of the WILPF, U.S. Section, series A5, box 1, literature and releases, 1919–1927; Libbey, *Gumberg and Soviet-American Relations*, 80.
67. Cyrus Huling to Hughes, April 21, 1921, RG 59, 661.1115/413; Kalinin and Secretary P. Zalutsky to the Congress of the United States and the president, March 21, 1921, RG 59, 661.1115/279.
68. W.A. Williams, *American-Russian Relations*, 182.
69. Perkins, *Charles Evans Hughes*, 188, 189; Glad, *Illusions of Innocence*, 151; Maddox, *Borah and American Foreign Policy*, 185.
70. Murray, *Harding Era*, 354; *The New York World*, April 24, 1922, JGP, clippings file.
71. Salzman, *Reform and Revolution*, 312.
72. The required adjustments included "guarantees of private property, the sanctity of contract and the rights of free labor." See Hughes to Albrecht, March 25, 1921, RG 59, 661.1115/275a.
73. Gompers to Hughes, March 15, 1921, RG 59, 661.1115/266; Hughes to Gompers, April 5, 1921, *FRUS, 1921* 2:773.
74. Boris M. Baievsky, Russian Division, to Klein, July 1, 1921, RG 151, 448-U.S. The SS *Vincennes Bridge* had 250,000 pairs of shoes and the SS *Panola* and *Plough City* had similar but undetermined quantities. The SS *Eastport* carried 10,000 cases of soap.
75. Report from John Tors, ARA representative in Reval, n.d., RG 151, 448-U.S; S. White, *Britain and the Bolshevik Revolution*, 180.
76. Horne quoted in A.J. Williams, *Trading with the Bolsheviks*, 62; see also *New York Times*, March 18, 1921. Highlights of the treaty included diplomatic immunity for commercial representatives and "reciprocity" in refraining from "any hostile act or propaganda." See Krassin, *Leonid Krassin*, 134, 133. On Soviet-British conflict in Central Asia after 1917, including the Bolshevik role in fomenting Indian revolution in 1920–1922, see Jacobson, *When the Soviet Union Entered World Politics*, 72–80.
77. *New York Post*, August 12, 1921; I. Nyurnberg, "In the Tsardom of the World Bourgeoisie," *Novy Mir* 1 (1922): 199. As Christine White notes, the treaty had great influence, despite the fact that its opponents could demonstrate that it did not bring trade back even to its prewar levels. Not only did the agreement contribute to a growing commercial relationship, but it also had an important "psychological impact," representing for the Soviets their first major success in what became a growing trend in foreign trade agreements, most spectacularly, the Rapallo Treaty with Germany in 1922. See White, *British and American Commercial Relations*, 174.
78. Hughes to Gompers, April 5, 1921, Hughes to Albrecht, March 25, 1921, *FRUS, 1921* 2:773, 768; Hughes to Hoover, March 22, 1922, container 35, reel 28, Hughes Papers; Poole, "Memorandum Concerning Trade with Soviet Russia," May 19, 1921, Poole to secretary, June 30, 1921, RG 59, 661.1115/333.
79. Poole to Hughes, March 7, 1923, box 4, Leland Harrison Papers; see Robert P. Skinner to Hughes, March 7, 1922, Robert F. Fernald to D.F. Murphy, May 26, 1922, RG 59, 861.50/285, 861.51/310.
80. See for instance, Wilbur J. Carr for the secretary of state to Evan E. Young, May 11, 1921, RG 59, 661.0015/-h; Hughes to William Wallace Breuer, May 8, 1922, RG 59, 661.1115/311; Poole to Hughes, April 20, 1922, RG 59, 661.1115/399.
81. See Samuel S. Hickop to Department of State, March 20, 1922, RG 59, 661.1115/389.

82. Poole to Dearing, May 5, 1921, May 16, 1921, Dearing to Poole, May 18, 1921, RG 59, 661.1115/333; Charles K. Rockwell to R.W. Bliss, April 12, 1921, RG 59, 661.1115/318.

83. D.C. Poole, memo, May 27, 1921, RG 59, 661.1115P81/180.

84. Baer, ed., *A Question of Trust*, 160. The East European Division replaced the Russian Division after recognition of the Baltic states in 1922.

85. See Libbey, *Gumberg and Soviet-American Relations*, 105; Salzman, *Reform and Revolution*, 312.

86. Robert P. Skinner to Hughes, March 7, 1922, RG 59, 861.50/285; Robins to Gumberg, November 7, 1922, AGP, box 2; Poole to secretary, April 28, 1922, RG 59, 661.1115/418.

87. W. Kliefoth to Hughes, August 1, 1922, RG 151, 448-U.S.

88. On the ARA's role in sustaining the Soviet regime, see Weissman, *Hoover and Famine Relief*, 201; Hoff Wilson, *Ideology and Economics*, 24.

89. Hoover to Wilson, March 28, 1919, box 20, PCP.

90. In this textbook, Hoover reflected his racist era by declaring that *"one white man equals from two to three of the colored races"* in mining work. See Hoover, *The Principles of Mining* (New York, 1909), 163, as cited in Nash, *The Engineer*, 505.

91. Nash, *The Engineer*, 479; Burner, *Hoover*, 54.

92. Burner, *Hoover*, 53–57; Nash, *The Engineer*, 444–45, 487–88.

93. See *Mining Magazine* (February 1914): 97, as quoted in Burner, *Hoover*, 56; Nash, *The Engineer*, 446.

94. Lloyd, *Aggressive Introvert*, 10; Burner, *Hoover*, 96; Best, *Politics of American Individualism*, 9; P. Johnson, *Modern Times*, 242.

95. See Coben, *Palmer*, 256; Burner, *Hoover*, 153–54; and on the attractions of Hoover's candidacy to both parties, see Newton D. Baker to Hugh Wallace, September 27, 1919, Baker Papers, reel 9, containers 11–12.

96. Murray, "Herbert Hoover and the Harding Cabinet," in Hawley, ed., *Hoover as Secretary of Commerce*, 21.

97. McFadden, "The Politics of Relief: American Quakers and Russian Bolsheviks, 1917–1921," unpublished conference paper, *Society for Historians of American Foreign Relations*, June 1994, 6, 21.

98. Henry C. Wolfe oral history file, October 17, 1969; Hoff Wilson, *Ideology and Economics*, 23.

99. The Soviet government was required to provide $10 million (20 million gold rubles) of the total. See Lenin, *CW* 43:163; "Declaration of the American Relief Administration," December 30, 1921, *RGAE, fond* 413, *op.* 10, *del.* 837, *l.* 35, 31.

100. Dr. Rufus Jones, the eminent chairman of the American Friends Service Committee (AFSC), assured Hoover that he himself was very concerned about "red-minded" people who were undermining the ARA's and AFSC's efforts. See Jones to Hoover, September 16, 1921, Jones Papers, box 54.

101. Hoover to Harding, February 10, 1922, JGP, box 24; Hoover to Liggett, January 23, 1922, draft letter, Hoover to senators on advisory council of American Committee for Russian Famine Relief, February 7, 1922, box 4, Misrepresentations File, HHPL. For additional material on Hoover's views about what he considered pro-Soviet relief groups, see Misrepresentations File, boxes 3 and 4.

102. Gilson Gardner to Harding, February 11, 1922, Harding Papers, box 2.

103. The vote was 187 to 71. Some congressmen were less than enthusiastic about the bill, such as West Virginian Woody Koontz, who felt that Americans also deserved money. See the *San Antonio Express*, February 14, 1921.

104. See discussion in Ball, *Russia's Last Capitalists*, 8–9; Trotsky, *Chto takoe SSSR i kuda on idët* [What kind of USSR and where is it going?] (Paris, n.d.), 16, as quoted in Pipes, *The Russian Revolution*, 672.

105. Conquest, *Harvest of Sorrow*, 57; "Isvesty of the Chairman of the Metelnich District Executive Committee of the Soviet of Workers, Army and Village Paupers Deputies," FBI Records, L0032, box 1. This was a commission attached to the Soviet of Peoples Commissars for combating the counterrevolution on the Czecho-Slovak front, Vyatsk section.

106. Nove, *Economic History of the U.S.S.R.*, 77, 120.

107. Evan E. Young to Hughes, April 10, 1922, RG 39, box 181, file 13. In 1921, Gosplan launched a fifteen-year plan called Goelro. This was not the first such blueprint of its kind; the Supreme Council of the National Economy (VSNKh), established in December 1917, had also promulgated a plan for industrial production in Soviet Russia. See Andres, *N.E.P.*, 4, 8; also, Lenin, "On a Unified Economic Plan: the New Economic Policy and Problems of Political Education," *Pravda* 39 (February 22, 1921). Excellent sources on NEP's development and implementation include Ball, *Russia's Last Capitalists*; Carr, *History of Soviet Russia*, vol. 3; and Nove, *Economic History of the U.S.S.R.*

108. See O'Connor, *Engineer of Revolution*, 166, and Ch. 9, passim; G.A. Smith, *Soviet Foreign Trade*, 31, 45, 49; Krassin, *Krassin*, 158; Kosikh, "Concession Policy of the Bolsheviks," 1.

109. "Five Years of the Russian Revolution and the Prospects of the World Revolution," report to the Fourth Congress of the Communist International, November 13, 1922, in Lenin, *CW* 33:421; Ball, *Russia's Last Capitalists*, 27–28; Libbey, *Gumberg and Soviet-American Relations*, 127–28; Sutton, *Western Technology*, 5.

110. "The Home and Foreign Policy of the Republic," December 23, 1921, *CW* 33:160. The American Communist party affirmed: "Official business relations, which we must support with the bourgeois government and representatives of capitalist world . . . is absolutely not 'treachery' to communism, but serves it. Authoritative representatives can and must use in their work the help of bourgeois specialists—not for political, but for technical work." See Central Committee to *Tovarishchi* (n.d.), *RTsKhIDNI, fond* 495, *op.* 1, *del.* 26, *l.* 136.

111. Nove, *Economic History of the U.S.S.R.*, 81–82.

112. Weissman, *Hoover and Famine Relief*, 199; Conquest, *Harvest of Sorrow*, 56; Hoover memorandum, January 1, 1919, box 40, PCP.

113. Levin, *Woodrow Wilson and World Politics*, 191; Mayer, *Politics and Diplomacy of Peacemaking*, 272.

114. Filene, *Americans and the Soviet Experiment*, 78; Weissman, *Hoover and Famine Relief*, 200; Hoff Wilson, *Ideology and Economics*, 23–24.

115. Lenin to Molotov for the Politburo of the Russian Communist party, August 11, 1921, Lenin to Zinoviev, August 22, 1921, *CW* 45:250–51, 263.

116. Gregory, "Stemming the Red Tide," *World's Work*, April 1921, 608–9; Yazikov to Plenipotentiary F.E.R. Kyshnarev, February 13, 1922, *RTsKhIDNI, fond* 5, *op.* 1, *del.* 2201; Robins to Gumberg, November 30, 1921, AGP, box 2.

117. Goodrich to Arthur K. Remmel, January 24, 1922, JGP, box 15; *Washington Globe*, December 21, 1921; *Washington Star*, December 23, 1921; *New York Times*, March 22, 1922.

118. Hoover to Haskell, February 16, 1922, JGP, box 19, Goodrich, "Manuscript on Various Trips to Russia, 1921–1922," Ch. R, 1, JGP, box 16.

119. See Gumberg to George Barr Baker, June 7, 1922; Gumberg to Robins, May 19, 1922; Alexander Gumberg to K.D. (Kenneth Durant), June 21, 1922; Gumberg to Robins, April 21, 1922, AGP, box 2. Hoover may have wanted to delay sending Gumberg until the negotiations were over for the Hague Conference. See Hoover to Robins, June 28, 1922, AGP, box 2. On Robins's views about Gumberg's role, see Robins to Gumberg, September 29, 1922, AGP, box 2.

120. Gumberg represented a Soviet-allied organization, the Far Eastern Republic, and more importantly, State Department Russian Affairs Chief Poole was aware that Gumberg

had orchestrated a "conspiracy to destroy Poole's credibility with Harding" in early 1922. See Libbey, *Gumberg and Soviet-American Relations*, 85, 192 n. 37.

121.   Golder, "Interview with Karl Radek Thursday Night, June 8, 1922," JGP, box 19; Goodrich, 1923, miscellaneous, JGP, box 15; Gumberg to Robins, December 19, 1921, AGP, box 2.

122.   Goodrich to Harding, June 1923 (undated), 3, JGP, box 16; *New York Herald*, November 1921, 11, JGP, box 15; Goodrich to Hoover, April 3, 1922, JGP, box 24, Goodrich, "The Situation in Russia," undated (1924?) JGP, box 15.

123.   Rhodes, "Goodrich and the 'Plain Facts,'" 3.

124.   Hoover to Will Hays, August 22, 1921, Herter to Fred W. Wile, April 8, 1922, box 276, ARA records, as quoted in Rhodes, "Goodrich and the 'Plain Facts,'" 21–22. In similar fashion, Hoover had limited his criticism of the Red Scare's domestic repression to private observations, believing that public opinion was "too reactionary [to heed] reason." See Rhodes, "Goodrich and the 'Plain Facts,'" 27; Hoover to Ray Lyman Wilbur, April 17, 1920, "1920 Campaign," PCP; Lloyd, *Aggressive Introvert*, 182.

125.   *Washington Post*, 1923 (no date given), WGP, clippings file. The travelers included Reps. James A. Frear of Wisconsin, Hamilton Fish, Jr., of New York, and William Beedy of Maine, and Sens. Edwin F. Ladd of North Dakota, William H. King of Utah, Burton Wheeler of Montana, Hiram Johnson of California, and Kenneth McKellar of Tennessee. Also see Rosta reports, October 10, 1923, October 16, 1923, *GARF, fond* 391, *op.* 2, *del.* 30, 1.172,1.71, *l.* 90; January 12, 1924, *GARF, fond* 391, *op.* 2, *del.* 45, *l.* 291–93.

126.   Goodrich to Hoover, January 30, 1923, CP, box 537; Golder to Herter, October 16, 1922, JGP, box 19.

127.   Goodrich to Arthur K. Remmel, January 24, 1922, JGP, box 15; Goodrich to Gumberg, March 16, 1923, Gumberg to Goodrich, March 22, 1923; AGP, box 3. The Sinclair concession is discussed in Ch. 7.

128.   C.A. White, *British and American Commercial Relations*, 180–81; Murray, *Harding Era*, 350; Poole to Hughes, September 20, 1921, RG 59, 661.1115/382.

129.   These government loans, according to the Treasury, "kept that great nation in the war and held the German troops upon the eastern front for six precious months," thus helping the Allied war effort. See *Annual Report of the Secretary of the Treasury on the State of the Finances for the Fiscal Year Ended June 30, 1919* (Washington, 1920), 65; and Russell Leffingwell's testimony in U.S. Congress, *Russian Bonds*, part 2, 91. Washington lent no money to the Imperial government during the First World War largely because of the tsar's anti-Semitic domestic policy. Banker Jacob H. Schiff was the leader in the campaign against American loans to tsarist Russia during the war. After the Provisional government took power, Schiff lent them $280,000 of his own money, which he would never see again. See Jacob Schiff to Boris Kamenka, May 31, 1917, Jacob Schiff to A.J. Sack, May 6, 1920, Schiff Papers. On Schiff, see Grayson, *Russian-American Relations in World War I*, 11, 29; Best, *To Free a People*, 210.

130.   See Burner, *Hoover*, 330, 187; *Combined Annual Reports of the World War Foreign Debt Commission, Fiscal Years 1922–27* (Washington, 1927), 81.

Chapter 4.
Economic Foreign Policy under Harding

1.   *Chicago News*, March 19, 1921, CP, box 536.

2.   Burner, *Hoover*, 161; Zieger, as quoted in Patrick J. O'Brien and Philip T. Rosen, "Hoover and the Historians: the Reconstruction of a President," in Dodge, ed., *Herbert Hoover and the Historians*, 98. A discussion of Hoover's interest in encouraging industrial organization and rationalization as well his sponsorship of the "associative" state is in Ellis Hawley, "Hoover and the Historians," in Dodge, ed., *Herbert Hoover and the Historians*,

23–24. For a rebuttal of the characterization of Hoover as a progressive, see Krog and Tanner, eds., *Hoover and the Republican Era*, x.

3.   *Commerce Reports*, January 16, 1922; Klein to Hoover, July 11, 1922; Klein to Hoover, May 24, 1924, box 393, CP; C.D. Snow, manager, Foreign Commerce Department, Chamber of Commerce, "A New and Enlarged Bureau of Foreign and Domestic Commerce," June 8, 1921, accession 160, U.S. Chamber of Commerce records, box 13; Stanley J. Quinn, "Centralization in Foreign Trade Matters," Seventh Annual Meeting, April 29, 1919, group III (foreign trade), 387, accession 160, U.S. Chamber of Commerce records, box 3; Brownlee, *Dynamics of Ascent*, 354; Hoover to Harding, June 15, 1923, CP, box 132.

4.   Christian A. Herter to Julius Klein, July 22, 1921, CP, box 393; Robins to Gumberg, March 8, 1921, CP, box 249; Hoover press release, March 25, 1921, CP. Jacobson notes that this lack of purchasing power was a main reason why the Germans had to look to the British and French to share the burden of investment in Russia in 1921; see idem, *When the Soviet Union Entered World Politics*, 83.

5.   The high value of the dollar helped attract gold to the United States. Hoover to Colby, March 16, 1921, *FRUS, 1921* 2:787, 762; Boris M. Baievsky, memo for the secretary of commerce, April 25, 1921, Barter and Commerce Corporation of America to Hughes, April 9, 1921, RG 59, 661.1115/285; S.P. Gilbert, undersecretary of the Treasury, to H.M. Foster, November 10, 1921, RG 59, 661.119/606; Federal Reserve *Bulletin* 7 (June 1921), 679, 681; Tass, March 30, 1928, *GARF, fond* 4459, *op*. 2, *del*. 328, *l*. 523, 524. For more on the willingness of anti-Bolshevik Western governments to accept Soviet gold, see C.A. White, *British and American Commercial Relations*, 160–169.

6.   Hoover to Hughes, December 3, 1921, Harding Papers, roll 181, box 2.

7.   It would be ironic if Hoover had neglected this idea, since the German rehabilitation scheme was strongly corporatist in nature. To work it required Western business interests to "balance self-interest and cooperation in such a way as to achieve stability and prosperity for all." Hogan, *Informal Entente*, 4.

8.   Frederick Dearing to Hughes, 21 December 1921, RG 59, 661.6215/1.

9.   Samuel A. Cross to E. Dana Durand, February 18, 1922, CP, box 534; Herrick, Paris, to secretary of state, January 23, 1922, RG 59, 661.1115/366.

10.   Dearing to American diplomatic and consular officers, November 19, 1921, RG 59, F.W. 661.1115/356a; document file note, May 3, 1929, from Kliefoth in Riga, RG 59, 661.1115/491.

11.   See *Who's Who in the Bureau of Foreign and Domestic Commerce* (1923), CP, box 536; E.D. Durand to Hoover, "Practicability of Private Investment by Americans," January 3, 1922, CP, box 535, 7; Durand, "Facts and Figures Concerning Russian Trade," *Proceedings of the Twenty-ninth Annual Convention of the National Association of Manufacturers*, May 19, 1924, 71–72; *Report of the Secretary of Commerce, 1921* (Washington, 1922), 68.

12.   Hoover to Charles A. Stone, December 7, 1921, CP, box 534.

13.   Harding to Hoover, December 10, 1921, Harding Papers, roll 181, box 2; Hoover to John M. Brewer, May 23, 1922, CP, box 535.

14.   Report of the Soviet Trade Delegation in London, March 6, 1922, "Legal Conditions for the Operation of Foreign Trade in Russia," CP, box 536.

15.   Poole to secretary, April 20, 1922, RG 59, 661.1115/399; C.A. White, *British and American Commercial Relations*, 182. Of this total, American sales comprehended almost 20 percent of Russia's imports for that year, in third place behind Great Britain at 29.1 percent and Germany at 25.3 percent. Between 1921 and 1923 over half of American shipments to Russia were related to the famine relief effort. See *Statistical Handbook of the U.S.S.R. for 1928*, 713, as cited in Budish and Shipman, *Soviet Foreign Trade*, 152–53; Hoover to John M. Brewer, May 23, 1922, CP, box 535; and Hoff Wilson, *Ideology and Economics*, 51.

16.   Hoover, press release no. 227, May 15, 1922; also see "United States Official Point of View," *Current History* 25 (February 1926): 624, CP, box 536; observations of

Consul Monnett B. Davis, at Department of State undergoing instruction, January 21, 1921, RG 59, no file no.; and discussion in Filene, *Americans and the Soviet Experiment*, 128–29.

17.   Gordon Lee to Thomas Taylor, May 1, 1922, RG 151, 448-U.S.; E.C. Ropes, "Foreign Credits to Soviet Russia," Special Circular no. 162, Finance and Investment Division (confidential), CP, box 536; E.C. Ropes to Mr. Stokes, July 13, 1925, CP, box 536; S.D. Winderman to Robert S. Alter, January 7, 1924, enclosed with letter, Robert S. Alter to W.H. Rastall, chief, Industrial Machinery Division, BFDC, BFDC 35/21/12.

18.   U.S. Department of Commerce, *Statistical Abstracts of the United States*, 1925, as cited in C.A. White, *British and American Commercial Relations*, 219. I. Taigin, "Why Soviet-American Trade Is Growing," *Izvestiia*, April 12, 1929, attached to letter, Coleman to secretary, April 19, 1929, RG 59, 661.111/10.

19.   This did not include the hefty transfer trade from the United States to Russia via Europe, necessitated by the primitive state of direct Soviet-American commercial and credit relations in the prewar era. Figures compiled from U.S. Department of Commerce, *Statistical Abstracts of the United States*, 1921, cited in C.A. White, *British and American Commercial Relations*, 26. White notes that in 1913 alone, American cotton exports to Russia were at least $50 million, "nearly *ten times* the amount given in the official U.S. returns"; idem, 13, emphasis in original. D.C. Poole reported that in 1913 two-thirds of the American cotton exported to Russia was actually indirectly provided through Germany. See Poole to Hughes, October 4, 1921, RG 59, 661.11/7.

20.   Hoover press release, July 15, 1925, CP, box 536. Despite the importance of this trade, Russia was still far behind Cuba or Canada, for example, in its ranking as a recipient of American exports. See "Russia: A Consideration of Conditions as Revealed by Soviet Publications," published by the Commission on Commerce and Marine, American Bankers Association, CP, box 535; D.C. Poole to Hughes, April 20, 1922, RG 59, 661.1115/399. See also Browder, *The Origins of Soviet-American Diplomacy*, 37.

21.   *Trade and Industrial Gazette* (February 24, 1928) declared that "contradictory tendencies run like a scarlet thread" through U.S. policy toward Russia; cited in A.J. Williams, *Trading with the Bolsheviks*, 47. For a critical discussion of Hoover's contradictions, see Hoff Wilson, *Ideology and Economics*, 29–30, and 130–31.

22.   Williams, *Trading with the Bolsheviks*, 47.

23.   For Soviet confirmation that the credit situation was improving also see Rosta, April 2, 1924, *GARF, fond* 391, *op.* 2, *del.* 69, *l.* 234; *Rosta* report, July 18, 1925, *GARF, fond* 391, *op.* 2, *del.* 21, *l.* 91.

24.   Hapgood to Borah, July 11, 1923, Gumberg to Borah, July 23, 1923, box 144, Borah Papers; Hurgin to Moisei Ilyich [Frumkin, acting people's commissar of foreign trade], June 25, 1923, *RGAE, fond* 413, *op.* 2, *del.* 1684, *l.* 42; Gumberg to Borah, September 24, 1925, November 24, 1925, Borah Papers, box 192.

25.   Lowitt, ed., *Journal of a Tamed Bureaucrat*, entry from May 11, 1925, 13–14.

26.   *New York Times*, October 10, 1925; Gumberg to Borah, October 15, 1925, Borah to Gumberg, October 16, 1925, George B. Baker to Gumberg, November 20, 1925, Gumberg to Baker, November 24, 1925, Borah Papers, box 192; Alexander Gumberg to Goodrich, November 28, 1925, AGP, box 4.

27.   Fink, *Genoa Conference*, 5–6; Lenin, comments on Draft Declaration, October 24, 1921, *CW* 45:356–58.

28.   Himmer, "Rathenau, Russia, and Rapallo," 149, 156–59; Jacobson, *When the Soviet Union Entered World Politics*, 82–84.

29.   Jacobson, *When the Soviet Union Entered World Politics*, 81, 82–84; O'Connor, *Diplomacy and Revolution*, 86; S. White, *Origins of Detente*, 46–47.

30.   Jacobson, *When the Soviet Union Entered World Politics*, 85; Fink, *Genoa Conference*, 40, 41 n. 19, 38–43, 193.

31.   See Jacobson, *When the Soviet Union Entered World Politics*, 84–85, 91–92.

32.   Himmer, "Rathenau, Russia, and Rapallo," 162–64, 171; O'Connor, *Diplomacy and Revolution*, 87.

33. Lenin to Chicherin, February 15, 1922, *CW* 45:469–70.

34. *New York World*, April 24, 1922.

35. See *Federal Reserve Bulletin* 8 (June 1922), 681; (August 1922), 935.

36. Himmer, "Rathenau, Russia, and Rapallo," 179.

37. See discussion in Fink, *Genoa Conference*, 168, 264–65.

38. In addition to concerns that participation would appear to imply recognition of Russia, the department also was perturbed that the issues of disarmament and reparations had been excluded from the agenda. Washington considered these to be major sources of Europe's financial problems. See Fink, *Genoa Conference*, 97–98.

39. *Free Press*, April 18, 1922, clippings file, JGP, box 16; Gompers, press release, January 12, 1922, Harding Papers, box 3; Central Committee of American Communist party to *Tovarishchi, RTsKhIDNI, fond* 495, *op.* 1, *del.* 26, *l.* 136. On communist infiltration of the AFL, see Gitlow, *I Confess*, 334–41; Draper, *Roots*, 304, 316–18.

40. *New York World*, April 24, 1922; Richard Child to Hughes, May 22, 1922, RG 59, IB 861.01/443.

41. Robins to Gumberg, April 9, 1922, May 13, 1922, AGP, box 2.

42. A discussion of British "consternation" and French "outrage" over Rapallo, is in S. White, *Origins of Detente*, 162–66; Lenin to Stalin, Kamenev, and L.D. Trotsky, April 18, 1922, *CW* 45:530–31.

43. O'Connor, *Diplomacy and Revolution*, 92.

44. Chicherin to Litvinov, April 11, 1923, on Lausanne Conference and foreign policy, *RTsKhIDNI, fond* 5, *op.* 1, *del.* 1988. See also Fink, *Genoa Conference*, 173, 306–7.

45. The party apparently found the efforts to have been successful, noting a few months after the conference that "those circumstances, which hindered European power[s] from taking [over] the Russian Soviet Government, were carried out exactly at the Genoa Conference." See Y.Y. Skololiev, "Our Relations with America," October–November 1922, *RTsKhIDNI, fond* 17, *op.* 84, *d.* 403.

46. See C.A. White, *British and American Commercial Relations*, 185.

47. See *New York World*, April 24, 1922; *Federal Reserve Bulletin* 8 (June, 1922), 681, 642, and (August 1922), 935; for the full text of the Soviet statement of May 11, 1922, see Degras, ed., *Soviet Documents in Foreign Policy*, 308–18 and especially 314–15.

48. See Fink, *Genoa Conference*, 304, 306.

49. P. Johnson, *Modern Times*, 232; Chamber of Commerce, *General Bulletin* 731 (July 24, 1925); 2229, accession 160, U.S. Chamber of Commerce Records, box 13; National Industrial Conference Board, *Trends in the Foreign Trade of the United States,* 11.

50. Hall, *International Transactions of the United States*, 106–7; Two recent interpretations of the folly of American loans to Weimar Germany, in particular, are Bernard V. Burke, "Ambassador Sackett, Chancellor Bruning, and the Nazis," and Manfred Berg, "'Safe for Democracy'? American Perceptions of Weimar Domestic and Foreign Politics, 1924–1929," both unpublished conference papers delivered at the annual meeting of the Society for Historians of American Foreign Relations, June 1994.

51. Hoover to Hughes, July 14, 1922, CP, box 286; Krasin to Central Committee, August 9, 1922, file 227, *DVP* 5:543.

52. Libbey, *Gumberg and Soviet-American Relations*, 98–99. Gumberg urged Robins to act quickly so as to coordinate the initiative with Goodrich's ongoing discussions in Russia. Also see Salzman, *Reform and Revolution*, 312.

53. Robins to Hoover, June 21, 1922, AGP, box 2.

54. Robins to Hoover, June 21, 1922, AGP, box 2.

55. Hughes to Hoover, July 15, 1922, CP, box 286; Alanson B. Houghton to State Department, August 28, 1922, RG 59, 861.50 Am 3/2; Hughes to Harding, August 21, 1922, Harding Papers, box 2; William Phillips to Houghton, August 29, 1922, RG 59, 861.50 Am 3/6. Houghton, former president of Corning Glass, had served on the board of directors of the Metropolitan Life Insurance Company, a firm that had lost substantial Russian holdings in the revolution. See Libbey, *Gumberg and Soviet-American Relations*, 99.

56. Bose, *American Soviet Relations*, 159.

57. Chicherin quoted in O'Connor, *Diplomacy and Revolution*, 114.

58. Chicherin to Stalin, August 8, 1922, file 226, Krasin to Central Committee, August 9, 1922, file 227, *DVP* 5:542–44.

59. Chicherin to Stalin, August 8, 1922, *DVP* 5:542–43; "Report of the Soviet Press on Conversations on the Revival of Russian-American Business Relations" (L.M. Karakhom to *New York Times*, August 19, 1922), September 15, 1922, file 252, *DVP* 5:579 (hereafter cited as "Report of Soviet Press").

60. Libbey, *Gumberg and Soviet-American Relations*, 99.

61. "Report of Soviet press," September 15, 1922, file 252, *DVP* 5:579, 580; Houghton to State Department, September 16, 1922, RG 59, 861.50 Am3/17; Krasin to Central Committee, August 9, 1922, file 227, *DVP* 5:543. For more on the Soviet press reaction to this "dispatch of an American investigative committee . . . [that] did not correspond to the principle of equality," see *GARF*, September 17, 1922, *fond* 391, *op*. 2, *del*. 15, *l*. 38.

62. Yazikov to Gillerson, August 1, 1922, *RTsKhIDNI, fond* 5, *op*. 1, *del*. 2201.

63. Houghton to State Department, September 16, 1922, RG 59, 861.50 Am3/17; Hughes to Houghton, August 23, 1922, container 35, reel 28, Hughes Papers; William Phillips to Houghton, August 29, 1922, RG 59, 861.50 Am 3/6.

64. Robins to Gumberg, August 19, 1922, AGP, box 2.

65. Robins to Gumberg, August 20, 1922, August 23, 1922, AGP, box 2.

66. Boris Skvirskii to C.I. Gillerson, September 18, 1922, 29, *DVP* 5:580; Harding to William Phillips, August 30, 1922, Harding Papers, roll 181, box 2; also see Murray, *Harding Era*, 353.

67. "*America*" (1922, n.d.), no author given, *RTsKhIDNI, fond* 17, *op*. 84, *del*. 403.

68. "*America*" (1922, n.d.), *RTsKhIDNI, fond* 17, *op*. 84, *del*. 403.

69. "*America*" (1922, n.d.), *RTsKhIDNI, fond* 17, *op*. 84, *del*. 403; Skvirskii to Litvinov, December 18, 1922, *RTsKhIDNI, fond* 5, *op*. 1, *del*. 2201.

70. "*America*" (1922, n.d.), *RTsKhIDNI, fond* 17, *op*. 84, *del*. 403; Bloomfield to Hughes, January 2, 1923, RG 59, 661.1115/430; *New York World*, December 31, 1922; Poole to Hughes, December 20, 1922, container 15, reel 12, Hughes Papers; Hughes to Bloomfield, January 5, 1923, RG 59, 661.1115/430; Goodrich to Gumberg, December 18, 1922, AGP, box 2.

71. S.R. Bertron to Hughes, November 23, 1922, RG 59, 661.1115/322. Chicherin had already told State Department representatives that he had no objection to such a businessmen's trip to Russia; it was the unilateral, state-sponsored inspection by a "committee of experts" that had bothered him that previous summer. See Chicherin to Houghton, August 28, 1922, attached to Houghton to Phillips, August 29, 1922, RG 59, 861.50 Am 3/7; Hughes to Bertron, November 21, 1922, Bertron to Hughes, November 17, 1922, Poole memorandum, November 20, 1922, RG 59, 661.1115/422, /423.

72. Skvirskii to Litvinov, December 18, 1922, *RTsKhIDNI, fond* 2201, *op*. 1; "Summary of conversation with Mr. Meyer Bloomfield on February 19, 1923," AGP, box 3.

73. Julian E. Gillespie to State Department, February 2, 1923, RG 59, 861.50 Am 3/34; Chicherin to Litvinov, January 14, 1923, *RTsKhIDNI*, fond 5, op 1, del 1988.

CHAPTER 5.
THE SOVIET COMMERCIAL MISSIONS UNDER
HARDING, COOLIDGE, AND HOOVER

1. Bureau of Investigation report, May 25, 1922, McNamee to Burns, April 19, 1922, RG 38, box 197, A8-5/EF61.

2. *Washington* Post, December 5, 1922, clippings file, JGP, box 17; Savitt, "To Fill a Void," 216; Maxim Litvinov to Skvirskii, November 28, 1922, *DVP* 6:22.

3. Skvirskii to Chicherin, November 22, 1922, *RTsKhIDNI, fond* 5, *op*. 1, *del*. 2201.

Skvirskii visited regularly with D.C. Poole. See Poole to William Phillips, February 9, 1923, Harrison Papers, box 4; Poole to Phillips, December 4, 1922, RG 59, 861.01/812.

4. *Washington Post*, December 5, 1922, clippings file, JGP, box 16. Gumberg doubted that their posts had been very effective, since they could get information only from the ARA or from "unofficial agents." Gumberg to Jerome Davis, May 7, 1923, AGP, box 3.

5. Skvirskii to Litvinov, December 18, 1922, *RTsKhIDNI, fond* 5, *op*. 1, *del*. 2201; Libbey, *Gumberg and Soviet-American Relations*, 96; Litvinov to Skvirskii, March 27, 1923, *DVP* 6:240.

6. Burns to Capt. Luke McNamee, director, Naval Intelligence, September 5, 1923, RG 38, A8-5/EF61.

7. Libbey, *Gumberg and Soviet-American Relations*, 111.

8. Burns to Capt. Luke McNamee, director, Naval Intelligence, September 5, 1923, RG 38, A8-5/EF61; Gumberg to Goodrich, March 22, 1923, Gumberg to Chamberlain, March 15, 1923, Burton K. Wheeler to Gumberg, June 23, 1923, AGP, box 3; *Washington Post*, Sept 19, 1923; Savitt, "To Fill a Void," 216.

9. Burns to director, Military Intelligence Division, October 29, 1923, RG 165, 10110-G-42; Corson and Crowley, *The New KGB*, 298.

10. *Krasnaya Gazeta*, January 21, 1926, as quoted in Finder, *Red Carpet*, 22. For records of Hammer's shipments, see, for example, *Tallina Tolliwalitsus* bills of lading, May 19, 1920, May 17, 1920; manifest, SS *Lake Frumet* and *Wheeling Mold*, June 30, 1920, *AVPRF fond* 507, *op*. 5b, *del*. 5, *papka* 35; *del*. 14, *papka* 3b.

11. Hammer, *Hammer*, 71, 48; Gitlow, *I Confess*, 25.The Wisconsin State Historical Society's records show that Armand's father did sign him up in 1915 as a member of the Socialist Workers party, but his age then (sixteen) undermines the significance of this act. Nevertheless, as Klehr, Haynes, and Firsov demonstrate with documents from the Communist party archive (see, for example, *RTsKhIDNI fond* 495, *op*. 19, *del*. 612, 613; *fond* 515, *op*. 1, *del*. 422 [I]), Hammer and his father served as conduits for Soviet funds to the American Communist party during the 1920s; see idem, *Secret World*, 26–30.

12. The causes of her death were unclear, since there was an epidemic of Spanish flu at the time. See Finder, *Red Carpet*, 11; Hammer, *Hammer*, 75–81, 88; Weinberg, *Hammer*, 35, 25, 31.

13. Weinberg, *Hammer*, 33; R.C. Williams, *Russian Art and American Money*, 197; Hammer, *Hammer*, 66–67.

14. Hammer, *Romanoff Treasure*, 3.

15. Americans were required to surrender their passports upon entering Russia for which they would receive a receipt redeemable upon their return. See F.M. Dearing to Rafailovich, April 23, 1921, RG 59, 661.1115/284. Also see Weinberg, *Hammer*, 35–36.

16. Hammer, *Romanoff Treasure*, 3; Lenin, *CW* 45:337.

17. Weinberg, *Hammer*, 36–37; Hammer, *Hammer*, 116–17, 121, 100, 109; Gillette, "Armand Hammer," 357; Lenin, *CW* 45:337.

18. Lenin to Zinoviev, May 11, 1922, Lenin to Martens, October 15, 1921, Lenin to Stalin, May 24, 1922, *CW* 45:544, 338, 559.

19. See C.A. White, "Ford in Russia," 85–86; Nevins and Hill, *Ford: Expansion and Challenge*, 2: 673; Hammer, *Hammer*, 135–38; Bryson, *The World of Armand Hammer*, 45. The combined capitalization of Hammer's clients added up to more than $1 billion. See Hoff Wilson, *Ideology and Economics*, 74.

20. Its first million dollars in sales included $250,000 in cotton, $40,000 in tin, $65,000 in Ford vehicles, $50,000 in typewriters, and $20,000 in mechanical tools. Hammer, *Hammer*, 138; *New York Times*, August 12, 1923, 6. On Soviet shipments to the United States, see R.C. Williams, *Russian Art and American Money*, 209; Hammer, *Hammer*, 160.

21. Herbert W. Gruber to New York District Office, March 19, 1924; A.J. Barnaud to BFDC, April 1, 1924, C.J. Mayer to director, BFDC, May 14, 1924, RG 151, 448-U.S, 448X-US.

22. Lewery to Mayer, July 23, 1924, RG 151, 448-U.S.

23. Hammer, *Hammer*, 138; Rosta Press Agency reports, April 1, 1924, April 2, 1924, and December 22, 1924, *GARF, fond* 391, *op.* 2, *del.* 69, *l.* 236, *del.* 69, *l.* 234, *del.* 66, *l.* 16; D.C. Poole to Phillips, September 6, 1922, RG 59, 661.1116/54; Sutton, *Western Technology*, 286; Charles D. Orth, Sisal Sales Coporation, to Fred M. Dearing, March 4, 1922, RG 59, 661.1115/388. Besides Dollar, other firms selling machinery to Russia were Arcos (the American branch of the British Soviet trading agency), Baker, Carver, and Morrell, and Mett Engineering Company. See Robert S. Alter to W.H. Rastall, January 12, 1924, S.D. Winderman to Alter, January 7, 1924, BFDC 35/21/12; Lewery to Mayer, July 23, 1924, RG 151, file 448-U.S.

24. Clinton W. Gilbert, "An American Banker Whose Advice Carries Weight in Russia," *New York Evening Post*, July 30, 1929. Gumberg was introduced to Borah by Robins in December 1922. See Libbey, *Gumberg and Soviet-American Relations*, 104, and W.A. Williams, *American-Russian Relations*, 202. Libbey's is the best book about Gumberg's role.

25. Gumberg to Chamberlain, March 15, 1923, AGP, box 3.

26. Gumberg to Chamberlain, March 15, 1923, AGP, box 3.

27. See Nogin, "On the work of the Chief Cotton Committee [*GKhK*]," 1922, *RTsKhIDNI, fond* 145, *op.* 1, *del.* 16; Libbey, *Gumberg and Soviet-American relations*, 129.

28. *The All-Union Textile Syndicate*, 3; "Report of Soviet Press," September 15, 1922, 252, *DVP* 5:579; the Chief Cotton Committee and the All-Russian Textile Syndicate in the Presidium of *Vesenkha*, "On the Question of Buying Foreign Cotton," October 9, 1922, *RGAE, fond* 4372, *op.* 11, *del.* 8, *l.* 186.

29. Rosta, January 19, 1924, *GARF, fond* 391, *op.* 2, *del.* 45, *l.* 183; February 15, 1924, *fond* 391, *op.* 2, *del.* 69, *l.* 76, 77; Viktor Pavlovich Nogin, "*Poezdka v Coedinennikh Shtatakh*" [Train journey in the United States], April 7, 1924, *RTsKhIDNI, fond* 145, *op.* 1, *del* 120; Edward T. Pickard to Mr. Taylor, April 26, 1926, CP, box 536; W.L. Clayton to Morris Sheppard, July 2, 1924, AGP, box 4. The cotton brokers of Bremen were not so pleased by the loss of their profitable trade. See Rosta, March 26, 1924, *GARF, fond* 391, *op.* 2, *del.* 69, *l.* 170.

30. Goodrich to Hughes, June 26, 1923, AGP, box 3; *RGAE, fond* 7770, *op.* 14, *del.* 14, *l.* 12. Gumberg to Robins, October 3, 1923, RRP, box 19; Rosta, April 2, 1924, *GARF, fond* 391, *op.* 2, *del.* 69, *l.* 234.

31. As Clayton wrote to Sen. Morris Sheppard, lobbying for a change in policy, "It seems to me rather inconsistent that our Government should not give some legal and official status to the acts which its citizens are at liberty to do." W.L. Clayton to Morris Sheppard, July 2, 1924, note from Goodrich to Gumberg, January 1924, AGP, box 4; *The All-Union Textile Syndicate*, 19.

32. Rosta, April 2, 1924, *GARF, fond* 391, *op.* 2, *del.* 69, *l.* 234; "Russia's Cotton Come-back," *Commerce and Finance* 14 (October 7, 1925): 1977; Smith to William Borah, February 24, 1925, Borah Papers, box 192.

33. Announcement, ARTS, February 4, 1925, Gumberg to Goodrich, February 20, 1924, balance sheet and statement of expenditure for the fiscal period from December 13, 1923, to September 30, 1924, prepared by the Marwick, Mitchell, and Company, "U.S. Hard Hit in Shipping to Russia," *New York Times* (n.d.), 1924, all in AGP, box 4.

34. "Russia's Cotton Come-back," *Commerce and Finance* 14 (October 7, 1925): 1977; Fithian, "Soviet-American Economic Relations," 128–29; Hoover, confirming telephone call from Mr. Phenix at the State Department, October 26, 1925, CP, box 269; K. (no name given) to Gumberg, confidential, 1925, AGP, box 4.

35. "Success of Conversations of Tov. Nogin," January 10, 1924, *GARF, fond* 391, *op.* 2, *del.* 45, *l.* 300; Chicherin to the Central Committee of the RKP, August 3, 1921, *RTsKhIDNI, fond* 17, *op.* 84, *del.* 234; Tass, February 12, 1928, *GARF, fond* 4459, *op.* 2,

del. 210, *l.* 267. National City ended up losing nearly $10 million. See Cleveland and Huertas, *Citibank*, 101. Schley, however, never reported Chase having any trouble collecting its Soviet bills. See Heymann, *We Can Do Business with Russia*, 139.
 36. "Russia's Cotton Come-back," 1977; Sutton, *Western Technology*, 278; Libbey, *Gumberg and Soviet-American Relations*, 129.
 37. Gumberg letter, July 25, 1925, AGP, box 4; *RGAE, fond* 413, *op.* 10, *del.* 838, *l.* 67–69, 70.
 38. Coleman to secretary, November 19, 1925, RG 59, 661.11/10; "Russia's Cotton Come-back," *Commerce and Finance* 14 (October 7, 1925):1977; I. Taigin, "Why Soviet-American Trade Is Growing," *Izvestiia*, April 12, 1929, attached to letter, Coleman to secretary, April 19, 1929, RG 59, 661.111/10.
 39. Rosta, April 1, 1924, *GARF, fond* 391, *op.* 2, *del.* 69, *l.* 236. Its president was Paul J. Ziev, former trade representative to Latvia, and other officers and participants included Dr. Isaac J. Sherman of Arcos, Johann G. Ohsol of Products Exchange Company, and Isaiah Hoorgin of Derutra. Amtorg had a three-year agreement with the People's Commissariat of Foreign Trade for licenses to import and export "all kinds" of raw and finished goods, and Amtorg would pay the commissariat 50–60 percent of its profit. See contract, Isaiah Hoorgin, chairman of the board of directors, Amtorg, and Moisei Frumkin, acting people's commissar of foreign trade, USSR People's Commissariat of Foreign Trade, November 28, 1924, 148285, enclosure 50732, Office of the General Counsel, Bureau of Internal Revenue, Washington.
 40. White, commissioner in Riga, to secretary of state, RG 59, 661.1115 Amtorg Trading Corporation/2; Rosta, April 2, 1924, *GARF, fond* 391, *op.* 2, *del.* 69, *l.* 234; Coleman to secretary, January 21, 1924, RG 59, 661.00/82.
 41. Minutes, meeting of the board of directors, accession 1411, National Association of Manufacturers, February 19–20, 1924, reel 1, 9; Durand to Benny, April 14, 1924, RG 151, 448-U.S.
 42. See Hoff Wilson, *Ideology and Economics*, 67–68; Hoover quoted by Earl Constantine, in Constantine to Hoover, May 7, 1924, RG 151, 448-U.S.
 43. Isaac J. Sherman, "Ways and Means for Trading with Russia," *Proceedings of the Twenty-ninth Annual Convention of the National Association of Manufacturers*, May 19, 1924, 52–55.
 44. Isaac J. Sherman, "Commercial Credits in Russia," *Proceedings of the Thirty-first Annual Convention of the National Association of Manufacturers*, October 6, 1926, 218–23 (hereafter cited as *Proceedings of the Thirty-first Annual Convention*).
 45. Norman J. Gould, introductory remarks, *Proceedings of the Thirty-first Annual Convention*, October 6, 1926, 26–27.
 46. Gumberg to Goodrich, June 2, 1925, Liebenstein to Gumberg, December 30, 1925, AGP, box 4.
 47. Carver to Gumberg, May 19, 1924, Carver letter, 1925 (n.d.) AGP, box 4; *New York Times*, June 25, 1926, ARCCP, box 21; Heymann, *We Can Do Business with Russia*, 85; Saul Bron, as quoted in *Ekonomicheskaya Zhizn*, June 1, 1928, attached to letter, Coleman to secretary of state, June 12, 1928, RG 59, 661.1111/19.
 48. Hugh L. Cooper, "Possibilities in Russia," *Proceedings of the Thirty-first Annual Convention*, October 5, 1926, 205; "Four Giant Electric Generators for Russia," undated, Hammond file L4142, G.E. historical file.
 49. Kargina, "Soviet-American Trade," 13; Libbey, *Gumberg and Soviet-American Relations*, 129; American Friends Service Committee, "The United States and the Soviet Union," pamphlet collection, Hoover Institution. On Chase's financing also see "Success of Conversations of Tov. Nogin," January 10, 1924, *RGAE, fond* 391, *op.* 2, *del.* 45, *l.* 300.
 50. Pamphlet, luncheon of the American-Russian Chamber of Commerce, Banker's Club of America, February 17, 1928, ARCCP, box 21; Kargina, "Soviet-American Trade," 131.

51.   Smith quoted in pamphlet, luncheon of the American-Russian Chamber of Commerce, Banker's Club of America, February 17, 1928, ARCCP, box 21. On Smith's concessions see Sutton, *Western Technology*, 284–85. Despite these patriotic sentiments, Smith most probably was a communist, according to Libbey, *"American-Russian Chamber of Commerce,"* 240.

52.   J.E. Hoover to H.H. Hough, March 30, 1925, Mark Brooke to Hough, April 3, 1925, RG 38, A8-5/EF61.

53.   Streloff's report, attached to W.R. Sayles to R.H. Grayson, December 16, 1926, RG 38, box 196, A8-5/23 (12–16); *"400 Smuggled Liberty Motors Traced to Soviet,"* *New York Herald Tribune*, November 26, 1930, AGP, box 8b.

54.   See Filene, *Americans and the Soviet Experiment*, 114; D. Smith, *Bainbridge Colby*, 68. On Amtorg's espionage, see, for example, Siegel, "Soviet Industrial Espionage in the United States during the Interwar Years and World War II," unpublished conference paper, Society for Historians of American Foreign Relations, June 1995; Corson and Crowley, *New KGB*, 317; Dallin, *Soviet Espionage*, 397–99, 411–12; Brown and MacDonald, *Field of Red*, 342; U.S. Congress, *Investigation of Un-American Propaganda Activities in the U.S.* 9:5810.

55.   Lenin to Stalin, May 24, 1922, *CW* 45:559.

CHAPTER 6.
TRADE AND FOREIGN POLICY, 1923–1929

1.   Budish and Shipman, *Soviet Foreign Trade*, 1; Rosta, *GARF, fond* 391, *op.* 2, *del.* 21, *l.* 713; *Izvestiia*, February 20, 1923, RG 59, 761.00/28.

2.   Rosta, *GARF, fond* 391, *op.* 2, *del.* 21, *l.* 714, 503.

3.   See Killen, "Search for a Democratic Russia," 253–54. For another example from the mid-twenties when the United States "recognized Russian sovereignty even as it refused to recognize the Soviet authorities" on a frozen Arctic island, see Richard G. Kurial, "Wrangle over Wrangel: Soviet-American Concord in the 1920s," unpublished conference paper, Society for Historians of American Foreign Relations, June 1994, 42–43.

4.   Guerra Everett, chief, section of legal information, Division of Commercial Laws, to Intelligence Division, June 2, 1925, attached to E.C. Ropes to Robert F. Kelley, June 6, 1925, RG 59, 811.607AQ/96.

5.   Hurgin to Krasin, August 24, 1923, *RGAE, fond* 413, *op.* 2, *del.* 1684, *l.* 138; Berzin to Litvinov, January 26, 1922, *DVP* 5:66.

6.   See, for instance, "Intercourse with Territory under Bolshevik Control," Phillips to Senator Wadsworth, November 1, 1919, Russian series, no. 2, RG 59, F.W. 661.119/471; Hughes to Quarton, December 18, 1923, RG 59, 711.61/71. Soviet historians Sivachev and Yakovlev claim that assertions of Soviet propaganda were "obviously unfounded," although they do not find this the case with American "counterrevolutionary propaganda." Still, they do allow that a "Trotskyist-Zinovievist bloc" within Russia was providing the West grounds "for accusing the USSR of unleashing 'world revolution'"; see idem, *Russia and the United States*, 69, 75–76, 82.

7.   See Soviet representative in Britain (Berzin) to Maxim Litvinov, January 26, 1922, and files 150–54, May 8, 1922, *DVP* 5:65, 293–349 passim.

8.   *Daily Worker*, May 16, 1924; *New York Herald*, March 25, 1921. On public opinion, see Filene, *Americans and the Soviet Experiment*, 264; Hoff Wilson, *Ideology and Economics*, 131; Bishop, *Roosevelt-Litvinov Agreements*, 7–8; Bennett, *Recognition of Russia*, 83.

9.   Ellis, *Kellogg*, 14; Maddox, *Borah and American Foreign Policy*, 183, 214.

10.   See committee to director of public safety, City Hall, Philadelphia, June 15, 1922, WILPF Pennsylvania branch papers, box 40; "From the Women's Committee for the Rec-

ognition of Russia Affiliated with the WILPF," 1923 (n.d.), Records of the WILPF, U.S. Section, series A5, box 1.

11. The chairman of the Foreign Policy Association, James G. McDonald, believed that the Soviets were "scrapping their communistic theories" and "Lenine tactics" in favor of "capitalistic methods" in business, farming, and trade areas. See *New York Herald Tribune*, June 21, 1926.

12. The description of Branham is Armand Hammer's in idem, *Romanoff Treasure*, 98; see also Elizabeth W. Clark to Kameneva, May 10, 1929, *GARF, fond* 5283, *op*. 3, *del*. 61, *l*. 24; R.C. Williams, *Russian Art and American Money*, 203, Libbey, *Gumberg and Soviet-American Relations,* 106. Branham taught in Columbia's extension program during 1920–1921.

13. Gumberg to Robins, November 14, 1922, AGP, box 2; Gumberg to Clinton W. Gilbert, May 13, 1925, AGP, box 4.

14. Hughes, press release, March 21, 1923, *FRUS, 1923,* 2:755, 756; WILPF *Bulletin* 6 (June 1923): 1; Branham to members, March 31, 1923, WCRRP.

15. See, for example, the *New York Times*, March 22, 1923, 1. By contrast, wrote Branham, "Our statement to Mr. Hughes . . . was smothered in the papers." See Branham to Members, March 31, 1923, WCRRP.

16. Yu. Steklov, "A Step Backward—And What a Step!" *Izvestiia*, March 27, 1923; Gumberg to Robins, March 22, 1923, RRP, box 19.

17. Ella Boynton and Louisa Atkinson, April 3, 1923, WCRRP.

18. See attack by R.M. Whitney, "Peace at Any Old Price," pamphlet on the annual conference of the WILPF in Washington, March 13–16, 1923; Maud Wood Park to John L. Weeks, secretary of war, April 2, 1924, Weeks to Park, April 16, 1924, all in Records of the WILPF, U.S. Section, general correspondence, 1919–1924, box 1, folder 13; undated statement relating to the withdrawal of the WILPF from the National Council of Women, January 1925, Hull Papers, reel 75.5, cited in Pois, "Politics and Process of Organizing for Peace," 198; Elizabeth Cope to Hannah Hull, February 4, 1925, and Women's Committee for the Recognition of Russia to members, January 27, 1925, Hull Papers, reels 75.1 and 75.5.

19. Gumberg to Borah, March 23, 1923, Gumberg to Robins, January 12, 1923, AGP, box 3. Also see discussion in W.A. Williams, *American-Russian Relations*, 203.

20. Robins to Gumberg, October 23, 1922, AGP, box 2.

21. Gumberg to Borah, April 20, 1923, Gumberg to Robins, April 1, 1923, AGP, box 1. On American reaction to the execution, see Libbey, *Gumberg and Soviet-American Relations*, 108.

22. Gumberg to Goodrich, June 4, 1923, Goodrich to Gumberg, June 18, 1923, draft letter, Robins to Harding, May, 1923, AGP, box 3.

23. Robins to Will Hays, June 5, 1923, AGP, box 3; W.A. Williams, "Raymond Robins and Russian-American Relations, 1917–1938," 95, discussion in idem, *American-Russian Relations*, 204, and Williams's note on letter, Robins to Goodrich, May 31, 1923, AGP, box 3.

24. Bennett, *Recognition of Russia*, 62. Harding's illness is addressed in Ferrell, *Ill-Advised*, 20–27.

25. Gumberg to Benjamin (B.E.) Gumberg, August 22, 1923, AGP, box 3; on Harding's death see also McCoy, *Quiet President*, 181.

26. See Isaiah Hurgin to Krasin, August 24, 1923; "New President," August 24, 1923, *RGAE, fond* 413, *op*. 2, *del*. 1684, *l*. 137, 87; minutes, board of directors, accession 1411, National Association of Manufacturers, November 6, 1919, reel 1, 5.

27. Gumberg to Wheeler, August 22, 1923, box 3, AGP; Hurgin to Krasin, August 24, 1923, *RGAE, fond* 413, *op*. 2, *del*. 1684, *l*. 137l.

28. Coolidge, first annual message to Congress, December 6, 1923, in Moran, ed., *Calvin Coolidge, 1872–1933*, 35; *Congressional Record*, 68th Cong., 1st sess., 65 (1923), 97, as cited in Bose, *American Soviet Relations*, 47.

29. Chicherin to Coolidge, December 16, 1923, *FRUS, 1923* 2:787. For the original Russian version, see Chicherin to Coolidge, December 16, 1923, file 613, *DVP* 6:547; on Gumberg and Robins's role, see Libbey, *Gumberg and Soviet-American Relations*, 115.
30. Hughes to Quarton (for transmittal to Chicherin), December 18, 1923, *FRUS, 1923* 2:788.
31. Baer, *A Question of Trust*, 147; RG 59, file 123K282/24a; on Kelley's testimony, see Propas, "Creating a Hard Line toward Russia," 211. On Borah's Senate fight, see discussion in Maddox, *Borah and American Foreign Policy*, 205–7, and Johnson, *Peace Progressives*, 144–45. The hearings are in U.S. Senate, *Recognition of Russia*.
32. Libbey, *Gumberg and Soviet-American Relations*, 116.
33. Borah to Don Marlin, December 10, 1924, Borah Papers, box 192.
34. Libbey, *Gumberg and Soviet-American Relations*, 146; Kargina, "Soviet-American Trade," 16.
35. *Narkomvneshtorg* to *S.T.O.* (Council for Labor and Defense), "Political Position in the United States" [description of secret and top secret papers sent to STO in 1924], documents from Berlin to the national commissar of foreign trade, July 18, 1924, *RGAE, fond* 413, *op.* 5, *del.* 1327, *l.* 23, 24. Skvirskii to Chicherin, November 16, 1922, *RTsKhIDNI, fond* 91, *op.* 1, *del* 72; Stalin, letter to the editor of the *Daily Worker*, 1922 (n.d.), *RTsKhIDNI, fond* 558, *op.* 1, *del* 2788.
36. *Narkomvneshtorg* to *S.T.O.*, "Political Position in the United States," July 18, 1924, *RGAE, fond* 413, *op.* 5, *del.* 1327, *l.* 23, 22; Rosta, November 24, 1923, *GARF, fond* 391, *op.* 2, *del.* 29, *l.* 82; *New York Times*, July 15, 1923.
37. Gumberg to La Follette, June 18, 1923, AGP, box 3; "America and the U.S.S.R.," Rosta, November 24, 1923, *GARF, fond* 391, *op.* 2, *del.* 29, *l.* 116. On the Progressives' attitude toward the Soviet issue, see Schuman, *American Policy toward Russia since 1917*, 237.
38. Robins to Gumberg, August 5, 1923, AGP, box 3; Robins as quoted in Salzman, *Reform and Revolution*, 315.
39. *Washington Post*, June 20, 1923, JGP, clippings file.
40. *New York American*, July 11, 1923, *RGAE, fond* 413, *op.* 10, *del.* 360, *l.* 1; Richard Child to Hughes, May 22, 1922, RG 59, IB 861.01/443.
41. Hughes to Irving T. Bush, president of Chamber of Commerce of New York, October 12, 1922, Hughes Papers, reel 12, container 17; Hughes to Coolidge, August 7, 1923, Hughes Papers, reel 16, container 21.
42. "Russian-American Relations," *GARF, fond* 391, *op.* 2, *del.* 45, *l.* 259, January 14, 1924; Etta Tuch, "Memorandum for Mr. Martens," April 10, 1920, FBI Martens, vol. 2.
43. Durant to Gumberg, February 21, 1925, AGP, box 4; American Foreign Service report from Riga to State Department, February 27, 1925, RG 59, 861.01/982. Durant was a Philadelphian who had formerly worked for George Creel in the Committee for Public Information during the war, and who had, according to William C. Bullitt, become "violently disgusted" when the U.S. published the fraudulent Sisson documents alleging that Germany was funding the Bolshevik revolution for its own expansionist purposes. Durant had subsequently "swung over completely" to the Soviet side. See Bullitt to R. Walton Moore, February 22, 1936, Moore Papers, box 18. On Japan's 1924 treaty with Moscow, see Borah to John A. Armbruster, July 17, 1924, Borah Papers, box 167.
44. Coleman to Kellogg, March 24, 1925, Coleman to Grew, March 24, 1925, RG 59, F.W. 861.01/984.
45. *New York Herald*, January 12, 1925; State Department memorandum, "The Essential Factors Involved in Establishing Normal Relations with the Russian Regime," February 1925, 4, 12, attached to letter from Hughes to Hoover, February 28, 1925, CP, box 286.
46. Elihu Root to Ivy Lee, March 2, 1926, enclosed in Lee to Borah, March 3, 1926, Borah Papers, box 218; on Communist advocacy, see William J. Burns to Norman Armour, August 30, 1923, RG 59, 811.00B/212.

47.   Kellogg to F.W.B. Coleman, March 25, 1925, RG 59, 861.01/984; Leland Harrison to James G. McDonald, May 18, 1926, CP, box 535; Ellis, *Kellogg*, 14, 235.

48.   Ellis, *Kellogg*, 6; Baer, ed. *A Question of Trust*, 168; Ellis, *Kellogg*, 8, viii.

49.   Kelley, quoted in Schulzinger, *Making of the Diplomatic Mind*, 131; M.J. McDermott, State Department memorandum of press conference, November 30, 1927, RG 39, box 188, 134; Robert F. Olds to Charles Muchnic, November 28, 1927, RG 59, 861.51 Am 3/1, *FRUS, 1927* 3:654; *Chicago News*, March 19, 1921.

50.   Young to secretary, February 23, 1924, RG 59, 661.1115/451.

51.   Enclosure, "Statement Concerning the Activities of the Department of State: Russia," in Kellogg to Senator Butler, February 23, 1928, *FRUS, 1928* 3:824, 825.

52.   See Propas, "Creating a Hard Line toward Russia," 209, 219, 221.

53.   See Ch. 7, n. 90 on Averell Harriman's loan to Moscow in 1928.

54.   Rather than taking the provocative step of sending gold with the Bolshevik mark, Reeve Schley had hoped the Soviets would send bullion with another government's imprint. See Libbey, *Gumberg and Soviet-American Relations*, 152; Tass, February 11, 1928, *GARF, fond* 4459, *op.* 2, *del.* 328, *l.* 664.

55.   Tass, March 7 and March 8, 1928, *GARF, fond* 4459, *op.* 2, *del.* 328, *l.* 606, 600; resolution of the board of directors of the American-Russian Chamber of Commerce, 1928, AGP, box 6A; Tass, 1929, *GARF, fond* 4459, *op.* 2, *del.* 329, *l.* 63; Libbey, *Gumberg and Soviet-American Relations*, 157–58. See also Libbey, "New Study Areas for Soviet-American Relations," 16–18.

56.   Tass, March 30, 1928, *GARF, fond* 4459, *op.* 2, *del.* 328, *l.* 523.

57.   See chapter 4.

58.   Leighton W. Rogers to J.C. Dunn, chief, Division of Protocol, September 29, 1928, note, Dunn to Myson, October 1, 1928, Kelley memorandum, October 8, 1928, Francis White to Rogers, October 12, 1928, RG 59, 579.6R1/104.

59.   Enclosure no. 2 to confidential dispatch 3028 of F.W.B. Coleman to Kellogg, July 9, 1925, RG 59, no file number. One reason that conditions had gotten easier for Russian travelers, and would continue to improve, was the Soviet government's ability to manufacture passports from the names of the dead. Jacob Golos was eventually arrested for this practice in 1941. See Corson and Crowley, *New KGB*, 450 n. 42; Bentley, *Out of Bondage*, 73.

60.   T. Bentley Mott, report to assistant chief of staff, October 20, 1928, Hoover to Col. Stanley H. Ford, November 21, 1928, RG 165, 10058-1287/2, /4.

61.   Stalin, discussion with Mr. Campbell, January 28, 1929, *RTsKhIDNI, fond* 558, *op.* 1, *del.* 2884; "Resolution of the Colonial Commission of the Executive Committee of the Communist International (*IKKI*) on the work of the Workers Party in American Colonies and Possessions," 1929 (n.d.), *RTsKhIDNI, fond* 558, *op.* 1, *del.* 3292.

62.   The Commerce Department reported in 1923 that "practically all sales of goods to the Russian government" have been in cash. Further, "very few sellers have granted any credit even for short periods" since credit transactions "for the most part have been unsuccessful." See Dr. E. Dana Durand, "Confidential Circular of the Eastern European and Levantine Division," April 9, 1923, 5, RG 151, 448-U.S.

63.   Rosta, April 2, 1924, *GARF, fond* 391, *op.* 2, *del.* 69, *l.* 234; Sutton, *Western Technology*, 278; Crissey, *Alexander Legge*, 174–75; Division of East European Affairs, Department of State, "Memorandum on the Soviet Monopoly of Foreign Trade," April 18, 1927, 61, RG 59, Office of East European Affairs, staff studies and memoranda, series E555, box 13; "Arcos and Amtorg, 1925," *RGAE, fond* 413, *op.* 10, *del.* 1025, *l.* 4.

64.   McAllister to Perkins, April 26, 1918, IHP, BA1-01, box 3, 1373; Fithian, "Soviet-American relations," 27–28; Fayette W. Allport to Chester Lloyd Jones, February 25, 1926, RG 59, 661.1115/474.

65.   Executive council report no. 24-30, cable of F.J. Brown, special council no. 24-8, March 11, 1924, O.H. Browning to George W. Koenig, IH Foreign Sales Department, October 15, 1924, IHP, BA1-01, box 1, 1348.

66.   By the end of 1925, ten thousand Fordson tractors had been shipped to Russia, and after Ford's new offer of a relatively meager ten-month, 25 percent credit, ten thousand more had arrived by April 1926. This compared with only 2,400 total shipped by the more generous Harvester in the same period. See C.A. White, *"Ford in Russia,"* 88, 89. Also see "Soviet Foreign Trade," *Russian Review*, February 15, 1926; on the Soviet view of Henry Ford, see Reuther, *The Brothers Reuther*, 91.

67.   Report of conference, December 17, 1924, Legge report, December 26, 1924, G.W. Koenig to McKinistry, August 18, 1925, IHP, BA1-01, box 1, 1348.

68.   Fayette W. Allport to Chester Lloyd Jones, February 25, 1926, RG 59, 661.1115/474. For a discussion of Ford's credit arrangements for Amtorg through Chase National Bank and Equitable Trust Company, see White, *"Ford in Russia,"* 87–88; G. Sandomirsky to Brittenham, December 3, 1925, IHP, BA2-01, box 2, 1383.

69.   Fayette W. Allport to Chester Lloyd Jones, February 25, 1926, RG 59, 661.1115/474.

70.   Sandomirsky to Brittenham, December 3, 1925, IHP, BA2-01, box 2, 1383.

71.   Sutton, *Western Technology*, 277–78. By the end of 1926 production problems developed at Ford's new plant in Cork, Ireland. Soviet Ford purchases shrank to five thousand between 1926–1929; by the latter year, Harvester was selling the majority of tractors. See C.A. White, *"Ford in Russia,"* 88–90; *New York Times*, December 15, 1925, and January 27, 1926, quoted in Fithian, "Soviet-American Economic Relations," 321.

72.   *Rosta* report, July 18, 1925, *GARF, fond* 391, *op.* 2, *del.* 21; *l.* 91. Promissory notes of up to three months duration were also available. See "Arcos and Amtorg, 1925," *RGAE, fond* 413, *op.* 10, *del.* 1025, *l.* 4. On the widespread use of 50 percent cash terms in sales to Russia, see BFDC to Robert F. Kelley, February 1, 1926, RG 59, 661.1115/466-1/2.

73.   This was a guaranteed credit, spread over four years, and 80 percent backed by the German government, individual German states, and a German bankers' consortium. See Fithian, "Soviet-American Economic Relations," 135, 137 n. 49.

74.   Davis, Polk, Wardwell, Gardiner, and Reed (Harriman's attorneys) to Assistant Secretary of State Leland Harrison, March 17, 1926; Leland Harrison to Davis, Polk, Wardwell, Gardiner, and Reed, April 2, 1926; G. Murnane to the secretary of state, July 19, 1926, Leland Harrison to New York Trust Company, July 15, 1926, *FRUS, 1926* 2:906–7, 907–10. See also Robert F. Kelley memorandum, October 28, 1927, RG59, 861.51 Am 3.

75.   In 1924–1925, the United States sold 201,821,000 rubles in goods to Moscow as compared with Germany's 102,668,000, and in 1929–1930, the United States sold 280,360,000 rubles to Germany's 234,389,000. See Budish and Shipman, *Soviet Foreign Trade*, 152; Amtorg, *Economic Statistics of the Soviet Union*, 79; "Foreign Trade over the European Frontier," June 1929, organ of the People's Commissariat of Foreign and Domestic Trade of the USSR, RG 59, 661.111. Overall, however, the two countries' exports to Russia were not far apart between 1923 and 1930: $708 million for Germany and $668.3 million for the United States. U.S. Department of Commerce, *Commerce Yearbook, 1926* 2:475; *1928* 2:556; *1929* 2:568; *1930* 2:345; *1931* 2:270. On the German-American competition for Russian trade, see American-Russian Chamber of Commerce, report no. 16, November 15, 1927, ARCCP, box 21; Ray Atherton, counselor of embassy, London, to secretary, RG 59, 661.00/1415.

76.   On the Dawes Plan's corporatist antecedents, see Hogan, *Informal Entente*, 68–71.

77.   H. Parker Willis, *Proceedings of the Thirty-first Annual Convention*, October 6, 1926, 213, 215–16.

78.   See *Ost Express*, "Germany, America and the Russian Market," no date, RG 59, 661.001/95; Reeve Schley to W.R. Castle, February 1, 1928, Kellogg to Schley, February 1, 1928, RG 59, 861.51 State Bank/3, /10; Jacob Gould Schurman to secretary of state, December 3, 1929, RG 59, 661.6215/56. In 1930–31 Germany did extend long-term guaranteed

credits to Russia that helped it take almost half of Soviet orders in 1932. See Jacobson, *When the Soviet Union Entered World Politics*, 252.

79.   Tass, 1928, *GARF, fond* 4459, *op.* 2, *del.* 329, *l.* 387; press release, October 16, 1928, Hammond file L3597, G.E. historical file; W.R. Castle to secretary, November 1, 1928, RG 59, 661.1115/488.

80.   Tass, October 22, 1929, *GARF, fond* 4459, *op.* 2, *del.* 329, *l.* 361.

81.   W.R. Castle to secretary, November 1, 1928, document file notes, November 6, 1928, November 22, 1928, RG 59, 661.1115/488, /489, /490.

82.   *Ekonomicheskaya Zhizn*, June 1, 1928, attached to letter, Coleman to secretary of state, June 12, 1928, RG 59, 661.1111/19.

83.   Bron, *Soviet Economic Development*, 57. In 1928, for instance, the Fulton Iron Works firm contacted the State Department to find out whether it would be allowed to extend credit terms for the Soviets for up to two years on beet and sugar machinery. Officials had no complaint, as long as the arrangement did not turn into a loan. Fulton Iron Works to State Department, February 11, 1928, RG 59, 661.1115/484.

84.   Sherman to Roamer Motors, May 26, 1927, attached to letter, special agent in charge to R.C. Bannerman, June 16, 1927, RG 59, 661.1116/58-1/2; Corson and Crowley, *New KGB*, 283. As Sherman did discount up to 40 percent on the Amtorg bills, then resold them in Europe for approximately 18 percent, manufacturers sometimes felt they had been gouged. See Fithian, "Soviet-American Economic Relations," 139. Sherman's agency was still operating in 1930. See Sherman to gentlemen, May 1930, AGP, box 7.

85.   Budish and Shipman, *Soviet Foreign Trade*, 11. See also U.S. Department of Commerce, *Commerce Yearbook, 1929* 2:568; *1930* 2:345; *1931* 2:270; *1932*, 135; *1937*, 149. The Soviets were in fourth-to-last place among nations exporting to the United States, selling just $22 million in 1930. See U.S. Department of Commerce Release, February 5, 1931, as cited in "Exports of the United States, by Leading Countries, 1929 and 1930," and "Imports of the United States, by Leading Countries, 1929 and 1930," December 7, 1931, accession 1057, National Industrial Conference Board Papers, box 3, series 5.

86.   "Prospects of Soviet-American Trade," S.G. Bron, *Ekonomicheskaya Zhizn*, June 10, 1928, attached to Cole to secretary, June 25, 1928, RG 59, 661.1111/20.

87.   See *Ford News*, February 17, 1927, quoted in Fithian, "Soviet-American Economic Relations," 307; "The Trade of the United States with the Soviet Union," extract from an article in the *Sovetskaya Torgovlia*, published in the Danish Foreign Office journal, attached to letter, Ellis A. Johnson and North Winship, legation in Denmark, May 14, 1929, RG 59, 661.11/13.

88.   "American Machinery Purchases for Soviet Union Show Large Increase," *Economic Review of the Soviet Union* 4 (August 1, 1929): 254 (a publication of Amtorg's Information Department). On American industry's role in the plan, see Sutton, *Western Technology*, 3–4, 319, 348; Hoff Wilson, *Ideology and Economics*, 96–97.

89.   See confidential memorandum, "Russian Conditions," May 7, 1930, 1, accession 1662, DPP, box 35.

90.   Tass, September 17, 1929, *GARF, fond* 4459, *op.* 2, *del.* 444, *l.* 212; Hoover to Jerome Davis, June 29, 1929, Hoover Presidential Papers, box 993; C.B. McClintock to Henry L. Stimson, October 10, 1929, Stimson to McClintock, October 22, 1929, RG 59, 361.11/4031; manager, Export Department, to State Department, November 8, 1929, Kelley to Worthington Pump, November 22, 1929, RG 59, 361.11/4032. Also see Kelley to Nicholas M. Stepnoff, December 30, 1939, RG 59, 361.11/4033.

91.   See memo to membership, n.d., (1929), ARCCP, box 21.

92.   See memo to membership, n.d., (1929), ARCCP, box 21.

93.   Travelers included Robert de Camp of Equitable Trust, James Gannon of Chase National Bank, A.L. Helwig of General Railway Signal Company, Parker Willis of the *Journal of Commerce*, and Dr. V.F. Boucar of International Business Machine Company,

Rio de Janeiro, Brazil. See *Economic Review of the Soviet Union* 4 (August 1, 1929): 263.

94. Report by Gumberg, "American-Russian Chamber of Commerce Delegation to the USSR, July–August 1929," (September 1929), Gumberg to Schley, April 15, 1929, report, American-Russian Chamber of Commerce delegation to the USSR, July–August 1929, (October 19, 1929), ARCCP, box 21.

95. See *New York Herald Tribune*, July 18, 1929, among others; and Gumberg to Schley, April 15, 1929, ARCCP, box 21.

96. *New York Herald Tribune*, August 4, 1929, *Time*, July 1929, Laurd S. Goldsborough to Reeve Schley, August 8, 1929, ARCCP, box 21.

97. "America's Capitalists and Stalin's Russia," *Stokholms Tidningen*, August 10, 1929, attached to letter, Leland Harrison of legation of Stockholm, to secretary, August 12, 1929, RG 59, 661.111/11; Gumberg to Reeve Schley and Frank Callahan, December 31, 1928, AGP, box 6A; Gumberg to Reeve Schley and Frank Callahan, June 3, 1929, AGP, box 7; Gumberg article, "Russian Trip of American Businessmen Brought Definite Results," ARCCP, box 21; White, "Ford in Russia," 91, 96–97. The Austin Company would go on to design six hundred Soviet plants; see Hoff Wilson, *Ideology and Economics*, 162–63. Among the American technicians who assisted at the Ford factory were Walter and Victor Reuther; see Reuther, *The Brothers Reuther*, Chs. 9–10 passim.

98. Gumberg article, "Russian Trip of American Businessmen Brought Definite Results," ARCCP, box 21.

99. "America's Capitalists and Stalin's Russia," *Stokholms Tidningen*, August 10, 1929, attached to letter, Leland Harrison to State Department, August 12, 1929, RG 59, 661.111/11.

100. Stalin, discussion with Mr. Campbell, January 28, 1929, *RTsKhIDNI, fond* 558, *op.* 1, *del.* 2884.

101. D.C. Poole to secretary, August 21, 1929, RG 59, 661.1116/70.

102. "Americans on Soviet Russia," *Vossische Zeitung*, August 22, 1929, ARCCP, box 21.

103. Gumberg article, "Russian Trip of American Businessmen Brought Definite Results," Schley to Norman J. Gould, November 27, 1929, ARCCP, box 21. On the British delegation, see Williams, *Trading with the Bolsheviks*, 213 n. 23, and idem, *Labor and Russia*, Ch. 6.

104. Gumberg to Schley, November 26, 1929, ARCCP, box 21; Libbey, "American-Russian Chamber," 242, 244.

105. Consul's letter, RG 59, 316-131-1/2, as quoted in Sutton, *Western Technology*, 284. Robins described Smith as someone who "performed great services for the Russian Revolution." Robins to Upton Sinclair, October 15, 1930, AGP, box 8C.

106. See Gumberg to A.A. Yazikov, Moscow, November 22, 1929; minutes of the meeting of the board of directors of the American-Russian Chamber of Commerce, October 7, 1929; Alexander Gumberg to Oswald L. Johnston, secretary and treasurer, ARCC, December 17, 1929; Schley to Smith, October 24, 1929; Schley to directors of ARCC, December 5, 1929, all in ARCCP, box 21. Large members included Sullivan Machinery, American Locomotive, Percival Farquhar, Averell Harriman, Johnson and Higgins, Westinghouse Electric, Remington Rand, Chicago Pneumatic Tool, Chase National Bank, Equitable Trust, Hugh Cooper, Allen Wardwell, and Simpson, Thacher, and Bartlett.

107. Memorandum regarding changes in personnel and activities of the chamber, October 15, 1929, Gumberg to Yazikov, November 11, 1929, Schley to Smith, October 24, 1929, ARCCP, box 21.

108. See Libbey, "American-Russian Chamber," 240 n. 33; news release, June 18, 1930, ARCCP, box 22.

109. Khinchuk to RusChamber, December 20, 1929; see telegram signed Binder, Chamberlain, Deuss, Duranty, Lyons and Mills to Schley, November 17, 1929, ARCCP,

box 21. On the Soviet-Nazi trade in American goods, see Libbey, "American-Russian Chamber," 240; and "'Moral Embargo' Against Moscow," *New York Times,* December 2, 1939.

CHAPTER 7.
AMERICAN BUSINESSMEN, THE NEP,
AND THE FIRST FIVE-YEAR PLAN

1. Nove, *Economic History of the U.S.S.R.*, 96.
2. Ball, *Russia's Last Capitalists,* 5; Nove, *Economic History of the U.S.S.R.*, 84; Lenin to Ninth All-Russia Congress of Soviets, December 25, 1921, *CW* 33:177, 151.
3. Lenin to Seventh Moscow *Gubernia* Conference, October 29, 1921, *CW* 33:107–8. Also see Carr, *Bolshevik Revolution* 3:445.
4. See Krasin to Vyacheslav Molotov, February 11, 1922, *RGAE, fond* 413, *op.* 2, *del.* 1517, *l.* 423; Lenin, *CW* 42:59.
5. Lenin, quoted in Shishkin, *Sovietskoe Gosudarstvo,* 417; ibid., 416; Sutton, *Western Technology,* 6, 9; Davies, *Economy in Turmoil,* 33 n. 129; W. Cohen, *Empire without Tears,* 87. In 1923, *Glavkontsesskom,* the Chief Concessions Committee, was established. This introduced a formal mechanism for conducting negotiations for concessions, ensuring that the Soviet government derived a fixed share of profits, even when margins were thin.
6. Lenin, *CW* 32: 223, 224, 298.
7. "Lenin's Speech," enclosure 11, with Alfred W. Kleifoth's report, February 11, 1921, RG 59, 661.001/21; List of *Vesenkha's* Concessions Committee, 1921, *RTsKhIDNI, fond* 5, *op.* 1, *del.* 2694.
8. Ball, *Russia's Last Capitalists,* x; Carr and Davies, *Foundations of a Planned Economy,* 1:628.
9. Carr and Davies, *Foundations of a Planned Economy* 1:717.
10. Day, *Trotsky and Politics of Economic Isolation,* 135; Trotsky cited in Day, 133; Jacobson, *When the Soviet Union Entered World Politics,* 149.
11. Day, *Trotsky and Politics of Economic Isolation,* 132; Trotsky, *My Life,* 519.
12. Trotsky, *My Life,* 519; Trotsky as cited in Day, *Trotsky and Politics of Economic Isolation,* 134, 135.
13. Young to secretary, February 23, 1924, RG 59, 661.1115/451.
14. Carstensen, *American Enterprise in Foreign Markets,* 120, 204–6; "A Step Ahead," *Pravda,* August 9, 1924, IHP, BA2-01, box 2, 1384. On Harvester's profits see Carstensen, 205. Its investment amounted to 60,450,000 gold rubles. Singer Sewing Machine, the next major investor, invested fifty million gold rubles in the USSR. See Lincoln Hutchison, August 8, 1922, "Confidential Supplement to Memorandum of July 24, 1922, on Foreign Capital in Russia Before the Revolution," AGP, box 2.
15. Halverson to Herbert F. Perkins, July 3, 1917, IHP, BA2-01, box 2, 1381; K. Kruming to August A. Halverson, November 6, 1917, IHP, BA1-01, box 1, 1345.
16. Selskosoyuz, which took over the assets of the Narodny Bank in December 1918, bought twenty thousand mowers and reapers in 1918–1919. When this independent cooperative was replaced by [Glav]selmash in October 1919, Harvester received two more annual contracts, which ran from October 1919 to October 1920 and again from October 1920 to October 1921. See McAllister to Perkins, April 16, 1918, IHP, BA1-01, box 3, 1373; "IHC in Russia: Lubertzy Works," IHP, BA2-01, box 2, 1384.
17. McAllister and Anderson to Perkins, IHP, November 19, 1917, BA1-01, box 3, 1373.
18. L.G. Gray, "Report on the Omsk Branch House," December 1, 1917, to January 3, 1919, BA1-01, IHP, box 1, 1368.

19.   McAllister to Perkins, May 15, 1918, April 26, 1918, IHP, BA1-01, box 3, 1373. Years later, DeWitt Clinton Poole, the consul general in Moscow in 1919, recalled that "Robins knew how to talk to the Bolsheviks." See Poole's diary, April 3, 1952, Poole Papers, box 10. On Robins's attempts to build a relationship with the Bolsheviks, see McFadden, *Alternative Paths*, Ch. 4 passim; on Harvester's exemption from nationalization, also shared by Singer and Westinghouse, see ibid., 118, and certificates dated December 28–29 and 31, 1920, "IHC in Russia: Lubertzy Works," IHP, BA2-01, box 2, 1384.

20.   For Harvester's reaction to exemption from nationalization, see A. Stephens to Chicago, IHP, December 12, 1918, BA1-01, box 2, 1365; Lenin, *CW* 32:189.

21.   Sandomirsky to Couchman, March 16, 1920, IHP, BA1-01, box 2, 1364.

22.   Lenin, *CW* 32:189; Ranney to Harold McCormick, May 24, 1920, Anderson telegram, included in letter from Couchman to Ranney, April 26, 1920, Harold McCormick to Cyrus McCormick, June 22, 1920, H.W. Westinghouse, C. Coleman, Allen Wardwell to Cyrus McCormick, June 11, 1920, Harold to Cyrus McCormick, April 21, 1920, Alexander Legge to Harold McCormick, April 20, 1920, IHP, BA1-01, box 2, 1364; also see Wardwell to McCormick, April 10, 1920, IHP, BA1-01, box 1, 1348.

23.   Lenin, *CW* 32:346. A discussion of the government's demands for general investment may be found in Hans Emch, F.J. Brown, George Sandomirsky, "Memorandum of Conference Held in the General Office on December 14, 1922," IHP, BA1-01, box 1, 1346.

24.   See N. Vashkoff (acting chairman, London section, Chief Concessions Committee, Russian Trade Delegation) to S.G. McAllister, March 6, 1924, IHP, BA1-01, box 1, 1350.

25.   Between December 1921 and March 1922, material prices rose at the factory from $12,805,603 to $232,783,667. Kruming to McAllister, April 5, 1922, Anderson to Harvester, Brussels, 1922 (n.d.), IHP, BA1-01, box 1, 1346; D.C. Poole to Phillips, September 6, 1922, RG 59, 661.1116/54.

26.   Emch to Brussels, December 28, 1922, IHP, BA1-01, box 1, 1346.

27.   Emch and Sandomirsky to P.A. Bogdanov, January 9, 1923, IHP, BA1-01, box 1, 1346.

28.   On the link between concessions and modernization see, for example, Lenin's comments on technical improvements to be derived from Western oil concessions, in *CW* 32:266.

29.   D.C. Poole to Mr. Phillips, September 6, 1922, RG 59, 661.1116/54; extract from protocol no. 83, "Meeting of the Presidium of the Central Committee of the All Russian Union of Metal Workers," December 8, 1922, IHP, BA1-01, box 1, 1346.

30.   Emch to Brussels, December 28, 1922, IHP, BA1-01, box 1, 1346; See Legge to Hoover, July 27, 1922, Hughes to Hoover, July 28, 1922, and Christian A. Herter to Legge, August 4, 1922, IHP, BA2-02, box 1.

31.   Vashkoff to Brussels, November 14, 1924, IHP, BA1-01, box 1, 1348; Emch and Sandomirsky to Brussels, January 2, 1923, IHP, BA1-01, box 1, 1346.

32.   Emch, Brown, and Sandomirsky, "Memorandum of Conference Held in the General Office on December 14, 1922"; Emch and Sandomirsky to P.A. Bogdanov, January 9, 1923, IHP, BA1-01, box 1, 1346; "IHC in Russia: Lubertzy Works," November 1924, IHP, BA2-01, box 2, 1384.

33.   Emch to McAllister, January 5, 1923, and Emch, Brown, and Sandomirsky, "Memorandum of Conference Held in the General Office on December 14, 1922," IHP, BA1-01, box 1, 1346.

34.   Emch to Brussels, December 28, 1922, and Emch, Brown, and Sandomirsky, "Memorandum of Conference Held in the General Office on December 14, 1922," IHP, BA1-01, box 1, 1346.

35. Emch, Brown, and Sandomirsky, "Memorandum of Conference Held in the General Office on December 14, 1922," and Emch to Brussels, December 28, 1922, IHP, BA1-01, box 1, 1346; McAllister to McCormick, January 31, 1923, IHP, BA1-01, box 1, 1346.

36. Obtaining such official authorization was generally a mere formality during the years when the United States did not recognize the Soviet Union. W.D. McHugh to Charles Henry Butler, March 26, 1923; Butler to McHugh, March 28, 1923, IHP, BA2-02, box 1.

37. "IHC in Russia: Lubertzy Works," November 1924, and Emch to McAllister, October 10, 1924, IHP, BA2-01, box 2, 1384; Emch and Brown to McAllister, October 20, 1923, IHP, BA2-01, box 3; Emch, Brown, and Sandomirsky, "Memorandum of Conference Held in the General Office on December 14, 1922," IHP, BA1-01, box 1, 1346.

38. Emch to McAllister, September 25, 1924, IHP, BA1-01, box 1, 1348; Chandler Anderson to Herbert F. Perkins, November 1, 1924, IHP, BA2-01, box 2, 1382. In 1924 the Soviets claimed that Harvester had been expropriated by a decree of June 28, 1918, although the company was never shown a copy of this nationalizing document. See Chandler Anderson to Perkins, October 22, 1924, IHP, BA1-01, box 1, 1348.

39. Perkins to McAllister, October 21, 1924, IHP, BA1-01, box 1, 1348.

40. Vashkoff to McAllister, November 14, 1924, IHP, BA1-01, box 1, 1350. See also Vashkoff to McAllister, March 6, 1924, IHP, BA1-01, box 1, 1350; Vashkoff to Brussels, November 14, 1924, McAllister to Vashkoff, December 26, 1924, McAllister to Vashkoff, March 10, 1924, IHP, BA1-01, box 1, 1348; Legge to McAllister, April 30, 1925, IHP, BA2-01, box 2, 1383.

41. See executive council report no. 25-12, February 13, 1925, "Russian Matters," IHP, BA2-01, box 2. Harvester officials continued to debate whether the firm had been "sequestered" or "nationalized." If it was the former, it should be easier to claim compensation, according to S.G. McAllister. See McAllister to Legge, February 10, 1925, IHP, BA2-01, box 2.

42. Legge to Chandler Anderson, January 22, 1925, and Anderson to Legge, March 13, 1925, IHP, BA2-01, box 2; *San Francisco Bulletin*, April 20, 1925, IHP, BA1-01, box 1, 1348.

43. This included $342,000 for the branch warehouses seized just after the revolution; $36 million in cash, assets, and collections when the branch inventories were seized and the nation's currency inflated in 1918; $1.7 million in Lubertzy inventory, work in progress, machines, and more inflation between 1917 and 1924; and finally, $4.9 million from the Lubertzy plant and its equipment taken in 1924. Lubertzy also lost potential interest income and forfeited accumulated goodwill, trademarks, and other intangibles. W.S. Elliott to Chandler Anderson, May 28, 1925, IHP, BA2-01, box 2, 1383.

44. Executive Council report no. 27-1, January 4, 1927, IHP, box 1, 1348; William B. Elliott to E.R. Lewis, August 4, 1932, IHP, BA3-01, box 2, 1340; Joseph Stein, director, Soviet Claims Division, Foreign Claims Settlement Commission of the United States, to International Harvester, March 4, 1959, IHP, BA2-02, box 1.

45. Parry, "'Khan of Kamchatka,'" 311, 313, 318–19, 324–25.

46. "Statement of the Narkomindel on the subject concession of the Vanderlip syndicate," November 2, 1920, *RTsKhIDNI, fond* 5, *op.* 1, *del.* 2090 Vanderlip; "W. Vanderlip in Petrograd and Moscow," *Novy Put*, March 9, 1921, RG 59, 661.1115/287; Parry, "'Khan of Kamchatka,'" 314–15; Gaddis, *Russia, the Soviet Union, and the United States*, 91–92; "Lenin's Speech," enclosure 11, with Alfred W. Kleifoth's report, February 11, 1921, RG 59, 661.001/21.

47. "W. Vanderlip in Petrograd and Moscow," *Novy Put*, March 9, 1921, RG 59, 661.1115/287; "An Interview with Comrade Martens," *Pravda* 40 (February 23, 1921), RG 59, 701.6111/538; Parry, "'Khan of Kamchatka,'" 329.

48. See Fithian, "Dollars without the Flag," 205–22.

49. See chapter 5.

50. "Project of Concession Agreement in Cultivation of Asbestos Production in Urals in the Wording of Concession Committee of *Vesenkha*," *RTsKhIDNI, fond* 5, *op.* 1, *del.* 2697; See M.D. Durand, memo in answer to letter of Asbestos and Mineral Corporation, dated October 19, relative to a concession granted by the Soviet government for an American capitalist to mine asbestos, October 28, 1921, RG40, 77295.

51. As quoted in Gillette, "Armand Hammer," 362.

52. Quoted in Hammer, *Romanoff Treasure*, 231. Some of Hammer's concession privileges included radio and telegraph access, the opportunity for (American) employees "to travel freely about Russia," unlimited freight and passenger rail service, and his own two-person committee to clear up red tape.

53. Wolfe, *Life in Two Centuries*, 172; Lenin, as quoted in ibid.

54. Lenin to Radchenko, October 27, 1921, *CW* 45:362, italics in original.

55. Alamerico to Voronetskii, April 1, 1922, Rablenko to Alamerico, April 4, 1922, *RGAE, fond* 413, *op.* 3, *del.* 1001a, *l.* 4, 5; *New York Times*, February 20, 1923, 6.

56. Hammer, *Hammer*, 154; Williams, *Russian Art and American Money*, 211.

57. F. Ia. Rabinov to Lenin and Lezhava, February 8, 1922, *RTsKhIDNI, fond* 5, *op.* 1, *del.* 2387.

58. See discussion on Genoa's oil dealings in C.A. White, *British and American Commercial Relations*, 186–88; F. Ia. Rabinov to Lenin and Lezhava, February 8, 1922, *RTsKhIDNI, fond* 5, *op.* 1, *del.* 2387.

59. Chadbourne to Gumberg, January 16, 1923, AGP, box 3; F. Ia. Rabinov to Lenin and Lezhava, February 8, 1922, *RTsKhIDNI, fond* 5, *op.* 1, *del.* 2387; *Baku Workman*, March 8, 1923, AGP, box 2.

60. "An Interview with Americans," *Labor*, Baku, March 25, 1923, AGP, box 2.

61. Translation from the *Baku Workman*, March 9, 1923, AGP, box 3.

62. Translation from the *Baku Workman*, March 9, 1923, AGP, box 3.

63. Chadbourne to Gumberg, May 18, 1923, Gumberg to Chadbourne, June 19, 1923, AGP, box 3.

64. Fithian, "Soviet-American Economic Relations," 173–75; Chandler Anderson to H.F. Perkins, October 16, 1924, IHP, BA1-01, box 1, 1348; Sutton, *Western Technology*, 23.

65. High commissioner at Constantinople to secretary of state, August 30, 1921, RG 59, 661.1115/346; secretary of state to the high commissioner, November 1, 1921, RG 59, 661.1115/346, *FRUS, 1921* 2:780, 784.

66. Poole to secretary, October 25, 1921, A.W. Lasker to secretary of state, August 11, 1921, RG 59, 661.1115/417, /336.

67. In 1918 Harriman considered getting involved in the development of Siberia and asked the State Department its view of the R. Martens Export Company, a firm that sought the financier's involvement in Russia. See Harriman to Jerome Landfield, September 20, 1918, AHP, box 674.

68. Derutra is an abbreviation for Deutsche-Russische Lager und Transportgesellschaft (German-Russian Storage and Transportation Company). See Finder, *Red Carpet*, 53–54; Krasin, *Questions of Foreign Trade*, 391; Harriman and Company, report, September 30, 1920, AHP, box 686; Carver to Harriman, Carver to Krasin, August 12, 1921, AHP, box 29.

69. See Max Warburg to Paul Warburg, December 18, 1922, and Paul Warburg to Harriman, January 2, 1923, AHP, box 118; Harriman, *America and Russia in a Changing World*, 2. The Warburgs and Harrimans were old friends. See Abramson, *Spanning the Century*, 139-40.

70. See Carver to Harriman, May 28, 1922, Harriman to Carver, May 11, 1922, AHP, box 29.

71. *New York Times*, June 19, 1924; Derutra report, December 1, 1922, AHP, box 29; *New York American*, June 11, 1923.

72.   Harriman to John North Willys, October 21, 1926, AHP, box 121; Carver to Harriman, September 24, 1926, and attached memo of September 27, AHP, box 29.

73.   Carver to Harriman, September 24, 1926, AHP, box 29; See Sutton, *Western Technology*, 86. Fourteen pounds of manganese were needed for each ton of steel. See John V.W. Reynders, "Manganese Resources in Relation to Domestic Consumption," from flyer on the American Institute of Mining and Metallurgical Engineers Spring Meeting, April 1927, AHP, box 699.

74.   Harriman telegram, May 13, 1925, AHP, box 692; Finder, *Red Carpet*, 56.

75.   The State Department's Division of East European Affairs soon learned about Harriman's venture and followed it closely. See Wilkins, *Maturing of Multinational Enterprise*, 108; Sutton, *Western Technology*, 89; and Harriman, *Peace with Russia?* 2.

76.   Minutes of the first meeting of the board of directors, August 7, 1925, AHP, box 692; also see concession agreement, AHP, box 695; Irving Rossi to Harriman, January 14, 1925, AHP, box 90.

77.   The final concession contract stipulated Harriman's "right to 'realize profits' from the sale and export of ore." Harriman thought the need for such a clause "absurd," but at his attorney's urging, he accepted it. Harriman to Elliott, March 13, 1925, AHP, box 697; E. Eckhardt, Georgia Manganese interoffice memorandum, July 21, 1926, AHP, box 691.

78.   Harriman memorandum, Cables, 1925, AHP, box 692; B.L. Thane to W.W. Newberry, July 2, 1925, AHP, box 698.

79.   Harriman held 51 percent of the firm, with 49 percent of it belonging to others. See U.S. embassy in Berlin, report 334, July 14, 1925, cited in Sutton, *Western Technology*, 87. Investors included two German firms—Gelsenkirchner Borgwerke A.-G. and the Disconte Gesellschaft—and two American ones—Lee, Higginson and Company, which invested $25,000, and the Morgan-controlled Guaranty Trust, which extended a loan for $1.1 million, personally guaranteed by Harriman. See Connett to Lee, Higginson, July 28, 1925, AHP, box 693; and George T. Scherzinger (assistant treasurer of Guaranty Trust) to Harriman, September 22, 1925, AHP, box 51.

80.   Elliott to Harriman, July 27, 1925, AHP, box 693; "Information from [Reporter] Vashadze Respecting the Status of Negotiations with Harriman," in *Zaria Vostoka* [Eastern dawn], March 20, 1927, AHP, box 699.

81.   B.L. Thane to W.W. Newberry, July 2, 1925, AHP, box 698. Yet in 1926, when the concession was foundering, Hoover brushed off Harriman's appeals, disclaimed any governmental responsibility for American investments in Russia, and drove the angry manganese magnate to switch parties and vote for Al Smith in 1928. See Finder, *Red Carpet*, 57.

82.   Liston M. Oak to Alexander Gumberg, May 18, 1925, AGP, box 4.

83.   Harriman to Charles L. Holman, December 17, 1925, AHP, box 693; Holman to Harriman, August 12, 1926, AHP, box 698; Rawack and Grunfeld (A-G) and Harriman (Georgia Manganese) memorandum of understanding, March 8, 1926, AHP, box 689. This development helped "confirm the fear of some State Department officials and U.S. businessmen" of German economic rivalry in the Soviet Union. See Hoff Wilson, *Ideology and Economics*, appendix B, 159; for Nikopol's output, see Sutton, *Western Technology*, 87.

84.   The Trade Union Council had recently announced a 300 percent wage increase for workers, and Trotsky was convinced that Stalin would try to force him to intervene on behalf of the capitalists. He would thus lose all credibility among his remaining supporters. See Trotsky, *My Life*, 518. In his four-hour meeting with Harriman, Trotsky was careful not to say anything off the subject, leading Harriman to guess, correctly, that the former Red Army chief was worried about his future. Trotsky also seemed concerned that he not be "tainted" by what he said to Harriman. Trotsky's attitude gave Harriman a hint that his own days as a concessionaire were numbered. See Harriman, *America and Russia*, 4, 5; and idem, *Peace with Russia?* 2.

85.   Robinson to Harriman, March 28, 1927, 8, AHP, box 90.
86.   John Speed Elliot, "Memorandum in Re Manganese Promotion Controversy," attached to Elliot to Charles Hayden, September 2, 1927, AHP, box 699; Wilkins, *Maturing of Multinational Enterprise*, 107.
87.   Robinson to Harriman, February 12, 1927, AHP, box 90; see "Information from Vashadze Respecting the Status of Negotiations with Harriman," *Zaria Vostoka*, March 20, 1927, AHP, box 699.
88.   See "Information from Vashadze Respecting the Status of Negotiations with Harriman," *Zaria Vostoka*, March 20, 1927, AHP, box 699; note on conversation with [concessions chief A.A.] Joffe by Schwenfeldt, December 27, 1926, AHP, box 699.
89.   See Robinson to Harriman, March 28, 1927, and enclosures "E" and "F," February 23, 1927, AHP, box 90. Harriman's engineers were buying rubles from the neighboring Turks and not from the Soviet state bank. See Wilkins, *Maturing of Multinational Enterprise*, 108.
90.   Harriman, *America and Russia*, 7; G.A. Kenney to Georgia Manganese, December 7, 1928, AHP, box 714; Harriman quoted in Wilkins, *Maturing of Multinational Enterprise*, 108; Amtorg quoted in Sutton, *Western Technology*, 298, note 11. See also Hoff Wilson, *Ideology and Economics*, 160.
91.   See Wilkins, *Maturing of Multinational Enterprise*, 108.
92.   Hammer, *Hammer*, 161–72; Sutton, *Western Technology*, 112; American-Russian Chamber of Commerce, report no. 16, November 15, 1927, ARCCP, box 21.
93.   The other successful concessionaire was Eitingon-Schild, an American fur and leather-trading firm headed by a Russian émigré. See Sutton, *Western Technology*, 147, 237, 287; on Hammer's successes, see Hammer, *Romanoff Treasure*, 231; Gillette, "Armand Hammer," 362.
94.   This was a trial of five German A.E.G. engineers accused of a wrecking plot in the Don mining region. See Sutton, *Western Technology*, 325–26. The Shakhta affair had followed an earlier instance of British "wrecking," as alleged at the Metropolitan-Vickers trial of 1927.
95.   *Economic Review of the Soviet Union*, April 15, 1930, 156, as cited in Finder, *Red Carpet*, 67, 68–69; R.C. Williams, *Russian Art and American Money*, 216. For a discussion of Hammer's other ventures in revolutionary states, Libya in particular, see Hammer, *Hammer*, Ch. 20.
96.   Lenin, quoted posthumously in *Komsomolskaya Pravda* (October 9, 1928), and cited in Sutton, *Western Technology*, 349.
97.   Jacobson, *When the Soviet Union Entered World Politics*, 248–49, 250; S.F. Cohen, *Bukharin and the Bolshevik Revolution*, 278–79, 287.
98.   Ball, *Russia's Last Capitalists*, 61.
99.   Jacobson, *When the Soviet Union Entered World Politics*, 250, 269; Stalin as quoted in Jacobson, 266–67.
100. See Kuromiya, *Stalin's Industrial Revolution*, 9; R.C. Williams, *Russian Art and American Money*, 211. Stalin, discussion with Mr. Campbell, January 28, 1929, *RTsKhIDNI, fond* 558, *op.* 1, *del.* 2884. See also the discussion in Sutton, *Western Technology*, 344–49.
101. Trotsky, "Trotsky Invites Capitalists to Get Russian Concessions," report, The World and North American Newspaper Alliance, August 19, 1925; Sutton, *Western Technology*, 346–47. Companies included Albert Kahn, MacDonald Engineering, the Austin Company, Ford Motor, and General Electric. Associated Press cables, March 17, 1930, *GARF, fond* 4459, *op.* 3, *del.* 92, *l.* 212. An excellent study of the challenges and difficulties faced by an American consultant in Russia during the First and Second Five-Year Plans is Gelb, ed., *American Engineer in Stalin's Russia*, based on the memoirs of Zara Witkin.

102.   See Heymann, *We Can Do Business with Russia*, 16; *Ekonomicheskaya Zhizn*, no. 225, September 29, 1929, 3, as cited in Sutton, *Western Technology*, 348.

103.   I. Taigin, "Why Soviet-American Trade Is Growing," *Izvestiia*, April 12, 1929, attached to letter, Coleman to secretary, April 19, 1929, RG 59, 661.111/10, emphasis in original.

104.   Fithian, "Soviet-American Economic Relations," 171, 356.

105.   Henry Green to Lammot Du Pont, May 3, 1927, and Lammot Du Pont to Henry Green, May 6, 1927, accession 1662, DPP, box 35. The firm that accepted the business, the French Nobel Company, "found it impossible to operate . . . because of labor troubles, Government regulations," and other problems and got out with a settlement of 33 million francs. See J.K. Jenney to Lammot Du Pont, October 3, 1930, accession 1662, DPP, box 35.

106.   See Sutton, *Western Technology*, 212.

107.   See Hugh L. Cooper, "Soviet Russia," address delivered before the Institute of Politics at Williamstown, Massachusetts, August 1, 1930, Cooper to Lammot Du Pont, July 15, 1929, Du Pont to Cooper, March 20, 1929, and Cooper to Du Pont, March 28, 1929, accession 1662, DPP, box 35. For more on Cooper's success, see Fithian, "Soviet-American Economic Relations," 267–68.

108.   Dr. Fin Sparre to Lammot Du Pont et al., April 20, 1929, and Dewey to Sparre, April 19, 1929, accession 1662, DPP, box 35.

109.   Cooper to Lammot Du Pont, July 15, 1929, Cooper to Sparre, April 12, 1929, Cooper to Lammot Du Pont, July 15, 1929, and R. Fastenburg to secretary, July 23, 1929, accession 1662, DPP, box 35.

110.   Du Pont to Saul G. Bron, August 7, 1929, and M.D. Fisher to Lammot Du Pont, August 8, 1929, accession 1662, DPP, box 35; Fin Sparre memorandum to E.G. Robinson et al., "Sale of Processes to Soviet Government," March 12, 1930, accession 1813, Harrington Papers, box 2; Lammot Du Pont to J.W. McCoy and W.M. Swint, March 30, 1936, accession 1662, DPP, box 35.

111.   The company expected that each plant should earn $12,000 annually. See draft agreement attached to letter of Sparre to T.S. Grasselli, March 19, 1930, accession 1813, Harrington Papers, box 2.

112.   Sparre to Grasselli, March 21, 1930, president to Sparre, April 4, 1930, accession 1813, Harrington Papers, box 2; Sutton, *Western Technology*, 212–13.

113.   Richter to Sparre, July 28, 1930, accession 1813, Harrington Papers, box 2.

114.   J.K. Jenney to Du Pont, February 19, 1930, accession 1662, DPP, box 35; Sparre to Delment, July 9, 1930, and Delment to Sparre, July 10, 1930, accession 1813, Harrington Papers, box 9.

115.   Lammot Du Pont to Hugh Cooper, January 19, 1931, accession 1662, DPP, box 35.

116.   Mooney to Sloan, October 20, 1930, 13, 14, and Mooney to Du Pont, November 21, 1930, accession 1662, DPP, box 35.

117.   Stalin, discussion with Mr. Campbell, January 28, 1929, *RTsKhIDNI, fond* 558, *op.* 1, *del.* 2884; Mooney to Sloan, October 20, 1930, 1–2, accession 1662, DPP, box 35.

118.   Mooney to Sloan, October 20, 1930, 2, 11–13, accession 1662 DPP, box 35. For more on Mooney's reflections about his trip to Russia, see his address before the American Automotive Club in Paris, October 7, 1930, accession 1662, DPP box 35.

119.   Mooney to Sloan, October 20, 1930, 6, 7, accession 1662, DPP, box 35.

120.   Du Pont to William Coyne, April 2, 1930, Du Pont to Peter A. Bogdanov, October 14, 1930, F.W. Pickard to Du Pont, May 26, 1932, and Du Pont to J.W. McCoy and W.M. Swint, March 30, 1936, accession 1662, DPP, box 35.

121.   F.W. Pickard to Lammot Du Pont, May 26, 1932, accession 1662, DPP, box 35.

122.   Sonkin, *Okno vo Vneshnii Mir*, 199.

CHAPTER 8.
SOVIET-AMERICAN RELATIONS, 1929–1933

1. See American-Russian Chamber of Commerce, *Handbook of the Soviet Union*, 352, 353; Budish and Shipman, *Soviet Foreign Trade*, 10, 11.
2. American-Russian Chamber of Commerce, *Handbook of the Soviet Union*, 352, 353; U.S. Department of Commerce, *National Income and Product Accounts*, 303, 344.
3. American-Russian Chamber of Commerce, *Handbook of the Soviet Union*, 361.
4. Sackett to secretary of state, February 16, 1931, RG 59, 661.1115/503;Gumberg to Louis Fischer, August 20, 1930, AGP, box 8b.
5. Yanson, *Foreign Trade in the USSR*, 84; American-Russian Chamber of Commerce, *Handbook of the Soviet Union*, 368. In descending order these were Illinois, Michigan, Ohio, Iowa, and Wisconsin. For more on the firms and states benefiting most from Amtorg's business, see Bron, *Soviet Economic Development and American Business*, 32, 51–52, 93; U.S. Department of Commerce, *Commerce Yearbook 1928* 2:556; *1931* 2:275.
6. See *New York Times*, May 4, 1930, 28; Gumerg to Fischer, August 20, 1930, August 5, 1930, AGP, box 8b.
7. Reeve Schley to Robert P. Lamont, May 19, 1930, S.R. Bertron, Allen Wardwell, Hugh L. Cooper, and H.H. Dewey to members of the American-Russian Chamber of Commerce, June 14, 1930, AGP, box 21; Gumberg to Louis Fischer, August 20, 1930, AGP, box 8b. Herbert Romerstein has, in fact, suggested that the forgeries may have been planted with police by a left-wing journalist, John L. Spivak. See Romerstein, *Against the Main Enemy*, 47–53; Klehr, Haynes, and Firsov, *Secret World*, 126.
8. Fish Committee quoted by Hugh Cooper, at American-Russian Chamber of Commerce luncheon, January 30, 1931, AGP, box 21. Ironically, Amtorg would become a more important player in "subversive activities" after 1930 as it became a center not for propaganda so much as for industrial espionage.
9. See Budish and Shipman, *Soviet Foreign Trade*, 14, 29; Filene, *Americans and the Soviet Experiment*, 234; Bogdanov address to American-Russian Chamber of Commerce luncheon, January 30, 1931; Bogdanov to Bertron, July 28, 1930, AGP, box 21.
10. See New York *Herald Tribune*, July 29, 1930, box 8b, AGP; American-Russian Chamber of Commerce to Hoover, Mellon, and Lamont, July 30, 1930, ARCCP, box 22; hearing with respect to pulpwood from Russia, before Gov. Seymour Lowman, Capt. F.X.A. Eble, commisioner of customs and Customs Board, August 1, 1930, AGP, box 8b; Libbey, "American-Russian Chamber," 242.
11. See telegram, S.R. Bertron, L.L. Fleming, and Hugh L. Cooper to the president, Andrew W. Mellon, and Robert P. Lamont, July 30, 1930, "Memorandum of Conference with Bureau of Customs Relative to New Regulations for Enforcement of Section 307 of the Tariff Act of 1930 (Convict Labor)," November 11, 1930, Robins to Gumberg, August 2, 1930, Gumberg to Louis Fischer, August 5, 1930, Gumberg to Schley, August 7, 1930, AGP, box 8B.
12. Robert Alter to Reed Smoot, February 24, 1931, George P. Oswald to Hugh L. Cooper, February 24, 1931, telegram from Oswald to Reed Smoot, February 24, 1931, "Delegation who accompanied Col. Hugh L. Cooper to Washington, January 23, 1931," AGP, box 21.
13. Bogdanov to Gumberg, August 9, 1930, AGP, box 8b; On the trade bans, see Hoff Wilson, *Ideology and Economics*, 104–9.
14. Browder, *Origins of Soviet-American Diplomacy*, 35.
15. American-Russian Chamber of Commerce, *Handbook of the Soviet Union*, 352.
16. A.J. Williams, *Trading with the Bolsheviks*, 159, 166; *Chicago Tribune*, October 26, 1931; Libbey, "American-Russian Chamber of Commerce," 243 n. 43. For Ameri-

can firms' reaction to this cutback, see Spencer Williams to Hugh L. Cooper, October 8, 1931, and Hugh Cooper to Andrew W. Mellon, November 27, 1930, AGP, box 21.

17. Jacobson, *When the Soviet Union Entered World Politics*, 254; Filene, *Americans and the Soviet Experiment*, 235.

18. See American-Russian Chamber of Commerce, *Handbook of the Soviet Union*, 316, 317.

19. Nikolai Krestinskii, as quoted in Libbey, "American-Russian Chamber of Commerce," 243.

20. Stimson did not *"overtly propose"* recognition, realizing that President Hoover refused to see how "a nation of Japan's size could unsettle the futures of two countries as large as China and Russia." Stimson, diary entry, May 16, 1932, reel 4, Stimson Papers, Library of Congress, as cited in A.J. Williams, *Trading with the Bolsheviks*, 167. Kellogg to Stimson, November 18, 1932, RG 59, 861.01/1841, as cited in Bennett, *Recognition of Russia*, 78–79. On cotton, see Jesse H. Jones to president, June 24, 1933, Jones to Henry Morgenthau, Jr., June 27, 1933, Morgenthau Papers, box 243.

21. Bennett, *Recognition of Russia*, 89–91, 104; Filene, *Americans and the Soviet Experiment*, 266; see newspaper stories emphasizing trade issues in the *Chicago Daily News,* October 20, 1933; *Providence Journal,* October 21, 1933; and *Philadelphia Public Ledger,* October 22, 1933; security is emphasized also in articles in the *New York Times,* October 23, 1933, and Scripps-Howard report, October 1933, all in Moore Papers, box 18; Duranty to John C. Wiley, June 13, 1932, Wiley Papers, box 6.

22. Bennett, *Recognition of Russia*, 86; Farnsworth, *Bullitt and the Soviet Union*, 89, Bishop, *Roosevelt-Litvinov Agreements*, 7, 10; Hoff Wilson, *Ideology and Economics*, 113, 120.

23. Undated memo, "Suggestions re Rusian Trade and Credit Agreements," Moore papers, box 18; "Asks Soviet Traffic for American Ships," *New York Journal of Commerce,* October 25, 1933, "Guarantee Sought for Soviet Credits," *New York Times,* October 23, 1933, Moore Papers, box 18.

24. Borah as quoted in "U.S.-Soviet Meeting Seen as World Peace Aid," Scripps-Howard newspapers, October 1933, Moore Papers, box 18; Bennett, *Recognition of Russia,* 77–79; idem, *Roosevelt and the Search for Security,* 22–23.

25. See Frank A. Golder, "Interview with Karl Radek Thursday Night, June 8, 1922," 1, Goodrich Papers, box 19.

26. Robert F. Kelley, "Daily Report for Eastern Europe," October 24, 1933, Moore Papers, box 18.

27. Farnsworth, *Bullitt and the Soviet Union,* 92; Bennett, *Roosevelt and the Search for Security,* 19–20; Bullitt memo, "Gentleman's Agreement," November 1933, attached to Kelley to Morgenthau, May 12, 1937, Morgenthau Diary, 68: 40.

28. Heymann, *We Can do Business with Russia,* 79; Sheinis, *Maxim Litvinov,* 250–51.

29. Bullitt to Department of State, June 16, 1934, September 13,1934, September 15, 1934, cited in Brownell and Billings, So Close to Greatness, 164–65; informal memorandum, Wiley to Kelley, August 10, 1934, Wiley Papers, box 1.

30. See Secretary Cordell Hull to American Embassy, Moscow, March19, 1934, PSF, Diplomatic Correspondence, Russia: 1934, box 49; Herbert Feis to Henry Morgenthau, Jr., June 16, 1939, Morgenthau Diary, 197: 185; Bennett, *Roosevelt and the Search for Security,* 19-20; Brownell and Billings, So Close to Greatness, 160, 162; Libbey, "American-Russian Chamber of Commerce," 244; Hoff Wilson, *Ideology and Economics,* 129.

31. See also Morgenthau Diary, May 11, 1937, 67: 242–49 passim; a digest of the ultimately inconclusive discussions is in Morgenthau Diary, 68: 43–67 passim.

32. See Department memo, September 3, 1935, Wiley Papers, box 2; Bennett, *Roosevelt and the Search for Security,* 62–63.

33.   On Bullitt's disillusionment with the Bolsheviks, see Bullitt to Wiley, January 7, 1935, Wiley Papers, box 2; Bullitt to Moore, July 15, 1935, November 24, 1936, Moore Papers, box 3; Bullitt to Secretary of State, April 27, 1935, PSF, Diplomatic correspondence, Russia: 1934.

34.   See Sumner Welles press release, August 7, 1940, Morgenthau Diary, 307: 57; A.J. Williams, *Trading with the Bolsheviks,* 173.

35.   Figures derived from table in Condoide, *Russian-American Trade,* 91.

CHAPTER 9.
CONCLUSION

1.   Legge to Chandler Anderson, January 22, 1925, IHP, BA2-01, box 2.

2.   Although technical assistance programs were profitable, American and other foreign engineers regularly saw their work frustrated by "solid walls of habit and hostility" resulting from the "subterfuge, duplicity, laziness, venality, jealousy, and stupidity" endemic under the Soviet system. Eugene Lyons as quoted in Gelb, ed., *American Engineer in Stalin's Russia,* 7, 8.

3.   Kelley, State Department Division of Eastern European Affairs, July 2, 1930, document file note, RG 59, 811.00B/1126.

BIBLIOGRAPHY

➤ MANUSCRIPT COLLECTIONS

American-Russian Chamber of Commerce. Papers. Wisconsin State Historical Society, Madison, Wisconsin.

Austin, William Liseter. Papers. Hagley Library, Wilmington, Delaware.

Baker, Newton D. Papers. Manuscript Division, Library of Congress, Washington, D.C.

Borah, William E. Papers. Manuscript Division, Library of Congress, Washington, D.C.

Brasol, Boris Leo. Papers. Manuscript Division, Library of Congress, Washington, D.C.

Bullard, Arthur. Papers. Seeley Mudd Manuscript Library, Department of Rare Books and Special Collections, Princeton University, Princeton, New Jersey.

Castle, William R. Papers. Herbert Hoover Presidential Library, West Branch, Iowa.

Colby, Bainbridge. Papers. Manuscript Division, Library of Congress, Washington, D.C.

Coolidge, Calvin. Papers. Herbert Hoover Presidential Library, West Branch, Iowa.

Davis, Norman H. Papers. Manuscript Division, Library of Congress, Washington, D.C.

E.I. Du Pont de Nemours and Company. Papers. Hagley Library, Wilmington, Delaware.

General Electric Company. Historical File, Publicity Department. General Electric Company Archives, Schenectady, New York.

Goodrich, James P. Papers. Herbert Hoover Presidential Library, West Branch, Iowa.

Gumberg, Alexander. Papers. Wisconsin State Historical Society, Madison, Wisconsin.

Harding, Warren G. Papers. Herbert Hoover Presidential Library, West Branch, Iowa.

Harriman, Averell. Papers. Manuscript Division, Library of Congress, Washington, D.C.

Harrington, Willis F. Papers. Hagley Library, Wilmington, Delaware.

Harrison, Leland. Papers. Manuscript Division, Library of Congress, Washington, D.C.

Hoover, Herbert. Papers. Commerce Papers. Herbert Hoover Presidential Library, West Branch, Iowa.

———. Misrepresentations File. Herbert Hoover Presidential Library, West Branch, Iowa.

———. Pre-Commerce Papers. Herbert Hoover Presidential Library, West Branch, Iowa.

———. Presidential Papers. Herbert Hoover Presidential Library, West Branch, Iowa.

Hoover War Collection. Hoover Institution on War, Revolution, and Peace, Stanford University, Stanford, California.

Hughes, Charles Evans. Papers. Manuscript Division, Library of Congress, Washington, D.C.

Hull, Hannah Clothier. Papers. Swarthmore College Peace Collection, Swarthmore, Pennsylvania.

International Harvester Company. Papers. Wisconsin State Historical Society, Madison, Wisconsin.

Jones, Rufus. Papers. Quaker Historical Library, Haverford College, Haverford, Pennsylvania.

Leffingwell, Russell. Papers. Manuscript Division, Library of Congress, Washington, D.C.
McCormick, Cyrus. Papers. Wisconsin State Historical Society, Madison, Wisconsin.
Moore, R. Walton. Papers. Franklin D. Roosevelt Library, Hyde Park, N.Y.
Morgenthau, Henry, Jr. Papers. Franklin D. Roosevelt Library, Hyde Park, N.Y.
———. Diary. Franklin D. Roosevelt Library, Hyde Park, N.Y.
National Association of Manufacturers. Vada Horsch Collection. Hagley Library, Wilmington, Delaware.
———. Minutes, Board of Directors, 1919–1926. Hagley Library, Wilmington, Delaware.
National Industrial Conference Board. Papers. Hagley Library, Wilmington, Delaware.
Pamphlet Collection. Hoover Institution on War, Revolution, and Peace, Stanford, California.
Poole, DeWitt Clinton. Papers. Wisconsin State Historical Society, Madison, Wisconsin.
Robins, Raymond. Papers. Wisconsin State Historical Society, Madison, Wisconsin.
Roosevelt, Franklin D. Papers. Franklin D. Roosevelt Presidential Library, Hyde Park, N.Y.
Schiff, Jacob. Papers. Hebrew Union College Annex Library, Los Angeles, California.
Sperry Gyroscope/Remington Rand Company. Papers. Hagley Library, Wilmington, Delaware.
U.S. Chamber of Commerce. Records. Hagley Library, Wilmington, Delaware.
———. Minutes, Annual Meetings, 1919–1923. Hagley Library, Wilmington, Delaware.
———. Minutes, Board of Directors' Meetings, 1919–1926. Hagley Library, Wilmington, Delaware.
Wiley, John Cooper. Papers. Franklin D. Roosevelt Library, Hyde Park, N.Y.
Wolfe, Henry C. Oral History File. Herbert Hoover Presidential Library, West Branch, Iowa.
Women's Committee for the Recognition of Russia. Records. Swarthmore College Peace Collection, Swarthmore, Pennsylvania.
Women's International League for Peace and Freedom. Records, U.S. Section. Swarthmore College Peace Collection, Swarthmore, Pennsylvania.

➢ Published and Unpublished Government Documents

American Relief Administration Records, Hoover Institution on War, Revolution, and Peace, Stanford University, Stanford, California.
Cumming, C.K., and Walter W. Pettit, eds. *Russian American Relations, March 1917–March 1920: Documents and Papers*. Westport, Conn., 1977.
Degras, Jane, ed. *Soviet Documents on Foreign Policy*. Volume I. 1917–1924. London, 1951.
Hughes, Charles Evans. *The Pathway of Peace: Representative Addresses Delivered during His Term as Secretary of State*. New York and London, 1925.
Joint Legislative Committee for the Investigation of Seditious Activities (Lusk Committee). Records, Russian Soviet Bureau Seized Files. New York State Archives, Albany, N.Y.
Lenin, V.I. *Collected Works*. Vols. 24, 28, 30, 32, 33, 42, 43, 44, and 45. London, 1965, 1966.
Ministry of Foreign Affairs of the USSR. *Dokumenty Vneshnei Politiki SSSR*. Vols. 1–6. Moscow, 1957–1962.
Moran, Philip R., ed. *Calvin Coolidge, 1872–1933: Chronology-Documents-Biblio- graphical Aids*. Dobbs Ferry, N.Y., 1970.
State Archival Administration of the Russian Federation (Rosarkhiv). *Arkhiv Vneshnei Politiki Rossiiskoi Federatsii* (*AVPRF*: Foreign Ministry Archive of the Russian Federation), Moscow.

————. *Gosudarstvennyi Arkhiv Rossiiskoi Federatsii* (*GARF*: State Archive of the Russian Federation), [formerly *Tsentral'nyi Gosudarstvennyi Arkhiv Oktiabr'skoi Revolutsii S.S.S.R.* (Central State Archive of the October Revolution, USSR)], Moscow.

————. *Rossiiskii Gosudarstvennyi Arkhiv Ekonomiki* (*RGAE*: Russian State Archive of the Economy) [formerly *Tsentral'nyi Gosudarstvennyi Arkhiv Narodnogo Khoziaistva S.S.S.R.* (Central State Archive of the National Economy, USSR)], Moscow.

————. *Rossiiskii Tsentr' Khraneniia i Izucheniia Dokumentov Noveishei Istorii* (*RTsKhIDNI:* Russian Center for the Preservation and Study of Documents of Modern History) [formerly *Tsentralnyi Partiinyi Arkhiv Instituta Marksizma-Leninizma pri Tsentral'nom Komitete Kommunisticheskoi Partii Sovetskogo Soyuza* (Central Party Archive of the Institute of Marxism-Leninism of the Central Committee of the Communist Party of the Soviet Union)], Moscow.

U.S. Congress, House. Committee on Expenditures in the State Department. *Russian Bonds.* 65th Cong., 3d sess., 1919.

————. Committee on Foreign Affairs. *Conditions in Russia.* 66th Cong., 3d sess., 1921.

————. Special Committee on Un-American Activities, *Investigation of Un-American Propaganda Actitivies in the U.S.* 77th Cong., 1st sess., 1939. H.R. 282. 10 vols.

U.S. Congress, Senate. Committee on Foreign Relations. *Relations with Russia.* 66th Cong., 3d sess., 1921. S.J. Res. 164.

————. Committee on Foreign Relations. *Recognition of Russia.* 68th Cong., 1st sess., 1924.

————. Subcommittee of the Committee on Foreign Relations. *Russian Propaganda.* 66th Cong., 2d sess., 1920. S. Rep. 526.

U. S. Department of Commerce. *Commerce Reports.* Washington, D.C., 1921–1922.

————. *Commerce Yearbook.* Washington, D.C., 1927–1942.

————. General Records, 1919–1927. Record Group 40, National Archives, Washington, D.C.

————. Records of the Bureau of Foreign and Domestic Commerce, 1919–1930. Record Group 151, File 448-U.S., National Archives, Washington, D.C.

————. *Report of the Secretary of Commerce, 1921, 1924.* Washington, D.C., 1922, 1924.

U.S. Department of Commerce, Bureau of Economic Analysis. *The National Income and Product Accounts of the United States, 1929–1974.* Washington, D.C., 1975.

U.S. Department of Justice. Federal Bureau of Investigation Records, Ludwig Martens Papers. Washington, D.C.

U.S. Department of the Navy. Office of Naval Intelligence (ONI) Central Administration Correspondence, 1930–1948. Record Group 38, National Archives, Washington, D.C.

U.S. Department of State. General Records, 1918–1929. Record Group 59, National Archives, Washington, D.C.

————. *Papers Relating to the Foreign Relations of the United States, 1920, 1921, 1922, 1923, 1928.* Washington, D.C.,1936–1943.

————. Records of the Department of State Relating to Internal Affairs of Russia and Soviet Union, 1919–1929. Record Group 59, National Archives, Washington, D.C.

U.S. Department of the Treasury. *Annual Report of the Secretary of the Treasury on the State of the Finances, 1919–1922.* Washington, D.C., 1920–1923.

————. General Records, 1917–1927. Record Group 39, National Archives, Washington, D.C.

U.S. Federal Reserve Board. *Federal Reserve Bulletin.* Washington, D.C., 1921–1926.

U.S. War Department. Records of the Department of Military Intelligence, 1919–1941. Record Group 165, National Archives, Washington, D.C.

World War Foreign Debt Commission. *Combined Annual Reports of the World War Foreign Debt Commission, Fiscal Years 1922–27.* Washington, D.C., 1927.

➤ NEWSPAPERS, PERIODICALS, AND INTERNAL BUSINESS PUBLICATIONS

American-Russian Chamber of Commerce. *Handbook of the Soviet Union*. New York, 1936.

Amtorg. *Economic Review of the Soviet Union*. New York, 1929.

Chase National Bank. *The Chase Economic Bulletin*. New York, 1922.

National Association of Manufacturers. *American Industries*. New York, 1919–1923.

———. *American Industries Pocket Bulletin*. New York, 1926.

———. *Confidential Bulletin of Foreign Trade Opportunities*. New York, 1919.

———. *Export American Industries*. New York, 1920.

———. *Proceedings*. New York, 1919–1926.

National Industrial Conference Board. *Conference Board Bulletin*. New York, 1929.

———. *A Picture of World Economic Conditions, 1928*. New York, 1928.

———. *A Picture of World Economic Conditions in the Summer of 1929*. New York, 1929.

———. *Trends in the Foreign Trade of the United States*. New York, 1930.

New York Times. New York, 1919–1926, 1930.

Russian Economic Review. New York, 1920.

U.S. Chamber of Commerce. *General Bulletin*. New York, 1919–1926.

———. *Foreign Commerce Handbook, 1922–1923*. New York, 1922.

———. *Foreign Commerce Handbook, 1923–1924*. New York, 1923.

➤ SECONDARY SOURCES: ARTICLES, BOOKS, DISSERTATIONS

Abrahams, Paul P. "American Bankers and the Economic Tactics of Peace." *Journal of American History* 56 (December 1969): 572–83.

Abramson, Rudy. *Spanning the Century: The Life of W. Averell Harriman, 1891–1986*. New York, 1992.

All-Union Textile Syndicate, The. Moscow, *Krasnyi Proletarii*, n.d.

Ambrosius, Lloyd. *Woodrow Wilson and the American Diplomatic Tradition: The Treaty Fight in Perspective*. Cambridge, Mass., 1987.

Amtorg Trading Corporation. *Economic Statistics of the Soviet Union*. New York, 1928.

———. *Soviet-American Trade Outlook*. New York, 1928.

Andres, Enrike. *The N.E.P.: Its Origin and Goal*. Moscow, 1969.

Baer, George W., ed. *A Question of Trust: The Origins of U.S.–Soviet Diplomatic Relations: The Memoirs of Loy Henderson*. Stanford, Calif., 1987.

Ball, Alan M. *Russia's Last Capitalists: The Nepmen, 1921–1929*. Berkeley, Calif., 1987.

Bentley, Elizabeth. *Out of Bondage*. New York, 1951.

Bennett, Edward M. *Recognition of Russia: An American Foreign Policy Dilemma*. Waltham, Mass., 1970.

———. *Franklin D. Roosevelt and the Search for Security: American-Soviet Relations, 1933–1939*. Wilmington, Del., 1985.

Best, Gary Dean. *The Politics of American Individualism: Herbert Hoover in Transition, 1918–1921*. Westport, Conn., 1975.

———. *To Free a People*. Westport, Conn., 1983.

Bishop, Donald Gordon. *The Roosevelt-Litvinov Agreements: The American View*. Syracuse, N.Y., 1965.

Bose, Tarun Chandra. *American Soviet Relations, 1921–33*. Calcutta, 1967.

Brandes, Joseph. *Herbert Hoover and Economic Diplomacy*. Pittsburgh, 1962.

Bron, Saul G. *Soviet Economic Development and American Business*. New York, 1930.

Browder, Robert Paul. *The Origins of Soviet-American Diplomacy*. Princeton, N.J., 1953.

Brown, Anthony Cave, and Charles B. McDonald. *On a Field of Red: The Communist International and the Coming of World War II*. New York, 1981.

Brownell, Will, and Richard N. Billings. *So Close to Greatness: A Biography of William C. Bullitt*. New York, 1987.

Brownlee, W. Elliot. *Dynamics of Ascent: A History of the American Economy*. 2d ed. Chicago, 1988.

Bryson, John. *The World of Armand Hammer*. New York, 1985.

Budish, J.M., and Samuel S. Shipman. *Soviet Foreign Trade: Menace or Promise*. New York, 1930.

Bullitt, William C. *The Bullitt Mission to Russia: Testimony before the Committee on Foreign Relations, United States Senate*. New York, 1919. Reprint, Westport, Conn., 1977).

Burner, David. *Herbert Hoover: A Public Life*. New York, 1979.

Carr, E.H. *A History of Soviet Russia*. Vol. 3, *The Bolshevik Revolution, 1917–1923*. London, 1953.

Carr, E.H. and R.W. Davies. *Foundations of a Planned Economy, 1926–1929*. 2 vols. New York, 1969.

Carstensen, Fred V. *American Enterprise in Foreign Markets: Studies of Singer and International Harvester in Imperial Russia*. Chapel Hill, N.C., 1984.

Chossudovsky, E.M. *Chicherin and the Evolution of Soviet Foreign Policy and Diplomacy*. Geneva, 1973.

Cleveland, Harold van B., and Thomas F. Huertas. *Citibank, 1812–1970*. Cambridge, Mass., 1985.

Coben, Stanley. *A. Mitchell Palmer: Politician*. New York, 1963.

Cohen, Stephen F. *Bukharin and the Bolshevik Revolution: A Political Biography, 1888–1938*. New York, 1980.

Cohen, Warren. *Empire without Tears: America's Foreign Relations, 1921–1933*. Philadelphia, 1987.

Colcord, Lincoln. "Absolutely No Russian Policy." *Nation* 110 (April 3, 1920): 427–478.

Condoide, Mikhail V. *Russian-American Trade: A Study of the Soviet Foreign-Trade Monopoly*. Columbus, Ohio, 1946.

Conquest, Robert. *The Harvest of Sorrow: Soviet Collectivization and the Terror-Famine*. New York, 1986.

Corson, William R., and Robert T. Crowley. *The New KGB: Engine of Soviet Power*. New York, 1985.

Crissey, Forrest. *Alexander Legge, 1866–1933*. Chicago, 1936.

Dallin, Robert J. *Soviet Espionage*. New Haven, Conn., 1955.

Davies, R.W. *The Soviet Economy in Turmoil, 1929–1930*. Cambridge, Mass., 1989.

Day, Richard B. *Leon Trotsky and the Politics of Economic Isolation*. Cambridge, England, 1973.

Debo, Richard K. "George C. Chicherin: Soviet Russia's Second Foreign Commissar." Ph.D. diss., University of Nebraska, 1964.

———. *Revolution and Survival: The Foreign Policy of Soviet Russia 1917–18*. Toronto, 1979.

———. *Survival and Consolidation: The Foreign Policy of Soviet Russia 1918–1921*. Montreal, 1992.

Dodge, Mark M., ed. *Herbert Hoover and the Historians*. West Branch, Iowa, 1988.

Draper, Theodore. *Roots of American Communism*. New York, 1957. Reprint, Chicago, 1985.

Dunn, Robert W., ed. *The Palmer Raids*. New York, 1948.

Ellis, Ethan. *Frank B. Kellogg and American Foreign Relations, 1925–29*. New Brunswick, N.J., 1961.

Evgen'ev, G., and B. Shapik. *Revolyutsioner, Diplomat, Uchenyi: L.K. Martens*. Moscow, 1960.

Farnsworth, Beatrice. *William C. Bullitt and the Soviet Union.* Bloomington, Ind., 1967.
Ferrell, Robert H. *Ill-Advised: Presidential Health and the Public Trust.* Columbia, Mo., 1992.
Filene, Peter G. *Americans and the Soviet Experiment, 1917–1933.* Cambridge, Mass., 1967.
Finder, Joseph. *Red Carpet.* New York, 1983.
Fink, Carole. *The Genoa Conference: European Diplomacy, 1921–22.* Chapel Hill, N.C., 1984.
Fithian, Floyd J. "Dollars without the Flag: The Case of Sinclair and Sakhalin Oil." *Pacific Historical Review* 29 (May 1970): 205–22.
———. "Soviet-American Economic Relations, 1918–1933: American Business in Russia During the Period of Nonrecognition." Ph.D. diss., University of Nebraska, 1964.
Foglesong, David S. "Xenophon Kalamatiano: An American Spy in Revolutionary Russia?" *Intelligence and National Security* 6 (January 1991): 154–95.
Forbes, John Douglas. *J.P. Morgan, Jr., 1867–1943.* Charlottesville, Va., 1981.
Gaddis, John Lewis. *The Long Peace: Inquiries into the History of the Cold War.* New York, 1987.
———. "New Conceptual Approaches to the Study of American Foreign Relations: Interdisciplinary Perspectives." *Diplomatic History* 14 (Summer 1990): 405–24.
———. *Russia, the Soviet Union, and the United States.* 2d ed. New York, 1990.
Gaworek, Norman H. "From Blockade to Trade: Allied Economic Warfare against Soviet Russia, June 1919 to January 1920." *Jahrbücher für Geschichte Osteuropas* 23 (1975): 39–69.
Gelb, Michael, ed. *An American Engineer in Stalin's Russia: The Memoirs of Zara Witkin, 1932–1934.* Berkeley, Calif., 1991.
Gillette, Peter S. "Armand Hammer, Lenin, and the First American Concession in Soviet Russia." *Slavic Review* 40 (Fall 1981): 355–65.
Gitlow, Benjamin. *I Confess.* New York, 1940.
Glad, Betty. *Charles Evans Hughes and the Illusions of Innocence: A Study in American Diplomatic History.* Urbana, Ill., 1966.
Grayson, Benson Lee. *Russian-American Relations in World War I.* New York, 1979.
Gregory, T.T.C. "Stemming the Red Tide." *World's Work* (April 1921): 608–9.
Hall, Ray O. *International Transactions of the United States.* New York, 1936.
Hammer, Armand. *The Quest of the Romanoff Treasure.* New York, 1932.
Hammer, Armand, with Neil Lyndon. *Hammer.* New York, 1987.
Harriman, W. Averell. *America and Russia in a Changing World: A Half Century of Personal Observation.* Garden City, N.Y., 1971.
———. *Peace with Russia?* New York, 1959.
Hawley, Ellis, ed. *Herbert Hoover as Secretary of Commerce: Studies in New Era Thought and Practice.* Iowa City, Iowa, 1981.
Heymann, Hans. *We Can Do Business with Russia.* Chicago, 1945.
Himmer, Robert. "Rathenau, Russia, and Rapallo." *Central European History* 9 (1976): 146–83.
Hoff Wilson, Joan. *Ideology and Economics: U.S. Relations with the Soviet Union, 1918–1933.* Columbia, Mo., 1974.
Hogan, Michael J. "Corporatism: A Postive Appraisal." *Diplomatic History* 10 (Fall 1986): 363–72.
———. *Informal Entente: The Private Structure of Cooperation in Anglo-American Economic Diplomacy, 1918–1928.* Chicago, 1977. Reprint, Chicago, 1991.
Howe, Irving, and Louis Coser. *The American Communist Party: A Critical History, 1919–1957.* Boston, 1957.
Jacobson, Jon. *When the Soviet Union Entered World Politics.* Berkeley, Calif., 1994.
Johnson, Claudius O. *Borah of Idaho.* Seattle, 1936. Reprint, Seattle, 1967.

Johnson, Paul. *Modern Times: The World from the Twenties to the Eighties*. New York and London, 1983.
Johnson, Robert David. *The Peace Progressives and American Foreign Relations*. Cambridge and London, 1995.
Jordan, Virgil. *The Inter-Ally Debts and the United States*. New York, 1925.
Kargina, Tatiana N. "*Politika Americanskogo Kapitala v Otnoshenii Sovietskoi Rossii v 1920 godov–nachale 30kh godov.*" In *Sovremennaia Istoriografiia Ekspansionizma SShA*, edited by A.A. Fursenko and V.N. Pleshkova. Leningrad, 1985.
———. "Soviet-American Trade: Economic Links in the 1920s." Ph.D diss., Leningrad University, 1988.
Kayden, Eugene M. and Aleksiei N. Antsiferov. *The Cooperative Movement in Russia during the War*. New Haven, Conn., 1929.
Kennan, George F. *Russia and the West under Lenin and Stalin*. Boston, 1960.
———. *Soviet-American Relations, 1917–1920: Russia Leaves the War*. Princeton, N.J., 1956.
Khovratovich, I.M. *G.V. Chicherin*. Moscow, 1980.
Killen, Linda. *The Russian Bureau*. Lexington, Ky., 1983.
———. "The Search for a Democratic Russia: Bakhmetev and the United States." *Diplomatic History* 2 (Summer 1978): 237–56.
Klehr, Harvey, John Earl Haynes, and Fridrikh Igorevich Firsov. *The Secret World of American Communism*. New Haven, Conn., 1995.
Klein, Julius. *Frontiers of Trade*. New York, 1929.
Kosikh, Elena Semenovna. "The Concession Policy of the Bolsheviks in the Twenties." Abstracted Ph.D. diss., Moscow Pedagogical State University, 1994.
Krasin, L.B. *Questions of Foreign Trade*. Moscow, 1928.
Krassin, Lubov. *Leonid Krassin: His Life and Work*. London, 1929.
Krog, Carl E., and William R. Tanner, eds. *Herbert Hoover and the Republican Era: A Reconsideration*. Lanham, Md., 1985.
Kuromiya, Hiroaki. *Stalin's Industrial Revolution: Politics and Workers, 1928–1932*. Cambridge, England, 1988.
Levin, N. Gordon. *Woodrow Wilson and World Politics: America's Response to War and Revolution*. New York, 1968.
Lewis, Cleona. *America's Stake in International Investments*. Washington, D.C., 1938.
Libbey, James K. *Alexander Gumberg and Soviet-American Relations, 1917–1933*. Lexington, Ky., 1977.
———. "The American-Russian Chamber of Commerce." *Diplomatic History* 9 (Summer 1985): 233–48.
———. *American-Russian Economic Relations, 1770s–1990s: A Survey of Issues and References*. Claremont, Calif., 1989.
———. "New Study Areas for Soviet-American Relations: The Case of Russian Gold." *Society for Historians of American Foreign Relations Newsletter* 6 (June 1975): 16–18.
Lloyd, Craig. *Aggressive Introvert: A Study of Herbert Hoover and Public Relations Management, 1912–1932*. Columbus, Ohio, 1972.
Lowitt, Richard, ed. *Journal of a Tamed Bureaucrat: Nils A. Olsen and the BAE (Bureau of Agricultural Economics), 1925–1935*. Ames, Iowa, 1980.
Lundestad, Geir. "Moralism, Presentism, Exceptionalism, Provincialism, and Other Extravagances in American Writings on the Early Cold War." *Diplomatic History* 13 (Fall, 1989): 527–545.
Maddox, Robert James. *William E. Borah and American Foreign Policy*. Baton Rouge, La., 1969.
——— "Woodrow Wilson, the Russian Embassy, and Siberian Intervention." *Pacific Historical Review* 36 (November 1967): 435–48.

Maddux, Thomas R. *Years of Estrangement: American Relations with the Soviet Union, 1933–1941.* Tallahassee, Fla., 1980.

Mayer, Arno. *Politics and Diplomacy of Peacemaking: Containment and Counterrevolution at Versailles, 1918–19.* New York, 1967.

McCoy, Donald R. *Calvin Coolidge, the Quiet President.* New York, 1967.

McFadden, David W. *Alternative Paths: Soviets and Americans, 1917–1920.* New York, 1993.

———. "The Politics of Relief: American Quakers and Russian Bolsheviks, 1917–1921." Unpublished conference paper, Society for Historians of American Foreign Relations, 1994.

Murray, Robert K. *The Harding Era: Warren G. Harding and His Administration.* Minneapolis, 1969.

———. *The Politics of Normalcy: Governmental Theory and Practice in the Harding-Coolidge Era.* New York, 1973.

———. *Red Scare: A Study in National Hysteria, 1919–1920.* Minneapolis, 1955.

Nash, George H. *Herbert Hoover: The Engineer.* New York, 1983.

Nevins, Allan, and Frank Ernest Hill. *Ford.* Vol. 2, *Expansion and Challenge, 1915–1933.* New York, 1957.

Nove, Alec. *An Economic History of the U.S.S.R.* Middlesex, England, 1969.

Novosti Press Agency. *USSR '90 Yearbook.* Moscow, 1990.

O'Connor, Timothy Edward. *Diplomacy and Revolution: G.V. Chicherin and Soviet Foreign Affairs, 1918–1930.* Ames, Iowa, 1988.

———. *The Engineer of Revolution: L.B. Krasin and the Bolsheviks, 1870–1926.* Boulder, Colo., 1992.

Parry, Albert. "Washington B. Vanderlip, the 'Khan of Kamchatka.'" *Pacific Historical Review* 27 (August 1948): 311–30.

Pavloff, J.M. "The Upbuilding of Soviet Russia: Five-Year Plan for Industrial Development of the Soviet Union." Amtorg pamphlet, April 1929.

Perkins, Dexter. *Charles Evans Hughes and American Democratic Statesmanship.* Boston, 1956.

Pipes, Richard. *The Russian Revolution.* New York, 1990.

Podlesnii, P.T. *SSSR i SShA: 50 Let Diplomaticheskikh Otnoshenii.* Moscow, 1983.

Pois, Anne Marie. "The Politics and Process of Organizing for Peace: The United States Section of the Women's International League for Peace and Freedom, 1919–1939." Ph.D. diss., University of Colorado, Boulder, 1988.

Pratt, J.W. "Robert Lansing." *Dictionary of American Biography,* edited by Dumas Malone, 5:609–10. New York, 1961.

Propas, Frederic L. "Creating a Hard Line toward Russia: The Training of State Department Soviet Experts, 1927–1937." *Diplomatic History* 8 (Summer 1984): 209–26.

———. "The State Department, Bureaucratic Politics and Soviet-American Relations, 1918–1938." Ph.D. diss., University of California, Los Angeles, 1982.

Radosh, Ronald. "John Spargo and Wilson's Russian Policy, 1920." *Journal of American History* 52 (December 1965), 548–60.

Reikhberg, G.E., and B.S. Shapik. *Delo Martensa.* Moscow, 1966.

Reuther, Victor G. *The Brothers Reuther and the Story of the U.A.W.* Boston, 1976.

Rhodes, Benjamin. "Governor James P. Goodrich of Indiana and the 'Plain Facts' about Russia." *Indiana Magazine of History* 85 (March 1989): 1–30.

Romerstein, Herbert. *The KGB against the "Main Enemy": How the Soviet Intelligence Service Operates against the United States.* Lexington, Mass., 1989.

Ropes, E.C. "American-Soviet Trade Relations." *Russian Review* 3 (Autumn, 1943): 89–94.

Salzman, Neil V. *Reform and Revolution: The Life and Times of Raymond Robins.* Kent, Ohio, 1991.

Savitt, Robert Paul. "To Fill A Void: Soviet 'Diplomatic' Representation in the United States Prior to Recognition." Ph.D. diss., Georgetown University, 1983.

Schulzinger, Robert D. *The Making of the Diplomatic Mind: The Training, Outlook, and Style of United States Foreign Service Officers, 1908–1931*. Middletown, Conn., 1975.

Schuman, Frederick L. *American Policy toward Russia since 1917: A Study of Diplomatic History, International Law, and Public Opinion*. New York, 1928.

Seppain, Hélène. *Contrasting U.S. and German Attitudes to Soviet Trade, 1917–1991: Politics by Economic Means*. New York and Hampshire, England, 1992.

Sheinis, Zinovy. *Maxim Litvinov*. Translated by Vic Shneierson. Moscow, 1990.

Shishkin, V.A. *"Polosa Priznanii" i Vneshneekonomicheskaia Politika SSSR*. Leningrad, 1983.

Siegel, Katherine A.S. "Loans and Legitimacy: Soviet-American Trade and Diplomacy, 1919–1929." Ph.D. diss., University of California, Santa Barbara, 1991.

———. "Technology and Trade: Russia's Pursuit of American Investment, 1917–1929." *Diplomatic History* 17 (Summer 1993): 375–98.

Sivachev, N.V. and N.N. Yakovlev. *Russia and the United States*. Chicago, 1979.

Smith, Daniel M. *Aftermath of War: Bainbridge Colby and Wilsonian Diplomacy, 1920–1921*. Philadelphia, 1970.

Smith, Glen Alden. *Soviet Foreign Trade: Organization, Operations, and Policy, 1918–1971*. New York, 1973.

Sonkin, M.E. *Okno vo Vneshnii Mir: Ekonomicheskie Sviazi Sovetskogo Gosudarstva*. Moscow, 1964.

Spargo, John. "Bainbridge Colby." In *The American Secretaries of State and their Diplomacy*, edited by Samuel Flagg Bemis, 10:179–218. New York, 1958.

Spolansky, Jacob. *The Communist Trail in America*. New York, 1951.

Sutton, Antony. *Wall Street and the Bolshevik Revolution*. New Rochelle, N.Y., 1974.

———. *Western Technology and Soviet Economic Development, 1917 to 1930*. Stanford, Calif., 1968.

Talbert, Roy, Jr., *Negative Intelligence: The Army and the American Left, 1917–1941*. Jackson, Miss., 1991.

Thompson, John M. *Russia, Bolshevism, and the Versailles Peace*. Princeton, N.J., 1966.

Trani, Eugene P. "Herbert Hoover and the Russian Revolution, 1917–1920." Presented at a seminar in memory of the 100th anniversary of Hoover's birth. West Branch, Iowa: Herbert Hoover Presidential Library Association, 1974.

Trotsky, Leon. *My Life*. Gloucester, Mass., 1970.

Tsvetkov, G.N. *Shestnadtsat' Let Nepriznaniia: Politika SShA v Otnoshenii Sovetskogo Gosudarstva v 1917–1933 gg*. Kiev, 1971.

Uldricks, Teddy J. *Diplomacy and Ideology: The Origins of Soviet Foreign Relations, 1917–1930*. London, 1979.

Ullman, Richard H. *Anglo-Soviet Relations, 1917–1921*. Vol. 2, *Intervention and the War*. Princeton, N.J., 1961.

———. *Anglo-Soviet Relations, 1917–1921*. Vol. 3, *The Anglo-Soviet Accord*. Princeton, N.J., 1973.

Unterberger, Betty M. "Woodrow Wilson and the Bolsheviks: The 'Acid Test' of Soviet-American Relations." *Diplomatic History* 11 (Spring 1987): 71–90.

U.S. Army Intelligence Center. *The Counter Intelligence Corps between Two World Wars, 1918–1941*. History of the C.I.C. Series, vol. 4. Fort Holabird, Baltimore, Md., May 1960.

Warth, Robert D. "The Palmer Raids." *South Atlantic Quarterly* 48 (January 1949): 1–23.

Weinberg, Steve. *Armand Hammer: The Untold Story*. Boston, 1989.

Weissman, Benjamin. *Herbert Hoover and Famine Relief to Soviet Russia, 1921–1923*. Stanford, Calif., 1974.

―――. "Herbert Hoover's 'Treaty' with Soviet Russia, August 20, 1921." *Slavic Review* 28 (1969): 276–88.

White, Christine A. *British and American Commercial Relations with Soviet Russia, 1918–1924*. Chapel Hill, N.C., 1992.

―――. "Ford in Russia: In Pursuit of the Chimeral Market." *Business History* 28 (October 1986): 77–104.

White, Steven. *Britain and the Bolshevik Revolution*. New York, 1980.

―――. *The Origins of Detente: The Genoa Conference and Soviet-Western Relations, 1921–1922*. Cambridge, England, 1985.

Wilkins, Mira. *The Maturing of Multinational Enterprise: American Business Abroad from 1914 to 1970*. Cambridge, Mass., 1974.

Williams, Andrew J. *Labor and Russia: The Attitude of the Labour Party to the USSR, 1924–1934*. Manchester, England, 1989.

―――. *Trading with the Bolsheviks: The Politics of East-West Trade, 1920–1939*. Manchester, England, 1992.

Williams, Robert C. *Russian Art and American Money, 1900–1940*. Cambridge, Mass., 1980.

Williams, William Appleman. *American-Russian Relations, 1781–1947*. New York, 1952.

―――. "Raymond Robins and Russian-American Relations, 1917–1938." Ph.D. diss., University of Wisconsin, 1950.

Wolfe, Bertram. *A Life in Two Centuries*. New York, 1981.

Yanson, J.D. *Foreign Trade in the U.S.S.R.* London, 1934.

INDEX

A.E.G. Corp., 67-68
agricultural policies, 127
Alamerico (Allied American Corp.), 4, 65,
  80-81, 84, 89, 101, 126, 167 n 20
Alapayevsk asbestos mine, 119
Albert Kahn Co., 182 n 101
Allen, W. E., 16
Allied American Corp. (Alamerico). See
  Alamerico
Allied Drug and Chemical Co., 19, 78-79
Allied embargo against Soviet Russia, 2, 9,
  12, 13, 14, 17-18, 24, 26, 146 n 28, 152-
  53 n 31; trade through Estonia during,
  26-27, 29; business opposition to, 28;
  ending of U.S. participation in, 28, 46,
  48; labor union opposition to, 28; ex-
  clusion of war-related materiel after U.S.
  lifting of, 30, 46, 153 n 49; trade through
  Estonia after lifting of, 30-31; State De-
  partment position on, 39; ending of, 42,
  45; and Russian civil war, 45; and humanitarian relief, 57; Allied Drug and
  Chemical trade with Soviets during, 79;
  claims for compensation for, 90
Allied powers: military intervention in
  Russia, 16, 20, 40-43, 44, 45, 90,
  157 n 28; diplomatic initiatives, 41-42
Allied Supreme Economic Council, 68
Allis-Chalmers Manufacturing Co., 80
Allport, Fayette, 101-2
All-Russian Central Executive Committee
  of Soviets, 49
All-Russian Textile Syndicate (ARTS), 4,
  81-84, 86, 89, 105-6
Alter, Robert S., 28
Amalgamated Clothing Workers, 36
American Bolshevik Bureau of
  Information, 7, 145 n 15
American Car and Foundry Co., 29

American Commercial Association to
  Promote Trade with Russia, 16, 24-25,
  37, 149 n 80
American Committee for Russian Famine
  Relief, 55
American Communist party, 1, 7, 25, 69,
  134, 151 n 3; the Hammers' role in, 78,
  167 n 11; under Coolidge, 100
American Export-Import Bank, 138
American Federation of Labor, 50, 69
American Friends Service Committee
  (AFSC), 160 n 100. See also Quakers
American Locomotive Sales Corp., 3, 29,
  30, 66, 98, 103, 139, 176 n 106
American Manufacturers' Export Assoc.,
  62
American Red Cross, 113. See also
  Robins, Raymond
American Relief Administration (ARA),
  124; relief activities, 3, 49, 53-60, 160
  nn 99, 103; and Hoover's proposed
  economic mission to Russia, 71, 72; and
  diplomatic relations with FER, 167 n 4
American-Russian Chamber of Commerce,
  13, 46, 75, 86-87, 105-9, 175-76 n 93,
  176 nn 105, 106; and tariffs, 134-35
American Screw Co., 149 n 81
American Ship and Commerce Corp., 123
American Society of International Law, 39
American Steamship Owners Assoc., 136
American Steel Export Co., 21
American Tool Works Co., 28, 80, 104
Amerikanskii Torgovlaia. See Amtorg
  Trading Corp.
ammonia oxidation technology, 130
Amtorg Trading Corp., 4, 65, 81, 84-88,
  94, 105, 126, 140, 169 n 39; financing
  for, 84, 85, 88, 101-2, 103-4, 175 n 84;
  Wolfsohn and Son suit against, 89-90;

representation at Civil Aeronautics Conference, 99; travel regulations and, 99-100; and Soviet propaganda in U.S., 100, 184 n 8; and E. I. du Pont de Nemours & Co., 130; OGPU section of, 134

Anderson, T.H., 114

Anglo-Soviet trade treaty of Feb. 1921, 11, 52, 60, 69, 154 n 52

Animal Trap Co., 106

Antheus Trading Co., 151 n 8

anticommunism: and loans to Kolchak, 6; and Soviet Bureau, 12-13, 14-17, 23, 147 n 56; and military intervention in Russia, 40; and recognition of Soviet Russia, 47-48, 52, 91, 94, 95; and trade with Soviets, 52, 75, 80, 90, 170 n 6; and humanitarian relief, 53, 57, 58; and recognition of Soviet Russia under Coolidge, 97; and trade with Soviets under Coolidge, 100

Apex Co., 16

Arcos Soviet purchasing agency, 85, 107, 168 n 23, 169 n 39

Armenia, 122

Armour and Co., 21

Asbestos and Mineral Corp., 180 n 50

asbestos mines, 119-20, 126

Austin Co., 106, 182 n 101

Austria, 2

autarky, 112, 134, 135

automobile industry, 131

Avezzana, Camillo, 47

Azerbaijan, 121, 122

Azneft oil agency, 121

Babbitt, B.T., Soap Co., 27, 28, 152-53 n 31

Baker, Carver, and Morrell, 168 n 23

Baker, George Barr, 66

Baker, R.J., 136

Bakhmetev, Boris, 8-9, 10, 146 n 26; and military intervention in Russia, 40; and FBI investigation of FER, 76

Baku Workman, 121

balance of trade, 135

Baldwin Locomotive Works, 28-29, 30, 52, 139

Ball, Alan, 127

Bank of Nova Scotia, 33

Barnsdall Corp., 120-22

Baron, S.L., 28, 33

Bausch and Lomb Co., 105

Belgium, 67, 70

Belting and Leather Products Assoc., 154 n 61

Bennett, Edward M., 137

Berkenheim, Alexander M., 17

Berkman, Aron, 152 nn 24, 27

Berlow, Elias, 152 n 27

Bertron, S.R., 75, 134

Berzin, P., 90

Bethlehem Steel Co., 124

Beyer, Capt. Otto S., Jr., 29, 30

Black and Decker Manufacturing Co., 105

Black Tom explosion, 8

Bliss, Gen. Tasker, 43

Bloomfield, Meyer, 74-75

Bobroff, B.L., 22, 37-38

Bobroff Foreign Trading and Engineering Co., 22

Bogdanov, P.A., 134

Bohlen, Charles E., 98

Bolsheviks: deportation of suspected, from U.S., 1; revolution of, 1, 8; and humanitarian aid from U.S., 3; and capitalism, 111

Borah, William E., 8-9, 16, 49, 52, 60, 67, 137, 140; and recognition of Soviet Russia, 70, 81, 90-92, 94; and Gumberg, 81, 168 n 24; and recognition issue under Coolidge, 96, 97

Borden Condensed Milk Sales Co., 24

Borodin, D.D., 66

Boucar, V.F., 175 n 93

Boyer, E.H., 21

Boyer and Sloan, 34

Brandeis, Louis, 16, 54

Branham, Lucy, 90-91, 140, 171 n 15

Breedy, William, 162 n 125

Brest-Litovsk, Treaty of, 12, 111

Briand, Aristide, 68

Bridgeport Rolling Mills, 21

Bristol, Mark L., 122

Bristol Patent Leather Co., 106

Brittenham, E.A., 102

Bron, Saul, 86, 100, 103-4, 130

Browder, Robert Paul, 135

Brown, F.J., 113

Brown, Walter L., 57

Brown and Sharpe Co., 104

Browning, O.H., 101

Bryant, Louise, 44

Buchavich, Fr. Constantine, 92

Buckler, William H., 41
Bukharin, Nikolai, 112, 127
Bullard, Arthur, 39-40, 156 n 5
Bullitt, William C., 41-43, 44-45, 137-38, 139, 157 n 23, 172 n 43
Bureau of Foreign and Domestic Commerce (BFDC), 62, 64, 65, 101
Bureau of Information for Soviet Russia, 9
Bureau of Investigation. *See* Justice, U.S. Department of
Burner, David, 61
Burns, William J., 77-78

Canada: trade with Soviet Russia, 28, 32-34, 101; Department of Labor of, 34
Cannes Conditions, 68, 69
capitalist reforms, with New Economic Policy, 56, 110-11, 161 n 110
Carr, E.H., 12
Carver, C.H., 86
Carver, Clifford, 123
Castle, William R., Jr., 103
Central Executive Committee (Ispolkom), 121
Chadbourne, Philip H., 120-21
Chamberlain, William Henry, 81-82, 109
Chamber of Commerce for the West (Torgpalata), 108-9
Chance-Vought Corp., 87
Chandler, Harry, 118
Chase National Bank, 3, 66; financing for Textile Syndicate from, 83, 86, 169 n 35; Soviet gold shipment consigned to, 99, 173 n 54; financing for Soviet railway bonds, 103; and American-Russian Chamber of Commerce 1929 delegation to USSR, 106, 175 n 93, 176 n 106
chemical industry, 129-31
Chemstroi chemical agency, 129-30
Chiaturi, Georgia, 123-25
Chicago Daily News, 6
Chicago Herald Examiner, 145 n 19
Chicago Pneumatic Tool Co., 176 n 106
Chicherin, Georgii, 2, 6, 8, 11, 35, 36, 60; and Soviet debt/reconstruction, 67, 68, 69, 70, 83; and Hoover's proposed economic mission to Russia, 71, 72; and Soviet-U.S. trade, 75, 94, 166 n 71; and diplomatic relations with U.S., 96, 156 n 5
Chief Concessions Committee, 72, 116,

119, 177 n 5
Child, Richard Washburn, 69, 70, 96
Chretien, John, 152-53 n 31
Christian Science Monitor, 109
Churchill, Sir Winston, 41, 43
Cincinnati Milling, 104
Civil Aeronautics Conference, 99
civil war, Russian; Red army victory, 45; humanitarian aid during. *See* humanitarian relief initiatives
Clark, Charles S., 12
Clark, Evans, 9, 16
Clayton, W.L., 82, 168 n 31
Clemenceau, Georges, 41, 45, 79
Colby, Bainbridge, 27, 46-48, 139
Colby note, 4, 46-48, 51, 66, 139
Colcord, Lincoln, 23, 24
Cold War; historical scholarship during, 4-5
Cole, Felix, 9, 35, 64, 144 n 6
Coleman, Frederick W.B., 51, 84, 97
collectivization, 135; limited, 127
Comintern, 11, 23, 69, 100, 138; and Amtorg Trading Corp., 134
Commerce, U.S. Chamber of, 62, 114, 119. *See also* American-Russian Chamber of Commerce
Commerce, U.S. Department of: and trade with Soviets under Harding, 51, 62-67; Hoover's appointment as Secretary of, 54-55; and war debts, 60-61, 62; Bureau of Foreign and Domestic Trade, 62, 64, 65; and trade with Soviets under Coolidge, 80-81, 82, 85, 94; and trade with Soviets under Hoover, 105; and Soviet Georgia, 122
commercial missions, Soviet, 76-88; Alamerico (Allied American Corp.), 4, 65, 78-81; All-Russian Textile Syndicate, 4, 81-84, 86, 94; under Harding, 76-77; Skvirskii as commercial representative, 76-77; under Coolidge, 77-78, 80-87, 94-95, 99-100; under Hoover, 87-88; under Wilson (*see* Soviet Bureau). *See also* Amtorg Trading Corp.
Commissariat of Food and Supplies, 114
Commissariat of Foreign Affairs (Narkomindel), 72, 77, 95; and Soviet Bureau under Martens, 10, 11-12, 19, 31-32, 154 n 61; Chicago Bureau, 14; and commercial missions during

Coolidge administration, 77-78, 95; and
Kamchatka Peninsula, 118; New York
bureau. *See* Soviet Bureau
Commissariat of Foreign Trade, 72, 101,
119, 169 n 39
Committee for Protection of Creditors,
83
Committee on Public Information (CPI),
39
Communist Labor party, 145 n 17,
154 n 54
Communist party of America, 19, 23, 140,
150 n 106, 151 n 3. *See also* American
Communist party; United Communist
party
concessions policy, 180 n 50; and New
Economic Policy, 111-14; and Kamchatka Peninsula, 118; end of, 127-28
Connors, Eugene F., 120
Constantine, Earl, 85
Converse, Clarence, 23, 24
Coolidge, Calvin, and administration, 3, 4,
140; Hughes' influence on, 50; and
Soviet commercial missions, 77-78,
80-87, 99-100; trade with Soviets under,
79-84, 86-87, 93-105, 167 nn 19, 20,
168 n 23, 174 nn 66, 71, 75, 175 n 83;
and Gumberg, 81; diplomatic relations
with Soviets under, 82, 84, 96-97,
168 n 31; and recognition of Soviet
Russia, 94-97, 98, 100; election of, 95;
and International Harvester, 117
Coombs, William H., 27
Cooper, Henry E., 25
Cooper, Hugh L., 86, 106, 129, 134, 176 n
106
cooperatives: Tsentrosoyuz, 13, 17, 26, 46,
84; Selskosoyuz, 26, 100, 113; British
trade with, 45, 46, 158 n 47; financing
for, 100-101
Corning Glass Works, 165 n 55
corporatism: New Era, 3; Hoover's practice
of, 62, 163 n 7
Corson, William R., 104
Council on Foreign Relations, 15
Cowham Engineering, 107
credit. *See* debt, Soviet; financing; loans
Cross, Samuel H., 64
Crowley, Robert T., 104
Cudahy and Co., 21
Cuse, Robert, 87
Czechoslovakia, 101

Daily Worker, 90
Dalinda (Russian representative to trade
conference), 49
Daugherty, Harry, 49
Davidov (Chairman of Selmash), 116
Davis, Jerome, 90, 136
Davis, John W., 95
Davis, Monnett B., 153 n 31
Davis, Norman H., 46, 48
Dawes Plan, 61, 64, 100, 102
Day, Henry Mason, 120-21, 122
Day, Richard, 112
Dearing, Frederick, 52, 63-64, 122
Debo, Richard K., 2, 42
Debs, Eugene V., 36
debt, Soviet, 45; and recognition issue, 60,
90; Hoover's position on, 60-61, 62;
total amount by 1926, 61; international
conferences on, 67, 68, 69; Coolidge's
position on, 94; and trade with U.S., 94.
See also financing; loans
de Camp, Robert, 175 n 93
Demidov San Donato, 7
Dennison Manufacturing Co., 149 n 81
deportations, of Russians from U.S., 1, 23
Depression. *See* Great Depression
Derutra (Deutsche-Russische Lager und
Transportgesellschaft), 78, 123, 169 n
39, 180 n 68
Detroit Twist Drill, 154 n 61
Deutsche Works, 102
Dewey, H.H., 129, 134
diplomatic initiatives, 1919-1923, 39-53,
156 n 5; and Colby note, 4, 46-48, 51,
66; Bullard's visit, 39-40, 156 n 5;
Bullitt's mission, 41-43, 44-45, 157 n
23; and trade embargo, 45-46; Hughes's
influence on, 48-53, 66, 159 n 72
diplomatic recognition. *See* recognition, of
Soviet Russia
Dirksen, Herbert von, 103
Disconte Gesellschaft, 181 n 79
Dnieprostroi power station, 129
Doheny, Edward L., 118
Dorpat Peace Treaty, 26
Duplex Machine Co., 28, 149 n 81
Du Pont, Lammot, 128, 130-32
Durand, E. Dana, 64, 80, 85
Durand, M.D., 180 n 50
Durant, Kenneth, 24, 29, 35-36, 96,
172 n 43
Duranty, Walter, 66, 109, 136

Eastman, Max, 58
Eberhard Faber, 126
economic mission to Russia, proposed, 71-75, 165 n 52, 166 n 71
Eddy, Sherwood, 90
E.I. Du Pont de Nemours & Co., 128-32
Eitingon-Schild, 182 n 93
Ekonomicheskaya Zhizn, 11
Elkus, Abram I., 15
Ellis, L. Ethan, 97
embargo. *See* Allied embargo against Soviet Russia
Emch, Hans, 115-16, 117
emigrants, to Soviet Russia from U.S., 18, 31
Equitable Trust Co., 3, 25, 66; financing for Textile Syndicate from, 83; Soviet gold shipment consigned to, 99; and American-Russian Chamber of Commerce, 175 n 93, 176 n 106
Estonia, 26-27, 29, 30-31
export licenses: for trade through Soviet Bureau, 16, 22; for trade in war-related material, 153 n 49

Fall, Albert B., 93
Far Eastern Republic (FER), 119; Soviet front government in Siberia, 58, 76, 161 n 120, 167 n 4; Special Trade Delegation of, 76
Far Eastern Trade Delegation, 81
Farmer-Labor party, 95
Farquhar, Percival, 176 n 106
Federal Reserve Board, 26, 99
Filene, Peter G., 3, 47, 57, 136
Financial America, 96
financing: for Canadian-Soviet trade, 101; for Czechoslovakian-Soviet trade, 101; for German-Soviet trade, 101, 102-3, 174 n 73, 174-75 n 78; for Swedish-Soviet trade, 101
financing, for U.S.-Soviet trade, 100-104, 175 n 83; for Soviet Bureau, 14-15, 18-19, 25, 26, 31, 148 n 71, 150 n 98, 151 n 13, 152 n 24; for Textile Syndicate, 83; for Amtorg Trading Corp., 84, 85, 88, 101-2, 103-4, 175 n 84; Kellogg's policy on, 98; for cooperatives, 100-101; and General Motors, 131-32; Commerce Department 1923 report on, 173 n 62
Fink, Carole, 68, 70-71

Finnish Information Bureau, 9
Finnish Workers' Government, 9
Fischman and Co., 22
Fish, Hamilton, Jr., 134, 162 n 125
Fithian, Floyd, 122
Five-Year Plan, First, 4, 5, 51, 104, 106, 139-40; and technical assistance contracts, 127-32
Five-Year Plans, 104, 182 n 101
Ford, Henry, 14, 18, 80, 124, 139
Ford Motor Co., 14, 18, 26, 80, 101, 102, 104, 149 n 81, 167 n 20, 174 nn 66, 71, 182 n 101; Nizhni Novgorod plant of, 106, 131, 176 n 97
Foreign Debt Commission, 61
Foreign Policy Association, 90, 171 n 11
Foster, Sir George E., 33
Fox, Albert W., 48, 76-77, 96
Fraina, Louis C., 7, 19, 34
France: trade with Russia, 2, 45, 67, 101, 163 n 4; military intervention in Russia, 40, 41, 43, 45, 157 n 23; and Soviet debt/reconstruction, 68, 70; claims to Soviet gold, 99. *See also* Allied powers; Supreme Allied Council
France, Joseph, 16
Frear, James A., 162 n 125
Free Press, 69
French Nobel Co., 183 n 105
Freyn, H.J., 105
Freyn Engineering Co., 105
Friends of Soviet Russia, 55
Fulton Iron Works, 175 n 83

Gannon, James, 175 n 93
Gardner, Gilson, 55
Gary, Elbert H., 21
Gaworek, Norman, 39
Gelsenkirchner Borgwerke A.-G., 181 n 79
General Electric Co., 3, 33, 66, 86, 103, 105, 136, 182 n 101. *See also* International General Electric Co.
General Motors Corp., 131, 136
General Paper Co., 97
General Railway Signal Co., 175 n 93
Genoa conference, 67-71, 120, 165 nn 38, 45
Georgia, 122; and Barnsdall Corp., 120
Georgia Manganese Co., 124-25, 181 nn 77, 83
German-Russian Storage and Transportation Co. *See* Derutra

German-Soviet Treaty of Brest-Litovsk, 12, 111

Germany: Soviet trade agreements with, 2, 25, 70, 97, 159 n 77; investigation of Martens background in, 15; Soviet trade with, 32, 59, 64, 101, 102-3, 104, 107, 163 nn 4, 15, 168 n 29, 174 nn 73, 75, 174-75 n 78; as broker for U.S. trade with Russia, 63, 64, 163 n 7; and Soviet debt/reconstruction, 68-69, 70; Rapallo Treaty, 70, 97, 159 n 77; technical assistance consultants from, 128; and credits, 133, 135, 137; and Bolshevik revolution, 172 n 43

Gillespie, Julian, 75

Gillette Safety Razor Co., 107

Gitlow, Benjamin, 154 n 54

Glavmetall metal industries agency, 117

Glover Machine Works, 24

Goelro fifteen-year plan, 161 n 107

gold, Russian: as payment from Russia to U.S. firms, 26-27, 30, 38, 52, 63, 152 n 30, 154 n 52; as payment from Russia to countries outside U.S., 33, 34; as payment to U.S. firms from other European countries, 63, 163 n 5; as payment from Russia to U.S. firms under Coolidge, 99, 173 n 54

Golder, Frank, 60

Goldman, Emma, 23

Golos, Jacob, 173 n 59

Gompers, Samuel, 50, 69, 95

Goodrich, James P., 67; and humanitarian relief effort, 49, 50, 58-59, 60; and trade with Soviets under Harding, 66; and Hoover's proposed economic mission to Russia, 71, 73; and All-Russian Textile Syndicate, 82; and recognition of Soviet Russia, 90, 92

Gorbachev, Mikhail S., 78

Gorky, Maxim, 55

Gosbank Soviet state financial institution, 83, 124

Gosplan Soviet planning agency, 56, 72, 161 n 107

Gostorg Soviet state trading agency, 84

Gould, Norman J., 85-86

grain exports, 127, 135

Grand Rapids Underwear Co., 14

Grasselli, T.S., 130

Grasselli Chemical Co., 130

Gray, Lacey G., 113

Great Britain: trade agreements with Soviet Russia, 2, 11, 25, 46, 50-51, 52, 69, 159 nn 76, 77; Martens in, 7; trade with Soviet Russia, 28, 45, 46, 50, 51, 67, 85, 107, 163 nn 4, 15; military intervention in Russia, 40, 41, 43, 157 n 28; and relief efforts, 55, 60; and Soviet debt/reconstruction, 68, 70-71; diplomatic relations with Soviets, 107, 108; Imperial Chemical of, 129, 130-31; and credits, 135. See also Allied powers; Supreme Allied Council

Great Depression, 5, 90; and American-Soviet trade, 135-38

Gregory, T.T.C., 58, 124

Guaranty Trust Co. (GTC), 3, 14-15, 27, 123, 148 n 71; opposition to embargo, 28; loans to Soviets, 66, 181 n 79

Gukovskii, Isidor, 26, 27

Gumberg, Alexander, 49, 58, 59, 66-67, 133-35, 140, 161 n 119, 161-62 n 120; and recognition of Soviet Russia, 70, 77, 81, 82, 84, 90-95, 168 n 24; and Hoover's proposed economic mission to Russia, 71, 72, 73, 75, 165 n 52; professional background, 81; and Textile Syndicate, 81-82, 94; and American-Russian Chamber of Commerce, 86, 106, 107-8; and U.S.-Soviet trade under Coolidge, 94; and concessions, 120-21; on U.S. consuls in Siberia, 167 n 4

Hague conference, 70

Haines, Anna, 55

Hamburg-Amerika Line, 123

Hammer, Armand, 18, 19, 26, 38, 77, 139; political affiliation, 78, 167 n 11; personal and professional background, 78-79; ventures in Russia, 79-81, 119-20, 126-27. See also Alamerico

Hammer, Julius, 9, 11, 19, 24, 78-79, 150 n 98, 167 n 11

Hammer, Victor, 126

Hanna, Paul Wallace, 16

Hapgood, Norman, 66

Harding, Warren G., and administration, 118-19, 140; humanitarian relief under, 3, 49, 53-60, 160 nn 99, 103; election of, 48; and recognition of Soviet Russia, 48-49, 50, 89-93; diplomatic relations with Soviets under, 48-53, 74-75, 89-93,

95-96, 159 n 72; Hughes' influence, 48-53, 66, 159 n 72; trade with Soviet Russia under, 48-53, 59, 60, 62-67, 69, 75, 92, 159 n 72, 163 n 15, 164 n 20; and Goodrich's trips to Soviet Russia, 58; economic foreign policy under, 62-75; and Genoa conference, 69-71, 165 n 38; proposed economic mission to Russia under, 71-75, 165 n 52, 166 n 71; Bloomfield visits to Russia during, 74-75; and Gumberg, 81, 121; illness and death, 93

Hardwick, Thomas, 24, 35

Harper, Samuel N., 34, 147 n 56

Harriman, Averell, 86, 112, 132, 180 n 67; and manganese concession, 122-26. See also W. Averell Harriman and Co.

Harriman, Edward Henry, 122

Harrison, Leland, 102

Haskell, Col. William, 60, 66

Hearst, William Randolph, 96

Heller, Abraham A., 9, 11, 13-14, 16, 17, 18, 20-21, 25, 128, 139; and investigations of Soviet Bureau, 24; and operations of Soviet Bureau, 152 n 27

Helwig, A.L., 175 n 93

Hemphill, Alexander J., 15, 148 n 71

Henderson, Loy, 52, 97-98

Hercules Powder Co., 130

Herter, Christian, 59

Hillquit, Morris, 8, 9

Himmer, Robert, 69

Hinger, A.W., 28-29

Hoff Wilson, Joan, 47, 57, 136

Hoover, Herbert, 3-4, 140; and humanitarian relief, 43-44, 53-60, 157 n 35; and trade with Soviets under Harding, 51, 62-67; personal and professional background, 53-54, 160 n 90; recognition of Soviet Russia under, 54, 60, 66, 108, 135, 185 n 20; and Goodrich's trips to Soviet Russia, 58, 161 n 119; Goodrich's influence on, 59, 60; and war debts, 60-61, 62; proposed economic mission to Russia under Harding, 71-75, 165 n 52, 166 n 71; and trade with Soviets under Coolidge, 82, 85, 94, 98; trade with Soviets under, 104-9, 174 n 75, 175 n 85, 181 n 81; diplomatic relations with Soviets under, 105; and International Harvester, 116; and anticommunism, 152 n 124

Hoover, J. Edgar, 1; and investigation of Soviet Bureau, 15, 16, 19-20; and arrest of Martens, 23; and investigation of Amtorg Trading Corp., 87; and recognition issue under Coolidge, 100

Horne, Sir Robert, 46, 50

Horowitz, I., 17

Horton, Loton, 21

Houghton, Alanson B., 71-72, 73, 165 n 55

Hourwich, Isaac, 9, 35-36

Hourwich, Nicholas, 11

House, Col. Edward M., 8, 39, 41, 43

Hughes, Charles Evans, 122; and diplomatic relations with Soviets, 48-53, 58, 60, 66, 74-75, 76, 159 n 72; professional background, 49-50; and U.S.-Soviet trade, 63, 69; and Genoa conference, 69; and Hoover's proposed economic mission to Russia, 71, 72, 73, 74; and recognition of Soviet Russia, 90-93; and U.S.-Soviet trade under Coolidge, 94; and diplomatic relations with Soviets under Coolidge, 96; opinion on media coverage, 96; resignation from State Department, 96, 97; and International Harvester, 116

Huling, Cyrus, 49

Hull, Cordell, 136, 137

humanitarian relief initiatives, 1919-1923: American Relief Administration (ARA) in, 3, 49, 53-60, 139, 160 nn 99, 103; Nansen plan for, 43-44, 53, 54, 157 n 33; other organizations, 55, 160 n 100; motivation for, 57-58; from Hammers, 79

Hurgin, Isaiah Yakovlevich, 66, 77-78, 87, 90, 93, 101, 123, 169 n 39

IBM. See International Business Machine Corp.

Imperial Chemical of Great Britain, 129, 130-31

Imperial Government. See Russian Imperial Government; Russian Provisional Government

Imperial Russian Transportation Ministry, 29

Industrial Credit Corp., 104, 175 n 84

industrialization, 133; and New Economic Policy, 111-12; and technical assistance, 128. See also New Economic Policy

inflation, in Russia, 31

Ingersoll Rand Co., 33
intelligence agencies, U.S., 12
International Association of Machinists, 36
International Business Machines Corp.
  (IBM), 107, 175 n 93
International Civil Aeronautics
  Conference, 99
International Free Trade League, 36,
  155 n 84
International General Electric Co., 103
International Harvester Co., 14, 51, 64,
  84, 100-2, 104-5, 139, 174 nn 66, 71;
  and New Economic Policy, 113-17,
  127
International High Speed Steel Co.,
  149 n 81
International Oxygen Co., 9, 128
International Workers of the World, 24
Interstate Pulp and Paper Co., 149 n 81
Irtysh Corp., 54
Ispolkom. *See* Central Executive
  Committee
Italy: trade with Soviet Russia, 28. *See
  also* Allied powers; Supreme Allied
  Council
Izvestiia, 91, 96, 128

Jacobson, Jon, 5, 12, 68, 112, 163 n 4
Japan: expansionism, 74; Soviet-Japanese
  treaty, 96; and Kamchatka Peninsula,
  118-19; and Sakhalin island, 119;
  and Soviet recognition, 137,
  185 n 20; *See also* Supreme Allied
  Council
Jennings, Emerson P., 24-25, 37,
  151 nn 13, 14, 155 n 93
Jews, intelligence agency investigations
  of, 15
J.I. Case Threshing Machine Co., 21, 28
Johnson, Hiram, 16, 49, 162 n 125
Johnson, Paul, 71
Johnson and Higgins Co., 176 n 106
Johnson and Johnson, 28
Johnson Debt Default Act (1934), 138
Journal of Commerce, 28, 86, 96, 175 n 93
Justice, U.S. Department of, Bureau of
  Investigation: investigation of Soviet
  Bureau, 12, 14, 15, 16, 19-20, 24, 25,
  26, 27, 34; investigation of FER, 76;
  investigation of Skvirskii's activities,
  77; investigation of Amtorg Trading
  Corp., 87

Kalamatiano, Xenophon, 45, 158 n 42
Kalinin, Mikhail, 49
Kamchatka Peninsula, 118
Kanseler, Ernest, 14
Kargina, Tatiana N., 6, 94
Kelley, Robert, 94, 98, 99, 105, 140
Kellogg, Frank B., 97-98, 136
Kellogg-Briand Pact, 98
Kempsmith Manufacturing Co., 151 n 117
Kendall bill, 135
Kennan, George F., 40, 98
Kerensky, Aleksandr Fyodorovich, 4
Kerr, Philip, 41, 42
Khinchuk, L.M., 109
Kidder Peabody, 144 n 4
Killen, Linda, 8, 40
King, William H., 162 n 125
Kirchwey, Freda, 9
Kleifoth, A.W., 52-53
Klein, Julius, 62
Klishko, N.K., 46
Koehler Motors Co., 12
Kolchak, Adm. Alexander V., 6, 8, 40, 43,
  144 n 4, 146 n 28
Koontz, Woody, 55
Kopp, Victor, 32
Kosikh, Elena Semenovna, 144 n 19
Kosmin (Soviet government
  representative), 114
Krasin, Leonid, 2, 11, 12, 30-32, 120, 123,
  154 nn 52, 61; and Soviet Bureau trade
  with Canada, 33, 34; and trade with
  Great Britain, 46, 52; and trade with
  U.S., 52, 86; and Soviet trade
  regulation, 56; Goodrich's meeting
  with, 58; and Soviet debt/
  reconstruction, 68, 69; and Hoover's
  proposed economic mission to Russia,
  71, 72-73
Krestinskii, Nikolai, 68
Kronstadt base, sailor revolt at, 110
Krupp, 102
Kyshtim Corp., 54

Labor, U.S. Department of, and
  deportation of Martens, 34-35, 36
labor unions, and trade with Russia, 28,
  36, 50
lacquer, manufacture of, 130
Ladd, Edwin F., 162 n 125
La Follette, Robert M., 95
Lamont, Thomas P., 134-35

Lansing, Robert: and Soviet Bureau, 8, 17; personal and professional background, 39; and military intervention in Russia, 40, 43, 44; and diplomatic initiatives, 41-42, 43, 44; resignation of, 44; and trade embargo, 45

Lausanne Conference, 75

League of Nations, 44, 68, 97

Lederle Antitoxin Laboratories, 28

Lee, Gordon, 65

Lee, Higginson and Co., 181 n 79

Leffingwell, Russell, 40

Left Wing Socialist party, New York, 7, 9, 11, 78

Legge, Alexander, 116, 117, 139

Legislative Committee for the Investigation of Seditious Activities. *See* Lusk Committee

Lehigh Machine Co., 21, 24, 151 n 8

Lenin, Vladimir Ilich, 1, 2, 4, 5; and Soviet Bureau, 6, 7, 12, 18, 20, 24, 156 n 95; "Letter to American Workers," 20, 24; and diplomatic relations with U.S., 42; and humanitarian relief, 44, 57; and trade with Great Britain, 46; and New Economic Policy, 56-57; and Genoa conference on Soviet debt/Soviet reconstruction, 69, 70; and Hammers, 78, 79-80; and trade with U.S., 88; and New Economic Policy, 110; and International Harvester, 114; and Kamchatka Peninsula, 118; and Armand Hammer, 119-20

Levin, N. Gordon, 57

Lewery, Leonard J., 80

Libbey, James K., 58, 94

Liebold, K.C., 14

Liggett, Walter, 55

Lima Locomotive Co., 29

lithopone, manufacture of, 130

Litvinov, Maxim, 10, 11-12, 13, 18, 26, 31, 37-38; and diplomatic relations with U.S., 41, 45; and trade with Great Britain, 46; and humanitarian relief, 57; Goodrich's meeting with, 58; and trade with U.S., 75, 77; and commercial representative Skvirskii, 77; at Waldorf-Astoria, 137-38

Lloyd George, David, 41, 42, 45, 46, 157 n 28; and Soviet debt/reconstruction, 68, 70-71

loans: to Imperialist Russia, 6, 60, 83, 144 n 4, 162 n 129, 169 n 35; to Provisional Government, 60, 146 n 26, 162 n 129; U.S., to Germany, 64; U.S., to foreign nations summarized, 71; Soviet, to FER, 76; from France to Imperialist Russia, 99; from Georgia Manganese Co., 125-26. *See also* debt, Soviet; financing

Lodge, Henry Cabot, 60, 94

Lomonosov, George, 9-10, 30, 32

London *Daily Mail,* 157 n 28

Long, Breckenridge, 40

Longworth, Nicholas, 28

Los Angeles *Times,* 118

Loucheur, Louis, 68

Lowman, Seymour, 135

Lubertzy. *See* International Harvester

Lucey Manufacturing Corp., 121

Luhring, Oscar R., 16

Lusk, Clayton R., 17. *See also* Lusk Committee

Lusk Committee (New York State Senate), 16-17, 19, 20-21, 24, 150 n 106

Lyons, Eugene, 109

MacDonald Engineering Co., 107, 182 n 101

Maddox, Robert, 90

Marshall Field and Co., 14

Martens, Ludwig C.A.K., 1, 2, 4, 6-8, 9-22, 139, 144 n 6; appearance, 7; career and personal life prior to opening of Soviet Bureau, 7; attempted arrest of, 23; deportation and return to Russia, 27, 34-38; personal life after closing of Soviet Bureau, 38; and Kamchatka Peninsula, 119; Senate hearing of, 134; on International Free Trade League advisory committee, 155 n 84. *See also* Soviet Bureau

Martin, Thomas, 18

Mason, William E., 16

Massey Harris Co., 101

Mayer, Arno, 57

Mayer, Carl J., 80

Mayer Boot and Shoe Co., 151 n 117

McAllister, Sidney, 100, 114, 116, 117

McClintock, C.B., 105

McCormick, Cyrus, 127

McCormick, Harold, 114

McDonald, James G., 171 n 11

McFadden, David W., 8, 47
McKellar, Kenneth, 162 n 125
media coverage: of Martens and Soviet
    Bureau, 6, 7, 15, 20, 21, 24, 145 n 19;
    opposition to embargo in, 28; of
    Russian retaliation for deportation of
    Martens, 36; of Allied military inter-
    vention in Russia, 43, 157 n 28; of trade
    with Soviet Russia under Harding, 48,
    67, 164 n 21; of British trade with
    Soviets, 50-51, 107; of Goodrich's trips
    to Soviet Russia, 58; of Genoa
    conference, 68-69; of withdrawal of
    U.S. consuls from Siberia, 76-77; of
    Washington Russian information bureau
    under Skvirskii, 77; of recognition issue
    under Harding, 90, 91, 95-96, 171 n 15;
    of recognition issue under Coolidge, 95,
    96-97; of trade with Soviet Russia under
    Coolidge, 96-97; of American-Russian
    Chamber of Commerce 1929 delegation
    to USSR, 106, 107
Medzikhovsky, C.J., 8
Mellon, Andrew W., 63, 98, 135,
    146 n 26
Menard, Frederick G., 120
Mennonites, in relief efforts, 55
Metropolitan Life Insurance Co., 165 n 55
Mett Engineering Co., 168 n 23
Miles, Basil, 35, 155 n 77
military initiatives, 1919-1923, 40-43,
    44, 45, 90, 157 n 28; Hoover's opinion
    of, 53
Military Intelligence Division (MID), U.S.
    War Department: investigation of Soviet
    Bureau, 12-13, 14-15, 24, 148 n 71;
    serving of subpoena on Martens, 12-13,
    14-15, 148 n 71; investigation of
    Jennings, 151 n 14; investigation of
    Communist Labor party, 154 n 54
Milwaukee Shaper Co., 151 n 117
mining concessions: asbestos, 119-20, 126;
    manganese, 122-26
Minor, Clark R., 103
Mississippi Valley Association, 28
Mitchell, Charles E., 83
mixed companies, 120, 123
Mooney, James D., 131
Morgan, J.P., 84
Morgenthau, Henry, 15, 185 nn 30-31
Morris, Edward, 21
Morris, Roland S., 35

Morris and Co., 21, 22
Morrow, Dwight, 71, 84
Morse Twist Drill and Machinery Co., 26
Moscow *Gubernia* Conference, Seventh,
    110
Moscow State Bank, 99
Moscow Union of Consumers' Societies,
    84
Moses, George E., 24
Mott, T. Bentley, 100
Mousabekoff (president of Azerbaijan),
    121
Muchnic, Charles, 29
Mulvey, Thomas, 33
Mulvihill, James P., 16
Murray, Robert K., 60

Nansen, Fritjof, 43, 44, 53, 54, 157 n 33
Narkomindel. *See* Commissariat of
    Foreign Affairs
Nation, The, 9
National Association of Manufacturers
    (NAM), 13, 46, 85-86, 102
National City Bank, 118; Russian assets
    held by, 8; and Tsentrosoyuz
    cooperative, 17, 84; and financing of
    Soviet Bureau, 26; loans to tsarist
    Russia, 83, 144 n 4, 169 n 35
National Defense Committee, 36
nationalization: and International
    Harvester, 115-17, 179 nn 38, 41
National Shoe, 14
National Storage Co., 151 n 8
nativism, in U.S., 6
Nazi-Soviet alliance, 109
Nearing, Scott, 90
Nelles, Walter, 9
NEP. *See* New Economic Policy
Nepmen, 112, 127
Newberger, Samuel, 105-6
New Economic Policy (NEP), 2, 4, 51,
    55-57, 67, 104, 144 n 19; and First
    Five-Year Plan, 110-32
New Era corporatism, 3
Newport News Shipbuilding and Dry Dock
    Co., 86
New Republic, 54
Newton, Charles B., 20
New York American, 96
New York Call, 16, 24
New York City Police Department, 9, 10
New York Commercial, 28, 96

New York County Committee, of the Socialist party, 145 n 17
New York Group of Social Revolutionists, 145 n 15
New York Herald, 15
New York Post, 50-51
New York Section of Russian Bolsheviks, 145 n 15
New York State Joint Legislative Committee for the Investigation of Seditious Activities. *See* Lusk Committee
New York State police, 16-17
New York Times, 20, 21, 23-24, 58, 67, 109, 136
New York Tribune, 20
New York World, 20
Nicholas II, 4, 54
Nikopol, Ukraine, 124-25
nitrocellulose, production of, 130
Nogin, Victor P., 82-84, 94
Nove, Alec, 110
Novy Mir, 7, 9, 145 n 15
Novy Put, 118
Nuorteva, Santeri, 7, 9, 10, 13-14, 15, 16, 17; and financing of Soviet Bureau, 19; and investigations of Soviet Bureau, 19-20, 23, 24, 25; and operations of Soviet Bureau, 25, 29; with Narkomindel, 31; and Soviet Bureau trade with Canada, 34; and humanitarian relief for Russia, 43; and diplomatic relations, 44; on International Free Trade League advisory committee, 155 n 84

Ohsol, Johann G., 10, 13, 33, 35-36, 169 n 39
oil concessions, 120-21, 180 n 58

Packard Motor Car Co., 28, 87
Palmer, A. Mitchell, 1, 23, 34, 54
paper manufacturing industry, 128-30
Paris Peace Conference of 1919, 26, 40-41, 42, 43, 44, 146 n 28; and humanitarian relief, 43, 53, 157 n 33
Parker Pens, 80
pencil concession, 126
People's Commissariat of Foreign Affairs. *See* Commissariat of Foreign Affairs
People's Commissariat of Foreign Trade. *See* Commissariat of Foreign Trade

People's Industrial Trading Corp., 26
Perkins, Herbert F., 117
Peterson, Ferdinand, 19
Pickard, F.W., 132
Pittman, Key, 16
platinum, as payment for shipment to Russia, 153 n 31
Poincaré, Raymond, 68
Poland, 2, 47
Politburo, 127
Polk, Frank, 8, 16, 17-18; and humanitarian relief for Russia, 43-44
Poole, DeWitt Clinton, 35, 51-52, 74, 75, 107, 122, 161-62 n 120, 167 n 3; and Skvirskii, 167 n 3
Poole, Ernest, 40
Porter, Stephen J., 16
Pratt and Whitney, 104
presidential elections, 48, 74, 95
Pressed Steel Car Co., 27, 29
Products Exchange Co., 169 n 39
Progressive party, 95
Provisional Government. *See* Russian Provisional Government
Public National Bank, 148 n 71

Quakers, in relief efforts, 55, 160 n 100

Rabinov, Max, 30, 38
Rabinovich, F.Y., 120
Radchenko, Ivan Ivanovich, 119
Radek, Karl, 52, 137; Goodrich's meeting with, 58-59; and Soviet debt, 68
Ragas. *See* Russian American Compressed Gas Company
Rahn-Larmon Co., 151 n 8
railroad equipment: purchases by Russia from U.S., 27, 28-31, 32, 34, 36, 38, 51-52, 153 n 49, 154 n 52; manufacture of, in Russia, 30, 34
railroads, 121, 125
Ranney, Austin, 117
Rapallo Treaty, 70, 97, 159 n 77
Rathenau, Walter, 67-68, 69
Rawack and Grunfeld, 124, 126, 181 n 83
reaping machines *(logobreiki),* 113
Recht, Charles, 8, 9, 24, 35, 89-90
recognition, of Soviet Russia, 179 n 36; Colby note on, 4, 47-48, 51, 66; and anticommunism, 47-48, 52, 91, 94, 95; under Harding, 48-49, 50, 89-93; Senate resolution for, 52; Hoover's position on,

recognition (cont.)
54; and Soviet debt to U.S., 60, 90;
Gumberg's role in, 70, 77, 81, 82, 168 n
24; Skvirskii's efforts toward, 77; and
Textile Syndicate, 82, 168 n 31;
acknowledgment of Soviet sovereignty
in U.S. courts, 89-90; under Coolidge,
94-97, 98, 100; American-Russian
Chamber of Commerce and, 108; under
Hoover, 108; under Roosevelt, 137-38;
meaning after 1913, 156 n 3;
reconstruction, of Soviet Russia, 68;
Genoa conference on, 69-71; and
Hoover's proposed economic mission to
Russia, 71, 74
Reconstruction Finance Corp., 136
Red armies, 22
Redfield, William, 13
Red Scare, 1, 2, 16, 21, 34, 162 n 124. *See
also* anticommunism
Reliance Yarn Co., 21
Remington Rand, Inc., 106-7, 176 n 106
reparations, German, to Soviet Russia,
69
Republican party, 4, 36, 49, 74, 95
Reuther, Victor, 176 n 97
Reuther, Walter, 176 n 97
Reval Industry Bank, 26
Revalis Co., 30-31
Rhodes, Benjamin, 59
Richter, William M., 130
Robert Dollar Co., 50, 81
Robespierre, Maximilien, 57
Robins, Raymond, 49, 50, 58, 59, 62-63,
135, 140, 156 n 5; on Genoa
conference, 70; and recognition of
Soviet Russia, 70, 91-94; and Hoover's
proposed economic mission to Russia,
71, 73, 165 n 52; and Gumberg, 81, 168
n 24; and U.S.-Soviet trade under
Coolidge, 94; opinion on 1924
elections, 95; and American-Russian
Chamber of Commerce, 108, 176 n 5;
and International Harvester, 113-14
Robinson, Robert H.M., 125
Romerstein, Herbert, 184 n 7
Roosevelt, Franklin D., 1, 5, 109, 139; and
Soviet recognition, 136-38
Root, Elihu, 97
Ropes, E.C., 66
Rosendal Reddaway Belting and Hose,
154 n 61

Rosta news agency, 95, 96
Royal Dutch Shell Co., 120
Russian American Compressed Gas
Company (Ragas), 128
Russian Branch, of Socialist party,
145 n 15
Russian Bureau for Trade Information,
proposed, 75
Russian [foreign language] Federation, 7,
11, 118, 145 n 15, 150 n 106
Russian Imperial Government, 14-15, 137.
See also Russian Provisional
Government
Russian information bureau, under
Skvirskii, 77
Russian Provisional Government, 9,
146 nn 26, 28; and Guaranty Trust,
14-15; loans from U.S. to, 60, 137,
146 n 26, 162 n 129
Russian Railway Mission to U.S., 9, 10
Russian Review, The, 77
Russo-Asiatic Consolidated, Ltd., 54
Russo-Polish war, 47
Rykov, Alexsei, 127, 129

Sabin, Henry, 14, 15, 148 n 71
Sackett, Frederic M., 133
St. Phalle, François de, 29, 30
Sakhalin Island, 119
Sandburg, Carl, 19
Sandomirsky, George, 101, 102, 114, 116
Scherzinger, George T., 181 n 79
Schiff, Jacob H., 162 n 129
Schley, Reeve, 83, 106, 108, 169 n 35,
173 n 54
Schurman, Jacob Gould, 103
Selmash agricultural machinery agency,
113, 115, 116
Selskosoyuz cooperative, 26, 100, 113
Senate. *See* United States Senate
Senior, John L., 107
Shakhta affair (1928), 126, 182 n 94
Sheffield Farms, 21
Sheppard, Morris, 168 n 31
Sherman, Isaac J., 85, 104, 169 n 39, 175 n
84
Shipping Board, U.S., 122
Shishkin, V.A., 1, 111
Siberia, U.S. Army intervention in, 40
Simpson, Thacher, and Bartlett, 83, 176 n
106
Sinclair, Harry, 81, 119, 122

Sinclair Exploration Co., 60, 93, 119
Sisson, Edgar, 39, 172 n 43
Sixth National Foreign Trade Convention, 13-14
Skinner, Robert P., 52
Skvirskii, Boris E., 75, 76-77, 95, 134, 167 n 3
Sloan, Alfred P., 131
Smith, Charles H., 87, 108, 170 n 51, 176 n 105
Smith, Daniel M., 46
Smith, Sherrill, 83
Smoot-Hawley Tariff Act (1930), 134
Socialist party of America, 9, 145 n 16; Russian Branch, 145 n 15; New York County Committee, 145 n 17
Socialist propaganda league, 145 n 15
Socialist Workers party, 167 n 11
Society for Technical Aid for Soviet Russia, 18
Sofiano, Tatiana, 108-9
Sonkin, M.E., 132
Sorenson, E.L., 14, 18
Soviet Bureau, 1, 2, 6-38; products shipped through, 6, 10-11, 18, 21-22, 26, 36, 50, 78, 144 n 7, 146-47 n 41, 152 n 24, 159 n 74; establishment of, 6-9; funds available for purchasing U.S. goods, 7, 145 n 19; and Socialist and Communist parties in U.S., 7, 11, 20, 24, 31, 34-35, 145 n 17, 150 n 106; offices of, 8, 9, 146 n 29; recognition by U.S., 8-9; staff, 9-10, 24, 78; operations concerned with U.S. trade, 9-18, 21-22, 28-32, 36-37, 146-47 n 41, 149 nn 80, 81, 150 n 114; and Narkomindel, 10, 11-12, 19, 31-32, 154 n 61; Justice Department investigation of, 12, 14, 15, 19-20, 24, 25, 26, 34; War Department (MID) investigation of, 12-13, 14-15, 148 n 71; financing for, 14-15, 18-19, 25, 26, 31, 148 n 71, 150 n 98, 151 n 13, 152 n 24; and Guaranty Trust, 14-15, 148 n 71; June 1919 raid on, 16-17, 18, 24, 149 n 80; Lusk Committee investigation of, 16-17, 19, 20-21, 24, 150 nn 98, 106; Senate investigation of, 23-24, 25, 34, 151 n 8; demise of, 23-38; operations concerned with Canadian trade, 32-34; and humanitarian relief, 43; Amtorg compared to, 88; bank accounts, 148 n 71

Soviet commercial missions. See commercial missions, Soviet; Soviet Bureau
Soviet Commissariat of Foreign Affairs. See Commissariat of Foreign Affairs
Soviet Information Bureau, 134
Soviet Russia, 13, 35
Soviet Russia Medical Relief Committee, 36
Soviet State Bank, 103
Spargo, John, 36, 47
Sparre, Dr. Fin, 129-30
Special Trade Delegation of the Far Eastern Republic, 76
Spivak, John L., 184 n 7
Spolansky, Jacob, 12
Stalin, Joseph, 5, 95, 100, 107; and New Economic Policy, 112; and concession operators, 126; and technical assistance contracts, 127
Standard Car Co., 29
Standard Oil Co., 20, 97, 120, 122
Standard Steamship Co., 28
State, U.S. Department of: and Soviet Bureau, 12, 16, 18, 21, 25, 34, 144 n 6, 147 n 56, 152 n 30; and Allied embargo of Russia, 28; and U.S.-Soviet trade under Wilson, 39; and diplomatic relations with Soviet Russia, 48-53, 58, 60, 66, 74-75, 76-77, 90, 159 n 72; and recognition of Soviet Russia, 50, 75, 90-93; and U.S.-Soviet trade under Harding, 51, 52-53, 60, 63-64, 66, 69, 75, 119; and Gumberg's proposed trip to Soviet Russia, 58, 161-62 n 120; and Genoa conference, 69, 165 n 38; and Hoover's proposed economic mission to Russia, 71, 72, 73, 74; Bloomfield's visits to Russia for, 74-75; restriction of travel to Russia by, 79; and U.S.-Soviet trade under Coolidge, 94, 98-100, 102-3, 175 n 83; and recognition of Soviet Russia under Coolidge, 96, 97-98; and U.S. financing for German-Soviet trade, 102-3; and U.S.-Soviet trade under Hoover, 105; Division of Eastern European Affairs of, 112, 181 n 75; and International Harvester, 115, 116; and concessions, 122; and Soviet debt repayment, 137, 140; and loans to Kolchak, 144 n 4; and export licenses for war-related material,

State, U.S. Department of (cont.)
153 n 49. *See also* diplomatic
initiatives; Hughes, Charles Evans;
Lansing, Robert
state capitalism, 56, 161 n 110
Steed, Henry Wyckham, 157 n 28
Steel Sole Shoe Co., 151 n 117
Steffens, Lincoln, 42
Stein, Joseph, 179 n 44
Stimson, Henry L., 105, 137, 185 n 20
Stockholms Tidningen, 107
Strauss, Oscar S., 15
Streloff, N., 87
Strom, Frederick, 19, 31
Stuart, Charles E., 106
Stuart, James, and Cooke, Inc., 106
Sudakov (Soviet representative), 117
Sullivan Machinery Co., 176 n 106
Supreme Allied Council, 144 n 4
Supreme Council of the National
Economy (VSNKh), plan for
industrial production, 161 n 107
Sutherland, George, 71
Sutton, Antony, 126
Sweden: Soviet trade agreements with, 2;
trade with Soviets, 33, 101; media
coverage of Soviet trade, 107
Swift, G.E., 21
Swift and Co., 21

tariffs, 134-35
Tass news agency, 99
Teapot Dome scandal, 93, 94, 122
technical assistance contracts, 127-32,
186 n 2
Thacher, Thomas D., 71, 86
Thomas, Edward B., 76-77
Thompson, John M., 42
Tiflis, Georgia, 120, 122
Time, 106
Torgpalata. *See* Chamber of Commerce for
the West
tractors, 14, 104
trade, U.S., with Soviet Russia: and
humanitarian relief, 43-44, 60; and end
of Russian civil war, 45-46; and Colby
note, 48, 66; under Harding, 48, 49, 50,
51-53, 59, 60, 62-67, 69, 75, 77, 92, 159
n 72, 163 n 25, 164 n 20; and
recognition of Soviet Russia, 49, 98;
prewar, 65, 164 n 19; under Coolidge,
79-84, 86-87, 93-105, 167 nn 19 and 20,
168 n 23, 174 nn 66, 71, 75, 175 n 83;

under Hoover, 104-9, 174 n 75,
175 n 85. *See also* Allied embargo
against Soviet Russia; commercial
missions, Soviet; financing
Trade and Industrial Gazette, 164 n 21
Trade Union Council, 181 n 84
travel regulations, 79, 99-100, 167 n 15,
173 n 59
Treasury, U.S. Department of the, 63, 99
Trevor, John B., 14-15, 148 n 71
Trotsky, Leon, 7, 15; and diplomatic
relations with U.S., 42, 156 n 5; and
Chief Concessions Committee, 112,
125, 181 n 84;
Tsentrosoyuz agricultural cooperative, 13,
17, 26, 46, 84
Tsvetkov, G.N., 47
Tuch, Etta, 24, 29
Tuck, S. Pinkney, 77
Turkey, 2, 182 n 89

Ughet, Serge, 9
Ukraine, power station in, 129
Underwood Elliott Fisher Co., 107
Underwood Typewriter Co., 80
Union Card and Paper Co., 21
Union of Georgia, Azerbaijan, and
Armenia for Foreign Trade, 120
Union Twist Drill Co., 80
United Communist party, 151 n 3
United Press, 109
United Shoe Machinery Corp., 33
United States: technical assistance
consultants from, 128, 140, 186 n 2;
trade with, 133-38; Soviet debt and,
136-38; *See also* Allied powers;
Supreme Allied Council
United States Machine Co., 80
United States Senate: subcommittee
investigation of Soviet Bureau, 23-24,
25, 34, 151 n 8; recognition resolution
in, 52; Foreign Relations Committee
and recognition issue, 90, 92; and
recognition issue, 90, 92, 94
United States Steel Corp., 20, 21
Unterberger, Betty, 40
Urquhardt, Leslie, 54
U.S. Rubber Co., 80
U.S. Steamship Co., 24

Vanderlip, Frank, 118
Vanderlip, Washington, 118-19
Vauclain, Samuel M., 29, 30

Versailles Treaty, 45, 69
Vesenkha, 111, 114, 116, 117. *See also* Chief Concessions Committee

Walsh, Joseph, 16
W. Averell Harriman and Co., 102-3, 123, 176 n 106
War, U.S. Department of: and sale of locomotives to Soviet Russia, 51-52. *See also* Military Intelligence Division (MID), U.S. War Department
Warburg, Max, 123
Wardwell, Allen, 71, 76 n 106, 86, 134
war materiel: U.S. trade regulations, 30, 46, 153 n 49; Amtorg trade in, 87
Washington Conference, 72, 119
Washington Globe, 58
Washington Post, 48, 76, 77, 95-96
Washington Star, 36, 58
Watts, Arthur, 55
Watts, H.W., 80
weapons. *See* war materiel
Weinberg and Posner, 7, 21, 28
Weinstein, Gregory, 9, 11, 14, 17, 24
Weissman, Benjamin, 57
Westinghouse Electric and Manufacturing Co., 33, 51, 106, 107, 176 n 106
Whalen, Grover, 134
Wheeler, Burton, 162 n 125
White, Christine A., 47-48, 60, 159 n 77
White, Henry, 43
White armies, 8

White Truck Co., 28
Williams, Andrew J., 66
Williams, Spencer, 109
Williams, William Appleman, 3, 47, 93
Willis, H. Parker, 86, 96, 102, 175 n 93
Wilson, Edith, 27
Wilson, William B., 34-35
Wilson, Woodrow, and administration, 4, 8, 27, 35, 36, 139-40; Colby note, 4, 46-48, 51, 66; diplomatic relations with Soviet Russia, 4, 39-48, 51, 157 n 33; military initiatives under, 40-43, 44, 45, 157 n 28; humanitarian relief under, 43-44, 53, 54, 157 n 33; and meaning of diplomatic recognition, 156 n 3
Wilson and Co., 21
Winderman, S.D., 65
Wolfsohn and Son, 89-90
Women's Committee for the Recognition of Russia, 49, 90-91
Women's International League for Peace and Freedom (WILPF), 90-91
World War Foreign Debts Commission, 61
Worthington Pump and Machinery Corp., 105

Yazikov, Alexander A., 58, 73, 76
Young, Evan E., 98, 112
Young Plan, 61, 103

Zieger, Robert H., 62
Ziev, Paul J., 101, 169 n 39
Zinoviev, Grigorii, 57, 119